A New
Significance

Commentaries by

    Richard Maxwell Brown

    Arnoldo De León

    Dan Flores

    Deena J. González

    Albert L. Hurtado

    Peter Iverson

    Patricia Nelson Limerick

    Sucheta Mazumdar

    Gary Y. Okihiro

    Robert W. Righter

    Vicki L. Ruiz

    Martha A. Sandweiss

    Barre Toelken

    Elliott West

Special concluding statement by

    Quintard Taylor

A New Significance

Re-envisioning the History of the American West

Edited by
CLYDE A. MILNER II

Essays by
Allan G. Bogue
William F. Deverell
David G. Gutiérrez
Susan Rhoades Neel
Gail M. Nomura
Anne F. Hyde
David Rich Lewis
Susan Lee Johnson

New York   Oxford   •   Oxford University Press   1996

Oxford University Press

Oxford   New York
Athens   Auckland   Bangkok   Bogotá   Bombay
Buenos Aires   Calcutta   Cape Town   Dar es Salaam
Delhi   Florence   Hong Kong   Istanbul   Karachi
Kuala Lumpur   Madras   Madrid   Melbourne
Mexico City   Nairobi   Paris   Singapore
Taipei   Tokyo   Toronto

and associated companies in
Berlin   Ibadan

Copyright © 1996 by Clyde A. Milner II

Published by Oxford University Press, Inc.
198 Madison Avenue, New York, New York 10016

Oxford is a registered trademark of Oxford University Press

All rights reserved. No part of this publication may be reproduced,
stored in a retrieval system, or transmitted, in any form or by any means,
electronic, mechanical, photocopying, recording, or otherwise,
without the prior permission of Oxford University Press.

Library of Congress Cataloging-in-Publication Data
A new significance: re-envisioning the history
of the American West / edited by Clyde A. Milner II;
essays by Allan G. Bogue . . . [et al.].
p.   cm.   Includes bibliographical references and index.
ISBN 0-19-510047-6. ISBN 0-19-510048-4 (paper)
1. West (U.S.)—History.
2. West (U.S.)—History—1890–1945.
3. West (U.S.)—History—1945–   .
I. Milner, Clyde A., 1948–   .
II. Bogue, Allan G.
F591.N47   1996   978—dc20   95-53151

9 8 7 6 5 4 3 2 1

Printed in the United States of America
on acid-free paper

Preface

Planning for this project began in the early spring of 1989 and may be neatly divided into two three-year periods: 1989–92 and 1992–95. All the names that appear below, including the shade of Frederick Jackson Turner, deserve my personal thanks for aiding me during this six-year trek. Initially, I had hoped to create a series of essays that would allow a new set of historians to comment on important topics that now shape our interpretation of the American West. I wanted these writings to demonstrate some of the "new significances" in western history that have arisen in the hundred years since Frederick Jackson Turner's seminal statement on "The Significance of the Frontier in American History." My plans included publication of these essays in the *Western Historical Quarterly.*

On 1 July 1989, with the retirement of my good friend and mentor Charles S. Peterson, I became the editor of the *WHQ,* the journal of the Western History Association. In 1984, Chas had appointed me his associate editor. He later gave me the designation of coeditor. Chas encouraged my efforts in creating this series and helped focus my thinking. Anne M. Butler took over my responsibilities as associate, and later co-, editor. Like Chas, Anne provided valuable advice on what topics to consider and which scholars to invite.

Before long, I felt that the selected authors might benefit greatly if we could all gather at a conference where early drafts of the articles could be read and improvements suggested. Plans for the conference soon began to anticipate a much bigger event. Utah State University's Mountain West Center for Regional Studies wanted to organize a national research conference in recognition of the centennial of Turner's frontier thesis. The center's director, F. Ross Peterson, suggested that we make a joint proposal to the National Endowment for the Humanities for some funding. We received generous support from the NEH, as well as additional funds from Utah State's Vice-President for Research, the university's Conference and Institute Division, the Department of History, and the Mountain West

Center. Shannon Hoskins, the center's associate director, oversaw many important details in our planning.

The conference took place from 29 July through 1 August 1992 on the campus of Utah State University in Logan, Utah. Over thirty graduate students from history programs across the United States received financial support to attend, as did numerous public school and community college teachers. Many others paid their own way to far northern Utah for our four-day gathering. An average of more than two hundred people attended each of the sessions. KUSU-FM, Utah Public Radio, recorded all the meetings. Lee Austin, the station's news director, then produced a series of five one-hour programs for regional broadcast.

Many people helped with the conference. What can be only a partial list must include special recognition to Utah State's Vice-President for Research, Bartell Jensen, now retired, as well as to Sherry L. Smith, Mikiso Hane, Carol A. O'Connor, Robert Parson, Richard White, Virginia Scharff, Zeese Papanikolas, Peggy Pascoe, Leonard Arrington, Kerry Soper, Carolyn Fullmer, Kimball Fife, Ian Craig Breaden, Bradley J. Birzer, David S. Trask, Gunther Peck, Päivi Hoikkala, Renée M. Sentilles, John Andrew Hardcastle, Hope Benedict, Scott Hughes, Brian Cannon, Alicia Rodriquez, Laura Santigian, and Kathryn Morse.

At the conference two individuals presented formal comments on each of the major essays. Allan G. Bogue graciously agreed to deliver our keynote address. By the time the commentators had become part of our project, I realized that we could produce a book that would contain the essays, the commentaries, and Al Bogue's address. All the participants agreed that the conference had allowed us to hear only preliminary drafts of what would later be published. The second three-year period, 1992–95, was a time of rewriting and rethinking for most of our contributors.

Bogue's keynote address and the seven major essays did appear in the *Western Historical Quarterly*. Nonetheless, each author has been permitted to make adjustments for publication in this book. The introduction, chapter 9, and all the commentaries are in print for the first time. The staff of the *Western Historical Quarterly* deserves my grateful thanks for preparing the main essays for publication. Barbara L. Stewart dealt with vital correspondence, whereas Jane A. Reilly and Ona Siporin oversaw production and copyediting. A group of student editorial assistants aided our production. They included Andrew M. Honker, John A. Hardcastle, Stephen K. Amerman, Kelly W. May, A. J. Taylor, Grant Martin, James W. Feldman, Jared Farmer, John W. Heaton, Eric Walz, Kevin D. Hatfield, Esther Hansen, and Tamara Martinez.

Once a book became the obvious goal, Sheldon Meyer of Oxford

University Press provided much encouragement. We were fortunate to have Sheldon's support. He is a peerless editor for important books in American history, and his attention to new writing on the American West is very welcomed. In addition, Sheldon sought out helpful readings of our collection by Peggy Pascoe and Sarah Deutsch. Peggy's report to the press provided important fresh ideas about our book's organization. D. Teddy Diggs copyedited our volume for the press. Andrew Albanese provided valuable editorial aid. Deborah C. Gessaman created uniform text files and a standard word-processing format. Jane A. Reilly and Sabine Barcatta compiled and edited the index. Dean Brian L. Pitcher of the College of Humanities, Arts, and Social Sciences at Utah State helped cover the cost of illustrations for this book.

Finally, I must express my sincere gratitude to the twenty-three scholars who contributed their writings to this project. They each applied their special gifts and precious time to a shared effort at re-envisioning the history of the American West. Because of their efforts, my six-year journey has been a wonderful collaboration. But our intellectual travels are not over. New generations of scholars will keep re-envisioning western history. With these future writers in mind, all of us who contributed to this book have agreed to place its royalty income into an account that will support graduate editorial assistants at the *Western Historical Quarterly.*

Logan, Utah   Clyde A. Milner II
March 1996

Contents

Introduction

Envisioning a Second Century of Western History

Clyde A. Milner II

Many people, especially many Americans, have a passion to honor anything that has existed for a century. These centennial enthusiasms may be explained by the fact that few people live for more than ten decades. Not all of these celebrations are created equally or are endowed with special importance. But for scholars interested in the history of the American West, one recent centennial deserved appropriate recognition. This collection of essays and commentaries began as an effort to recognize the centennial of Frederick Jackson Turner's first presentation, in 1893, of "The Significance of the Frontier in American History." Instead of yet again considering Turner's frontier thesis, this project tried to capture the *spirit* of intellectual excitement that Turner's essay created. For this reason, I wanted the authors of the major essays to be at a point in their scholarly careers that approximately equaled Turner's status in 1893. This approach meant that the "new significance" advocated in this volume is stated by a new generation of western historians—a generation newer even than those scholars currently identified with the "new western history."

Turner first presented his famous essay as a thirty-two-year-old historian from the University of Wisconsin. He gave the final talk at the last session on the second day of the World's Congress of Historians and Historical Students, organized by the American Historical Association as part of the Columbian Exposition in Chicago. His audience did not respond with any enthusiasm, but it was an especially warm July evening, and four other speakers had preceded him. Eventually, his thesis would gain an amazingly durable prominence.

During the past century, perhaps no other single essay on an American historical topic has received such extensive critical attention or lasted so long in terms of scholarly and popular interest. In addition, few other

American historians have been so praised and pounded—revived, revised, or dismissed—as has Frederick Jackson Turner. His ideas have remained both lively and controversial, especially for historians of the American West. This current volume was *not* conceived to extend the historiographical debate over Turner's frontier thesis, although a few readers may choose to use it for such a purpose. Instead, this book recognizes Turner's legacy of intellectual inquiry by publishing a set of "new significance" essays.

This collection gave numerous scholars an opportunity to examine topics that have emerged in the study of the American West in the century since that warm July evening. Many of the essays use examples drawn from the twentieth century. The topics either are ideas suggested in Turner's essay, such as the significance of the natural environment or the role of perception, or are subjects that Turner ignored, such as Native Americans, Mexican Americans, Asian peoples, and gender. In either case, the intellectual challenge to each author is drawn from a pedagogic technique that Turner used with his graduate students at Wisconsin and later at Harvard. In his seminars, as Merle Curti has reported, Turner had each student write a "problem paper" that focused on a narrow and well-defined research question. He then required a "correlation paper" that tried to synthesize the entire seminar in relation to the specific research problem examined by the individual student. As William Cronon has shown, Turner's own writings followed this same pattern. His most successful efforts were "correlation papers" that considered the "significance" of a historical question.

This volume is built around a set of seven "correlation papers." Preceding these, Allan Bogue's essay introduces readers to Turner and his professional career, especially his contribution to the teaching of western American history at colleges and universities. Bogue also considers the origins of the "new western history" and how it fits the pattern of other "new histories." The seven essays that follow avoid extended consideration of Turner and his ideas, since such considerations have been done and even overdone. Instead, these essays begin to chart the course for the next century of scholarship on the history of the American West. They ask us to consider, "What will be the 'newer' western history?"

The debate over the history of the American West has become as energetic as the older debate over the meaning of the frontier in American history. Contrived confrontations are tedious, but legitimate intellectual inquiry can be exciting. Other voices needed to be included in this intellectual conversation. For this reason, other scholars of diverse backgrounds and interests were invited to contribute shorter essays that responded to one of the seven major essays. In this way, the significance of each topic could be tested by sharing ideas and building additional insights. Two of these shorter commentaries accompany each of the longer essays. The authors of these responses could choose to consider directly the ideas presented in the main essay, or they could expand on the possibilities that the larger topic suggested. In most cases, the commentaries for each major essay divide between these two approaches.

The topics presented in this volume are not the exclusive "seven ways to understand the American West." Quintard Taylor's concluding statement in chapter 9, "Through the Prism of Race," and the jointly written afterword recognize that other "significant" topics are worthy of extended consideration. This collection also does not argue that each topic is a "new" way to explain western history. *Significance* for historical understanding, not the novelty of presentation, was the organizing principle. Among the mountains of historiographical writings on Turner's famous essay are studies that show his frontier thesis was not a fully original idea in 1893. Indeed, some of the immediate responses to his essay claimed that the basic concept had been known for a while. Ironically, these early critics missed the espoused *significance* of Turner's thesis because his central idea, the "frontier," did not seem "new." Similarly, the topics for each of the seven essays are not novel, yet each is important. Native Americans, Mexican Americans, Asia and Asian Americans, gender, the natural environment, human perception, and the role of the West itself in the nation's history are all vital subjects. To think about each of these is not new, but I hope that for many people reading this book, some of the ways to think about the *significance* of these topics will indeed be new.

A New
Significance

1

The Course of Western History's First Century

Allan G. Bogue

After the annual meeting of the American Historical Association in December 1888, John Franklin Jameson wrote to his father: "The meetings . . . were extremely stupid. . . . We had much Western history warmed-over from [the canceled meeting in Columbus]. Western history is stupid anyway, I think." Seven years later, the *Catalogue* of the University of Wisconsin carried a new course heading, "The History of the West," and the instructor, young Frederick Jackson Turner, was to become Jameson's trusted adviser in the latter's important roles in the developing profession.[1] Jameson's letter, the inception of Turner's course, and the latter's emergence as a person of professional consequence were all related to major changes under way in the history discipline. This essay considers the origins and development of western history in American institutions of higher learning, examines the changing face of the western history textbooks used by generations of college students, and tries in some degree to evaluate the past and future significance of the history of western America as a curricular offering.

Origins

In 1883, Herbert Baxter Adams of Johns Hopkins University confided to one of his correspondents that history was "booming." Actually, higher education was booming and continued to do so. Percentage growth in college enrollments was matched by that of college faculty. The University of Wisconsin claimed an enrollment of 722 students in the academic year 1887–88; its *Catalogue* of 1909–10 recorded a student body of almost 4,400 students.[2] As the only instructor in history and political studies at Johns Hopkins in 1876, Herbert Baxter Adams had provided "one exercise

a week." Ten years later there were "three regular instructors and one tutor" giving twenty-eight exercises each week. Pleas came to Adams, particularly from trans-Appalachian and southern institutions, for him to
recommend good men to assist in developing curricula in history and political science. In self-congratulation, he prepared a map of the United
States showing the "institutions of learning" that had employed his students, as a "graphical illustration" of "the colonial system of the Johns
Hopkins University."[3]

After his appointment as a classicist at Wisconsin in 1867, William F.
Allen came to specialize in history, having been progressively relieved of
other commitments. Pleading for help by the late 1880s, he shared the services of an M.A. candidate and former reporter, Fred Turner, with the Department of Rhetoric and Oratory. Soon President Thomas C.
Chamberlin recognized the need for a second full-time appointment, and
rather than looking abroad to fill this position on a full-time basis, Wisconsin released its own fingerling into the Hopkins pool for further training. After strategic maneuvering by all concerned, Chamberlin and Allen
reclaimed Frederick J. Turner at the end of the academic year 1888–89, his
horizons greatly expanded as a member of a group of young scholars who
would become the elite of their emerging discipline. Turner was intelligent, handsome, pleasant and resonant of voice, and infused with enthusiasm for scientific history. Aiding also in his rapid emergence as a force on
the Madison campus were the political lessons learned in a home headed
by an influential Republican politician.[4]

At the time of Professor Allen's death in late 1889, he and Turner constituted the history faculty at the University of Wisconsin. In Turner's last
year at Wisconsin (1909–10) the university *Catalogue* named eight history
professors, three instructors with Ph.D.'s in hand, and eleven teaching fellows or scholars.[5] At Wisconsin, as elsewhere, this period of expansion in
faculty and students allowed the development of historical curricula in
which there was a place for specialized courses.

The Wisconsin *Catalogue* of 1895–96, wrote Ray A. Billington, "announced a completely new course: 'History 7. The History of the West.'"
"Particular attention," explained Turner, "is paid to the advance of settlement across the continent, and to the results of this movement." "Here,"
wrote Billington, "was innovation, indeed—this was the first course on
the history of the frontier to be offered anywhere." Citing the pride of the
local press in this departure, he absolved Turner of provincialism by noting the continental sweep of the course. Interest in regionalism was widespread, he added, making it reasonable for Turner to believe that the
history of regions must be known before that of the nation could be un-

derstood. Billington suggested also that Turner's "decision to explain the 'West' to his students" followed arrangements to have Professor William P. Trent offer a lecture series on southern history at Wisconsin during the academic year 1895–96.[6]

"History of the West" was a novel catalogue entry; that it announced a "completely new course" is arguable. The description of course content can be traced back to the 1891–92 *Catalogue* when Turner introduced a course titled "Economic and Social History of the United States." Among the topics to be considered in that offering was "the process of American settlement across the continent." By the next year Turner was promising, "Particular attention will be paid to the spread of settlement across the continent, and to the economic and social causes of sectional and national sentiment." In the *Catalogue* of 1893–94, Turner dropped the second half of this description, substituting "and to the economic and social results of this movement." Two years later he changed the title of the course to "History of the West."[7]

Indeed, other antecedents of the course of 1895–96 had appeared as early as 1888 when Turner prepared a syllabus entitled "Outline Studies in the History of the Northwest" for the National Bureau of Unity Clubs. Turner listed undergraduate "seminary" study in the "History of the Northwest" in the Wisconsin *Catalogue* before his year at Johns Hopkins and, in planning course offerings for 1889–90 with Professor Allen, proposed that seminary work in "Northwestern development and influence" should be a string in his bow. The frontier hypothesis—the marvelously winning synthesis of ideas and evidence that derived from many sources and that he delivered as "The Significance of the Frontier in American History" in the summer of 1893—was thus being formulated during the early 1890s and earlier, in Turner's classroom as well as in his study and preliminary published statements.[8]

When Turner proclaimed the importance of the presence and recession of free land and declared that the first period of American history had ended with the passing of the frontier, he was justifying his western origins and intellectual commitments and protesting against eastern myopia. He was also forging a weapon in the competition for educational leadership beyond the Appalachians. Assisting in the efforts in 1891–92 to bring Professor Richard Ely to Wisconsin from Johns Hopkins to head a new School of Economics, Political Science, and History, Turner discussed the history program and his hopes for it. Ely's acceptance of the Wisconsin offer, Turner wrote, "will make it certain that the University of Wisconsin will not content itself with giving undergraduate instruction and becoming a feeder to Chicago; but that it will be a center of postgraduate work for the Northwest." He added: "This . . . has long been an ambition of mine . . . Such a school will be a new departure in the West, and I believe our earnest western boys will supply the best sort of material." He thanked Ely for his assurance that he and his colleague, Charles H. Haskins, would be freed for more advanced work. "I am myself becoming anxious to open some of the many fields for original work in American History that lie about me. If we are to contend with Chicago we must adhere strongly to the maxim—quality rather than quantity." A few days later Turner returned to this theme: "Chicago's funds enable her to carry things by a coup de main. . . . Ought we not to meet this policy by developing certain special features that will attract men. . . . In the line of western, local, and newspaper & periodical material, as well as in Dr. Draper's ms collections for Ky. Tenn. & N.W. history, we are *un*rivalled." A decade or so later, Turner still emphasized the contest with Chicago in a memorandum endorsing the usefulness of the summer school.[9]

On 19 February 1892, Turner described his own teaching preferences to Ely: "I would prefer to give two advanced courses in place of Modern history, viz. Social and Economic History of U.S.—(especial reference to progress of western settlement, immigration, internal improvements, land legislation, labor, manufactures, literature, etc.)—And a course in the general history of *Colonization*." Although Turner once presented an extension course on the history of colonization, his second advanced offering at Madison emerged in the *Catalogue* as "History of the West," and it had been gestating within "Economic and Social History"—curricular parthenogenesis.[10]

The delivery of the Chicago paper sounded the trumpet call "Charge" in the very keep of the academic enemy. It may also have proclaimed an important history agenda within Professor Ely's school, where there must have been a strong tendency for everything to be sucked into the wake of the dynamic director. In his way, Turner was no less committed to development than the western town promoters who rallied community support by invoking the threat of rivals. But we should not denigrate Turner's efforts; he had observed Adams's empire building at Johns Hopkins, and development and progress were part of the Yankee ethos in which Turner had been reared.

Turner and the Course

In effect, Turner set his teaching agenda in advanced courses for the rest of his career at Wisconsin in the *Catalogue* of 1895–96. Thereafter, throughout his career, the "History of the West" was his usual advanced undergraduate offering, accompanied by a graduate seminar in American history. Although Turner announced central topics in western history for the seminar for a few years around 1900, he focused the seminar each year after 1903 on one of the presidential administrations of the early national period, except in the year 1904–5, when the subject was nullification.[11]

How did western history spread out of its spawning ground at Wisconsin? In a recent evaluation of frontier historians, John R. Wunder identified seventy-eight deceased writers who had made major contributions to the history of the West. Sixty-two of the seventy-eight were academic historians; the remaining one-fifth were journalists, creative writers, lawyers, a gold rush merchant, and so on. The academic historians had trained in twenty different graduate schools, ten claiming degrees from Wisconsin and six from Harvard. The graduate schools of the University of Pennsylvania and the University of Chicago each prepared five scholars, and the University of California at Berkeley was represented by four graduates. Other historians had trained in schools scattered from Oxford, England, to Palo Alto, California. Although Wisconsin and Harvard produced sixteen of the academic western specialists, or a quarter of the total, Turner was the doctoral adviser for only five of the sixteen—two at Wisconsin and three at Harvard.[12]

Eighteen doctoral candidates completed degrees under Turner's direction at Wisconsin and a comparable number at Harvard University and Radcliffe College combined. Both the Wisconsin and the Harvard groups included historians with distinguished futures—Carl L. Becker, Louise P. Kellogg, Joseph Schafer, Marcus L. Hansen, and Frederick Merk, for example. Although Cornell, Wisconsin, and Northwestern employed Turner students, the Wisconsin Ph.D.'s in general pursued their careers in state universities of the second rank—West Virginia, Oregon, North Dakota University, North Dakota Agricultural College, Tulane—and small midwestern colleges. In the East, Turner's Harvard students served at the Universities of Pennsylvania, Pittsburgh, and Virginia, at Yale, Harvard, and Brown Universities, and at Clark and Williams Colleges, among others. In the West, they were at Oklahoma, Minnesota, Colorado, Northwestern, and Reed. Several found employment as researchers. But only three of the Harvard Ph.D.'s took their degrees before 1920. Also, some of Turner's advisees left the field, so we can hardly visualize a small army of his doctoral graduates seeding the profession during his career.[13]

But Turner's influence was potent. At both Wisconsin and Harvard some of his students remained to complete their degrees after his departure, and others became influential professionals without completing the Ph.D. At a farewell party in Madison in 1910, students presented him with a map of the United States; across the top a map-toting Turner pursued a trapper and a pioneer farmer, and dots and concentric circles located some eighty former members of his seminars. Numerous young scholars heard and were influenced by his message as visiting students in the Wisconsin summer sessions or as students in other schools at which he lectured. Financial considerations drew some with Wisconsin or Harvard credits elsewhere for the doctorate, but they remained committed to western history. However, the history of the West rapidly developed an identity larger than Turner and his students. Other scholars accepted his thesis, and it rapidly found its way into textbooks in American history and government. Beyond the Appalachians, Turner found able coworkers like Clarence W. Alvord, Benjamin Shambaugh, and Frederic L. Paxson eager to help develop the field. And graduate directors, little known as western historians, allowed students to develop doctoral topics in the field.

In 1922, Turner responded to a request for information about his "connection with Western history" and about himself. "Something like half the states have such a college course," he wrote, "and many of the leading universities, east and west, include it in their curriculum. A considerable portion of the instructors were trained in my seminary." The curricula of ninety leading history programs throughout the contiguous United States in 1931–32, the year of Turner's death, show that 63 percent of the institutions offered some variant of western or frontier history. From Ohio through Iowa and Minnesota, every state university plus the University of Chicago listed the course. Of the eastern schools surveyed, 49 percent had such an offering, compared with 69 percent of those in the trans-Mississippi West, but all seven Ivy League schools for which data are available gave the course. Of the southern schools examined, 47 percent offered western history, a figure exactly equal to the proportion listing southern history.[14]

Surveying the state of western American history during the early 1960s, W. N. Davis Jr. discovered that 194 of the 375 institutions queried reported a course in western history, 51 percent of the total. American Historical Association data for 1991–92 show that, in 191 of 610 American history programs listed, 245 faculty members (excepting emeriti) reported a research interest in the West or the frontier; 62 schools reported specialists in western subareas above the state level. Eliminating duplication provides 238 institutions with avowed western specialists, about 40 percent. The western tilt in the location of this interest was more visible than in the past. Of the seven Ivy League institutions teaching western history in 1931–32, only Yale and Dartmouth persevere. Of the eight leading midwestern schools of the earlier date, only Wisconsin, Indiana, and Iowa maintain the faith.[15]

Examining regional history offerings in 1990, Carl Abbott suggested that western history had suffered more recent erosion than had southern.[16] But western history studies are still important, and part of the apparent decline is explained by the fact that topics once presented as an integral part of western history are now often separate areas of interest, for example, Native American and environmental history.

Western History as Course

To the sorrow of publishers, Turner never wrote a western history text. However, preserved lecture notes and published reading lists reveal much of the organization and content of his course in western history. Well set by the time that he went to Harvard, the basic structure gave heavy coverage to the colonial frontiers and broke, probably at the end of the first semester, at about 1850. There were fifty-two reading units in the *List of References on the History of the West* of 1913, the last five dealing with the West after 1900: "The New West, 1900–1910," "Combinations and the Development of the West," "Conservation and the West," "The Progressives," and "Contemporaneous Western Ideals." In the edition of 1922, Turner and Frederick Merk added a section on "The West in the World War and Reconstruction." Despite his pronouncement of 1893, Turner's course apparently ended with the morning paper.[17]

Destined for a distinguished scholarly career in political science, John M. Gaus enrolled in Turner's western history lecture course during the second semester of the academic year 1919–20, and his notes have been preserved.[18] After discussing the extension of transportation facilities westward from the Appalachians and the territorial system, Turner turned his attention to the trans-Mississippi West. The Gaus notes reveal a course that melded economic, diplomatic, and political history. Turner did not disregard social institutions and the role of ideas—he called it idealism—but these were less emphasized. When he brought his presentation into the twentieth century, he still used the basic concepts of frontier and section to give broader meaning to his material. Gaus recorded descriptive statistics only occasionally, but Turner's slides probably provided such data. If Turner often emphasized colorful incidents or told anecdotes, Gaus did not record them. As a teacher, Turner was basically a question asker or a proposer of hypotheses, although he introduced illustrative individuals and crafted telling aphorisms. "The logic of events does not assume a logic of purpose," noted Gaus on one occasion.

Critics have correctly argued that Turner's interpretation of the westward movement revealed blind spots and a lack of sensitivity. Let us briefly examine his treatment of material bearing on those currently pop-

ular social variables—ethnicity, gender, and class. Although he did not ignore the indigenous population, Turner's use of the phrase "Indian Barrier" in his lists of references is cited as revealing the one-sidedness of his
approach, and he apparently did not dip deeply into the anthropological
and ethnographic literature. But on 29 March he included an evaluation
of American Indian policy and introduced the concept of conquest—a
term now much in vogue.

> The spread of population [scribbled Gaus] is fundamental in explaining
> the Mexican War—rather than any conspiracy of slave holders and using
> diplomacy to get more territory. Previous spread had been into unoccu-
> pied areas—unorganized by civilized people, not expansion by conquest.
> But we had conquered the Indians. Was this just? Failure to use resources
> will submit people to subordination of a superior type which does. An in-
> evitable process. But a better way could have been found for dealing with
> [the] Indians than was found.

Later Turner referred to the occupation of the Black Hills as a "betrayal" of
the Sioux. So we find a mingling in Turner of Spencerian inevitability, acknowledgment of injustice, and regret at past policies, but hardly moral
outrage.[19]

Turner taught numerous women in his seminar at Wisconsin and lectured for years at Radcliffe College, but Kit Carson's mother is the only
woman in the frontier essay. The record was not much improved during
the spring of 1920. Describing the background of the Grange, however,
Turner drew a picture of the farmer: "Isolated and ignorant. Wife still
worse off. Only an occasional religious meeting—no normal social functions." The children were "lured" away by "city growth and urban improvements." He noted that women were full-fledged members of the
Patrons of Husbandry and as such played important ceremonial roles, but
he ignored the female orators of the Populist movement. Although
Turner's *Reference List* of 1922 shows that he was somewhat interested in
the family's role in the westward movement, the gender issues and matters
of domestic economy that our generation has made an integral part of social history did not appear in his lectures or, to be fair, in those of his contemporaries.[20]

And what of class and its influence? Turner sketched at length the
great changes that occurred in the American economy during the late
nineteenth and early twentieth centuries and western involvement—the
spread of settlement, changes in transportation and marketing, the impact
of western minerals, the denuded pineries, and the growth of great corporations and combinations. Increased agricultural production and deflation
put the West and its farmers at a disadvantage. The latter Turner described

as a "class in a *region*." The passage of the Granger laws, John Gaus learned, meant that "individualistic competition and fear of govt [had] now [been] deserted by the farmer. *A turning point in the history of American development.* But a system of socialism was not sought."[21]

The recently settled West constituted a new section and joined with the South in a "free silver" group, but the northeastern wing of the Republican party overwhelmed the midwestern presidents, and "bloody shirt" rhetoric was diverting as well. Turner described the building of a great industrial empire in the West as a "new type of pioneering—a pioneering of capital and organization by men of imagination." James J. Hill was "a type of the new western man." "The capitalist," wrote Gaus, "was applying the principle of the squatter, but at the very time when such individualism [was becoming] a new thing because of disappearance of land." Where once the squatter farmer had ruled, now "combinations of industry and capital were predominant," and large stockmen dominated the range country by organizing associations. The basic principle, Turner explained, was that of the old farmers' protective associations and mining camp vigilance committees, but this was a "squatter sovereignty by business interests."[22]

The Populists, Turner told his class, represented a stage in the "advance of industrialism." William Jennings Bryan was thoroughly a "frontier type," one whose family had followed the frontier; his great speech of 1896 was a "remarkable effort" destined to "stand in history as a landmark." In concluding lectures Turner emphasized the concentration of control over natural resources, the Progressive reaction that this produced, and the enhanced role of government visualized by Theodore Roosevelt and Gifford Pinchot. Where squatter individualism had once prevailed, now government paternalism worked to provide "new functions due to western needs." Although there were "some areas yet to be developed in the West . . . [it would] be under conditions unlike the Old West." It would, forecasted Turner, "be through government or corporations—possibly through tenantry or peasantry." Gaus wrote, "The Old West will remain a disembodied idea."[23]

In his last lecture, Turner explained that the concentration of control in natural resources and other industries made political discontent "natural in our time." "Revolting political movements pass one into another— Bryanism, Insurgency—Progressivism." Gaus summarized Turner's conclusions as the lecture and semester ended:

> The frontier [was] important—settlement pressing forward into the wilderness—a new type developing different from Europe—opposite to every thing Prussian.

The movement had ended by 1900. With it had gone on the formation of provinces or sections. Each show signs of persistence—The U.S.
in terms of sections—Danger in intolerance. We must realize the com-
posite quality of our life. Made up of pieces of Europe. Study the house
raising of [the] West.[24]

Scholarly Cumulation

While Turner's career proceeded, great collections of monographs, period-
icals, society transactions, local and regional manuscripts, and government
documents relevant to his interests grew in library after library. His famous
Reference List expanded to 156 pages by 1922. Accumulation continues;
the western historian is singularly blessed. Given the many fine critiques
available, discussion of the western research frontier can be brief. Subsequent to Turner's retirement there were patterns of both continuity and
change; some scholars remained firmly committed to his ideas, whereas
others mined rewarding veins of western history that peers recognized as
important, irrespective of their relationship to a Turnerian framework.
One thinks of the work of Marcus L. Hansen, Frederick Merk, Paul W.
Gates, Arthur P. Whitaker, Thomas P. Abernethy, Edward E. Dale, Everett
Dick, and Herbert E. Bolton, for example. At about the time of Turner's
death, Walter P. Webb and James C. Malin were developing invigorating
reinterpretations of regionalism and human adaptation.[25]

Meanwhile criticism of Turner's ideas mounted, focused to some extent by George W. Pierson's survey of scholarly opinion about the frontier
thesis, a study that he reported in late 1941. Turner, critics said with some
justice, used social theory that was now obsolete, underemphasized the
continuities in the lives of the pioneers and their institutions, ignored important aspects of American development, and was blind to much of the
seamy side of frontiering. If some historians compounded Turner's faults
in the years following World War II, new approaches and perspectives
somewhat muted the protests. Henry Nash Smith and other specialists in
American studies, for example, demonstrated that reality did not always
rule in thinking about the West and that myths, symbols, images, and
stereotypes, developed in response to the conditions of a particular time,
could become embedded in American culture and be transmitted to subsequent generations.[26]

During the 1950s, behavioral science also began to influence many
historians. Stanley Elkins and Eric McKitrick, David M. Potter, and others suggested that aspects of Turner's argument made sense in the light of
contemporary social theory. The mixing of anthropologists and historians

in Indian claims cases nurtured ethnohistory, with its enhanced understanding of Indian values, objectives, and actions. Behavioralism also implied a more rigorous examination of evidence, and quantitative analysis was applied to old themes. Paul F. Sharp and Herbert Heaton called for the development of a comparative approach to the history of the West, and Earl Pomeroy and Robert F. Berkhofer Jr. urged western historians to pay more attention to continuities. Other scholars brought overly romanticized themes into perspective, such as when Richard M. Brown reassessed American violence. Howard Lamar found new meaning in so Turnerian a subject as territorial development. Biographers like Dale Morgan and Wallace Stegner found the West to be a magnificent canvas. Ray A. Billington conceived the "Histories of the American Frontier" series; if less integrated than hoped, many of the volumes are almost indispensable. Now too, Billington and Wilbur R. Jacobs began to enrich our understanding of Turner by their research in the Turner Manuscripts collection at the Huntington Library. The twenty-five years after 1945 were productive ones.[27]

By the late 1960s and 1970s, significant numbers of western historians were invading the twentieth century, and the era of the new social history was beginning with its changed emphasis, interdisciplinary concerns, and interest in identifying and understanding the members of ignored or oppressed social groups. Here, thus far, the contributions in women's history, Native American history, and environmental issues, particularly those relating to aridity and water supply, have been striking.[28]

Along these trails institutional landmarks appear. In 1929, former students of Turner's at the University of Colorado convened a regional conference at Boulder on the history of the trans-Mississippi West. Papers presented there showed increasing interest in western social history and continued progress in describing western economic development. Bolton, Carl O. Sauer, Schafer, and Webb presented papers that are still impressive.[29] Some three decades later, the Museum of New Mexico in Santa Fe was the site, in 1961, of a conference on the "History of Western America." This meeting triggered the organization of the Western History Association, whose early leaders mobilized a significant historical constituency. The papers delivered in Santa Fe revealed a growing interest in the twentieth century and indicated that intellectual and social history, including that of women, held great promise. But there was no Webb or Sauer on the program. Unfortunately, one promised paper, "The History of the West: The Worst Scholarship in America," was not published in the volume of conference papers.[30]

In September 1989, the National Endowment for the Humanities sponsored the exhibit "Trails through Time" and the symposium "Trails: Toward a New Western History," marking the initial presentation of the display in Santa Fe. The papers presented there prompted the editor of *Montana The Magazine of Western History* to commission complementary essays on the nature of western history. The two sets of papers are presented, with additional views, in *Trails: Toward a New Western History*. That history, say the critics here, has been too much a triumphal account of an advancing empire, of the development of a mythic garden, and of the nineteenth century. Now we must look at the grimmer side of a story of conquest, tally the human and environmental waste involved, study the victims of the advance of empire and those neglected in the storytelling, analyze intercultural relations, and examine the twentieth-century West. These are sound precepts, although the enthusiasm of these critics recalls, to some, Arthur Guiterman's concluding couplet celebrating Edinburgh's fixation with Mary, Queen of Scots, and suggests a revised wording:

> And send us good historians to restore the many blots
> That rest upon the titles of all those western lots.[31]

The Textbook Writers

When Davis surveyed the state of western American history during the early 1960s, he noted the "immense importance" of textbooks in determining course content: the teachers of 169 out of 194 courses used a standard text. Such texts did much to shape the conception of the American West in the minds of generations of college-educated Americans. They are worth consideration.

In the year that Turner retired from teaching, the *History of the American Frontier, 1763–1893* by Frederic L. Paxson appeared. A University of Pennsylvania Ph.D. and Turner's successor at the University of Wisconsin, Paxson recalled the state of western history around 1900, when he had begun to teach at the University of Colorado:

> The frontier was gone; and the frontiersmen there . . . were adapting themselves to the life of a new century. Turner had already pointed out the significance of the frontier . . . but the occasional historical pioneer who followed his lead must make his own tools. . . . This is all changed today. . . . The time is ripe for this synthesis. . . . My successors will . . . do better, but none will complete his task with a firmer conviction . . . that the frontier with its continuous influence is the most American thing in all America. In future generations we . . . shall still possess and be shaped by a unique heritage.[32]

Viewing frontiers east of the Proclamation Line of 1763 as European frontiers, Paxson focused on settlement west of the Appalachians. Although briefly acknowledging Turner's preeminence in western history, Paxson was more the narrative historian. He muted Turner's use of social science concepts and showed less interest in the relation between physiography and settlement patterns. Like Turner, he undervalued the urban component, and if more detailed in describing settlement processes than Turner, he was also less accurate. Paxson did express some sympathy for the Indians, and although he mentioned Emma Smith in his text, no woman appears in his index. Describing the frontier mother as heroic, he disposed of her unique problems and contributions in one paragraph. There were other gaps; John Wesley Powell, for example, does not enter the story. Like Turner's course—strongest in its treatment of western diplomatics and political and economic development, weakest in its approach to social history—Paxson's text is genteel. Members of the Donner party suffered without resort to cannibalism, and the cattle towns knew no prostitutes or female temperance advocates. Paxson concluded:

> The frontier had disappeared, and with it had been removed . . . that special influence that had made American history unique. . . . There was still no cessation in the steady pressure of the new West upon the Nation. . . . But the distinctive frontier influence was undergoing transmutation into agrarian influence, and the struggle was henceforth to be less a contest between the older sections and the young, and more a struggle of the agricultural elements of society against the industrial.[33]

Paxson's book won a Pulitzer prize, and Richard Etulain recently termed it "just the text" that professional historians "needed and used in their classrooms," the "core text" in western history until Ray A. Billington published *Westward Expansion* in 1949.[34]

In addition to Paxson, we identify his former student Robert E. Riegel, Dan E. Clark, Ray A. Billington, and Thomas D. Clark as traditionalists.[35] All were essentially committed to a Turnerian analysis of the West. Publishing first in 1930, Riegel, like his teacher Paxson, made few explicit references to Turner. But in his edition of 1947, Riegel responded to the criticism of the frontier hypothesis, made Turner central to a new concluding chapter, and stigmatized as "ridiculous" the "trend toward developing the thesis that the frontier had *no* significant influence." He wrote, "No one of intelligence can really believe that the conquering of three thousand miles of wilderness did not leave some stamp on American history and character."[36] In 1937, Dan E. Clark affirmed his support of the major elements of Turner's thesis but also maintained that the successive stages of economic development described by Turner were more typical of the Middle West than the Far West.

Ray A. Billington (initially collaborating with James B. Hedges) maintained that his text "attempt[ed] to follow the pattern that Frederick Jackson Turner might have used." In this impressive and most used of western texts, Billington outlined western processes of development as he believed Turner had seen them, but with perhaps some surreptitious amendment. In this respect consider the concluding lines of the first edition: "The hardy, self-reliant men and women who through three centuries conquered the continent have played their role in the drama of American development; as they pass from the scene a new generation, freed from the prejudices of an outworn past where the needs of individuals transcended the needs of society, will blaze the trails into the newer world of co-operative democracy that is America's future." The last of the traditionalists to produce a text, Tom Clark, was more qualified in his Turnerian commitments, admitting in 1959 that the contribution of the frontier to American democracy might "remain an open question" forever. But he saw it as a "fiery test of sinew and courage" that confirmed the nation's understanding of its great potential, contributed "a keen sense of progress," and prepared Americans to accept "large challenges."[37]

The traditionalists tended to affirm Turner's assertion of progressive adaptation frontier by frontier, without much specific citation of evidence. Women played extremely minor roles in their accounts, and these writers followed Turner in omitting other significant aspects of pioneer life, although they edged toward a fuller presentation of the contributions of towns and cities in western development. Paxson and Riegel began their accounts with the 1760s; the others treated the earlier colonial frontiers as well. All five, however, terminated their accounts with the 1890s. Initially, Paxson, Riegel, and Clark used few maps, whereas Billington's attention to physiographic regions and cartography would have gladdened Turner's map-loving heart. In contrast to Paxson, Riegel introduced memorable characters—Mike Fink, Calamity Jane, and Jesse James among them—and included humorous doggerel. Clark quoted sources freely and emphasized colorful details, including Henri de Tonty's prosthetic iron hand. The chapter bibliographies in Billington's text were, of themselves, valuable research tools.

The traditionalists were ethnocentric and uniformly believed that the westward movement was a great achievement, but one also finds admission of treacherous U.S. policy regarding Indians, of wastefulness in the use of resources, of failure as well as success. Although they might have emphasized such matters more, these authors did not picture the westward movement as a process of unalloyed progress and development.

At the end of the 1960s, writers of western texts began to break new ground, to innovate. From a background in American studies, Kent L. Steckmesser identified himself as a neo-Turnerian, humanistic in perspective and emphasizing "biography, social institutions, and folkways." But it was Robert V. Hine who most clearly showed the influence of American studies, writing in 1973 of a West that was "part economic and social fact, part myth" and that "had a history peculiarly revised by dream," a place of "native races" and "motley actors . . . spilling over from old cultures and helping to begin a new history." Hine made violence, the western hero, and community-building the subjects of separate chapters and dotted his text with revisionary evaluations. The four major characteristics of the American frontier had been "rapid growth, dynamic expansion, violence, and disdain for authority." Racist but intolerant of slavery and highly inconsistent in other attitudes and positions as well, "the West," wrote Hine, "with its recurrent cycle of growth from primitive conditions, motivated by and continually selecting its own myths and legends, pervaded American life and will continue to color tomorrow." Turner, Hine argued, had accurately predicted the consequences of the frontier's closing: imperialism, intensified class struggle, and a trend toward socialistic politics.[38]

In 1974, Richard A. Bartlett viewed the westward movement as "a great sweep westward, unbroken, inevitable, of epic proportions." He emphasized the movement of population westward, its composition, everyday life, western families, and society. But he entitled one of the eight chapters in his social history of the American West "Despoilment: The Rape of the New Country" and emphasized "The Urban Frontier." Such "complexities" as the Louisiana Purchase or Indian treaties were "mere incidents washed away by the flood tide of the white man's advance." And "different nationalities" were less important than "the story of [the settlers'] acculturation and adjustment to the new country," one with "incredible opportunity for the reasonably healthy, stable, and hard-working person." America's frontier years were perhaps "the happiest time," he mused, "for a whole people in all history."[39]

Two years later, Arrell M. Gibson completed *The West in the Life of the Nation*, positing an "Old West" lying between the Appalachians and the western boundaries of the first tier of trans-Mississippi states and a "New West" stretching beyond to the Pacific. His, he wrote, was a "pluralistic approach" emphasizing the "social, cultural, and intellectual dimensions" of western history and tempering Turnerian "absolutes." To Gibson, the

"emergent American nation . . . surging with incredible velocity and ir-
repressible force westward across the continent into the Pacific Basin" was
one of "the grandest epics of human history." The West, he argued, had
"been the prime determinant of national economic direction and development." Westerners did "refine and expand . . . democratic processes,"
but western pioneering experiences were not "the principal determinants
of a distinctly American character or . . . cultural institutions." But
Gibson accepted Turner's theory of successive economic stages, expanding
their number considerably. Unlike Hine and Bartlett, he carried his account deep into the twentieth century. Like them, he stressed the wastefulness of westerners, entitling a chapter "Plundering the New West's
Natural Bounty."[40]

In 1976, Turner's student, collaborator, and heir at Harvard, Frederick
Merk, completed the text that probably best fit Turner's mold. But Merk's
extended coverage of twentieth-century issues places his book among the
works of the innovators. Turner, in 1893, argued Merk, had merely stated
that "the line of the continuous frontier" had ended and not that "the frontier in all its aspects had ended." To Merk the frontier still persisted, although "increasingly . . . in the realms of science and technology . . .
the environment . . . the relations of man to man." Affirming that the
westward movement was "the greatest migration of peoples in recorded
history," Merk noted that it also involved "conquest, speculation, exploitation, and violence."[41]

Authors also examined subareas or chronological subdivisions of western history in books of sufficient scope to be used for textual reading: Cardinal Goodwin's treatment of the trans-Mississippi West, written in 1922;
Webb's 1931 monograph *The Great Plains*, immediately enshrined—at
least in Texas—as gospel and text for understanding adaptation to the
plains country; and LeRoy Hafen and Carl Rister's *Western America*, first
available in 1941. The last two authors explained that they were primarily
concerned with "the problems of conquest and settlement" and portrayed
a settler "sprung from a new soil, transformed by contact with forest and
Indian, an admixture of non-English blood in his veins, he was a newly
molded type—an American." Despite this flourish, Hafen and Rister were
severely factual. Their edition of 1970 included accounts of twentieth-century territorial, agricultural, industrial, and urban development. By this
time, Earl Pomeroy's thoughtful and pathbreaking *The Pacific Slope: A
History of California, Oregon, Washington, Idaho, Utah, and Nevada* had
appeared, developing a countertheory of western development and emphasizing cultural continuities and urban growth. Less prophetic of future

scholarly trends than Webb's or Pomeroy's volumes was John A. Hawgood's well-written but essentially traditional *America's Western Frontiers*, published in 1967.[42]

In 1973, Gerald D. Nash provided the first textual survey of the West's history during the twentieth century—using the phrase "urban oasis" in his subtitle. "Culture," wrote Nash, "and environment . . . have been the two great formative factors in the development of the twentieth-century West." Westerners were unique and faced a singular challenge in developing and melding dry and humid subregions. Influence between nation and region ran in each direction, but the West threw off its status as a colonial periphery to become a pacesetter in meeting the challenges of interacting cultures, in developing new industrial and technological solutions in both urban and agricultural settings, and in adopting metropolitan and suburban lifeways.[43]

Of the participants in the Santa Fe "Trails" symposium in 1989 and the contributors to its related publications, Richard White alone has written a full-scale western text: *"It's Your Misfortune and None of My Own."* White's West, however, is the trans-Missouri West, which he believes forms a coherent, but somewhat heterogeneous, western America today. Turner does not appear in White's index, and gone is the idea that the social processes associated with a moving frontier were unique in form and impact or even usefully comparative, although he delineates interaction between his West and the nation. To White, "the American West is a product of conquest and of the mixing of diverse groups of peoples. The West began when Europeans sought to conquer various areas of the continent and when people of Indian, European, Asian, and African ancestry began to meet within the territories west of the Missouri that would later be part of the United States."[44]

"It's Your Misfortune and None of My Own" repeats some of the ideas of the innovators and the subdividers but also strongly shows the influence of the new social history. Here we find concepts unknown to the traditionalists: transformations, two-tiered labor systems, household production, gender and the cult of domesticity, models, metaphors, myths, irony, and much else. If the traditionalists believed that they were presenting their readers with a golden key to American history, White, some may suggest, offers them a salad bowl of middle-range generalizations. In summarizing the research in western history during the last thirty years and especially that research relating to cultural interaction, modern western society, and the interactions between urbanization, corporations, and federal presence, White's book is a *tour de force*. But he also abandoned much that some his-

torians find hard to surrender. He also, others believe, revealed the westerner's proverbial land hunger by claiming the midwestern fringe states for his province even though the economic and cultural ties of the inhabitants still run primarily to the East.

Obviously, western textbook writers have changed and adapted their emphases, ideas, and material over time, although they held to some themes with unwise tenacity—particularly the magical significance of the 1890s. All scholars of stature, they have, of necessity, reflected the state of the periodical and monographic literature of their times. None of them have stood independent of the work of earlier scholars. They have, we suspect, been less responsible for romantic notions about the West than more popular writers.

Significance of Western History

In 1941, Samuel Eliot Morison, once a member of Turner's seminar, wrote:

> Turner's thesis served a very useful purpose. It stimulated study and interest in American history, served to differentiate our history from that of other lands, removed the inferiority-complex of the West and made that section proudly conscious of her immediate past, struck at the intellectual complacency of New England, and the romanticism of the South— and, not least, gave to hundreds of young westerners topics for books they could integrate with their environment.[45]

Although ranging from regional psyches to the pragmatism of book topics, Morison left much unsaid.

At its most elemental level, western history was the foundation on which a charismatic young scholar rose to eminence in a growing and professionalizing academic discipline. To read Frederick Jackson Turner's correspondence, to trace his daily routines, and to try to rethink his thoughts is to relive much of our own experience. His was the generation that established modern academic history—its interaction with administrators, its sense that graduate instruction and research are more important than undergraduate teaching, and its understanding that offers of jobs power the academic escalator. At the institutional level, the history of the West was also a weapon in a contest for regional educational hegemony that reflected the booming, developmental aspirations of western educators. Emphasis on the history of the West at the University of Wisconsin represented in part an effort to capitalize on local assets in a race with the University of Chicago for midwestern educational leadership.

In regional terms, the academic history of the West demonstrated that the country beyond the Appalachians also had a proud history and was an integral and important part of the American experience. Western soldiers had played a major role in saving the Union, and between 1850 and 1890 the economic transformation of the north-central region of the country was phenomenal. There had been approximately 438,000 farms there in 1850; by 1890 there were almost two million. Studying the national and regional economic development of this era, a team of economists later termed the Lake States "one of the greatest resource regions in the American economy," providing "a firm foundation for its own burgeoning manufactures and commerce" and "strength to the continuing thrust of industry elsewhere."[46] Between 1860 and 1900, western men almost monopolized the presidency, and after the 1890 redistricting, the north-central census region of the United States provided 36 percent of the nation's congressmen. Thus historians of trans-Appalachia had substantial ground for believing that they had an important and hitherto unappreciated story to tell.

It was Turner's genius, or luck, that he was able to meld basic facts of western growth with long-held ideas of western uniqueness and the scientific theories and popular concerns of the day into a rhetorical statement that became one of the most powerful explanations of American development and character. Although the western history course in important elements preceded the statement of the thesis, the thesis in turn provided a conceptual core that other history courses lacked. To study western history was to understand American growth, institutions, and values. Spread in hundreds of classrooms, the message could also be used by specialists elsewhere in the discipline—diplomatic history, for example—or as a baseline in the study of national cultures, and it could be useful to the psychologist or to Aldo Leopold advocating the retention of wilderness.[47] Absorbed within American culture, it could reinforce the American sense of uniqueness and accomplishment, strengthening our very nationalism.

At a less rarefied level, the history of the West gave generations of college students the best and, often, only introduction to their region and locality. In college history courses they learned how the Indians were dispossessed from their area, how the land was distributed to their ancestors, how their local and state governments came to be, and how these contrasted with experiences in other regions. Explicitly or implicitly, depending on the instructor and the time, the survey course in western history was a record of American aspirations, dreams, and myths. For many, it was an unmatched exercise in self-identification.

It was significant also that Turner's model of American development was interdisciplinary. Graduate students at Johns Hopkins absorbed large amounts of political economy. Turner, in 1892–93, was a faculty member of the School of Economics, Political Science, and History at the University of Wisconsin. In 1904, he wrote to Albion Small that there should be more sociology in history and more history in sociology.[48] The influence of other disciplines is apparent in his early publications. One of the most interesting aspects of western studies has been the fact that interaction with other disciplines has recurrently led to change in the content of western history.

What may we ask is the significance of the new western history? In part, the critics within the *Trails* detachment articulated ongoing tendencies, but the institutional expression of their discontents and dreams and the storm of popular and professional reaction have produced an intellectual ferment of unprecedented magnitude in western history. In broader perspective the new western history is one in a series of revitalizations that have occurred in American history since World War II but one that is unique in that elements of the general public apparently are also interested. In 1957, new economic historians were raising the standard of revolt in a conference at Williams College, and a less heralded meeting on political history at Rutgers University focused the behavioral thrust that produced a so-called new political history. By the mid-1960s, a new urban history was apparent, and somewhat later a transformation occurred in labor history when working-class history emerged; still later some historians proclaimed a new agricultural history. While older fields of interest underwent significant change, cadres of researchers energetically developed relatively ignored areas of American social history, such as the history of women and racial minorities.

Typically, in such revitalization, dissatisfaction with the values, concerns, and methods of historians in a subarea of the discipline have led individuals, usually those of a new generation, to reconceptualize the field by introducing new topical focuses, different assumptions, and new methods and by exploiting new source material or using old sources in different ways. As interest builds in conversations at professional meetings and in seminars, networks emerge to legitimize and spread the new approaches. Often a particular conference or meeting serves as a catalyst, solidifying opinion into holy cause. (The messianic gleam detected in the eyes of some new western historians is no more pronounced than that observed in the eyes of leading cliometricians during the early 1960s.)

The proposals of the new historians excite each other and draw adherents, especially senior graduate students. Particularly "hot" exponents of the new departures are deluged with invitations to appear on the programs of professional associations or to give lectures at other institutions of higher learning or in public forums. Their lecture fees escalate, and some suffer from jet lag and nervous exhaustion. Critics point out that the new prescription is not as new as claimed—citing examples—or note that the analysis involves sins of both omission and commission. Various older scholars take strong exception to the missionary message. Some frauds, sloppy workers, or overexuberant practitioners attach themselves to the movement, giving the critics particularly inviting targets. In the end the new historians are judged not by their preachments but by their scholarly product. Does their work help significantly in understanding important outcomes? Judging from past experiences, we see that so far no group of new historians in the post–World War II era has failed to alter the perspective and content of its field. But the most extreme positions taken by the new historians are sometimes rejected. In general, a stronger and more useful history has been the result, and there is every reason to believe that this will be true in western history as well.

Turner once wrote, "Each age writes the history of the past anew with reference to the conditions uppermost in its own time."[49] We have read this as a more devastating restriction on historical understanding and achievement than it needs to be. Whether implicitly or explicitly, historians ask questions about past human actions and historical events. The changing human condition dictates that new generations will ask different questions. That does not mean that their predecessors did not ask important questions or that all of their answers were wrong, then or later. But not all of those questions, or all of the answers, may be useful to a succeeding generation. One of the significant aspects of the history of the American West is that four-plus generations have found it possible to ask important questions about the subject matter around which Turner drove his claim stakes. Patricia Nelson Limerick has correctly noted, "In the second half of the twentieth century, every major issue from 'frontier' history reappeared in the courts or in Congress."[50]

Population mobility and change, community-building, intercultural relations, natural resource policy and management, the characteristics and problems of extractive industries, adaptation to natural environment as well as to technological, economic, and institutional change, urbanization, and the problems of development generally, including colonialism and its other face, dependency—these were and still are important processes, uniquely combined in the American West. In that fact lies the vitality of western history. Adjusting the curriculum to best convey an understanding of these issues and processes in relation to the problems of the future—that is our great challenge. Will subinfeudation continue until the survey course in western history disappears? Will western historians shrink their field to make a regional stand—perhaps their last—behind some midcontinental barrier? Will a new "holistic" formula emerge? Will fresh thinking and imagination carry an old heritage through new times and challenges? Our students and their students will decide.

Notes

An earlier version of this essay appeared under the title "The Significance of the History of the American West: Postscripts and Prospects," by Allan G. Bogue. Previously published in the *Western Historical Quarterly* 24 (February 1993): 45–68. Copyright by Western History Association. Reprinted by permission.

1. John Franklin Jameson to John Jameson, 5 January 1889, in *An Historian's World: Selections from the Correspondence of John Franklin Jameson,* ed. Elizabeth Donnan and Leo F. Stock (Philadelphia, 1956), 46; University of Wisconsin, *Catalogue, 1895–96* (Madison, 1895), 140.

2. William E. Foster to Herbert B. Adams, 5 April 1883, in *Historical Scholarship in the United States, 1876–1901: As Revealed in the Correspondence of Herbert B. Adams,* ed. W. Stull Holt (Baltimore, 1938), 61; University of Wisconsin, *Catalogue, 1887–88* (Madison, 1887), 35–36; University of Wisconsin, *Catalogue, 1909–10* (Madison, 1909), 601–2.

3. Herbert B. Adams to the president and executive committee of the Johns Hopkins University, 29 May 1886, in Holt, *Historical Scholarship in the United States,* 82–83; Herbert B. Adams, *The College of William and Mary,* U.S. Bureau of Education, Circulars of Information, No. 1, 1887, 73–74, as cited in Holt, *Historical Scholarship in the United States,* 94 n. 1.

4. The fullest account of Turner's emergence is provided by Ray Allen Billington, *Frederick Jackson Turner: Historian, Scholar, Teacher* (New York, 1973), 34–131. See also Wilbur R. Jacobs, *The Historical World of Frederick Jackson Turner with Selections from his Correspondence* (New Haven, 1968). Note also Fulmer Mood, "The Development of Frederick Jackson Turner as a Historical Thinker," *Publications of the Colonial Society of Massachusetts: Transactions, 1937–1942* (Boston, 1943), 283–352.

5. University of Wisconsin, *Catalogue, 1909–10,* 173.

6. Billington, *Frederick Jackson Turner,* 135–36; University of Wisconsin, *Catalogue, 1895–1896,* 140.

7. University of Wisconsin, *Catalogue, 1891–92* (Madison, 1891), 98; University of Wisconsin, *Catalogue, 1892–93* (Madison, 1892), 62; University of Wisconsin, *Catalogue, 1893–94* (Madison, 1893), 72; University of Wisconsin, *Catalogue, 1895–96,* 140.

8. Frederick Jackson Turner, *Outline Studies in the History of the Northwest* (Chicago, 1888); Frederick Jackson Turner to William F. Allen, 16 January, 14 March 1889, Frederick Jackson Turner Papers, Henry E. Huntington Library, San Marino, Calif. Turner's earlier statements are collected in *The Early Writings of Frederick Jackson Turner,* with an introduction by Fulmer Mood (Madison, 1938). Note

the criticism of Hermann Von Holst, a University of Chicago professor, in Frederick Jackson Turner, *The Frontier in American History* (New York, 1920), 24, and the bouquet tossed to Herbert B. Adams in ibid., 25.

9. Frederick Jackson Turner to Richard T. Ely, 29 January, 1 February 1892, Richard T. Ely Papers, State Historical Society of Wisconsin, Madison; undated memorandum (circa 1903) concerning the importance of maintaining a summer school, Frederick Jackson Turner Papers, University of Wisconsin Archives, Madison.

10. Turner to Ely, 19 February 1892, Ely Papers.

11. University of Wisconsin, *Catalogue,* for years 1889–1910.

12. John R. Wunder, ed., *Historians of the American Frontier: A Bio-Bibliographical Sourcebook* (New York, 1988).

13. The roster of those completing the Ph.D. under Turner's direction was compiled from Billington, *Frederick Jackson Turner,* and Jacobs, *Historical World,* from various lists in the Turner Papers at the Huntington Library, from the *Blue* and *Red Books* of testimonials in that collection, and from former students mentioned in Merle E. Curti, "The Section and the Frontier in American History: The Methodological Concepts of Frederick Jackson Turner," in *Methods in Social Science: A Case Book,* ed. Stuart A. Rice (Chicago, 1931), 353–57, as well as from the entries in Warren F. Kuehl, *Dissertations in History: An Index to Dissertations Completed in History Departments of United States and Canadian Universities, 1873–1960* (Lexington, 1965).

14. Frederick Jackson Turner to Constance Lindsay Skinner, 15 March 1922, in Jacobs, *Historical World,* 55–62. The 1931–32 data are based on a questionnaire circulated to the archivists in two major institutions in each state and the District of Columbia. I wish to thank the archivists who cooperated so promptly and helpfully.

15. W. N. Davis Jr., "Will the West Survive as a Field in American History? A Survey Report," *Mississippi Valley Historical Review* 50 (March 1964): 672–85; *Directory of History Departments and Organizations in the United States and Canada, 1991–92,* ed. Robert B. Townsend (Washington, D.C., 1991).

16. Carl Abbott, "Tracing the Trends in U.S. Regional History," *Perspectives* 28 (February 1990): 6. I owe thanks to Paul Andrew Hutton, who provided me with membership lists of the Western History Association.

17. In analyzing syllabi, I have used Frederick Jackson Turner, *List of References in History 17: History of the West* (Cambridge, Mass., 1911); Frederick Jackson Turner, *List of References on the History of the West* (Cambridge, Mass., 1913, 1915); Frederick Jackson Turner and Frederick Merk, *List of References on the History of the West* (Cambridge, Mass., 1922).

18. John M. Gaus, "Lecture Notes," February–June 1920, Turner Papers, University of Wisconsin Archives.

19. Ibid., 29 March, 5 May 1920.

20. Turner, *The Frontier in American History,* 19; Gaus, "Notes," 14 May 1920; Turner and Merk, *List of References,* 7–12. Turner's role as an adviser of women graduate students and his views on their place in the history teaching profession will be considered in another publication.

21. Gaus, "Notes," 14 May 1920.

22. Ibid., 19, 24 May 1920.

23. Ibid., 26, 28 May, 2 June 1920.

24. Ibid., 2 June 1920.

25. Illustrative works include the following: Marcus Lee Hansen, *The Atlantic Migration, 1607–1860: A History of the Continuing Settlement of the United States* (Cambridge, Mass., 1941), published posthumously; Frederick Merk, *The Oregon Question: Essays in Anglo-American Diplomacy and Politics* (Cambridge, Mass., 1967); Paul W. Gates, *History of Public Land Law Development* (Washington, D.C., 1968); Arthur P. Whitaker, *The Spanish-American Frontier, 1783–1795: The Westward Movement and the Spanish Retreat in the Mississippi Valley* (Boston, 1927); Thomas P. Abernethy, *From Frontier to Plantation in Tennessee: A Study in Frontier Democracy* (Chapel Hill, 1932); Edward E. Dale, *The Range Cattle Industry: Ranching on the Great Plains from 1865 to 1925* (Norman, 1930); Everett Dick, *The Sod-House Frontier, 1854–1890: A Social History of the Northern Plains from the Creation of Kansas and Nebraska to the Admission of the Dakotas* (New York, 1937); Herbert E. Bolton, *The Spanish Borderlands: A Chronicle of Old Florida and the Southwest* (New Haven, 1921); Herbert E. Bolton, *Wider Horizons of American History* (New York, 1939); Walter P. Webb, *The Great Plains* (Boston, 1931); James C. Malin, *The Grassland of North America: Prolegomena to Its History* (Lawrence, 1947).

26. George W. Pierson, "American Historians and the Frontier Hypothesis in 1941," parts 1 and 2, *Wisconsin Magazine of History* 26 (September 1942): 36–60; (December 1942): 170–85. For other representative criticism, see George Rogers Taylor, ed., *The Turner Thesis Concerning the Role of the Frontier in American History* (1949; 3d ed., Lexington, 1972), and Henry Nash Smith, *Virgin Land: The American West as Symbol and Myth* (1950; reprint, Cambridge, Mass., 1970).

27. Stanley Elkins and Eric McKitrick, "A Meaning for Turner's Frontier, Part 1: Democracy in the Old Northwest," *Political Science Quarterly* 69 (September 1954): 321–53. See also Richard Hofstadter and Seymour Martin Lipset, eds., *Turner and the Sociology of the Frontier* (New York, 1968); David M. Potter, *People of Plenty: Economic Abundance and the American Character* (Chicago, 1954); Herbert Heaton, "Other Wests than Ours," *The Tasks of Economic History*, supplement to *Journal of Economic History* 6 (1946): 50–62; Paul F. Sharp, "Three Frontiers: Some Comparative Studies of Canadian, American, and Australian Settlement," *Pacific Historical Review* 24 (November 1955): 369–77; Earl Pomeroy, "Toward a Reorientation of Western History: Continuity and Environment," *Mississippi Valley Historical Review* 41 (March 1955): 579–600; and Robert F. Berkhofer Jr., "Space, Time, Culture, and the New Frontier," *Agricultural History* 38 (January 1964): 21–30. For old assumptions tested, see Allan G. Bogue, "The Iowa Claim Clubs: Symbol and Substance," *Mississippi Valley Historical Review* 45 (September 1958): 231–53; Richard Maxwell Brown, *Strain of Violence: Historical Studies of American Violence and Vigilantism* (New York, 1975), essays extending back to the 1960s. Howard R. Lamar, *The Far Southwest, 1846–1912: A Territorial History* (New Haven, 1966); Dale L. Morgan, *Jedediah Smith and the Opening of the West* (Indianapolis, 1953); and Wallace Stegner, *Beyond the Hundredth Meridian: John Wesley Powell and the Second Opening of the West* (Boston, 1954). See also Billington, *Frederick Jackson Turner*, and Jacobs, *Historical World*.

28. For bibliographical reviews to the mid-1980s, see Michael P. Malone, ed., *Historians and the American West* (Lincoln, 1983), and Roger L. Nichols, ed., *American Frontier and Western Issues: A Historiographical Review* (New York, 1986). See also the reviews and bibliographical lists in the *Western Historical Quarterly*.

29. James F. Willard and Colin B. Goodykoontz, eds., *The Trans-Mississippi West: Papers Read at a Conference Held at the University of Colorado, June 18–21, 1929* (Boulder, 1930).

30. K. Ross Toole et al., eds., *Probing the American West: Papers from the Santa Fe Conference* (Santa Fe, 1962).

31. Patricia Nelson Limerick, Clyde A. Milner II, and Charles E. Rankin, eds., *Trails: Toward a New Western History* (Lawrence, 1991); Arthur Guiterman, "Edinburgh," in *The Pocket Book of Humorous Verse,* ed. David McCord (New York, 1945), 109–10. Just as defining "Turnerian" and "neoTurnerian" is difficult, so also, at times, is distinguishing "new" from "old" western history.

32. Frederic L. Paxson, *History of the American Frontier, 1763–1893* (Boston, 1924), v.

33. Ibid., 573.

34. Richard W. Etulain, ed., *Writing Western History: Essays on Major Western Historians* (Albuquerque, 1991), 152.

35. Robert E. Riegel, *America Moves West* (New York, 1930); Dan Elbert Clark, *The West in American History* (New York, 1937); Ray Allen Billington, *Westward Expansion: A History of the American Frontier* (New York, 1949); Thomas D. Clark, *Frontier America: The Story of the Westward Movement* (New York, 1959).

36. Robert E. Riegel, *America Moves West,* 2d ed. (New York, 1947), 624.

37. Billington, *Westward Expansion,* vii, 756; Clark, *Frontier America,* 24, 762.

38. Kent L. Steckmesser, *The Westward Movement: A Short History* (New York, 1969), v; Robert V. Hine, *The American West: An Interpretive History* (Boston, 1973), vii, 320, 334.

39. Richard A. Bartlett, *The New Country: A Social History of the American Frontier, 1776–1890* (New York, 1974), vi, 448.

40. Arrell M. Gibson, *The West in the Life of the Nation* (Lexington, 1976), viii–ix.

41. Frederick Merk, *History of the Westward Movement* (New York, 1978), 616–17.

42. Cardinal Goodwin, *The Trans-Mississippi West (1803–1853): A History of Its Acquisition and Settlement* (New York, 1922); Webb, *The Great Plains*; LeRoy R. Hafen and Carl Coke Rister, *Western America: The Exploration, Settlement, and Development of the Region beyond the Mississippi* (New York, 1941), viii, 74; Earl Pomeroy, *The Pacific Slope: A History of California, Oregon, Washington, Idaho, Utah, and Nevada* (New York, 1965); John A. Hawgood, *America's Western Frontiers: The Exploration and Settlement of the Trans-Mississippi West* (New York, 1967).

43. Gerald D. Nash, *The American West in the Twentieth Century: A Short History of an Urban Oasis* (Englewood Cliffs, N.J., 1973), 2. Michael P. Malone and Richard W. Etulain, *The American West: A Twentieth-Century History* (Lincoln, 1989), provides an eclectic alternative.

44. Richard White, *"It's Your Misfortune and None of My Own": A New History*

of the American West (Norman, 1991), 4. Depending on the other reading assigned, Patricia Nelson Limerick, *The Legacy of Conquest: The Unbroken Past of the American West* (New York, 1987), might also serve as a text.

45. Morison quoted in Pierson, "American Historians and the Frontier Hypothesis," 41–42.

46. Harvey S. Perloff et al., *Regions, Resources, and Economic Growth* (Baltimore, 1960), 175.

47. Curt Meine, *Aldo Leopold: His Life and Work* (Madison, 1988), 233, 244, 345, 352.

48. Frederick Jackson Turner to Albion Small, 4 November 1904, Turner Papers, University of Wisconsin Archives.

49. Turner, "The Significance of History," *Early Writings,* 52.

50. Limerick, *Legacy of Conquest*, 31.

2

Fighting Words:
The Significance of the American West
in the History of the United States

William Deverell

"Somebody's always looking for something in this part of the West," rancher Reno Smith says in the middle of the dark western film *Bad Day at Black Rock*. "To the historian it's the Old West. To the book writer it's the Wild West. To the businessman it's the underdeveloped West. They say we're all poor and backward and I guess we are. We don't even have enough water. But to us this place is our West, and I wish they'd leave us alone."[1]

Made in 1954, the film takes place in the California desert just after the end of the Second World War. Spencer Tracy's character John J. Macready, coolly investigating a murder, is unimpressed by Reno Smith's plaintive speech. But it is these words that I remembered when I began thinking about this essay. Somehow Smith succeeds in touching on some of western history's most important concepts. Spoken in cinematic sound bites, here are the organizing tools used by several generations of western scholars. The notion of an "old" and "wild" frontier West appears first, suggesting a boundary on the other side of which is the tame, new West. "We don't even have enough water," Smith laments, a blunt declaration of the West's arid barrier running north and south at the ninety-eighth meridian. Here too is the outpost colonial economy in which natural resources become valued commodities exchanged for eastern and foreign goods or cash. We even get a glimpse of that macho icon of western American lore, that "leave us alone" defensiveness: the West as refuge for defiant individuals brandishing cherished individualism.

Hollywood depends on scriptwriters who can, for better or worse, reduce American history and American culture to just a few lines. Rarely do such writers have the option or inclination to wander historical terrain with care. Shared facility with words notwithstanding, screenwriters and historians do not usually share the same West. But Reno Smith's quick recital of critical frames of western historical analysis did a remarkable thing: it smartly captured, in a few concise sentences, the concerns of this major subfield of the American historical enterprise.

Even though Hollywood has never lost its fascination with the West, such cinematic simplifying would today be impossible. Outside of an act-long soliloquy or a tedious interview, it is hard to imagine a film figure doing justice to the field's wide-ranging concerns. Western history is simply a different sort of pursuit from what it was a generation or two ago. These days it is concerned with issues beyond six or seven catchphrase ideas. No longer comfortable with the familiar in western American history—arid environmental determinism, frontiers giving way to postfrontiers, national character expressed as western masculinity—historians now seek to defamiliarize the field and its icons. They hope to disassemble that which was once solid so that a scholarly reassembly may yield new insight into the whole of American history. What is more, western historians increasingly ask whether there are new patterns to see in the mosaic of western America or even new patterns of *seeing*. Can our work be reconceptualized, from the outset of inquiry, with new questions about the West and about western history? Can those stories that make up the understandings of the western and American past be supplemented with other views? Can the fragmentary, even mythic, lives that historians make into history be altered or supplemented so that partial narratives get better at representing the richness of the American past? If so, will anyone pay attention? Will anyone care?

There have been encouraging signs. The Turner Centennial Conference held in the summer of 1992 at Utah State University, Logan, Utah, brought several dozen scholars together, united, if but temporarily, in the common pursuit of "western significance." Each went about her or his respective tasks differently. Some sought to analyze threads of regional history, leaning analysis against the West as place. Others were concerned with the West as process. Still others wandered a vague middle ground. All the Logan papers, comments, and discussions raised hard questions about how to begin thinking about the West in a new way. For instance, can western historians uncover truths about American history by pairing process with place? Can or should such pairing come in chronological sequence? Do we learn more about the West when we think of process giving way to place at some point in time?[2]

Questions such as these separated us as we tried to determine various ways to approach our work and our Wests. Deeper than any differences ran a shared, unspoken certainty: the historical West—place, process, whatever—is breathtakingly complicated. The work gets harder when we wonder what, exactly, is significant about the place, the process, and our analyses of both.[3] What exactly is *significance* in the first place?

I begin with a simple premise: the collected stories that make up the history of the West are ideal texts for the analysis of power throughout American history. That alone makes the West significant, but "Fighting Words" seeks also to exchange certain significances for others. In other words, significance itself is elastic: different truths, events, and meanings about the West have been determined as significant at different points in national history. That "determination of significance" is a dramatic contest—between political points of view, between scholarly generations, between the public and the academy, between the West and the outside. Simply put, western significance is no mild thing: as much as it is thought about, it is fought about.

Looking West

The American West plays an immense role in shaping and explaining American history. This truism has been molded into a popular understanding that the West—particularly the story of nineteenth-century frontiering—remains heroically detached from anywhere and anytime else in the nation and the nation's past. Companion to this "tyranny of the frontier" is a notion that the remote, heroicized West is itself more representative of national character than any other chronological or regional chapter in the text of popularized American history. These are troubling concepts to many western historians, scholars who argue that the West's sequential demographic catalog, with its familiar successive stages of explorer, trapper, settler, and on and on, hardly begins to tell the story. What is more, the western field is in the vanguard of an exciting reassessment of the entire supposed progression of American history: the story itself is in question.

Better analytic tools help western historians re-envision the West. These include a more sophisticated understanding of power, particularly that wielded by the state, and the ways in which power fills space on the western conceptual landscape. Power is being chased from its obvious and less obvious hiding places, particularly by scholars engaged in arenas within and across categories of race, class, gender, and environment. This essay closes with a suggestion that historians need to think more about addressing power through the prism of dependence and independence, especially by using a concept borrowed from legal studies, the ward/guardian relationship. Regardless of method, recent acclaim makes it clear that western historians are breaking new historical ground in all varieties of settings.

One deceptively simple contribution of recent work is the idea that we can learn a great deal more about the West and its significance when we render plural that which has been regarded as singular. This essay is about different significances and about different Wests; what I am concerned with here is probing the meanings behind those plurals. At the heart of this investigation is an interrogation of a compelling stereotype: "the West."[4]

What does this mean? My expedition is bracketed by an assumption that there exists one great narrative of the American West. It is a mythic image cultivated by all sorts of entities, from journalists to politicians to corporations, and it is a view fiercely protected by nostalgia and sentiment. It is a West both understood and explained by Ralph Lauren, Frontierland, Levi's, High Noon, rodeos, and Ronald Reagan, as well as countless history texts and tests. We all know about this West, the West of little houses and prairies, good and bad guys, Conestogas, and lusty days of yesteryear. This image is one that, as one writer put it, casts the West as "America's primordial sandbox." This is the mega-narrative, the supernarrative of many names, one equally as good as another: the legend of national fulfillment, the saga of cowboys and Indians, the hardy pioneer epic.[5] It is not necessarily true, and it is not necessarily false, but it is powerful. It is what so many people, adults and schoolkids alike, still think and believe when they imagine the West: that it is somehow different from the rest of the country and its history is different from the rest of the country's history, that it is marked by adjectives like *rugged*, *brave*, and *true* more than is any other time or any other place in all the American past.[6]

There is a quieter alternative working its way through parallel streams of public and academic consciousness. This vision of the West, or bundle of visions, does not exactly flip the other on its head, but there is great animosity between the two. At the very least, this collection of new stories (exactly that rendering of West into Wests) is trying to seize conceptual and explanatory power from the Super West that has, in Richard White's apt phrasing, taken "pride of place in the American imagination."[7] Wresting the history of the American West from the jealous grasp of myth calls for fighting words, precisely because possession of that past is so important to the present.

Competing visions of the western past assume different western significances. Newer versions of western history and understanding explicitly claim that the significance of particular, formerly unfamiliar western histories need now to be scrutinized, even emphasized. Not the least of these concerns is the necessity of stretching western American history beyond the raw limits of last century's imperial westward expansion, a period the supernarrative adores as much as it misrepresents. Similarly, much of the work challenging older notions expresses a wariness and exasperation over supposed western distinctiveness and exceptionalism, a tendency that invites marginalization on all sorts of political, cultural, and academic fronts.[8]

Assumptions of the West's exceptionalism are not new: remember, for instance, James Bryce's impenetrable reduction that took the equation even a step further: "What America is to Europe, what Western America is to Eastern, that California is to the other Western States."[9] Exceptionalism assumes western isolation, a belief that the West, by geography, history, and circumstance, is somehow outside of America. But, of course, except for a dividing mountain range or two, the West is not separate from the rest of the nation, nor has it ever been. Scholars of the American West err if they offer their insights as mere regional history, unable to transcend geography in addressing problems of the American, much less human, condition. That serves merely to reinforce the assumption of an isolated West, a West that, when it comes to explaining American history, is either special enough to be purely representative—an American mirror, as Bryce would have it—or so disappointingly distinctive that it tells us nothing at all about history outside regional divides.[10] The West is less than a perfect representation of, and more than only a regional variation on, American history, life, and character. Between those poles, scholars active in western American research and teaching take up Wallace Stegner's charge that the West "could use a little more confidence in itself" as they demonstrate the significance of the American West both to itself and to America.[11]

A first step is to encounter the region in its own terms. Think of experiencing this built and unbuilt West: standing atop Yosemite's Half Dome at sunset, hiking the Gore Range in Colorado, maneuvering through the canyons of Los Angeles skyscrapers, wandering the Texas hill country, visiting the pueblos of New Mexico, gazing out across miles of central Oregon wheat, navigating the endless grasslands of the central plains. It would be difficult not to have a visceral response to the West's sheer grandeur. This is one West, a well-known West, a much-photographed, much-painted, awe-inspiring place. This is the West of wide-open spaces, the West as last great place, the West of Manifest Destiny, the Big Sky, a dreamscape accepted as fundamental to America and fundamentally American.

Gut response to beauty is not the same thing as significance. This is not to say that this Big West is entirely without meaning, of course, but it is an image often divorced from the dramas of people's lives and the attachment of the living and the dead to the landscape. There is significance when beauty and grandeur are utilized as interpretive prisms; observers *explain* the people of (and peopling of) the West when they argue that human behavior is environmentally determined in the West in ways different from (or stronger than) those seen elsewhere in America.

As complement to the built and natural environment, the West exudes human historical bigness. The western embrace—however geologically or geographically defined—collects the histories of people, living and dead, the raw stuff of social and political history. Too many of these men, women, and children remain historically mute and invisible. As Elliott West has noted:

> We are obliged to study everyone who has ever lived in the West—and for the length of time they have lived there. That sounds obvious, but in fact the story of many peoples have [*sic*] been told only in relation to the frontier epic of the last century. Reading older texts, for example, it is easy to get the impression that Indians and Hispanics were significant only as barriers to the bold frontiersmen who pushed beyond the Missouri after 1820. One wonders how the Nez Perce and Navajos survived the boredom of long centuries waiting for invaders from the East to show up.[12]

The West is conceptually massive as well, at once place and many places, process and many processes, even something akin to ideology in popular conception.[13] Any slice of western time or space reveals that complexity: the vagaries of geopolitical history that have defined the West, the region's permutations of American social process and demography, the clash of cultural and political contests. When gathered as a collection of Wests, the loose package of western landscape, ideas, and people becomes all the more meaningful, all the more significant.

No less obvious than a giant mountain range is that scholars study the American West because it is dangerous not to, because wrapped in any significance test or demonstration are interpretive agendas worth fighting over and fighting for. Scholars tussle with themselves and those outside the academy in a contentious debate over representations of the West as true America. The so-called new western history adds an edge to western scholarship along with an inclination to saddle the West with different representations, different significances. Membership in the new western history club is hardly so important as learning from the insights of reinvigorated thinking.

Perhaps more so than their predecessors, new western historians admit just how extraordinarily slippery history can be. We are history's prisoners:

something happened *sometime* to create the world we inhabit, to render the past into the present. Less comforting, and far less absolute, is the realization that history is frighteningly malleable if it can be run down, gathered up, packaged, and sold. Interpretation alters how the present views the past by virtually changing that past. With past as cause and present as effect, western historians test public reactions to historical lessons.

Such interpretive tinkering rarely leads to uncritical celebration. The West can no longer be memorialized because it fulfilled or fulfills some vague, unsettling expectation of national destiny or greatness. To do so smooths the rough edges of the western past. Instead, historians go West to work in a laboratory ideally suited to investigating an American history that falls short of destiny and epic.

Environmental study offers a good example of this invigorated scholarship. Sophisticated analyses of the West juxtapose environmental despoilment with grandeur. That juxtaposition itself pushes scholars into new understandings, since it does little good simply to add an example of degradation as counterpart to each picture of beauty. An environmental grid prompts an entirely new conception of the West, one pointing toward failure far more often than triumph. Given the game of chicken now being played with environmental catastrophe, a greater understanding of western environmental history may help dull the impact of inevitable crisis. This requires that scholars push beyond the banality of landscape fascination to uncover root causes of environmental distress. In what may be the field's most important collective act, western historians increasingly turn out works (and students) that ask tough and disruptive questions about the all-too-obvious legacies of environmental damage.

The Once and Future West

Years ago, Richard Hofstadter cautioned scholars about mixing their "nows" with their "thens," about stirring too much present into too little past. The resulting blend would be short on "respect for the integrity, the independence, the pastness, of the past."[14] Just that sort of blurred past and present gave birth to the western supernarrative in the first place, in a kind of societal loss of the historical integrity to which Hofstadter referred. Think of the ways in which the mythic West informed understandings of nationalism, those all-too-well-known ties between a particularized understanding of western culture and emergent national identity. The West prevailed as that last best place for "free labor" in the debates of antebellum politics; to many, the western landscape looked like the causeway that could spill sectional angst onto the spacious plains. That vain hope found an ally in myth. Think of what the frontier suggested, particularly regarding the turmoil of nineteenth-century industrial expansion and sectional rivalry. Did the West ensure the maintenance of American democracy? Did the West relieve class, ethnocultural, and racial stress? So it was argued, a concept enshrined in the national psyche well before the outbreak of Civil War hostilities. Yet the West, and disagreements over the future of the West, also played a fundamental role in provoking the bloodbath that killed hundreds of thousands of Americans and nearly killed America in the process: here was a new western significance, ugly and unsubtle (and precisely the opposite of what myth promised).

Even so, the supernarrative lived on, invulnerable to the power of the paradox. How else to explain the West emerging from the fires of sectionalism as "America Triumphant" or "America Newly Defined"? In part this may have been because the West, oddly enough, escaped most of the war and the human and environmental carnage. And it can be argued that the West did not fully align with either side, thus enabling the region to exist as something again outside the war, outside its aftermath. But ideology loves vulnerable circumstance. As the nineteenth century closed, the West operated perfectly as the morality play for the emergent world power engaged in the drama of reestablishing national identity; history, specifically that centered on the western region, had become a vocabulary of validation. The West rode in ever so heroically to save the day, to escort an America eager to see the world. White, Anglo Saxon, cowboy and cavalry man, gunfighter and lawman, town-builder and banker: the West was heroic, grand, tough, and above all, ruggedly masculine. Theodore Roosevelt's public and political persona might have been equal parts coincidence and calculation but nonetheless speaks volumes about the timely coalescence of international American power and supposed western vitality.

This relationship between the spirit of the West and nationalism is troubling given its tried-and-true status as a storybook recitation of the history of America. But as George Lipsitz has succinctly pointed out, the Turnerian narrative thread "does not prepare us to think about the Americans who crossed the Pacific rather than the Atlantic, or about the people who did not come to America . . . but instead had America come to them with the brutality and sadism of conquest, slavery, and genocide."[15] Yet the crux of the problem is not necessarily that the West inspired dreams of national destiny and a brand of peculiarly gendered and racially specific heroism. We cannot make that vision go away simply by being disturbed by its narrowness. Nor should we try, since the West "worked" for many, especially those who fit into narrow race, class, and gender channels. The problem is the story's sheer inclusive power, its ability to stand as

"America" and not one tiny fraction of that America. Too many people seem to buy it as representative. So we get the perverse cause-and-effect equations of western American history. *Because* Horace Greeley said that the West operated as a safety valve to skim off both eastern laborers and class discontent, it must have done so. *Because* Henry David Thoreau and Walt Whitman insisted that the West was a special place, it must have been so. Thomas Moran, Albert Bierstadt, and John Hillers captured beautiful western landscapes. The unintended collaboration worked far beyond any individual artist's expectations, petrifying a particular West as much as simply representing it.[16] One of the region's greatest characteristics is its ability to inspire the hyperbolic "This is America!" exultation of a master painting or stunning photograph that memorializes freedom and equality simply by reference to space and landscape. On such assurances are imperial confidences formed.

Awe skews analysis. The Wests captured in paint, poem, and photograph (again, with particular reference to the nineteenth century) are synthetic: they say too much to too many by relying on the stories of too few. Yes, the West is, was, a beautiful place—it is the place of dreams—but it is the ways in which people act out their lives on and against that dreamscape that make a difference.[17] And that world is not always graced by the beauty of a western sunset or a canyon vista or a Rocky Mountain meadow. Nor is it an existence neatly tied up in the morally determined plot of a nineteenth-century dime novel or the breathless expectation of "new beginnings."

Some understood the burden placed upon the West better than others. The fervent hopes of Thomas Jefferson and the poetic cadences of Thoreau and Whitman gave way to the failed vision of John Wesley Powell and the ominous "What now?" pronouncements of Frederick Jackson Turner. Either Powell was right, and democracy would die of western thirst, or Turner was right, and democracy and the West could exist symbiotically until that fabled frontier line disappeared from the maps. The frontier is demographically erased, or it is destroyed by land monopolies and giant corporate farms; either way the democracy factory shuts down.

These darker images suggest a new West, the West of Populist fervor and passion, the West of utopian escapism, the West of anarchic dreamers and socialist hopefuls and industrial saboteurs. It is a West demanding equal time from older understandings. Not a West of Currier and Ives orderliness, this is a place-process amalgam of a dangerous, threatening landscape and an equally scary drama in which people get squashed by the weight of a capitalist nation-state swapping industrial demands for corporate ones. Again, the power motif emerges: these are Wests suited to analyses centered on the collection, utilization, maintenance, and mystification of power. The region offers hard lessons about the indiscriminate use of power as land- and gold-hungry Anglo Americans became the shock troops of a nation flexing its imperial muscles. The West witnessed all those legal, militaristic, and ideological constructs and institutions that made possible and glorified the continental stretch to full length. It is an often dark and bloody ground, this West, stained by the shame of genocidal combat, greed, and environmental destruction.[18] Again, significance lies in blunt ugliness, expressed as tales we only recently seem to think of as important. What can these do but force reassessment of the canonical triumphalism that has been western history, and how can we be surprised when some seek to make such revision the core memory of the West's or even the nation's heritage?[19]

Fond stereotypes of western meaning and history—such as "national fulfillment" and "Manifest Destiny"—remain alive and well for obvious, intuitive reasons. As is the case for most stereotypes, there may be some truth lying behind that caricature of the decent western lawman out to do good, some reality shadowing the memories we have of the independent farmer, the rugged cowboy, and the schoolteacher. It is important to acknowledge the truth in these stereotypes when we can, to display the individuals who give stereotype shape and form as real people whose lives deserve to be rendered true stories.[20]

But let us not forget that stereotypes cannot be allowed to stand in for history, that they do the labor of dehumanization. One-dimensional, quaint portraits exist because they take the edge off truth and invariably render history a neat, if not pretty, moral package. Stereotypes are dull: severe attention changes them into something else, something sharp, cutting, potentially painful. Scrutiny uncovers the "hurts and heartbreaks of history."[21] The West was not so much cowboys fighting Indians as it was indigenous people battling a ragtag, cacophonous infantry unit that was carrying out orders to starve natives off the land. Or we find Native American against Native American within these worlds, instances that were once dismissed or ignored and that now demand explanation. We reevaluate violence, we rethink crime, we find that for every duel at high noon, there were legions of lonely suicides, cold-blooded killings, and innumerable atrocities committed by the strong against the weak, the unprotected, and those simply overwhelmed—culturally, numerically, immunologically—by the proportions of Anglo-American penetration, settlement, and expansion.

So too are we careful about degree. The overwhelmed may not have been rendered powerless in any absolute sense; that is too easy a zero-sum game to pursue, and it is an exercise too wedded to the absolutes of conquest. Historians have gotten much better at understanding negotiation and contest among groups, genders, and ethnicities. We explore, for example, dynamics of gender and power not only when we write of western prostitution but also when we ponder the social relations between western men and women in all varieties of settings.[22] We describe cultural maintenance and evolution as well as discrimination and racism when we write of Spanish and Mexican encounters with Anglo conquistadors disguised as trappers, sailors, and merchants. The common denominator here is power, and we sense a vague uncomfortableness that everything was far more complicated than we once thought. The West—these Wests—display "power enacted" at specific and critical times in American history. In other words, these Wests are both the place and the process of national fulfillment—imperially defined—in a remarkable coincidence of timing and geography. The interplay between the temporal and situational arenas describes the West and its role in American life. This is the setting around which historians are adding complexity to the previously narrow understandings of national experience. These are the Wests around which new syntheses will be tried out and tried on, when and if synthesis is possible.[23]

If it is to mean anything at all, western history will be written as an exercise in demonstrating broad and potentially troubling significance at that meeting ground between past and present. The West today has the most important arenas of multicultural expression and the greatest hope for ethnic political coalescence in the history of the nation; so too does the West exhibit the possibility of an American version of international ethnic conflagration. No less momentous, the West will in large part determine how well the country handles environmental imperatives too long ignored.

Where did these imperatives come from? And how can we use historical insight to emphasize the West's significance in American history? Let me suggest a few important ways. For one, the West is an extraordinarily rich place in which to study state power and, in particular, the state's role in manufacturing and maintaining important relationships between groups and individuals. Since the federal government remains critically intertwined in western development, scholars have obligations to tease out the salient issues regarding the state's role in western lives. Rugged individualism free from state gaze and reach has ceased to mean as much under the open sky as it does on the big screen. We need fewer studies of hardy settlers, in whatever century, and more studies of the faceless and nameless pioneers of the Bureau of Land Management, the Immigration and Naturalization Service, the Forest Service, and the Army Corps of Engineers.[24] The looming presence of the federal government in and on the western landscape makes this place a highly significant region for this avenue of inquiry. We must ask big, bold questions about the ways in which bureaucracies (and bureaucrats) are formed, about the roots of state policy, about the ways in which the presence of state dollars, employees, and installations affects the everyday realities of people's lives. That state presence is here to stay, although it may change forms, despite disingenuous western pleas to the government to "leave us alone, but don't ignore us."[25] Through focused research in the West, we have a great deal to learn about the ways in which national power gets consolidated and extended, attracted and wooed, not to mention contested.[26]

It is the state's key relationships with groups and individuals that make the opportunity for study all the more compelling. For one, the federal government's sponsorship of industrial capitalism demands (always) more scholarly scrutiny. In a field full of arbitrary chronological and thematic frontiers and divides, there is at least one near-constant: state care, indeed massage, of a particular capitalistic political economy. Yet this is a research angle oddly and mysteriously untracked in western history. Given the timing of industrial expansion and transcontinental conquest, the West stands as the last proving ground of nineteenth-century American capitalism, complete with critical protest and opposition movements. Look to the West to see the lightning bolts of American political economy strike the landscape: imperial expansion, colonial management, industrial explosion, and the quieting and tamping—hushing and crushing—of conflict.[27] That takes us to the turn of the century. After that, it is the Progressive Era West that best displays the transitions inherent in a massive economy's move from industrial to corporate capitalism. From there the story gets more dense as the West becomes the weapons factory for the prosecution of wars hot and cold and the dormitory for millions of weapons makers and weapons users.

Given such factors as federal control and ownership of western lands, state involvement in natural resource "management" is as critical in the political economy of the American West as anywhere else in the nation. This feature of state involvement transcends boundaries conveniently designed to separate the old and the new Wests. "The West as colony" has long been an important conceptual arrangement by which to study the region's past. But such a conception absolves westerners of their part played in the drama, of their own colonizer roles. Investigations of the federal role in altering the natural environment at the request of various western constituencies, often well-removed from eastern or foreign settings, would generate both heat and light.[28] Where does degradation begin and internal improvement end—or do they coexist and overlap? Who decides? Which constituencies proved best able to entice federal engineering, financial, and legal capital to weigh in on their side? What is the frontier between conservation and environmentalism? Between conservation and preservation? How do we begin to arrange conceptually, even thematically, the multitude of federally sponsored projects that drastically affect the ways in which all living things go about their lives in the West?

Wards and Guardians, Land and Language

Other critical issues of power remain to be explored, and one way to get at them is through the ward and guardian concept. I mean to suggest here a broader social and political use of the terms and the relationship than that suggested by the strict legal relationship existing between a child and his or her adult guardian, although the analogy is an apt one. The state's guardian role played vis-à-vis Native Americans is closer to the conception I have in mind. If we cast the state as guardian, how does the relationship sketch itself out in the American West? And with what wards?

Wardship assumes a dependent role assigned to a class, group, or individual. The independent role is assigned to an agent with power over that ward, not unlike that of a parent over a child, although there is clearly room here for negotiation and its own dramas. The parental analogy is especially appropriate given the state view of dependents as infants, a view that lends new clarity to the Anglo propensity to utilize childlike adjectives in paternal regard to Native Americans, African Americans, Mexican Americans, or the gendered divisions separating citizen men from dependent women (or feminized, dependent men).

We know that one important way in which nineteenth-century America (or, more accurately, the narrowed America of the state) addressed wardship or dependence was through landownership. And we know the "land" and "the West" could often become conceptually interchangeable in the political and popular discourse of the era. According to the tenets of nineteenth-century American liberalism, landownership ensured the property owner protected access to the supposedly egalitarian marketplace. In other words, dependency could be (and ought to be) erased once title to land had been gained. For all its flaws—not the least of which was a stuck safety valve that stalled western landowning by eastern dependents—the idea itself was pure enough to become a staple of American political theory.[29] Landowning need not be the encompassing virtue that Jefferson so clearly articulated; it was important enough solely as protection from dependency. The access and acquisition of land in turn was supposed to woo the embrace of egalitarian enlightenment. And once the state got involved in the equation, the process became all the more momentous. Through the ordering and selling of the public domain, through the 1862 Homestead Act, through the Dawes Act, and through the forty-acre-and-a-mule redistribution schemes of Radical Reconstruction, the land-equality idea got played out again and again as the government sought to make real a scheme built on sand, sod, or dust.

The land-independence equation assumes that, in a world energetically embracing capitalism and its hierarchies, ownership of a freehold could create—indeed must create—equality. Or at least it could create some equality, enough to stave off Jefferson's nightmare of European crowdedness and inevitable social revolution. But the arrangements did not prevent failure for nearly enough Americans to make the equation representative. How could they?

When are wards supposed to grow up? The suggestion, indeed the expectation, embedded in American political discourse was that some mystical relationship existed among the triad of land, independence, and citizenship. Dependence was erased by the privileges of citizenship when landownership dissolved ward status. Yet although landholding might alleviate dependence in a sort of Jeffersonian wish fulfillment, it could not mitigate the problems of those people characterized as "different," beyond the ability of mere property to rectify. In addition to the obvious class specificity of the arrangement, nineteenth- and even twentieth-century American history offers a less than laudatory portrait of the power of land to, say, whiten the skin. And the triangular equation does not allow for the subtleties of western geography and geology. Land could shore up a tidewater planter's gendered, racial, and class bulwarks. But drag that same man west and grant him 160 acres, and the neat formula might just disintegrate in a single dry season. Jefferson's Virginia and Powell's arid West simply demanded different geopolitical schemes, not to mention something more tangible than an alchemic self-assurance that because it made sense, it must be true.

We know that ownership of that vaunted freehold meant tough political and economic sledding. Look to the prosaic story where life is just plain hard. Farmers squeezing that individual parcel of land hardly held the ticket to success that popular understanding suggested. As Gilbert Fite has written of many a western landowner, those fortunate enough to get onto land hardly had an independent life handed to them: "Rather than realizing their Jeffersonian dreams of establishing a successful farm and living a happy, contented life under their own vine and fig tree, they were battered and defeated by nature and ruined by economic conditions over which they had no control. Many western pioneers . . . filed on government land in a spirit of hope and optimism only to find that natural and human-made barriers defeated their hopes and aspirations."[30] Eden?

Studies departing from the old scripts of western history tell us about these difficulties, these failures. They call into question the narrow tale of western history that promises reward and independence for the patriotic hardy. Failure and the description of failure, particularly when that failure can be ascribed to victimization, tell us more than succeeding and accomplishing and making it work. Why? Because success is so casually expected, tossed off as a given in the discourse between state and individual, between government and governed.[31] Surely this was the suggestion in the codified conversation between the nation and the citizen, a dialogue replete with obligatory nods toward democratic ideals and meritocratic ideals, open access, and free exchange. Take up the yoke of Manifest Destiny, the state exhorts the people. Go West, own land, shed dependence, succeed.[32]

But when that equation breaks down, it signals one of two things. If it fails in isolated instances, we can marginalize failure as anecdotal, an easily dismissed outlier, unimportant. But when the arrangement breaks down in a systematic fashion, or looks unnervingly like a systematic pattern, there may be something else going on. Then the entire experiment— democracy, egalitarianism, the American Dream—is brought into question. Like so many latter-day Henry Georges, western historians tackle the Edenic vision of happy yeomen and contented families. Of course, maybe the equation itself is far too simplistic; maybe the acquisition of, say, land by a nineteenth-century western settler will address only symptomatic dependence? Perhaps the state-sponsored conversation wrapped around landholding independence is simply so much smoke and mirrors, deception, even conspiracy? In any event, the West offers great opportunity for the study of the arrangement and its drawbacks, and much of the best work in western American history is either implicitly or explicitly focused on the interaction of independence and dependence, usually through the prisms of gender, race, and ethnicity.[33] Exciting new research even pushes the relationship into an environmental arena, drawing from the attempts of groups to establish themselves as guardians to both animate and inanimate wards.[34]

Even so, many studies that discuss failure and drawback often tell us the "what" better than the "why." In other words, they tack bits and pieces onto the old narrative of western conquest without necessarily proposing a new one, remaining content usually to offer data as merely contradictory to perceived wisdoms. The West is a rich place to witness the limits of the American promise of success and upward mobility. But we must make sure to contextualize those studies within a framework that allows speculation about the roots of failure. Catalogs of disappointment, genocidal conflict, and racial disharmony and hatred tell us little beyond the obviousness of example. These findings will teach us more when they add analysis to descriptions of "who is doing what to whom" and when they attack the power of the old narrative.

This requires that old notions get scrapped, one being the arbitrary divide between the nineteenth and the twentieth centuries. The analysis has to be pushed across this invisible, largely meaningless boundary. For instance, if the nineteenth-century key to the vault of independence was supposedly land, it remains unclear what the America of the twentieth century has hit on as its equation. The key may simply be money, now standing in for property. Or it might be education. But more intriguingly, it may be language. For there is a way in which land and language compare in the realm of independence and "equal access" promises, one for the last century and one for this. Again the critical arena is the American West. The most important conflict in the twentieth-century West—and in America, I would argue—is that between native and alien, or insider and outsider.[35] Often, it is race that decides the issue, a reminder of the centrality of race in the nineteenth century (i.e., whites do not have to be natives to be insiders).

But beyond that crude denominator exists language—or more specifically, one language. The proponents of English-only initiatives sound much like the reformers of the nineteenth century working diligently toward that forty-acre-and-a-mule utopia for the dependent, dark-skinned burdens of white imperialism. We want only to level the playing field, reformers claim, to help dependent peoples *grow up*. The parallels are striking. Landholding was to provide protection from the slings and arrows of a monstrously transformed industrial economy. Today, language acquisition is said to foster entry into that economy, transformed again from industrial to corporate capitalism. English makes for better workers. Again, the dependency issue is stark. Just as land could be "given" by a hegemonic race-class-state structure a century ago (that giving itself an indication of the reality of haves and have-nots), language can be delivered—by law or symbol—to the dependent and, the myth suggests, dependency will cease. But it has not worked, and the mere notion of this "land-giving" and "language-giving" has at its core cultural arrogance and cultural thievery. After all, many a dependent group had their own land—or earned it—and they all had their own language. But their land was not commodified correctly, and their languages fell somewhere short of the accepted dialogue. As the Northern Cheyenne teacher Dick Littlebear noted, in a statement that highlights both the connectedness of land and language and this problem of giving: "We need *our* land and we need *our* language. The two are inseparable."[36]

Such is an unlikely dream. The American playing field is still rocky, and there looms a possibility that citizenship—or at least many of its privileges—will be predicated on language acquisition. Forcing non-English speakers to speak English by law will do little except create greater resentment between the independent and the dependent. Non-English speakers—and there are millions of them in the American West—are not dependent because they speak Spanish, Chinese, or Portuguese. They are dependent because the dominant society has determined that *difference* (particularly racial, ethnic, and class difference) must justify dependence and has gone about ensuring that this is so. Language cannot change this nearly so much as has been claimed. In the meantime, ethnic enclaves will remain safe harbors for people made to feel unwelcome by the broader society; traditional language maintenance will remain part of cultural and emotional defense mechanisms against a different world.[37]

Speaking English, like owning land a century before, will not erase class and race hierarchies made convenient, made legitimate, by difference. Language is not that powerful—nor is, nor was, land. The presumption that English proficiency produces societal "success" is both naive and insulting; such an equation has never worked for entire subsets of the 97 percent of the American population who speak English, whether they be Anglo Saxon, African American, Latino, or any other population slice. Again the West is the nation's headquarters for many of these contests: watch the Denver school boards, watch Los Angeles supervisors, watch Nevada's statehouse and Utah's town councils.[38]

The South has of course been the great example of historical unevenness between those independent and those dependent. The sort of inquiry that interrogates race, difference, and dependence ought now to shift to this world of the American West.[39] No doubt we can also learn a great deal from comparative studies; clearly, southern regional scholarship has much to teach us about racial tension, about herrenvolk conceptions of the world, and about group political formation based on racial unities and racist fears. These insights ought to be paired with similar analyses of western America.[40] But the West has as much to teach other fields. The West offers great opportunity for developing arguments that weave together race and class, ethnicity and dependence, citizen and noncitizen.[41]

These ways of investigating the West, these ways of insisting on western significance, rest on the realization that there is no longer a single, all-powerful conceptual model by which to explain the American West;

neither can we explain America by looking at the West. That is a potentially dangerous, at least lonely, position to take. There are sure indications
of a storm on the horizon, a battle taking shape over the West's ability to
define and to explain certain key traits of national character. The battle
lines this time around (in the fight "for the West") are not so simple as debates over the representativeness of Turner's demographic sequences. And
that complexity is perhaps why the debate is so exciting.[42]

Western historians already contribute to and further the contest. Interpretations of the West will continue to provide particularized, and no
doubt politicized, narratives around which to refine our understandings of
American history writ large. Western history will help increase awareness
that no single seamless narrative of American history or experience can
possibly be truthful. Western history will further divorce the particular
from the general in such a way as to call into question the legitimacy of any
consensus in (or regarding) the American past—or present.[43]

To paraphrase the film dialogue with which this essay began, someone
is always looking for something in the West. Historians are obligated to
explain that quest and to puzzle out the larger meanings therein. In doing
so, scholars further defamiliarize the West in attempts to reshape understandings of the big American picture. As William Cronon has encourag-
ingly written of western history, it "has been the one branch of American
history that has consistently looked at the nation as a whole to explore
similarities and differences in regional economies, environmental dynamics, political conflicts, and cultural identities."[44]

The West's revered place in American popular consciousness is as
strong now as ever. In a *New York Times* essay titled "Again, That Hankering," Deanne Stillman discussed the West's seductive hold on American
imagination. "In times of cultural travail, the country heads west to a frontier forever open," Stillman wrote. Historians, as merely "socially acceptable spin doctors," have protected tradition by twirling stories into
myths.[45] But many western historians no longer have those same concerns;
we no longer feel compelled to line up stages of national development in
categories of progressive advancement separated into the specifics of race,
ethnicity, and gender. Our task now is not to reveal such a one-dimensional portrait or story; it is to add richness and propose alternatives.

Frameworks abound for exploring and commenting on diversity and
the dramas that diversity produces. Relationships between power and dependence, ward and guardian, insider and outsider, and nature and humankind invite exploration in western time, place, and circumstance.
Western history can further help us determine why these socially deter-

mined categories, as well as those of race, gender, and ethnicity, have been so successful in dividing the world into groups and subgroups.

Scholars who study the American West find themselves up against powerful images that inform a protected narrative embedded in the national psyche. There is a western vision "out there," in popular culture and popular understanding, made up of stereotypes pasted together. But none are so true as to never be false. Equally obvious is the quality of works readdressing and reworking the entire frameworks of western American significance. These articles, addresses, and books contain scholarly fighting words, and they ought to.[46]

Many of the most important proponents of a new view of the western past have been unfairly accused of windmill-tilting because of pique and pessimistic funk. Nonsense. It is simpleminded to suggest that western historians are so disturbed about the present that they write disturbingly about the past. As historians, we revere the region's grandeur and beauty and can ourselves become carried away by the stirring rhetoric that comes out of this place. But we see the faults inherent in the human interaction with and on this landscape. That is not to say we see beyond the beauty: we simply are obliged to see things *in addition* to the beauty. The history of the American West is hardly all heroic, all natural splendor, all beatified democracy. Emphatically pointing this out is an implicit suggestion that things can be made better. As Howard Lamar has noted, we may one day again celebrate the image of the West offered to us by thinkers such as Turner and Jefferson not so much because they were right but because they (and their imagined, mythic West) gave us all something to shoot for, as a region, as a nation, and as a people.[47]

One hundred years ago, at that juncture of the nineteenth and twentieth centuries, this country happened on the West as a vital if not the most vital component in explaining the structure of national identity. As the country exerted international influence, it turned inward in search of self-referents. The process had an inescapable logic to it: exporting America required packaging it first. That package had to be defined and explained before it could be commodified or quantified. Hence, the West as America: rugged, free, independent, ambitious. Given the shape of the infant American historical profession, scholars tried to answer the era's call for scientific history to uncover the origins of Americanness.

At the same time, prophets of the American future looked West and saw the loss of free land as both fundamental challenge and inevitable eventuality. Scholars and social commentators look West today and are similarly resigned and exhilarated by massive demographic change. Across the arbitrary boundary of the fast-approaching century beckons a richly diverse and different world. Historians have a poor batting average when it comes to predictions of the future. But one "prediction" is easy to make, since it has already happened: the multicultural world that so many people think will arrive with the twenty-first century has always existed. It may not always have worked very well—hence one of our critical explanatory duties—but it has always been there. Rediscovery and refamiliarity lie in the new West we study.

Notes

This essay is dedicated to the memory and example of Wallace Stegner. If not for the help, insight, and advice of colleagues, this essay would have been much poorer. Special thanks go to David Gutiérrez and Patty Limerick, who spent time and care with an earlier draft. My gratitude also goes to Richard Maxwell Brown, Doug Flamming, Anne Hyde, Wilbur Jacobs, Clyde Milner, Martin Ridge, Bryant Simon, and Jennifer Watts. I am grateful to Clyde Milner for asking me to take on this essay. Its many shortcomings are, of course, entirely my responsibility. I urge colleagues to consult "Becoming West," the opening essay in William Cronon, George Miles, and Jay Gitlin, eds., *Under an Open Sky: Rethinking America's Western Past* (New York, 1992). Written by the volume's editors, "Becoming West" covers much of the same western ground I try to cross in this essay.

An earlier version of this essay appeared under the title "Fighting Words: The Significance of the American West in the History of the United States," by William Deverell. Previously published in the *Western Historical Quarterly* 25 (Summer 1994): 185–206. Copyright by Western History Association. Reprinted by permission.

1. *Bad Day at Black Rock*, produced by Dore Schary, directed by John Sturges, 81 min. (MGM, 1954).

2. At the risk of oversimplifying a sometimes contentious debate, scholars who emphasize place in their studies of the West implicitly argue that regional significance can alone justify their analytical attention. Process enthusiasts, on the other hand, explain that western significance lies in the region's laboratory status for analyses of national and international trends, themes, and relationships. Try as I might, I cannot rid myself of the suspicion that these two positions are symbiotic. For an engaging analysis of western regional definition, see David M. Emmons, "Constructed Province: History and the Making of the Last American West," *Western Historical Quarterly* 25 (Winter 1994): 437–459, as well as the roundtable responses that follow.

3. I am indebted to William Cronon for his reminder regarding the pitfalls of such an inquiry. As he has pointed out regarding another broad essay, "The emphasis on 'significance' was a black box that avoided the necessity of more rigorous analysis and theory." William Cronon, "Turner's First Stand: The Significance of

Significance in American History," in Richard W. Etulain, ed., *Writing Western History: Essays on Major Western Historians* (Albuquerque, 1991), 89.

4. I readily confess that reliance on "Wests" produces several conceptual dilemmas. It would be defensible to suggest that such reliance on a multiplicity of geographical-conceptual-ideological locations (in time, space, otherwise) called "the West" is but a backdoor escape from complexity. Using an apt metaphor, Wilbur Jacobs notes just how difficult it is to come up with "the West." "As you move back and forth," he wrote, "the West as a place floats on the map, almost like a puddle of mercury. The sub-puddles, spinning around, have so many socioeconomic, political, environmental, and cultural eddies that they are almost impossible to control when we try to write a coherent account." (Wilbur Jacobs to author, 19 September 1992, letter in author's files.) I do not doubt that this is true, and I suspect it is far more difficult for me to "control" these Wests than it is for my distinguished colleague. However, I would like to suggest that claiming—and trying to explain—many Wests over one coherent West has much merit. I am indebted to Dave Gutiérrez, who helped shape my thinking regarding the political nature of significance tests and significance testing.

5. This is the West that Richard White wrote about near the end of his fine textbook. "To many people the idea of a modern West seems to be an oxymoron—a combination of words that is inherently contradictory. The 'real' West can't be modern. It is nineteenth-century Dodge City or Virginia City; it is not late-twentieth-century Los Angeles or Dallas. Symbolically, the West in American culture stands for certain qualities and events that cannot survive the process of development; they vanish as a place matures." Richard White, *"It's Your Misfortune and None of My Own": A New History of the American West* (Norman, 1991), 537. See also the closing section on "The Imagined West," including its description of Ralph Lauren's time-warped activities in the Colorado Rockies (613–32). The sandbox quotation is from Deanne Stillman, "Again, That Hankering," *New York Times*, 22 August 1993, sec. 2, p. 20.

6. Nothing proved the power of the supernarrative to me more than a recent stint grading high school Advanced Placement history exams. The essays written in response to a westward expansion question revealed the overwhelming degree to which students remain wedded to Turnerian notions of the West as America. About the only indication that things may be slowly, slowly changing (although in which direction is unclear) was high schoolers' references to the ideas of "Jesse Jackson Turner," "Andrew Jackson Turner," the frontier historian "Ted Turner," and "Frederick Douglass Turner."

7. White, *"It's Your Misfortune,"* 617.

8. The recent past offers, I think, an example of this. In the spring of 1992, the American West was the site of the single most volatile urban uprising in American history. Yet in the presidential campaign that followed shortly thereafter, little of the conflagration seemed pertinent. Why? Is it because the turmoil of Los Angeles was not significant? That seems an unsustainable argument given the stark empirical realities of rage and destruction. Two other interpretations must be pondered—one crudely methodological, one crudely ideological. The uprising and its aftermath *may* have played a critical role in determining the outcome of the fall elections, something

that thoughtful electoral analysis will in time reveal. More germane to this essay and its purposes, events in Los Angeles were apparently pushed aside, allowed to seem less important (and unrelated) to other policy concerns and nationwide economic dilemmas in the midst of the run for the White House, as if western events might be more *interesting* (tragic, dangerous, frightening) than *important*.

9. See James Bryce, *The American Commonwealth*, vol. 2 (New York, 1889), 372.

10. Such obstinance is all the more frustrating given the obviousness of historical ties—in transportation, trade, and politics—between the West and other regions of the country, continent, and world. As William Robbins has noted in a recent essay, "The historic connectedness of the West to a wider geographical world . . . [has] never been central to scholarly discussions about the region." See William G. Robbins, "Laying Siege to Western History: The Emergence of New Paradigms," *Reviews in American History* 19 (September 1991): 313. On a purely anecdotal level, vis-à-vis the perceptions of scholars outside the western field, I well remember being involved in a discussion regarding the significance of the American West with a distinguished southern historian who dismissed the importance of the West because "the West had no Civil War."

11. Wallace Stegner, "Out Where the Sense of Place Is a Sense of Motion," *Los Angeles Times Book Review*, 3 June 1990, originally given as an address before PEN USA Center West. Virginia Scharff notes that western historians have staked out boundaries in part because of defensive reactions to dismissive responses from other fields of American history. "Western historians have long been derided by practitioners of other histories as cowpoke scholars. . . . The best western historians have produced sophisticated and significant work equal to any in American history, but have nevertheless been unable to escape this redneck stereotype." Virginia Scharff, "Else Surely We Shall All Hang Separately: The Politics of Western Women's History," *Pacific Historical Review* 61 (November 1992): 548.

12. Elliott West, "A Longer, Grimmer, but More Interesting Story," in *Trails: Toward a New Western History,* ed. Patricia Nelson Limerick, Clyde A. Milner II, and Charles E. Rankin (Lawrence, 1991), 107.

13. An analogy lurks here aligning the West with, of all things, postwar American suburbia. Think of that ostensibly inane explosion of 1950s American prosperity: the suburban world stretching American cities outward was at once place, certainly process, and, it has been argued, an ideological arena as well. The West seems similar. Like suburbia, the West is a moving and fluid entity, itself somehow wrapped up in compelling and often competing visions of the American dream.

14. The full text of Hofstadter's caution reads: "The activist historian who thinks he is deriving his policy from his history may in fact be deriving his history from his policy, and may be driven to commit the cardinal sin of the historical writer: he may lose his respect for the integrity, the independence, the pastness, of the past." Richard Hofstadter, *The Progressive Historians: Turner, Beard, Parrington* (New York, 1968), 464–65, quoted in William E. Leuchtenburg, "The Historian and the Public Realm," *American Historical Review* 97 (February 1992): 8.

15. George Lipsitz, "Facing the Music in a Land of a Thousand Dances," re-

marks delivered at "Art of Teaching History" conference, Los Angeles, 30 October 1992, printed in the California Council for the Social Studies magazine *Sunburst* (February 1993), 7.

16. See Anne Farrar Hyde, *An American Vision: Far Western Landscape and National Culture, 1820–1920* (New York, 1990), for a fine discussion of nineteenth-century artists and "their" West.

17. As Cronon, Miles, and Gitlin argue in *Under an Open Sky,* focused regional study of the American West, as place *and* process, "[reminds] us that the continent itself has been both the principal object of human struggle and the stage on which that struggle has taken place" (8).

18. I agree with William Robbins on this point: "But that is part of the beauty in the debates swirling about the New Western History, a vision tempered by a less optimistic view of American culture, one that self-consciously focuses on the darker, tragic element." Robbins, "Laying Siege to Western History," 316.

19. Insofar as this paragraph relates to the controversies over new western history and new western historians, I defer to Walter Nugent, with whom I agree: "I like to regard the New Western Historians as part of a long and honorable tradition of American anti-imperialism and resistance to aggression." See Walter Nugent, "Happy Birthday, Western History," *Journal of the West* 32 (July 1993): 4.

20. "However bored historians may be with such images, they retain a strong hold over our collective imaginations." Cronon, Miles, and Gitlin, *Under an Open Sky,* 5.

21. Lipsitz, "Facing the Music," 7.

22. I have learned much from Karen Anderson, "Work, Gender, and Power in the American West," *Pacific Historical Review* 61 (November 1992): 481–99.

23. I share scholar Judy Nolte Lensick's concern about the danger of quick synthesis and demand for incorporation of new work into old narratives. As she has written, a "highly suspicious subtext is embedded in the ongoing call by concerned historians for 'synthesis,' in which the 'subfields' of women's and ethnic history are cajoled to reenter the confines of History writ large, to 'wrestle inside the ring.' A major strength of feminist history is that thinkers stand on the *margins* of 'the' story so as to see it as freshly as possible." Judy Nolte Lensick, "Beyond the Intellectual Meridian: Transdisciplinary Studies of Women," *Pacific Historical Review* 61 (November 1992): 479.

24. Why federal bureaucracies in the West have not received more scrutiny is a mystery to me. As an example of a given institution acting on individuals and of individuals in turn acting on that institution, bureaucracies would seem to offer studies of great importance across a wide range of disciplines.

25. Patricia Limerick has wryly suggested that the quotation could as accurately read, "Leave us alone, but don't stop funding us."

26. I do not mean for this to be stretched beyond reason (and I think it can be). I have, for instance, been asked in a newspaper interview if one could compare the rebellious republics of the Baltic states with the Bear Flag Republic in nineteenth-century California. Aside from the fact that Estonia, Lithuania, and Latvia end in "ia" as does California, I am at a loss to make comparisons, meaningful or otherwise, across

so wide a gulf of time, space, and circumstance. White's *"It's Your Misfortune"* is to my mind a model of the ways in which state authority, patronage, and power can be analyzed in a western setting.

27. As such, we cannot ignore the critical western role played by the U.S. Army and, particularly as the nineteenth century yielded to the twentieth, various state militia and national guard units called into the field at the cooperative request of state and industrial officials during outbreaks of radical protest against the status quo. I would add to this the role played by the Army Corps of Engineers as well, in terms of both environmental manipulation and implantation of an additional bureaucratic structure in the West.

28. Water is, of course, the great, but by no means sole, natural resource subject here. The U.S. Bureau of Reclamation, for instance, demands greater study, in terms of not only dams and aqueducts but also patronage, bureaucracy, and politics.

29. See Fred A. Shannon, "A Post Mortem on the Labor-Safety-Valve Theory," *Agricultural History* 19 (January 1945): 31–37, and William F. Deverell, "To Loosen the Safety Valve: Eastern Workers and Western Lands," *Western Historical Quarterly* 19 (August 1988): 269–85.

30. Gilbert C. Fite, "A Family Farm Chronicle," in *Major Problems in the History of the American West*, ed. Clyde A. Milner II (Lexington, Mass., 1989), 431–32. I have also profited from the insights of Rowland Berthoff, "Conventional Mentality: Free Blacks, Women, and Business Corporations as Unequal Persons, 1820–1870," *Journal of American History* (December 1989): 753–84.

31. Patricia Limerick has made a similar point in arguing that the American West "underwent Anglo-American conquest at a time when the United States was a fully formed nation, providing, thereby, a more focused and revealing case study of how the United States as a nation conducted conquest and especially how the federal government adopted a central role for itself." See Patricia Limerick, "The Trail to Santa Fe: Unleashing the Western Public Intellectual," in Limerick, Milner, and Rankin, *Trails*, 71.

32. I know of no better popularization of this than in the person and practiced persona of Ronald Reagan. "Big Hat, No Cows" Reagan, always ably assisted by shrewd speechwriters, masterfully melded patriotism and western history as the democratic-promise script for the age. As Patricia Limerick notes in *The Legacy of Conquest: The Unbroken Past of the American West* (New York, 1987), the progressive view of American—hence western—history (and not the other way around) became a siren song for the conservative revolution of Reaganism, a blinded vision of Eurocentric cultural values and mean-spiritedness. Listen to both the historical understanding and the contemporary call to arms inherent in Reagan's oratory: "The men of the Alamo [and we must not forget the gendered specificity of the new Right's new America] call out encouragement to each other; a settler pushes west and sings his song, and the song echoes out forever and fills the unknowing air. It is the American sound: It is hopeful, bighearted, idealistic—daring, decent and fair. That's our heritage, that's our song. We sing it still. For all our problems, our differences, we are together as of old." Quoted in Limerick, *Legacy of Conquest*, 324. It is just that image, as well as the power that comes with being the messenger, that makes this entire approach to the history of the American West worth all the "fighting words."

33. The November 1992 issue of the *Pacific Historical Review* is devoted to discussions of western women's history and the ways in which recent scholarship is forcing scholars to rethink western America. See especially Antonia I. Castañeda, "Women of Color and the Rewriting of Western History: The Discourse, Politics, and Decolonization of History," *Pacific Historical Review* 61 (November 1992): 501–33.

34. The best case of this is the entire "should trees have standing?" debate over the Disney Corporation's attempts to build a resort at Mineral King, California. See especially Christopher D. Stone, "Should Trees Have Standing? Toward Legal Rights for Natural Objects," *Southern California Law Review* 45 (Spring 1972): 450–501. The western connections between early-twentieth-century debates over conservation and preservation and late-twentieth-century wrangles over "Deep Ecology" versus "Shallow Ecology" remain largely unexplored.

35. In terms of independence and dependence, it is clear that one category is "in" and that the other lacks the prefix and all the privileges that membership entails.

36. Dick Littlebear quoted in James T. Crawford's untitled essay in the "Quotable" section of the *Chronicle of Higher Education* (30 September 1992), B5 (italics added). As Crawford wrote: "Coercive anglicization has taken more from Native Americans than a set of linguistic skills. It has isolated them from cultural resources they need to define themselves."

37. Dennis Baron pointed out, "Fluency in English is universally advanced as a sine qua non for assimilation, yet the abandonment of a minority language in favor of English has seldom convinced American society at large to welcome into its midst former speakers of other tongues, while switching to English is all but certain to produce feelings of anxiety, guilt, or alienation in those experiencing language loss." Dennis Baron, *The English Only Question: An Official Language for Americans?* (New Haven, 1990), 194.

38. I have learned much from four recent publications addressing the English-only controversy and its historical roots. See Baron, *English Only Question;* Sandra Lee McKay and Sau-ling Cynthia Wong, eds., *Language Diversity: Problem or Resource* (New York, 1988); Karen L. Adams and Daniel T. Brink, eds., *Perspectives on Official English: The Campaign for English as the Official Language of the USA* (Berlin, 1990); and Harvey A. Daniels, ed., *Not Only English: Affirming America's Multilingual Heritage* (Urbana, 1990).

39. This is Robbins's argument in "Laying Siege to Western History."

40. I am reminded of the following lines from an essay by C. Vann Woodward: "What but confusion of the undergraduate mind can possibly come from comparing Colorado and Alabama? I apologize for this travesty against sound canons of the profession." C. Vann Woodward, "Reconstruction and Revision," unpublished manuscript, copy in author's files.

41. See, for instance, Howard Lamar, "From Bondage to Contract: Ethnic Labor in the American West, 1600–1890," in *The Countryside in the Age of Capitalist Transformation: Essays in the Social History of Rural America*, ed. Steven Hahn and Jonathan Prude (Chapel Hill, 1985).

42. Take the controversy over a recent (March-July 1991) exhibition at the National Museum of American Art in Washington, D.C. Called "The West as America:

Reinterpreting Images of the Frontier, 1820–1920," the short-lived show sparked a spirited debate over competing interpretations of the West. Controversy arose over the captions used to describe and analyze the exhibit's paintings. Smithsonian curators "pushed the envelope" and attempted to include much of what newer scholarship has suggested about the gender, cultural, and ethnic realities of the American West. We may agree with the historians Eric Foner and Jon Wiener that, in comparison with other crises in American life and on American campuses, this battle over the significance of the American West seems at first a tempest in a teapot—the Right's rejoinder to the Left's often shrill declarations. But there is more to it than this, evident in the words of Senator Ted Stevens (Republican, Alaska), who told officials at the Smithsonian that they were "in for a battle" over the exhibit, which, in the senator's mind, impugned his understanding of the West of America. I think that there is depth to this debate; at stake, in the words of Wiener and Foner, is "nothing less than an entire interpretation of the American past." See Eric Foner and Jon Wiener, "Fighting for the West," *The Nation* (29 July–5 August 1991), 163–66. See also William H. Truettner and Alexander Nemerov, "What You See Is Not Necessarily What You Get: New Meaning in Images of the Old West," *Montana The Magazine of the Western History* 42 (Summer 1992): 70–76; Alexander Gulliford, "Visitors Respond: Selections from 'The West as America' Comment Books," *Montana the Magazine of Western History* 42 (Summer 1992): 77–80; and Bryan J. Wolf, "How the West Was Hung; Or, *When I Hear the Word 'Culture' I Take Out My Checkbook,*" *American Quarterly* 44 (September 1992): 418–38.

43. This notion itself renders the "mere regional history" spin often applied to western history all the more meaningless. If western scholars suggest that the West *does not* fit the cultural norms of the whole, that may help reveal the problems inherent in any assumed notions of national identity or national fabric.

44. Cronon, "Turner's First Stand," 93. I disagree with, for instance, Michael Malone's view—in regard to a search for broader conceptualization—that "tracing national trends and events in western settings" is an "unrewarding task." Michael P. Malone, "Beyond the Last Frontier: Toward a New Approach to Western American History," *Western Historical Quarterly* 20 (November 1989): 415–16. On the contrary, as this essay is meant to suggest, it is precisely this "tracing" that may illuminate the gaps in the assumed narrative of American history.

45. See Stillman, "Again, That Hankering," sec. 2, pp. 1, 20.

46. See, for example, White, *"It's Your Misfortune"*; Limerick, *Legacy of Conquest*; Cronon, Miles, and Gitlin, *Under an Open Sky;* the November 1992 issue of the *Pacific Historical Quarterly*; William Cronon, *Changes in the Land: Indians, Colonists, and the Ecology of New England* (New York, 1983); Richard White, *The Middle Ground: Indians, Empires, and Republics in the Great Lakes Region, 1650–1815* (Cambridge, Mass., 1991) and *The Roots of Dependency: Subsistence, Environment, and Social Change among the Choctaws, Pawnees, and Navajos* (Lincoln, 1983); Peggy Pascoe, *Relations of Rescue: The Search for Female Moral Authority in the American West, 1874–1939* (New York, 1990); and Ramón A. Gutiérrez, *When Jesus Came, the Corn Mothers Went Away: Marriage, Sexuality, and Power in New Mexico, 1500–1846* (Stanford, 1991). I would also refer readers to the other chapters of this book. Two anthologies of earlier conferences are important compilations of newer western scholar-

ship: Susan Armitage and Elizabeth Jameson, eds., *The Women's West* (Norman, 1987); Lillian Schlissel, Vicki Ruiz, and Janice Monk, eds., *Western Women: Their Land, Their Lives* (Albuquerque, 1988).

47. "Turner, like Jefferson, insisted on talking about an ideal West rather than a real West. We may celebrate the names of both men one day, not for their presentation of the grim facts, but for their vision of what the West and America itself could mean." Lamar, "From Bondage to Contract," 317. See also Howard Lamar, "Much to Celebrate: The Western History Association's Twenty-Fifth Birthday," *Western Historical Quarterly* 17 (October 1986): 397–416.

Courage without Illusion

Richard Maxwell Brown

Written with verve and insight, William Deverell's "Fighting Words" is a wise and eloquent contribution to the series of essays growing out of the 1992 conference "Re-Envisioning the History of the American West." I do not have a single word of disagreement with what Professor Deverell has written. Instead, I am using a passage in his essay as a point of departure for my remarks, the passage in which he says that the West "is the place of dreams—but it is the ways in which people act out their lives on and against that dreamscape that makes a difference," a dreamscape littered with the failed hopes arising from the false illusions of many a westerner, including the father of the late Wallace Stegner, to whose memory and example Deverell dedicates his essay.[1]

We all know about the new western history, but there is something else just as new that might be called and probably has been called the "new western literature." By the new western literature, I mean the luminous stream of writing about the West in the last fifteen years or so—a period that roughly coincides with the rise of the new western history. I am not going to focus on the fictional output of the new western literature but, rather, on what has been one of its most striking products: autobiography. This, in turn, might be called the "new western autobiography." The new western autobiography is as much family history as it is individual autobiography. From the beginning of the new western autobiography—with *This House of Sky: Landscapes of a Western Mind* by Ivan Doig (New York, 1978)—to more recent examples such as Mary Clearman Blew, *All But the Waltz: Essays on a Montana Family,* and William Kittredge, *Hole in the Sky: A Memoir,*[2] western autobiography is thriving. The new western historians have been presenting a new conceptual history of the West while the new western autobiographers are giving us a new emotional history of the West.

In 1992 the dean of western letters, Wallace Stegner, published a book of essays on living and writing in the West entitled *Where the Bluebird Sings to the Lemonade Springs.*[3] Stegner won both the Pulitzer Prize and the National Book Award, but he never won what his nearly thirty books of fiction, history, biography, and essays over more than half a century earned him: the Nobel Prize for literature. In his last book, *Where the Bluebird Sings to the Lemonade Springs,* Stegner tells us what his literary mission was. Born in 1909 and growing up close to the bone of the North American West, Stegner wrote: "I grew to hate the profane Western culture, the economics and psychology of a rapacious society. I disliked it as reality and I distrusted it when it elevated itself into the western myths that aggrandized arrogance, machismo, vigilante or

sidearm justice, and the oversimplified good-guy/bad-guy moralities."4 Of
the mythic cowboy hero whose prototype is Owen Wister's Virginian, Stegner
wrote that the hero had "irritated" him all his life. "I would obviously like to
bury him. But I know I can't. He is a faster gun than I am. He is too attractive
to the daydreaming imagination. It gets me nowhere to object to the self-
righteous, limited, violent code that governs him."5

Of course, Stegner was more successful in a career of writing against the
western myth than he would have us think. The realism of his writing has had
a major impact.6 Yet there is still much to be done, and it is being done by a
younger generation of western writers who are giving us the new emotional
history I referred to. For writers of the southern renaissance—William
Faulkner and all the others from the 1920s to the 1950s—the great issue and
problem was black-white race relations.7 For the new western writers—at
least for many of them and certainly for the ones I am going to discuss—the
great issue and problem is the myth of the West: what that myth has meant to
them and what it has done to their own lives.

In 1939 the writer Mary Clearman Blew was born Mary Hogeland in the
Judith River range country of Fergus County in central Montana. She grew
up as a fourth-generation Montanan, with a father who came to mistake the
myth of the West for its reality. Her book *All But the Waltz* is the story of the
Hogelands and, on her mother's side, the Welches—three generations of men
and women who were ranchers and teachers among the plains and mountains
northwest of Lewistown, Montana. Mary's father, Jack Hogeland (born in
1913 and died in 1987), was a cowboy who became a successful rancher until he sold the medium-size family ranch in order to buy one that was not as
good but was located close to Lewistown, allowing his daughters, including
Mary, to live at home but ride the bus to high school in the county seat. Having no sons, Jack reared Mary like a cowboy and not like a little lady. His
dream was for Mary to go to college and become, like her mother and Grandmother Welch, a schoolteacher. Jack's plan was for Mary to come home from
college, find a country school to teach in during the winter, and live a ranch
life during the summer: breaking horses, tending the hay meadows, and running a little stock. "Of course," wrote Blew in *All But the Waltz*, "we did no
such thing."8 Instead, Mary went on to graduate school and an academic career, leaving her father feeling betrayed and angry. But Mary was angry too—
angry because her father had "tried too hard" to keep her tied to a tradition
that she saw as "illusory." She added, "He had given everything he had for me;
[but] all I wanted was to be free of the cowboy." By "the cowboy" she meant
her father, and she wanted to be free of his control as well as what he stood
for.9

Her father's life as a rancher dwindled away. "The price of beef cattle
plummeted, and he sold the Herefords and tried" dairy cows. "Tried sheep,
tried a little logging. Nothing did well. The economy was changing, ranching
was changing and the cowboy"—her father—"grew more and more bewil-

dered. Finally he gave up and leased out the pasture and went to work at the stockyards in town."[10] In his last years, with ranching behind him (and probably long before that), Mary's father, she tells us, had acquiesced "to that romantic and despairing mythology which has racked and scarred the lives of so many men and women in the West."[11] Looking back on Jack's life, Mary wondered whether his reading of the popular western fiction by the likes of Louis L'Amour "offered a pattern for his sense of himself, or a mirror"—"so strongly did he believe in a mythic Montana of the past, of inarticulate strength and honor and courage irrevocably lost."[12]

But as Mary's own life wore on in the 1960s, 1970s, and 1980s, she had her own problems. Mismated in a rash first marriage that eventually broke up, Mary reared her children and carried on a successful career as an administrator in a small state college in Montana. Then came a second marriage in which, for a long time, she was deeply happy—a marriage that, in the waning years of her fertility, yielded a love child. But the marriage tragically failed when her husband, an oil wildcatter from Kansas who lived on dreams and bravado and the highs and lows of a boom-and-bust career, became incurably ill. He reacted to his illness with denial and with a search, against all reason, for one more bonanza in a faltering oil industry. To Mary's frantic efforts to help he reacted with irrationality and abuse. She had no choice but divorce, and from twelve hundred miles away, she watched her former husband die as he continued to believe in his illusions to the last.

Still persisting in her academic career, Mary survived her ordeal through her writing and her western heritage of three Montana generations. Through study of private family writings and photo albums and through conversations with and memories of her mother and grandmothers and aunts, Mary resolved the emotional history of herself and her family and triumphed with a combination of courage without illusions. From her mother, with whom she often had a contentious relationship, there came a lesson of bravery, for her mother had survived a hard, cheerless girlhood followed by married life in bleak teacher cottages and on the luckless family homestead. As Mary listened to her mother's stories, she was awed by her mother's courage.[13] Mary's mother, father, aunts, and uncles were the children of Montana's early-twentieth-century homestead frontier; they would "take adversity for granted, poverty as pervasive," and "smile for the box cameras, as proud of their horses and proud of each other as though they had money in their pockets or whole shoes on their feet."[14]

Hole in the Sky by William Kittredge is a book in which the scope of triumph and tragedy and of failed illusions is on an even grander scale than that of the Hogelands and the Welches in Mary Clearman Blew's Montana. *Hole in the Sky* is the story of the 1930s–1960s rise and fall of a family ranching empire in the isolated but vast Warner Valley, a lush oasis in the desert country of southeastern Oregon. The book chronicles the environmental wounding of the fragile wetlands physical environment of the Warner Valley by the Kittredges' agribusiness farming and ranching that made the property intensely productive at first but ultimately sterile and degraded. It is the story also of how the human values of love in the Kittredge family were sacrificed to the excessively selfish values of economic gain. In a book that comes close to the Faulkneresque, Kittredge presents three generations: his own; that of his father, Oscar; and that of his grandfather William, after whom he was named. It was the steely resolve and lust for power of the domineering grandfather that ruled the far-flung Warner Valley ranch of twinkling marshes and bounteous pastures. In the second generation, Oscar Kittredge wanted nothing so much as to get away from it all—to attend Stanford University and forge a professional career—but his will to make a new life of his own was broken by his father, the patriarch. Instead, Oscar Kittredge threw himself into making the ranch a huge success, and he did. As he hobnobbed with, among others, the governor of Oregon, Oscar created an innovative, intricate network of irrigation canals that made the ranch the nation's greatest producer of heavy oats during World War II.

Meanwhile, the scion of the third generation and the family historian and autobiographical writer of *Hole in the Sky,* William (Bill) Kittredge, born in 1932, lived the life of a summertime teenage cowboy on the large family spread. When he went away to college at Oregon State in Corvallis, Bill found that the home ranch in the Warner Valley was the agriculture professors' classroom model of a technologically and scientifically up-to-date western producer of grain and beef. Imbued with the cowboy myth, the young Bill Kittredge grew up to operate the giant ranch with a pride and arrogance beyond his years.[15]

But it all collapsed in family discord and recrimination. The relentless pursuit of profit had enriched the family coffers but impoverished its emotions. Like so many other families in the early- and middle-twentieth-century West, the Kittredges lived by "a stern code, an unstated rule: *Never speak aloud of what you feel deeply.*"[16] The long marriage of Bill's father and mother fell apart, and Bill's father finally faced the fact that he had thrown away his life on a barren ethic of unfulfilling work, property, and ownership. A like realization came to the son, Bill, but not before Bill had ruined his own marriage with debauchery and faithlessness. Thus, William Kittredge was a damaged soul until he forsook the ranch and finally found redemption—as had Mary Clearman Blew—in an academic life of writing and teaching.[17]

Hole in the Sky is not only a searing story of a family ruined by false illusions and the inability to express love but also, interwoven with the family memoir, a disquieting environmental history of the Warner Valley. Without moralizing, the book is a cautionary tale about how illusions without love destroyed a family and how commercial values degraded an ecology and an environment.[18] Not until the members of the Kittredge family sold the ranch in the late 1960s were they able, at last, to find satisfaction in other pursuits.

Yet these two remarkable examples of the new western autobiography,

All But the Waltz and *Hole in the Sky*, do not leave the reader sunk in pessimism. After reading them, one is left with both purged and purified emotions and with hope. These two books—like others in the new western autobiography—engrave a lesson of courage without illusions. That is a principal achievement of the new western autobiography: the way its authors have held to the grassroots western heritage of courage without the disabling illusions that have misled so many into failed and fruitless lives across the western dreamscape.

Notes

1. William Deverell, "Fighting Words: The Significance of the American West in the History of the United States," *Western Historical Quarterly* 25 (Summer 1994): 194. (Reprinted this volume, pages 29–55.)

2. Mary Clearman Blew, *All But the Waltz: Essays on a Montana Family* (New York, 1991); William Kittredge, *Hole in the Sky: A Memoir* (New York, 1992).

3. Wallace Stegner, *Where the Bluebird Sings to the Lemonade Springs: Living and Writing in the West* (New York, 1992).

4. Ibid., 175–76.

5. Ibid., 111.

6. "Essays on Wallace Stegner," *Montana The Magazine of Western History* 43 (Autumn 1993): 52–76. See also Wallace Stegner and Richard W. Etulain, *Conversations with Wallace Stegner on Western History and Literature* (Salt Lake City, 1983).

7. A recent study is Joel Williamson, *William Faulkner and Southern History* (New York, 1993).

8. Blew, *All But the Waltz*, 54.

9. Ibid.

10. Ibid., 53.

11. Ibid., 45.

12. Ibid.

13. Ibid., 161–76 and passim.

14. Mary Clearman Blew, *Balsamroot: A Memoir* (New York, 1994), 4. *Balsamroot* is a sequel to *All But the Waltz* and, like its predecessor, is a combination of family history and autobiography.

15. *Hole in the Sky*, 105–15, 150–75.

16. The quotation is from Blew, *Balsamroot*, 4, but the "stern code" enunciated there by Blew on behalf of the Hogeland and Welch families certainly applied with equal force to the Kittredges and many other rural western families of that time.

17. *Hole in the Sky*, 173–238.

18. Ibid., 170–75 and passim. The theme of commercial values degrading a rural ecology and environment is also strong in Jane Smiley, *A Thousand Acres* (New York, 1991), an authentic, highly regarded work of fiction chronicling the rise and fall of a well-to-do Iowa family brought low by the heedless pursuit of profit from its thousand-acre farm.

Bibliographical Note

In addition to *This House of Sky, All But the Waltz, Hole in the Sky*, and *Balsamroot*, other notable examples of the new western autobiography include Juanita Brooks, *Quicksand and Cactus: A Memoir of the Southern Mormon Frontier* (Salt Lake City, 1982); Cyra McFadden, *Rain or Shine* (New York, 1986); Terry Tempest Williams, *Refuge: An Unnatural History of Family and Place* (New York, 1991); Ivan Doig, *Heart Earth* (New York, 1993); and Pete Sinclair, *We Aspired: The Last Innocent Americans* (Logan, Utah, 1993). With the exception of the book by Sinclair, all of these works combine family history with autobiography. All are distinguished for their literary quality. These books are part of an even broader trend, the "new grassroots biography of the West" (my own term) that I discuss in "Perspectives on Biography and on the New Grassroots Biography of the American West" (unpublished remarks delivered at the annual Evans Biography Award ceremony, Utah State University, August 17, 1993). Women are unusually prominent in this trend, both as authors (for example, four of the seven authors cited in this bibliographical note are women) and as subjects. All seven authors mentioned in this bibliographical note are trained intellects who are notably reflective and often explicitly conceptual in their autobiographical writings. The new western autobiography and the even broader new grassroots biography of the West are crucial meeting grounds of the literary talent and the social history of the West. Although the current trend began in 1978 with Ivan Doig's *This House of Sky*, there were, of course, earlier precedents, a striking example being Mari Sandoz, *Old Jules* (Boston, 1935), a book combining autobiography, biography, and family history.

The New Significance of the American West

Patricia Nelson Limerick

At Disneyland in my childhood, there were as many lessons to be learned as there were rides to be taken, and the lessons were decidedly mixed. The moral to the story of "Mr. Toad's Wild Ride," for instance, was that driving horribly and nearly killing yourself and others could be exhilarating. The moral to the story of the "Flying Saucers" was that if you cleared your path and leaned hard into the task, you could slam into your sister's saucer hard enough to take her to the borders of whiplash. With all this negativity on the grounds in Anaheim, the designers of Disneyland must have felt that they had to counter with one dose of complete, unbroken positivity. Therefore Disneyland assembled a ride in which multicolored, internationally costumed dolls danced, bobbed, and sang, in penetrating tones, "It's a Small, Small World."

I have not taken that cheerful ride in years, but it is impossible not to re-member it, and impossible not to resent it. Driving responsibly around Boul-der, halting at stop signs and signaling one's turns, one can remember with some envy how it felt to drive with the maniacal and unrestrained Mr. Toad. In various academic exercises, from department meetings to conference pre-sentations, one can draw on the lessons learned about momentum and impact from the "Flying Saucers." But when one thinks of that "Small, Small World" ride, one feels overdosed on sweetness, in deep need of a dill pickle or a spoon-ful of vinegar. The image of human life without conflict or friction, with everyone chirping away at the same squeaky song, drives one to imagine a counterride. In this ride, the dolls would dance, bob, and take an occasional swipe at one another. "It's a Small, Small World," they would sing, "But It's a Mean One."

For quite a long time, my understanding of the American West tilted to-ward the spirit of Disney's ride and away from the spirit of the counterride I propose here. In the preface to *The Legacy of Conquest*, I admitted that I was closer to Eleanor Roosevelt than to Angela Davis in my point of view. In the last lines of *The Legacy of Conquest*, I came as close to singing "It's a Small, Small World" as a historian can and still retain a shred of dignity: "Indians, Hispanics, Asians, blacks, Anglos, businesspeople, workers, politicians, bu-reaucrats, natives, and newcomers, we share the same region and its history, but we wait to be introduced. The serious exploration of the process that made us neighbors provides that introduction."[1]

One might imagine that a person who would write those lines was a per-son who observed National Brotherhood Week as her major annual holiday. And yet, against all probability, some imaginative readers were able to find in *Legacy* a dark and grim version of the West, a story centered on misery and op-pression. In fact, the good-hearted, earnest faith recorded in that book pushes past the edges of probability. If the people of the American West would only sit down and examine their shared history, the author of *Legacy* was trying to believe, the common ground that they would discover would persuade them to behave equitably toward each other. If they were tolerant and appreciative of each other's distinctive ways, they could live in peace. Regional identity, I had almost convinced myself, could give westerners a bridge across the canyons of ethnic and gender inequality. In its furthest reaches of hopefulness, *The Legacy of Conquest* walked right up to the edge of this proposition: if peo-ple from backgrounds of material abundance took seriously the histories of people from backgrounds of scarcity, the privileged people would redistribute their wealth, pay equitable wages, and forswear economic advantage.

Western America has played host to more improbable utopian visions than this one. I state it now without reservation, without an effort to cloak its improbability. If I wanted to make it to sound a little less improbable and a lit-tle more practical, I would accent the way in which I wanted to redefine west-ern legitimacy. I wanted to expand the boundaries of the definition of "real westerners" to include the descendants of nineteenth-century white pioneers, descendants of African-American people who came to the West to work in World War II's defense plants, descendants of Spanish conquerors and Mexican immigrants, descendants of Asian immigrants, descendants of people of mixed Indian and European heritage. I wanted to widen the pool of people who could be considered, to use a term of our times, "stakeholders" in the destiny of the West—past, present, and future. This was not a matter of utopian visions but simply historical accuracy. My more inclusive definition of westerner had, however, the inadvertent effect of mystifying birthplace, drawing a distinction between those "born" western and those who "became" western by immigration and choice. I was, unintentionally, glorifying a kind of pedigree, treating humans as others treat show dogs, determining legitimacy by the accident of birth. Here, I was missing the fact that living in the West by conscious, adult choice could carry considerably more meaning than living in the West by virtue of a biological event in which one was not a self-determining participant. Moreover, this definition of legitimacy invited a kind of existential application of the western doctrine of "prior appropriation." "First in time, first in right" had not always produced the most reasonable practices when applied to water, and there was no reason to think it would do much better when applied to human identity.

My "Small, Small World" vision of tolerance and equity, arrived at by a common historical claim to western legitimacy, has pretty well unraveled since the publication of *Legacy*. There have been plenty of good reasons for the unraveling: ongoing American hostility to Mexican immigrants; the bitterness of recent fights over western resource use; the 1992 uprising in south-central Los Angeles; the dramatic gap between the lives led by privileged westerners and the lives led by poor westerners; the adoption, by many audible and articulate white men, of the position of beleaguered victims of prejudice. I encountered, as well, my own doubts about how effectively regionalism provides a framework for understanding ethnic history.[2] Mexican Americans in Los Angeles and Mexican Americans in Chicago have shared and do share many concerns, whether or not the Mississippi River runs between them. San Francisco's Chinatown and New York's Chinatown have to figure in any understanding of Chinese-American history.[3] Indian people setting up gaming businesses in Connecticut face challenges in common with Indian people setting up casinos in California. When the boundaries of regionalism interrupt the understanding of ethnic experience, the only sensible choice is to defy those boundaries.[4]

Contemporary western historians, William Deverell tells us, can draw on "a more sophisticated understanding of power . . . and the ways in which power fills space on the western conceptual landscape."[5] It is the topic of power that knocks the pins out from under any effort to portray region as a unifying factor transcending ethnicity, gender, and class. The proposition that requires a reckoning is a simple one: people who have had power in western

American life have been consistently reluctant to give it up. Thus, all the attention directed to the cultural diversity of the western past, all the invocations of understanding and tolerance, all the recognitions of how completely everyone's stories are intertwined with everyone else's—all this runs up against the fact that people who have held power have tried to keep it.

Underneath, then, all these issues of cultural understanding and tolerance lies a story of contests to control property, labor, and profit. Consider, for instance, the lament that one sometimes hears over the ethnocentrism of nineteenth-century white Americans. Whites and Indians, this argument proceeds, met in a clash of cultures, a jangle of misunderstanding and prejudice. "If only," the presumption here seems to be, "white Americans had been more open-minded toward, more tolerant of, even enthusiastic about the rich and interesting ways of Indian people." And yet, even if one tries to imagine a "Small, Small World" version of nineteenth-century white consciousness, there remains an uncomfortable fact: the Indians had control of the land, and whites wanted to take it from them. Admiring the Indians' religious sincerity, appreciating their art, envying their warm ties of kinship, praising their oratory—none of that would have altered the power dynamics of the fact that some people occupied land that other people wanted. In truth, whites in the nineteenth century did a surprising amount of that admiring, appreciating, envying, and praising. Not much deterred, the land developers went about their business.

A clear appraisal of power and its operations in the American West knocks the wind out of innocent visions of historical understanding as the sponsor of tolerance and good nature. In truth, western America *is* a small world; for all the region's great spaces, a network of cultural and economic interactions has pulled people in remote places into interwoven narratives. For more than two centuries, everyone has been influencing everyone else. There is little in the way of cultural "purity" left for any group to claim; the enormous and consequential factor of intermarriage is the most powerful reminder of how intertwined our destinies are. But even though it is a small world, it has often enough been a mean world. Power—sometimes subtly expressed, sometimes openly wielded—has structured most cross-cultural interactions, with those in power directing land, resources, labor, markets, and laws toward their own benefit. Ironically, this ungenerous reality provided the underpinning for many of the most generous statements on behalf of the tolerance of difference. When, for instance, the owners of the Central Pacific Railroad supported the Chinese right to immigrate, or when southwestern farmers advocated an open border with Mexico, these spokesmen for tolerance were taking their direction from their wallets and account books and not from their consciences.

In 1987, in *The Legacy of Conquest,* I fudged the facts of power in the interests of offering a historical vision that might make westerners into better neighbors to each other. In 1996, I would *like* to fudge and cannot. This is not a statement of regret for or recantation of the part I played in campaigning for a new western history. I do not regret that campaign in the least. Ten years ago, most American historians were, in actual practice, regional historians. Whether they recognized it or not, what they called American history was primarily the history of the eastern United States. Half the nation waited for attention, recognition, and inclusion.[6]

That situation is by no means entirely reversed, but it has shifted remarkably. One feels unexpectedly—and prematurely—cast as the old-timer, sitting on the porch in the rocking chair and telling the youngsters what it was like in the olden days, when the field of western American history was on the ropes. The young people, the ancients necessarily feel, do not know how bad things were before the renaissance and recovery. A decade and a half may have passed, but this old-timer can still hear the voice of a distinguished American historian at a job interview, saying, "Patricia, we're curious why you would go into this *backwater* of a field."

"Backwater," huh? I'd show him. In fact, I—and several hundred other historians—*did* show him. Western American history got out of its slump. The field is thriving. When I am struggling to read all the important and instructive new monographs, I wish that the field would thrive a little less insistently. I may have fallen permanently behind in my reading, but it was a privilege and a very memorable adventure to play a part in the campaign to bring that restored vitality to the attention of mainstream American historians and to the attention of the public.

But like most adventurers, campaigners in the cause of the new (increasingly, the middle-aged) western history confront the passage of time with some bewilderment. Ten years ago, one's self-image was crystal clear. One was young, untenured, unorthodox, unintimidated, determined to challenge the assumptions and pieties of a complacent older generation. Within the space of a few years, everything reversed: youth to middle age; assistant professor to full professor; Young Turk to Old Bird; intentional challenger of an old orthodoxy to unintentional defender of a new orthodoxy; unintimidated questioner of established power to intimidator if others did not watch their step. As a historian, I had long recognized that intentions and outcomes stand in an ironic relationship. It is a different matter to *experience* this proposition rather than to study it.

Unpredictable outcomes, however, have their charms. Surely Disneyland's dullest ride, with the sorriest moral to the story, was the Autopia, in which one drove a little car around a track. The narrowness of the road and the big curbs on either side meant that choice was not at issue in this ride; one went where the road went. Neither was speed a temptation; press the accelerator as much as one wanted, and a snail-like forward movement was the best that could result. In fact, the wildest (and the only) choice one could exercise at the Autopia was *not* to press the accelerator and simply to block the road, permitting the car behind to rear-end one's own car and transform the ride into at least a pale imitation of the "Flying Saucers." The lesson of this ride was a deeply discouraging one: life followed a preset track, and all that the driver could do was to press the accelerator and go, with the most exciting prospect for creative self-assertion being a pileup.

Any melancholy, any mourning for lost hopes, any regret that region did not prove to be the loom on which a united, cross-ethnic western identity could be woven, any negativity at all, disappears when one contrasts the "Autopia" experience with the excitement and surprise of the last decade's change in the field of western history. The experience has been considerably closer to "Mr. Toad's Wild Ride," with twists and turns and sudden stops and sudden accelerations. The saccharine vision of a region of multicultural harmony, with the American West as the equivalent of Disney's multicolored, costumed dolls living together with full justice, mutual understanding, and a sustainable economy, collapsed of its own sweetness. But I hold on to another vision, the vision of western scholars engaged in fruitful and vigorous debate over these trying issues, using their "fighting words" in a spirit of personal respect and affection, living up to the motto of my undergraduate college, "The Pursuit of Truth in the Company of Friends." This vision may be nearly as improbable as the one of a "Small, Small World," but it carries, in my mind, one great advantage: I have, from time to time, seen this one work.

Notes

1. Patricia Nelson Limerick, *The Legacy of Conquest: The Unbroken Past of the American West* (New York, 1987), 349.

2. I am particularly indebted to David Gutiérrez for making it impossible to avoid these doubts.

3. See Patricia Nelson Limerick, "Common Cause? Asian American and Western American History," in *Privileging Positions: The Sites of Asian American Studies*, ed. Gary Okihiro (Pullman, Wash., forthcoming).

4. The project that most dramatically calls the remarks in this paragraph into question is Quintard Taylor's forthcoming book on western African American history, in which the unit of the region does not limit Taylor's inquiry in any way and in which Taylor's evidence calls into question many taken-for-granted propositions of western history.

5. William Deverell, "Fighting Words: The Significance of the American West in the History of the United States," *Western Historical Quarterly* 25 (Summer 1994): 187. (Reprinted this volume, pages 29–55.)

6. Patricia Nelson Limerick, "The Case of the Premature Departure: The Trans-Mississippi West and American History Textbooks," *Journal of American History* 78 (March 1992).

3

Significant to Whom?: Mexican Americans and the History of the American West

David G. Gutiérrez

In this period in which we mark both the quincentenary of Christopher Columbus's voyages and the centennial of Frederick Jackson Turner's ruminations on the significance of the frontier to American history, it has become fashionable to pose questions about minority peoples' contributions and significance to the pluralistic culture of the United States. Although most of the institutions sponsoring such observances appear to be well-intentioned, too few seem to recognize that framing these questions in this manner (once again) encourages a reproduction of modes of analysis that virtually guarantee that the categories "minority" and "majority"—and the asymmetrical relationships of power that they imply—will continue to persist and will be reinforced. When we ask questions in this manner, at some level we accept the premise that the significance of one group of people must be explained with reference to some other group.

This is not to assert, however, that thinking about the relationship of minority peoples to the history of the West cannot provide useful insights. On the contrary, in considering Mexican-American history, one might argue that the debate about the significance or importance of ethnic Mexican people in the West has reflected the central themes of the social and political history of the region. Whether one considers initial Mexican resistance to American exploration of the Mexican Northwest (a territory now encompassing the five southwestern states plus Nevada and Utah), Mexicans' active resistance to American imperialism during the Mexican American War, or ethnic Mexicans' subsequent campaigns to achieve the full rights of citizenship, we might argue that on one fundamental level, ethnic Mexican residents of the American West have been involved in a

protracted struggle to prove their importance, to prove themselves significant in American society.[1]

One might argue more generally that (like much of the interethnic
conflict that has erupted in the rest of the world) a substantial portion of
the ethnic conflict that has occurred in the American West has involved
subject peoples' efforts to contest and resist attempts to impose ascriptive
social judgments on them, particularly by interpreting and representing
their histories in certain ways. Much of the most compelling recent theoretical work in social history, cultural criticism, and feminist studies relies
on this central premise: military conquest or absorption of one society by
another usually represents only the first step of the process by which one
society imposes itself on another. Ultimately, however, the most crucial development as a result of expansion and domination is the subsequent construction of elaborate sets of rationales that are designed to explain why
one group has conquered another and to establish and perpetuate histories
that help "set . . . and enforce . . . priorities, [repress] some subjects
in the name of the greater importance of others, [naturalize] certain categories, and [disqualify] others."[2]

Myth and Myopia

The salience of applying such a perspective to historical analysis of ethnic
Mexicans in the American West is clear, for any such exploration must begin with an acknowledgment of how American ideologies of expansion
have powerfully influenced historical representations of and about "Mexicans" (and other subject groups) after the United States acquired the region. Of course, this process was well under way even before the actual
annexation of the West. Indeed, Americans had developed a rather detailed demonology about Mexicans (and about Spaniards before them)
even before establishing regular contact with Spanish-speaking people in
the region in the 1820s. Building on the so-called Black Legend, in which
European rivals portrayed Spaniards as bloodthirsty, sexually depraved
tyrants, Americans tended to transfer many of these negative stereotypes to
the descendants of the first Spanish explorers of South America, arguing
that their mixed-blood offspring combined the absolute worst traits of
both the conquistadors and the local Indians. With the advent of the clus-
ter of racist and nationalist ideas collectively known as Manifest Destiny
in the early 1840s, these stereotypes assumed a more virulent form. Although the specific ideas that contributed to the notion of Manifest Destiny seemed diverse and complex, virtually all of them derived from

Americans' belief in the superiority of U.S. civilization, culture, and political institutions.[3]

Mexicans were aware of Americans' tendency to explain their territorial aggrandizement as part of "God's plan" even before John L. O'Sullivan coined the term "Manifest Destiny" in the 1840s. In the 1820s, for example, a series of dispatches written from the Texas frontier by Inspector-General Manuel Mier y Terán made it clear that American designs on Mexico's northern territories deeply concerned the Mexican government:

> Texas is contiguous to the most avid nation in the world. The North Americans have conquered whatever territory adjoins them. In less than half a century, they have become masters of extensive colonies which formerly belonged to Spain and France, and even of spacious territories from which have disappeared their former owners, the Indian tribes. There is no power like that to the North, which by silent means, has made conquests of momentous importance.[4]

The general's observations, of course, proved prescient, anticipating both the Texas Revolution and the Mexican War. But Mier y Terán was perhaps even more foresightful in recognizing the Americans' tremendous ability to rationalize and justify westward expansion. "If considered one by one," the general noted wryly, the Americans' methods of expansion "would be rejected as slow, ineffective, and at times palpably absurd." He continued: "They begin by assuming rights . . . which it is impossible to sustain in serious discussion, making ridiculous pretensions based on historical incidents which no one admits. . . . In the meantime, the territory against which these machinations are directed . . . begins to be visited by adventurers [who gradually] complicate the political administration of the coveted territory by discrediting the efficiency of the existing authority and administration." Mier y Terán indignantly concluded that, to add insult to injury, the Americans "incite uprisings in the territory in question [while] manifesting a deep concern for the rights of the inhabitants."[5]

Although General Mier y Terán had no way of knowing it then, he had touched on one of the most important elements of Americans' expansionist impulses. The U.S. penetration and conquest of Mexican territory was, of course, important, but Mier y Terán seemed to recognize that this represented only the first step in American expansion. Ultimately, the critical aspect of the annexation of the West proved to be the power that conquest bestowed on Americans to *explain* what had occurred there. As Reginald Horsman noted in his analysis of the Mexican War: "Total Mexican defeat convinced the Americans that their original judgement of the

Mexican race had been correct. . . . Americans were not to be blamed for forcibly taking the northern provinces of Mexico, for Mexicans . . . had failed because they were a mixed, inferior race."[6]

Acceptance of these fundamental premises in turn enabled Americans to demean, and ultimately to dismiss, the people they had incorporated into their society. This process was sped along by the segregation of ethnic Mexicans, an activity that occurred in varying degrees throughout the region. As Mexican Americans were slowly forced, by population pressures and discrimination, to withdraw into shrinking urban barrios and isolated rural *colonias*, they seemed to gradually disappear from the landscape, thereby fulfilling the prophecies of those proponents of Manifest Destiny who had predicted that the West's indigenous peoples would "recede" or "fade away" before the advance of American civilization. By the turn of the century, Mexican Americans had become, to use the words of one well-known historian, America's "forgotten people."[7]

To assert, however, that America forgot this ethnic group oversimplifies a far more complicated story. What actually occurred was a rather peculiar re-envisioning of the role Mexicans played in the region's past. Gradually released from the necessity of viewing Mexicans as any kind of political or military threat, Americans were able to indulge themselves in romantic reveries about what the landscape must have looked like before the war. In a process no doubt similar to the one that allowed Americans to construct the notion of the noble savage after Indians had been effectively removed from lands they coveted, the consolidation of American control over former Mexican domains allowed westerners to construct what Carey McWilliams aptly called "the Spanish fantasy heritage." With historians and history buffs, artists, travel and fiction writers, amateur ethnographers, and eventually local chambers of commerce and real estate boosters all contributing, Anglo-American residents of the region helped to construct a benign history of the not-so-distant past, one in which gracious Spanish grandees, beautiful señoritas, and gentle Catholic friars oversaw an abundant pastoral empire worked by contented mission Indians. As McWilliams, Kevin Starr, and more recently, Anne Hyde have demonstrated, this creation not only fit nicely with the images that Americans held of themselves but also allowed them the freedom to extol and selectively appropriate for their own use those aspects of the region's culture that amused them. These pastoral images seemed to capture the imagination of people living in the region. By the early decades of this century, it was rare to find a town of any size in the "Old Spanish Southwest" that did not celebrate its illustrious past by restoring missions, erecting historical markers, and holding what seemed to be a nearly endless round of annual

Spanish fiestas, replete with dons and doñas (usually Anglos) wearing full "Spanish" regalia and sitting astride matched palominos.[8]

Resistance, Excavation, and Recovery

Although some may persist in arguing that the elaborate historical and popular reimaginings constituting "the Spanish fantasy heritage" were harmless examples of romantic myth-making, Mexican Americans have long been aware of the ways such myths have helped to obscure, and thus to diminish, the actual historical producers of the culture that Anglos ostensibly celebrated. It was one thing to suffer the humiliation of conquest and the subsequent indignity of relegation to an inferior caste status in the emerging social order of the American-dominated West, but it was quite another to sit idly by and watch the Americans appropriate, for their own amusement, aspects of Mexican culture they found quaint and picturesque reminders of the past. Moreover, many Mexican Americans knew, to a painful degree, that the seemingly harmless celebration of Spanish fiestas masked the disdain so many Americans felt about the remaining representatives of Hispanic culture in the West. One can easily imagine the bewilderment and anger of Mexican Americans who, knowing that the very term *Mexican* had already become deeply embedded in the vocabulary of the region as a label of derision and stigma, watched gringos celebrate appropriated cultural events.

In many ways, ethnic Mexicans' awareness that they had been rendered insignificant as human beings in this manner has provided one of the major forces driving both their efforts to achieve full political rights in American society and their attempts to recapture and rewrite their own history. In fact, these two objectives have worked hand in hand since the 1850s, even if the resultant efforts went largely unheeded until very recently. Even a cursory knowledge of the region's ethnic history reveals that Mexican Americans have long considered the struggle to represent their own history and to be represented accurately in the West's history generally as crucial components of their ongoing campaign to achieve their full rights as American citizens and as human beings.

The dual nature of this struggle is readily apparent in the work of the first generation of scholars who began publishing research on the West's ethnic Mexican population in the years following World War I. Most of this generation of Mexican Americans either were descendants of the Spanish-speaking people whose presence predated that of the conquest or, more commonly, were the children of the huge numbers of Mexican immigrants who settled in the United States after 1910, so they had firsthand knowledge of what it meant to grow up with the stigma of being Mexican in the American West. Thus, when reviewing the work of pioneering intellectuals such as George I. Sánchez, Arthur L. Campa, Carlos Castañeda, Ernesto Galarza, Jovita González, or Américo Paredes, one immediately sees that these individuals were driven by more than a merely dispassionate pursuit of knowledge for knowledge's sake. Although most of these scholars (particularly the professional academicians) attempted to adhere to the so-called ideal of objectivity that mainstream scholarship demanded, they recognized that before they could ever hope to gain a fair reading of their work, it would be necessary to break through the deeply entrenched, dehumanizing stereotypes that Americans had come to accept since the early nineteenth century. This first generation of intellectuals also faced the burden of having come of age during an era of heavy immigration from Mexico. Forced to do their work in an atmosphere of intensifying anti-Mexican sentiment, this generation of Mexican-American scholars had to be even more careful in the way they framed their research questions and in the language they used to represent the subjects of that research.

The work these scholars produced stands on its own as research, yet I would argue that the more important legacy of the scholarship produced during this era is its quietly political nature rather than its specific topical content. This is not to assert that the scholarly efforts of this group were part of some coordinated, monolithic project; to the contrary, these scholars came from diverse disciplinary backgrounds and training and held various research interests and political orientations. When viewed in hindsight, however, the body of work produced by these individuals is unified in several important respects. The most important theme unifying this research was these scholars' obvious concern to represent ordinary working-class Mexican Americans and Mexican immigrants as complex, fully formed, and fully functional human beings. Although this might not seem to be a significant point, when viewed in the context of the times this work should be seen as the first stage of a bold—and inherently political—project of excavation and recovery that was designed, at least partially, to upset the prevailing regional social order by demonstrating the extent to which stereotypes about Mexicans were the products of Americans' active, and truly powerful, imaginations.

A brief discussion of George I. Sánchez's research helps illustrate some of the ways Mexican-American scholars of this period used their work both to advance objective knowledge and to alter what had become the master discourse used to describe Mexicans in the United States. Superficially, the work of the longtime University of Texas history and education professor appears to be an example of fairly straightforward academic research. But a closer analysis of his work reveals that Sánchez pursued a self-consciously political agenda throughout his long career. But this was not "politics" in the sense that most Americans associate with the word. Although Sánchez actively participated in the civil rights efforts of organizations such as the League of United Latin American Citizens, the American G.I. Forum, and the American Council of Spanish-Speaking People, in some ways his attempts to get the readers of his research simply to recognize Mexican Americans as human beings represented the most radical political position he could have advanced in the 1930s and 1940s. From the time he wrote his earliest work on general issues concerning education, Mexican-American bilingualism, and intelligence testing, Sánchez focused intently on destroying prevailing notions of Mexican Americans as a culturally monolithic, socially unstratified population by demonstrating the complexity and utility of the Southwest's syncretic Mexican-American culture. Writing in 1941, Sánchez maintained: "The Spanish-speaking population is not a monogenous [sic] group—in economic status, in education, in cultural background and history, or even in the degree to which its members are, in truth, Spanish-speaking! There is as much cultural variety within the group as there is to be found in any similar sector of population in the nation."[9]

Sánchez's point here, and in much of his other work, was not merely that the Mexican-American population was heterogeneous and internally stratified. On the contrary, Sánchez sought to illustrate, in a subdued and scholarly way, that because Mexican Americans disagreed about politics and were divided, among other things, by class, religion, customs, and language preference, their community was as internally complex and functionally cohesive as any other. Building on this basic premise, Sánchez systematically dissected theories that attributed Mexican-American poverty and low educational achievement to putative flaws inherent in Mexican culture or biology. "Poverty and its social effects," he wrote, "are not peculiar to any one racial, language, or cultural group. These effects are the attributes of poor people—irrespective of race, nationality, or language."[10]

For Sánchez, the implications of such insights were clear: the ethnic Mexican population's internal heterogeneity proved that they were human beings entitled to the same chances as any other people. Although Sánchez's published work usually focused on ethnic Mexican schoolchildren, his proposals for reform—both in his academic work and in his tireless political efforts—encompassed issues relevant to the entire Mexican-origin population. As he put it: "'The problem of the Spanish-speaking child' is a fictitious generalization insofar as it presupposes uniformity in the educational status or prospect of Latin Americans in the United States. Any educational practice based on that assumption is ill-advised and dangerous." From his point of view: "Insofar as the fundamental approaches of the school are concerned, Spanish-speaking children are no different from other children. They learn just as readily, they require just as good teachers and instructional facilities, and they need the same careful study of their *individual differences* as do other children."[11]

Though Sánchez's assertions may now seem to be little more than common sense, such notions held potentially revolutionary implications. On the most fundamental level, Sánchez's arguments, and those made by other Mexican-American scholars and activists of this generation, undermined an ideological edifice that had long maintained notions of American superiority and Mexican inferiority as fact. Although Sánchez and his generation would be criticized in the 1960s and 1970s by some Chicano activists for not having been quite strident enough in their resistance to discrimination, in the context of their own times these individuals' efforts represented a serious and inherently subversive assault on the entire system of meanings that Americans had constructed about the annexation of the West and, perhaps more important, about the significance of the ethnic Mexican people living there. By attacking Americans' common assumptions of racial, cultural, and political superiority—using scientific and objective research methods that could not be faulted by mainstream scholars—Sánchez and his generation issued a crucial first challenge to the very core of the ethnically stratified social order in the American West.[12]

The Chicano Moment

Although few Chicano activists of the 1960s and 1970s seemed willing to acknowledge the accomplishments of their immediate forebears, Sánchez's generation of scholar-activists in many ways anticipated the research agenda, modes of analysis, and political rhetoric of the generation of intellectuals and social activists that came of age during the era of the Chicano movement. The members of this second generation of intellectuals and social critics, however, were in a much better position than their predecessors to take the project of humanization several crucial steps further. Coming of age during a period of social ferment symbolized by the civil rights movement, inner-city revolts, and intensifying protests over the war in Vietnam, by the mid-1960s young Mexican Americans in scattered locales across the Southwest had embarked on a series of political campaigns that became known collectively as the Chicano movement. These protests played a crucial role in transforming regional politics by forcing the majority population to acknowledge and act on Chicano demands, but one of the least noticed yet most important effects of the Chicano movement was the extent that it helped force open the doors of colleges and universities to Mexican-American students. The opening of such previously restricted institutions not only allowed unprecedented numbers of students the opportunity to pursue a higher education but also helped fuel a renewed drive among Mexican Americans to recapture and rewrite their own history.

If the hallmark of the first generation of Mexican-American scholars and social critics was to try to accomplish this task within what they understood to be the framework of American liberal democracy, scholars and activists of the Chicano generation raised the stakes of this endeavor by insisting that Mexican Americans should be much more militant in challenging Anglo political, social, cultural, and intellectual authority. Whereas many members of the generation active in the 1940s and 1950s seemed to accept the integrationist premises of American liberalism, Chicano radicals of the 1960s and 1970s wanted to engage in a full frontal assault on this ideology. Rejecting liberalism and the notion of assimilation as parts of a mystifying, imperialist regime of thought that helped reinforce notions of Mexican inferiority by holding up Anglo-American society as the ideal to which Mexican Americans (and other people of color) should aspire, Chicano activists advocated the development of a new positive sense of ethnic and cultural identity.[13]

From the point of view of many Chicano militants, history would play a central role in the project to reconstruct Chicano identity. Indeed, from the very outset of the movement, Chicano activists argued that ethnic Mexicans must learn their true history before they could even hope to develop a strong sense of community and solidarity. As Jesus Chavarría, a historian active in the Chicano movement, recalled:

> Chicano history emerged as a product of the Chicano Movement because of our people's social and psychic need for self-knowledge. We . . . gradually recognized . . . hat we were the social and cultural product of a racial and cultural [process] which had attained such a degree of deranged assimilation that it had produced a monstrous distortion of our true past. Thus, we set out . . . self-consciously to identify and reconcile ourselves with our true past, which [to us] meant a positive identification with our indigenous forebears.[14]

Of course, constructing a record of the true past and establishing a positive identification with that past meant different things to different people, a fact that many activists seemed to forget in the flush of the Chicano movement. Although the ideological struggles of the 1960s served as important catalysts that provoked historians to renew their inquiry into the significance of (or, to quote this same activist-historian, "the meaning and value of") Chicano history, at its worst the history produced during this period helped to create a different totalizing discourse that in some ways was as distorting, essentialistic, and exclusionary as the one that activists were attempting to transform. Drawing from quasi-nationalistic or ethnic separatist perspectives that were never completely thought through, some Chicano activist-scholars showed a tendency to reify "Chicano culture" into a set of codes and symbols designed to offset what they argued was the inherent acquisitiveness, materialism, chauvinism, and rapaciousness of Anglo culture. Although the more thoughtful of these intellectuals argued that such temporary distortions were unfortunate but necessary mechanisms designed to build solidarity, ethnic pride, and a basis for concerted political action among Americans of Mexican descent, few seemed to realize that much of the rhetoric of the Chicano movement—and the scholarship that drew inspiration from that rhetoric—slid perilously close to replicating the same kind of exclusionary, hierarchical, and dehumanizing ideologies that Anglo Americans had used so effectively for so long to suppress minority peoples.[15]

At their best, however, scholars writing during this period broadened and deepened comprehension of the social history of the West by pulling Mexican Americans and Mexican immigrants out of obscurity, by rendering them visible and significant in regional history. And perhaps more important, the best of this generation of historians gave new life to the humanizing project their predecessors had initiated nearly fifty years earlier. At the level of the academic production of history, scholars such as Rodolfo Acuña, Tomás Almaguer, Mario Barrera, Arnoldo De León, Mario T. García, Juan Gómez-Quiñones, Richard Griswold del Castillo, Ricardo Romo, David Weber, and others published important works that compelled scholars—and at least some of the general public—to replace the traditional, stereotypical representations that had long dominated regional history with more complex and subtle renderings of individual Mexicans and Mexican culture. Employing the same sophistication in conceptualization, methodology, and argument that other so-called new social historians were developing at this time, Mexican-American scholars publishing in the 1970s and early 1980s produced work that gained increasing notice, respectability, and legitimacy in mainstream academic circles.

Of the many studies published in this era, however, it was Albert M.

Camarillo's pathbreaking 1979 monograph, *Chicanos in a Changing Society,* that most suggested the possibilities inherent in exploring the implications of the wide variation in the experiences of the region's ethnic Mexican residents. Combining a close analysis of manuscript census data with extensive oral history interviews to develop a detailed portrait of Mexican Americans and Mexican immigrants in Santa Barbara and other southern California communities, Camarillo provided one of the most nuanced social histories of this particularly fruitful era of Mexican-American historiography. The postannexation imposition of American political and economic hegemony runs as a strong theme throughout the study, but Camarillo broke new ground in a number of areas by indicating the ways Mexican Americans and gold rush–era Mexican immigrants used traditional cultural practices to adapt to and survive their changed status as an ethnic minority in a larger society. More important, building on the insights first touched on in the work of pioneering scholars such as Manuel Gamio, George I. Sánchez, Paul S. Taylor, and Carey McWilliams, Camarillo performed crucially important spade work by emphasizing how important the heterogeneity of southern California's ethnic Mexican population was to Mexican-American social, cultural, and political development. By demonstrating the ways that Mexican Americans and subsequent immigrants manufactured social barriers that divided them along class, regional, generational, nativity, and other lines and by exploring some of the ways that Mexican immigrants differed from Mexican Americans with regard to their specific cultural and religious observances, linguistic practices, and political orientations, Camarillo's book challenged previous interpretations by both mainstream *and* Chicano scholars, who had depicted Mexicans (or Chicanos) as a monolithic, internally undifferentiated population. Although many reviewers apparently missed the significance of this point at the time, Camarillo's emphasis on the internal diversity of the ethnic Mexican population was crucial in that it eventually encouraged both Chicano and non-Chicano readers to recognize that—contrary to the monolithic images projected (albeit in very different ways) by mainstream western historians on the one hand and militant Chicanos on the other—the syncretic Mexican-American culture of the Southwest was just as intricate and variegated as any other.

Camarillo's study and similar works published in the 1970s and early 1980s played an important role in establishing Mexican-American studies as a viable area of research, but the ultimate significance of this scholarship derived from its ability to challenge Anglo Americans' authority to determine both the appropriate (or significant) subjects of historical research and thus the dominant interpretations of the region's past. The scholarship produced during this era alerted westerners—and other Americans—that ethnic Mexicans henceforth were to be not only included in the West's history but included on their own terms.

The Changing Significance of Difference in Western History

Though some would argue that the project of humanization pursued by historians of the ethnic Mexican experience since early in this century continues in the present period, the character of this enterprise has recently undergone a significant transformation. In fact, members of the present generation of ethnic Mexican and other Latino intellectuals and social activists seem intent on pushing their demands for recognition and inclusion even further than did the militants of the 1960s and 1970s. Moving well beyond the rhetoric of mere inclusion, many in the present intellectual and political generation are insisting on developing a fundamental reconfiguration in the ways minority peoples are conceived of, categorized, and analyzed in history and contemporary American society.

On one level, this strident interventionist initiative can be seen as the outcome of a much larger process of social flux in which the character of ethnic, racial, gender, and class politics has changed in the West, and in the United States generally, since the civil rights upheavals of the 1960s. Although it is clear that civil rights activists' efforts to overthrow the established racial hierarchy of the United States have been only partially successful, the civil rights movement has succeeded in transforming the debate over race and ethnicity by providing American minority groups with powerful new bases of collective identity. By confronting, and ultimately rejecting, the ascribed negative identity categories (such as "Negro," "Oriental," or "Mexican") that had provided the necessary first steps in the construction and maintenance of the traditional racial hierarchy of American society, by the late 1960s "Blacks," "Asians," and "Chicanos" not only had redefined their own identities but also had served notice that other Americans would henceforth have to deal with them on new terms. As the sociologists Michael Omi and Howard Winant noted in their analysis of the civil rights era: "The ability of racially based movements to . . . challeng[e] . . . past racial practices and stereotypes [helped] initiate . . . a trajectory of reform which exposed the limits of all previously existing political orientations. . . . In transforming the meaning of race and the contours of racial politics, the racially based movements transformed the meaning and contours of American politics itself."[16]

The effect of this political sea change on historical scholarship has been no less profound. The widespread challenges to established authority that were issued on the streets and in the universities during the 1960s contributed to a sharpening of debate about the politics of representation of minority peoples and, more broadly, about the nature of historical authority itself. As Peter Novick noted in his sweeping study of the historical profession, when combined with the parallel challenges being issued to the notion of "objective," "value-free" history and social science by other dissident scholars, minority scholars' intellectual assault on the presumed "universalistic norms" of the American historical profession helped to throw the enterprise of historical scholarship into a deeply divisive "epistemological revolution" that continues to rage today.[17]

Although it is impossible in this limited space to assess the full impact of this revolution on questions concerning the historical significance of minority populations in the West (and even more difficult to predict the future trajectory of these ongoing political and intellectual developments), the emergence of three interrelated trends in recent regional historical interpretation is particularly relevant to this discussion. First, consider the dramatic increase in the number of scholars who are bringing interdisciplinary or transdisciplinary approaches to their study of the history of ethnic Mexican peoples in the West. Drawing theoretical, methodological, and critical insights and research questions from what used to be much more discretely demarcated disciplines, the recent "blurring of genres" (to borrow Clifford Geertz's phrase) so evident in western historiography has brought a variety of new perspectives to the study of minority populations. It is also contributing to a rapid dismantling of the kind of victor's history that has dominated regional historiography since the Mexican Cession. Whether one considers the recent explorations in autobiography and literary theory by scholars such as Hector Calderón, Angie Chabram, Clara Lomas, Genaro Padilla, José David Saldívar, Ramón Saldívar, or Rosaura Sánchez,[18] the musings of anthropologists such as Renato Rosaldo or Roger Rouse,[19] the historical investigations of folklorists such as María Herrera-Sobek, José Limón, or Manuel Peña,[20] the ruminations on regional history by sociologists such as Tomás Almaguer or David Montejano,[21] or the work of formally trained interdisciplinary social historians such as Deena J. González, Camille Guerin-Gonzales, Ramón A. Gutiérrez, Lisbeth Haas, Douglas Monroy, George J. Sánchez, or Devra Anne Weber,[22] one cannot help but be struck by the extent that old "us versus them" interpretations of interethnic relations have given way to extremely subtle analyses in which Mexicans, Anglos, Indians, and others emerge as complex, multifaceted, sometimes cooperative, and often contradictory actors on the regional stage. For example, it is impossible to read the work of González, Padilla, or Gutiérrez on New Mexico, Montejano or Peña on Texas, or Hass, Monroy, or Almaguer on California and not come away with the understanding that the conquest of the Mexican Northwest in the 1840s involved more than the abject subjugation of ethnic Mexicans and Indians. As Montejano reminds us in the case of Tejanos, although the history of relations between Anglos and Mexicans in Texas has undeniably been harsh and at times brutal, extensive contact over time forced "uneasy accommodation[s]" in which "paternalism and protection, the exchange of obligations and commitments, and justice [were all] sometimes possible."[23] In short, work of this type shows the extent to which Mexicans were simultaneously objects of subordination and active agents of political and cultural opposition and resistance.

Whereas the move toward interdisciplinary analyses represented by such work has accelerated the project of humanization initiated by pioneering ethnic Mexican activists and intellectuals, an even more fundamental challenge to "business as usual" in regional history has been issued by western historians of women, gender, and sexuality. Spurred by developments similar to those that stimulated women in the civil rights, antiwar, and New Left movements to reassess their relationships to male activists in the 1960s and 1970s, the recent florescence of Chicana history grew out of Mexican-American and Mexican immigrant women's experiences in the Chicano movement. Ethnic Mexican women played central roles in the myriad organizations that made up the Chicano civil rights struggle, but like their counterparts in the other social movements of the times, they quickly discovered that they were expected to conform to traditional subordinate gender roles within their culture.[24]

Exposed through their political activities to the raw dynamics of continuing gender subjugation within a movement ostensibly dedicated to their liberation, Chicana and Mexicana activists soon began asking more comprehensive questions about the nature of their oppression in society. Logically, the answers to these questions initially tended to focus almost exclusively on the dynamics of male-female relationships within contemporary Mexican-American and Mexican culture. However, as increasing numbers of women activists gained access to higher education along with their male counterparts in the Chicano movement, such inquiries inevitably began to influence the production of regional historical scholarship and interpretation.

The work of a new generation of women scholars influenced by these political and intellectual developments began to appear in the 1980s. Led by women's historians such as Vicki L. Ruiz, Rosalinda González, Sarah Deutsch, Deena J. González, Antonia Castañeda, Peggy Pascoe, Susan Johnson, and others, this generation of scholar-activists immediately transformed the research agenda in the West by systematically including, often for the first time, women as primary subjects of analysis in regional, social, and cultural history.[25] Perhaps just as important, from the time they first entered graduate school, women scholars made it a fundamental part of their business to insist that male historians rethink the ways they framed and pursued their own research.[26]

Although this insistence played a crucial role in reducing the glaring distortions resulting from traditional research methods that had obliterated at least half of the putative subjects of social history, it proved to be just the first step in a series of logical steps that led women's historians and feminist theorists to ask deeper questions about the nature of gendered systems more generally construed. The importance of the critique that arose from such a realization extended far beyond its proximate concentration on women per se. On the most basic level, scholars who sought to analyze gender—that is, the complex systems of social and cultural meanings assigned to sexual difference—insisted that it played at least as powerful a role in ordering and stratifying men *and* women in society as does race or class. Using this basic premise as a point of departure, women's historians and feminist theorists explicitly and implicitly raised important theoretical questions about the production and reproduction of all kinds of subjective identities, including those based on race, ethnicity, and class. As one theorist noted recently, by engaging in "genealogical investigations of the generative power of male dominance within the production of knowledge," feminist scholars opened the door to new ways of thinking about other aspects of social life and knowledge, including "the suppression of knowledge of gender and its essential role in the structuring of individual experience, social relations, and knowledge itself."[27] Just as important, such a line of inquiry eventually led feminist scholars to reject notions of unified naturalized identity categories in favor of those that treat identity as "a contested terrain, the site of multiple and conflicting claims."[28]

Although regional historical scholarship that draws on such insights is still in a probing, experimental stage of development, several projects published since 1980 suggest the possibilities inherent in pursuing these experiments. Perhaps the earliest and best-known example of such innovative work is the best-selling anthology *This Bridge Called My Back,* edited by Gloria Anzaldúa and Cherríe Moraga and first published in 1981. Although not specifically a work of historical scholarship, the collection stands out as an important example of early experimental efforts to extend and explicitly link insights generated from feminist and cultural theory with explorations into other asymmetrical relationships of power, including those involving the historical legacies of racial, ethnic, and class stratification.[29]

Beyond the thematic content of the anthology, the importance of this and similar work lay in the rich possibilities it suggested for the continuation and expansion of the general project both to humanize the objects of historical inquiry and to add to our comprehension of what traditionally has been termed "ethnic relations" in the West. By dismissing essentialistic renderings of individuals, communities, and cultures and by paying particularly close, critical attention to the ways men, women, and children are socialized to take up prescribed roles within gendered systems, studies such as *This Bridge* represent an important example of these social critics' willingness to interrogate and challenge naturalized categories such as race, culture, ethnicity, sex, and nation.

Moreover, the authors of innovative works such as *This Bridge* accomplished another breakthrough by demonstrating the courage to be openly self-reflective and self-critical. Although a strong critique of the hegemonic power of white colonizers is evident throughout the anthology, the women represented in *This Bridge* spent at least as much energy calling into question the painfully sexist, racist, homophobic, and culturally chauvinistic tendencies evident in their own cultural and/or social groups and thus contributed to the process of self-determination that activists had called for during the Chicano movement. Both majority and minority readers undoubtedly will continue to find it painful to consider this type of criticism, but the authors of *This Bridge* and more recent works make it clear that close attention to the structures that *internally* stratify and divide communities must be a central component of any project that aspires to render human *all* of the historically subject peoples who have lived and now live in the West.[30]

The third and potentially greatest contribution made by the members of the present generation of critical scholars to the project to render significant the ethnic Mexican population of the West is their unwavering commitment to explore and illuminate the intrinsic relationship between power and knowledge in scholarship and in society at large. Although many academics refuse to acknowledge that the production of *any* historical knowledge is an inherently political act, it is clear that many (if not most) scholars of the ethnic Mexican experience in the West have accepted the view that, as Peter Novick notes of those who believe this, "postures of disinterestedness and neutrality [in historical scholarship are] outmoded and illusory."[31]

The production of knowledge based on the acceptance of such a premise has not occurred without cost to those actively engaged in it. On the contrary, as the recent proliferation of highly critical books, articles, and political rhetoric attests, scholars pursuing this type of innovative, nontraditional research will continue to face charges that the inherently political nature of their work renders their project an exercise in polemics rather than rigorous, objective historical scholarship.[32] Moreover, to recognize that the challenge to deeply ingrained ways of thinking undoubtedly will continue to elicit strong and perhaps even violent opposition, one need think only of the intensifying debate over cultural values in the most recent American presidential campaigns, the bitter ongoing battle to challenge and restructure curricula at all levels of American public education, the increasingly rancorous interethnic and intraethnic disagreements over the efficacy and desirability of affirmative action approaches to structural discrimination, the recent increase in both racial and ethnic tensions, gang violence, and "hate crimes," and in the West especially, the renewal of the bitter debate over U.S. immigration policy. Clearly, practitioners of this kind of research—and activists who espouse similar views in their political work at the community level—will inevitably continue to attract the ire of those in society who feel personally threatened by the implicit and explicit challenges to the social status quo (or who have a vested interest in *preserving* the status quo).[33]

In a fundamental way, however, this kind of research is *intended* to threaten existing social structures that serve to maintain the subordination of certain groups at the same time that they mystify the dynamics of this subordination. By drawing from and building on theoretical and methodological insights developed by those involved in interdisciplinary cultural studies and, more recently, by women's historians and feminist theorists, historians interested in analyzing other kinds of socially constructed systems of difference and power seem committed to struggle to transform the ways we conceive of and understand the histories of subordinated peoples in the region. This exceedingly diverse and complex work should not be thought of as a monolithic project or as some magical device that will provide historians the means to bridge the gap between the lived experiences of ethnic Mexicans (or, for that matter, any group) and the historians' representations of this social history. Activist-scholars need also to guard against, to paraphrase Henry Louis Gates, the academic profession's "propensity for offering lexical redress to political grievances" and our tendency to believe that a more complete representation of various underrepresented minority groups in historical texts is somehow necessarily equivalent to a more complete *political* empowerment.[34]

Taken as a whole, however, all research of this type suggests a number of innovative ways to reconceptualize historical inquiry, ways that perhaps will help us to challenge more effectively the racist, sexist, and culturally chauvinistic stereotypes and structures that have for so long permeated thought and discourse about the significance of different peoples in the American West. By exposing and painstakingly analyzing the constructed, manipulated nature of social hierarchies of all types, scholars and social critics working from this point of view might help change the terms of debate about the historical and contemporary significance of ethnic Mexicans and other minority peoples. They might also have an unprecedented opportunity to change the way people think about the significance of differences between and among people generally. If these trends continue, to paraphrase the recent musings of two scholars of the emergence of multiculturalism, we may be witnessing "the development of a new definition of what comprises 'mainstream' culture."[35] If such hopeful prognostications turn out to be true, the question of who is, and who is not, considered significant in this society will itself take on an entirely new significance.

Notes

I am deeply indebted to a number of friends and colleagues for reading and critiquing several earlier drafts of this work. Special thanks go to Tomás Almaguer, Al Camarillo, Arnoldo De León, Bill Deverell, Ramón Gutiérrez, Susan Johnson, Michael Meranze, Clyde Milner, Raúl Ramos, and Vicki Ruiz. I would also like to express my thanks to Susie Porter for her research assistance and my heartfelt gratitude to Peggy Pascoe and Andrea Otañez for encouraging me to listen to the ideas that most informed this essay.

An earlier version of this essay appeared under the title "Significant to Whom?: Mexican Americans and the History of the American West," by David G. Gutiérrez. Previously published in the *Western Historical Quarterly* 24 (November 1993): 519–39. Copyright by Western History Association. Reprinted by permission.

1. In this essay, when I speak of "Mexican Americans" I am referring to American citizens of Mexican descent, regardless of their length of residence in the United States. The term *Chicano*, as will become clear in the text, refers to persons of Mexican descent who used that term as a self-referent during the 1960s and 1970s. I use the term *Mexican immigrants* when referring to citizens of Mexico residing in the

United States. Although all of these groups have historically recognized important distinctions between and among themselves, all have been subject to varying degrees of prejudice and discrimination in the United States, regardless of their formal citizenship status. Thus, when referring to the combined population of all people of Mexican ancestry or descent living in the United States, I employ the term *ethnic Mexicans*. For an extended analysis of the historical significance of difference within this population, see David G. Gutiérrez, *Walls and Mirrors: Mexican Americans, Mexican Immigrants, and the Politics of Ethnicity* (Berkeley, 1995).

2. Joan Wallach Scott, *Gender and the Politics of History* (New York, 1988), 9. This is, of course, a point a number of scholars have made in other contexts. My analysis here has drawn on, in addition to Scott, Michel Foucault, *The Order of Things: An Archaeology of the Human Sciences* (New York, 1970) and *The Archaeology of Knowledge* (New York, 1972); Abdul R. JanMohamed, "Negating the Negation as a Form of Affirmation in Minority Discourse: The Construction of Richard Wright as Subject," in *The Nature and Context of Minority Discourse*, ed. Abdul R. JanMohamed and David Lloyd (New York, 1990), 102–23; and especially Edward W. Said, *Orientalism* (New York, 1978).

3. For the evolution of such attitudes, see Raymund A. Paredes, "The Origins of Anti-Mexican Sentiment in the United States," in *New Directions in Chicano Scholarship*, ed. Ricardo Romo and Raymund Paredes (La Jolla, Calif., 1978), 139–65; David J. Weber, "'Scarce More than Apes': Historical Roots of Anglo Stereotypes of Mexicans in the Border Region," in *New Spain's Far Northern Frontier: Essays on Spain in the American West, 1540–1821*, ed. David J. Weber (Albuquerque, 1979), 295–307; Reginald Horsman, *Race and Manifest Destiny: The Origins of American Racial Anglo-Saxonism* (Cambridge, Mass., 1981); and Arnoldo De León, *They Called Them Greasers: Anglo Attitudes toward Mexicans in Texas, 1821–1900* (Austin, 1983).

4. Mier y Terán to Pablo Viejo, Mexican Minister of War, 14 November 1829, in Ohland Morton, *Terán and Texas: A Chapter in Texas-Mexican Relations* (Austin, 1948), 99–101. Excerpts of these dispatches are reprinted in David J. Weber, ed., *Foreigners in Their Native Land: Historical Roots of the Mexican Americans* (Albuquerque, 1973), 101–4.

5. Mier y Terán in Morton, *Terán and Texas*.

6. Horsman, *Race and Manifest Destiny*, 246, 210.

7. George I. Sánchez, *Forgotten People: A Study of New Mexicans* (Albuquerque, 1967).

8. On the creation and evolution of the Spanish fantasy heritage, see Carey McWilliams, *North from Mexico: The Spanish-Speaking People of the United States* (New York, 1949) and *Southern California Country: An Island on the Land* (Salt Lake City, 1973), 70–83; Kevin Starr, *Americans and the California Dream, 1850–1915* (New York, 1973), 390–401; and Anne Farrar Hyde, *An American Vision: Far Western Landscape and National Culture, 1820–1920* (New York, 1990), 235–38. Although the Spanish fantasy heritage of the Southwest was constructed largely at the level of the popular imagination, professional scholars also played their part in building this view of the region's past. The earliest histories (such as Hubert Howe Bancroft's massive series of volumes) and more recent works by American borderlands

scholars characteristically include sympathetic depictions of Spanish colonial and Mexican institutions and culture, but the reader cannot help but come away from these histories with the sense that they reflect a kind of "victor's history," which above all else seeks to analyze and explain the "objective reasons" for American "successes" and Hispanic "failures" in the region. For a recent review and critique of this literature, see Gerald E. Poyo and Gilberto M. Hinojosa, "Spanish Texas and Borderlands Historiography in Transition: Implications for United States History," *Journal of American History* 75 (September 1988): 393–416.

9. George I. Sánchez, "North of the Border," *Proceedings and Transactions of the Texas Academy of Science, 1941* 26 (1942): 79.

10. Ibid., 82.

11. Ibid., 80, 81, emphasis added.

12. For a recent study that makes this case, see Mario T. García, *Mexican Americans: Leadership, Ideology, and Identity, 1930–1960* (New Haven, 1989).

13. That Chicano intellectuals were no longer content to suffer the appropriation or colonization of their people's history was made crystal clear in a series of scathing critiques of Anglo-American interpretations of the Mexican-American experience. Among the most notable published during this period were Tomás Almaguer, "Toward the Study of Chicano Colonialism," *Aztlán* 2 (Spring 1971): 7–21, and "Historical Notes on Chicano Oppression: The Dialectics of Racial and Class Domination in North América," *Aztlán* 5 (Spring and Fall 1974): 27–56; Octavio Ignacio Romano-V, "The Anthropology and Sociology of the Mexican Americans: The Distortion of Mexican-American History," *El Grito* 2 (Fall 1968): 13–26, "The Historical and Intellectual Presence of Mexican-Americans," *El Grito* 2 (Winter 1969): 32–46, and "Social Science, Objectivity, and the Chicanos," *El Grito* 4 (Fall 1970): 4–16; Nick C. Vaca, "The Mexican-American in the Social Sciences, 1912–1970," part 1 (1912–35), *El Grito* 3 (Spring 1970): 3–24, and part 2 (1936–70), *El Grito* 4 (Fall 1970): 17–51; and Miguel Montiel, "The Social Science Myth of the Mexican American Family," *El Grito* 3 (Summer 1970): 56–63.

14. Jesus Chavarría, "On Chicano History: In Memoriam, George I. Sánchez, 1906–1972," in *Humanidad: Essays in Honor of George I. Sánchez*, ed. Américo Paredes (Los Angeles, 1977), 44.

15. For recent critical discussions of some of the intellectual and ideological inconsistencies that characterized the Chicano movement, see José E. Limón, "The Folk Performance of 'Chicano' and the Cultural Limits of Political Ideology," in *"And Other Neighborly Names": Social Process and Cultural Image in Texas Folklore*, ed. Richard Bauman and Roger D. Abrahams (Austin, 1980), 197–225; Tomás Almaguer, "Ideological Distortions in Recent Chicano Historiography: The Internal Colonial Model and Chicano Historical Interpretation," *Aztlán* 18 (Spring 1987): 7–28; Alex M. Saragoza, "Recent Chicano Historiography: An Interpretive Essay," *Aztlán* 19 (Spring 1988–90): 1–78; Juan Gómez-Quiñones, *Chicano Politics: Reality and Promise, 1940–1990* (Albuquerque, 1990); and David G. Gutiérrez, *"Sin Fronteras?* Chicanos, Mexican Americans, and the Emergence of the Contemporary Mexican Immigration Debate, 1968–1978," *Journal of American Ethnic History* 10 (Summer 1991): 5–37.

16. Michael Omi and Howard Winant, *Racial Formation in the United States: From the 1960s to the 1980s* (New York, 1986), 138.

17. Peter Novick, *That Noble Dream: The "Objectivity Question" and the American Historical Profession* (Cambridge, England, 1988), 470, 546.

18. Such work has proliferated at such a rapid rate that it is impossible to summarize here. For some representative examples, see Angie Chabram, "Chicano Critical Discourse: An Emerging Cultural Practice," *Aztlán* 18 (Fall 1987): 45–90; Genaro M. Padilla, "'Yo sola aprendi': Contra-Patriarchal Containment in Women's Nineteenth-Century California Personal Narratives," *Americas Review* 16 (Fall-Winter 1988): 91–109, and "The Recovery of Chicano Nineteenth-Century Autobiography," *American Quarterly* 40 (September 1988): 286–306; Clara Lomas, "Mexican Precursors of Chicana Feminist Writing," in *Multiethnic Literature of the United States: Critical Introductions and Classroom Resources,* ed. Cordelia Candalaria (Boulder, 1989); Ramón Saldívar, *Chicano Narrative: The Dialectics of Difference* (Madison, 1990); Rosaura Sánchez, *Chicano Discourse: Socio-Historic Perspectives* (Rowley, Mass., 1983) and "Postmodernism and Chicano Literature," *Aztlán* 18 (Fall 1987): 1–14; Asunción Horno-Delgado et al., eds., *Breaking Boundaries: Latina Writing and Critical Readings* (Amherst, 1989); and Héctor Caldereón and José David Saldívar, eds., *Criticism in the Borderlands: Studies in Chicano Literature, Culture, and Ideology* (Durham, N.C., 1991).

19. Renato Rosaldo, *Culture and Truth: The Remaking of Social Analysis* (Boston, 1989); Roger Rouse, "Mexican Migration and the Social Space of Postmodernism," *Diaspora* 1 (Fall 1991): 8–23.

20. María Herrera-Sobek, *The Bracero Experience: Elitelore versus Folklore* (Los Angeles, 1979) and *The Mexican Corrido: A Feminist Analysis* (Bloomington, 1990); José E. Limón, *Mexican Ballads, Chicano Poems: History and Influence in Mexican American Social Poetry* (Berkeley, 1992); Manuel H. Peña, *The Texas-Mexican Conjunto: History of a Working-Class Music* (Austin, 1985).

21. Tomás Almaguer, *Racial Fault Lines: The Historical Origins of White Supremacy in California* (Berkeley, 1994); David Montejano, *Anglos and Mexicans in the Making of Texas, 1836–1986* (Austin, 1987).

22. Deena J. González, *Resisting the Favor: The Spanish-Mexican Women of Santa Fe, 1820–1880* (New York, forthcoming); Camille Guerin-Gonzales, *Mexican Workers and American Dreams: Immigration, Repatriation, and California Farm Labor, 1900–1939* (New Brunswick, N.J., 1994); Ramón A. Gutiérrez, *When Jesus Came, the Corn Mothers Went Away: Marriage, Sexuality, and Power in New Mexico, 1500–1846* (Stanford, 1991); Lisbeth Haas, *Conquests and Historical Identities in California, 1769–1936* (Berkeley, 1995); Douglas Monroy, *Thrown among Strangers: The Making of Mexican Culture in Frontier California* (Berkeley, 1990); George J. Sánchez, *Becoming Mexican American: Ethnicity, Culture, and Identity in Chicano Los Angeles, 1900–1945* (New York, 1994); Devra Weber, *Dark Sweat, White Gold: California Farm Workers, Cotton, and the New Deal* (Berkeley, 1994).

23. Montejano, *Anglos and Mexicans*, 11.

24. Adelaida Del Castillo, "Mexican Women in Organization," in *Mexican Women in the United States: Struggles Past and Present*, ed. Magdalena Mora and Ade-

laida Del Castillo (Los Angeles, 1980), 9. Many women activists had come to the painful realization that the patterns of gender subordination they experienced in society generally were being replicated, and even intensified, within the Chicano movement. For discussion of these issues in the Chicano movement, see Adaljiza Sosa Riddell, "Chicanas and El Movimiento," *Aztlán* 5 (Spring and Fall 1974): 155–65, and Sonia A. López, "The Role of the Chicana within the Student Movement," in *Essays on La Mujer,* ed. Rosaura Sánchez and Rose Martinez Cruz (Los Angeles, 1977), 16–29. For more general discussions, see Maxine Baca Zinn, "Mexican-American Women in the Social Sciences," *Signs* 8 (Winter 1982): 259–72; Patricia Zavella, "The Problematic Relationship of Feminism and Chicana Studies," *Women's Studies* 17 (1989): 25–36; Alma M. Garcia, "The Development of Chicana Feminist Discourse, 1970–1980," in *Unequal Sisters: A Multicultural Reader in U.S. Women's History,* ed. Ellen Carol DuBois and Vicki L. Ruiz (New York, 1990), 418–31; Denise A. Segura and Beatriz M. Pesquera, "Beyond Indifference and Antipathy: The Chicana Movement and Chicana Feminist Discourse," *Aztlán* 19 (Fall 1988–1990): 69–92; and Antonia I. Castañeda, "Women of Color and the Rewriting of Western History: The Discourse, Politics, and Decolonization of History," *Pacific Historical Review* 61 (November 1992): 501–33.

25. See Antonia I. Castañeda, "Comparative Frontiers: The Migration of Women to Alta California and New Zealand," and Vicki L. Ruiz, "Miles to Go...: Mexican Women and Work, 1930–1950," both in *Western Women: Their Lands, Their Lives,* ed. Lillian Schlissel, Vicki L. Ruiz, and Janice Monk (Albuquerque, 1988), 283–300, 117–36; Antonia I. Castañeda, "The Political Economy of Nineteenth Century Stereotypes of Californianas," in *Between Borders: Essays on Mexicana/Chicana History,* ed. Adelaida R. Del Castillo (Encino, Calif., 1990), 213–36; Sarah Deutsch, *No Separate Refuge: Culture, Class, and Gender on an Anglo-Hispanic Frontier in the American Southwest, 1880–1940* (New York, 1987); Deena J. González, "The Widowed Women of Santa Fe: Assessments on the Lives of an Unmarried Population, 1850-1880," in *On Their Own: Widows and Widowhood in the American Southwest, 1848–1939,* ed. Arlene Scadron (Urbana, 1988), 65–90; Peggy Pascoe, *Relations of Rescue: The Search for Female Moral Authority in the American West, 1874–1939* (New York, 1990); Susan L. Johnson, "Sharing Bed and Board: Cohabitation and Cultural Difference in Central Arizona Mining Towns, 1863–1873," in *The Women's West,* ed. Susan Armitage and Elizabeth Jameson (Norman, 1987), 77–92; Rosalinda M. González, "Chicanas and Mexican Immigrant Families, 1920–1940: Women's Subordination and Family Exploitation," in *Decades of Discontent: The Women's Movement, 1920–1940,* ed. Lois Scharf and Joan M. Jensen (Westport, Conn., 1983), 59–84; and Vicki L. Ruiz, *Cannery Women, Cannery Lives: Mexican Women, Unionization, and the California Food Processing Industry, 1930–1950* (Albuquerque, 1987).

26. For critiques of the resistance of Chicano men to the inclusion of gender in their historical research, see Cynthia Orozco, "Chicana Labor History: A Critique of Male Consciousness in Historical Writing," *La Red/The Net* 77 (January 1984): 2–5, and "Sexism in Chicano Studies and the Community," in *Chicana Voices: Intersections of Class, Race, and Gender,* ed. Teresa Cordova et al. (Austin, 1986), 11–18, and Vicki

L. Ruiz, "Texture, Text, and Context: New Approaches in Chicano Historiography," *Mexican Studies/Estudios Mexicanos* 2 (Winter 1986): 145–52.

27. Jane Flax, "The End of Innocence," in *Feminists Theorize the Political,* ed. Judith Butler and Joan W. Scott (New York, 1992), 454.

28. Joan W. Scott, "Experience," in ibid., 31.

29. Cherríe Moraga and Gloria Anzaldúa, eds., *This Bridge Called My Back: Writings by Radical Women of Color* (New York, 1981). Although this collection does not explicitly focus on "the West," the authors of many of the essays write of lives experienced in the region.

30. For recent publications that build on the project first articulated in *This Bridge,* see Gloria Anzaldúa, ed., *Making Face, Making Soul—Haciendo Caras: Creative and Critical Perspectives by Women of Color* (San Francisco, 1990), and Gloria Anzaldúa, *Borderlands/La Frontera: The New Mestiza* (San Francisco, 1987); Norma Alarcón, "Traddutora, Traditora: A Paradigmatic Figure of Chicana Feminism," *Cultural Critique* 13 (Fall 1989): 57–87; Angie Chabram-Dernersesian, "I Throw Punches for My Race, but I Don't Want to Be a Man: Writing Us—Chica-nos (Girl, Us)/Chicanas—into the Movement Script," in *Cultural Studies,* ed. Lawrence Grossberg, Cary Nelson, and Paula A. Treichler (New York, 1992), 81–95; Norma Alarcón, Ana Castillo, and Cherríe Moraga, eds., *Third Woman: The Sexuality of Latinas* (Berkeley, 1989); and Tomás Almaguer, "Chicano Men: A Cartography of Homosexual Identity and Behavior," *Differences* 3 (1991): 75–100.

31. Novick, *That Noble Dream,* 523.

32. For recent articulations of this kind of criticism, see Arthur M. Schlesinger Jr., *The Disuniting of America* (New York, 1992), and Dinesh D'Souza, *Illiberal Education: The Politics of Race and Sex on Campus* (New York, 1991). For a broader view, see James Davison Hunter, *Culture Wars: The Struggle to Define America* (New York, 1991).

33. For explications of such research agendas in interdisciplinary Chicana/o studies that, in my view, have direct implications for historical scholarship (in addition to the previously cited works by Norma Alarcón, Antonia Castañeda, Angie Chabram, Deena J. González, Ramón A. Gutiérrez, Genaro Padilla, Renato Rosaldo, and Ramón Saldívar), see also Chela Sandoval, "U.S. Third World Feminism: The Theory and Method of Oppositional Consciousness in the Postmodern World,"*Genders* 10 (Spring 1991): 1–24, and articles by Richard Chabrán, Angie Chabram, Norma Alarcón, Alvina Quintana, Rosa Linda Fregoso, Yolanda Broyles González, Rosaura Sánchez, Michael Soldatenko-Gutiérrez, and Raymond Rocco in a special issue of *Cultural Studies* entitled "Chicana/o Cultural Representations: Reframing Alternative Critical Discourses," *Cultural Studies* 4 (October 1990).

34. Henry Louis Gates Jr., "The Weaning of America,"*New Yorker* (19 April 1993), 114; see also Henry Louis Gates Jr., "Trading on the Margin: Notes on the Culture of Criticism," *Loose Canons: Notes on the Culture Wars* (New York, 1992), 173–93.

35. Rick Simonson and Scott Walker, eds., *The Graywolf Annual Five: Multicultural Literacy* (Saint Paul, 1988), xi.

In Pursuit of a Brown West

Arnoldo De León

Professor David Gutiérrez informs us that the most important new perspectives currently being utilized to re-envision the American West may be traced to the influence of the social movements of the 1960s. He is particularly struck by the effect of interdisciplinary concepts in rewriting western history and by the approaches used by scholars interested in women, gender, and sexuality. Of course, space limits him from speculating at length on how to revise the story of the West. Let me, therefore, take up where Professor Gutiérrez left off by offering further possibilities.

A careful consideration of geographic areas and how they influence Mexican-descent peoples might serve as a framework for understanding the diversity of Hispanic communities in the West. Historians have long acknowledged the distinctions among Tejanos, Nuevo Mexicanos, and Californios, and though they recognize environment as a determining factor in the complexity of the Mexican experience in the West, they have not pursued it decisively. In 1989, I focused on this issue in an article entitled "The Tejano Experience in Six Texas Regions,"[1] and if the claim may be made that particular settings such as the agricultural orientation of South Texas or the ranching ambient of West Texas shape personalities as well as regional variants of Mexican-American culture, then similar arguments may be advanced concerning the impact that mountains, rivers, plains, deserts, and forests have on Mexican residents in the southwestern states or on inhabitants of Montana, Utah, Kansas, and Nebraska.

Cultural geographers might chime in with historians and find fertile grounds for their own perspectives. Already historians are engrossed in a lively debate over the origins and preservation of Hispano culture in northern New Mexico; the catalyst has been Richard L. Nostrand's conception of the "Hispano Homeland." As Nostrand sees it, the Hispanos' isolation over the generations begot a culture that is distinctive from that of Mexicanos in the rest of the New Mexico and certainly in other regions of the West, and although other geographer-historians have contested his thesis, Nostrand marshals a credible group of fellow scholars to uphold his conclusions.[2] Similarly, Daniel D. Arreola of Arizona State University has looked at a variety of Mexican-American cultural manifestations including houses and house fences, plazas, restaurants, and murals. He finds that cultural tastes that are traceable to Mexico are not entirely muted by residence in the United States and that such sentiments produce favorite cultural expressions that distinguish a Mexican-American identity from that of other peoples in the West.[3] The historian

Antonio Ríos-Bustamante of the University of Arizona is currently directing a major project tentatively titled "Atlas of Mexican American History."

Historians might test the relevance of the frontier thesis to the experience of ethnic Mexicans. Research need not necessarily focus on Frederick Jackson Turner's major premises—that the West engendered rugged individualism, democracy, self-reliance, improvisation, and the like—although it might. A more appropriate interpretive framework might borrow from the musings of Ray Allen Billington. As Billington explained his own understanding of cultural geography, frontiers do not necessarily shape cultural folkways or societal traits. Instead, a healthy interaction occurs between a society and a wilderness setting. A frontier people's cultural baggage can influence survival responses.[4] Consequently, Tejanos might have reacted somewhat differently than did Californios or Nuevo Mexicanos to a similar environmental setting, and the consequences make up different stories of assimilation and adaptation.

The continuity of cultures across nationhoods might have to be taken into account in new periodizations of western history. Studies in the 1980s showed that the year 1848—the date of the signing of the Treaty of Guadalupe Hidalgo, which transformed Mexican residents of the Far North into American citizens—is not the feasible beginning date for Mexican-American history (as the early practitioners of Chicano history had argued). The works of Gerald E. Poyo, Gilberto M. Hinojosa, and Jesús F. de la Teja in Texas, of Ramón A. Gutiérrez and Deena González in New Mexico, and of Douglas Monroy and Antonia I. Castañeda in California are but a sampling of recent studies that undermine that earlier notion.[5] This reconceptualization has meaningful implications for western history. For one thing, the once antagonistic relationship that prevailed between the Bolton-Bannon Borderlands school of New Spain's Far North and the newer revisionist "Chicano history" finds common ground in the linkage between the Spanish-Mexican and Chicano experiences. More significant, historians will have to rethink notions of the "American West" and push their beginning point to the years of the earliest Spanish *entradas*. Recent studies have been doing this, and the recognition given to Ramón A. Gutiérrez's *When Jesus Came, the Corn Mothers Went Away* by scholars of the West encourages this consideration.

Simultaneously, historians should turn their attention to notions of "community," "identity," and "nationalism." Historians who have made recent probes into the subject have sought to determine how Mexican Americans and their predecessors in what is today the continental United States grappled with forces such as changing sovereignties (Spain, Mexico, and the United States), economic systems, population movements, intellectual currents, and a plethora of other variables. New realities ordinarily lead to a process of readjustment or of redefinition of feelings regarding allegiance (when different governments take power), self-identity, community values, and nationalistic tendencies, especially among immigrant communities. The last case brings up the related topic of how international episodes touch on events in the United States. Select examples of transnational incidents that have determined Mexican-American history include the roles of Mexican exile Ricardo Flores Magón and the activities of his Partido Liberal Mexicano in Los Angeles during the era of the Mexican Revolution and the diplomatic strategy of Mexico's President Venustiano Carranza in Texas making use of the Plan de San Diego (1915), which called for establishing a republic in the U.S. Southwest for Mexican-origin people.[6] Nationalism has also been evident in heightened *mexicanidad* within Mexican-American communities, such as in the first three decades of the twentieth century and even later at the time of the Chicano movement (1960s and 1970s), when Mexican Americans reaffirmed their pre-Columbian origins.

Indeed, Professor Gutiérrez's essay refers to the Chicano movement, noting its impact on how historians, especially Chicanos, came to revise the way western scholars interpreted their history. How do social movements determine the direction of intellectual discourse, then? Was the movement an advancement of sentiments previously advocated by those political leaders before the 1960s, or was it a "militant" expression with ambiguous antecedents? Historians today generally posit that the programs advanced by the "Chicano Generation" (the politicized cohorts of the 1960s and 1970s) amounted to little else than a recycling of ideas pressed by Mexican-American leaders since the U.S. conquest of the borderlands in 1848, albeit more precisely advocated by men such as Ernesto Galarza, Alonso Perales, and George I. Sánchez (to name only a few individuals) since the 1930s. Thus the movement was a moderate reformist one resting squarely on the American political tradition: it called for an opening of society in which Chicanos might gain social, economic, and political parity with Anglos.[7] But there is room for others to argue that unprecedented ideological currents characterized the *movimiento*. Youths inspired it: they renounced the acculturation process and looked to their pre-Columbian past or the Mexican Revolution for inspiration, called for liberation, criticized gringo society, and advocated a return to Aztlán. They engaged in demonstrations, marches, and school boycotts, all methods shunned by earlier generations of leaders. Supposedly, the movement took new directions, departing from old platforms proposed by earlier spokespeople. Once the movement petered out by the 1970s, Hispanic ideology reverted to its more natural ties to the politics of the pre-1960s generation.[8]

Julie Leininger Pycior's study titled "Lyndon Johnson, Mexican Americans, and the American Saga" gives us a glimpse of the type of study that western historians will inevitably undertake to discern connections between national and regional politics. Based on a wealth of sources garnered from the National Archives, the LBJ Archives at the University of Texas, the Hector P. García Archives at Texas A&M University–Corpus Christi, and many smaller collections, Pycior's work in progress is a model study of the relevance of U.S.

history to a minority group experience.[9] Other candidates for scrutiny may be governors such as Octaviano Larrazolo, senators such as Bronson M. Cutting, congressmen such as Maury Maverick or Dennis Chávez, or even another president. Such political figures need not always have had the best interest of *la raza* at heart, but the manner in which their politics affected ordinary folks at more localized levels will move us away from the tendency to concentrate almost exclusively on microhistory.

Historians might also consider allocating a more prominent role to Anglos in Mexican-American history and for that matter to African Americans and Native Americans, as Neil Foley and Ramón Gutiérrez have done respectively.[10] Presently, for instance, Anglo Americans rarely play a part other than oppressor and exploiter of powerless minorities in the West. Yet there are numerous figures that spring to mind as "friends of Mexicans," among the most obvious being Carey McWilliams (the journalist-historian who championed Mexican-American causes from the 1930s to the 1960s) or even Billy the Kid. Historians might try to unravel cordial relationships extant between barrio members and social workers, religious figures, educators, labor union leaders, and even political bosses who took a caring attitude toward a people they perceived as being downtrodden. Other sympathetic Anglos no doubt worked closely with ethnic Mexicans to survive the rigors of the West, to found settlements, or in the twentieth century, to help in civil rights movements. One should expect to find Anglo allies as much a part of Mexican-American history as white people have long been performers in African-American history. Such research would end the stock portrayal of the Anglo as a villain and lead to a more completely integrated history of the West.[11]

Scholars might make more deliberate efforts to present the unsavory role that Mexican Americans have played in western history. Mexican-American scholars still feel it is almost treasonable to bring up the darker side of their people's history, whereas Anglo writers think it is politically hazardous to attempt the same thing. The newer western history should include honest doses of self-analysis and self-criticism. In this revisionism, scholars would realistically identify the forms of self-oppression that have characterized Chicano communities throughout time. How have segments of the Mexican-American population used means—similar to the type that historians associate with white racial control—to oppress fellow Chicanos? Did men hold restrictive feelings regarding schooling for women in the nineteenth century? What stands did communities take on issues such as women's suffrage or women's political activism? Have some members of the community colluded with Anglos to profit from economic change, even when it meant exploiting poorer elements in their neighborhoods? In the realm of politics, how did bossism work at the barrio and rancho levels? Very little is known of midlevel bosses, only that they existed as lieutenants within the urban boss structure. As middlemen who came from the barrios, were they motivated by genuine concerns for residents of their districts, or did they seek personal aggrandizement? Writers of Chicano history, the majority of whom are Mexican Americans, may take a cue from the work of southern historians, most of them white, who display little restraint in attacking mainstream white society for its treatment of African Americans.

Lastly, historians should revive the issue of "race" as an analytical frame of reference for understanding western history. For a time in the 1970s, race received a great deal of attention as a causal factor in the formation of ethnic relations in the West, but then historians turned their attention to other subject matters. In the 1990s, a discussion concerning the place of racism in the development of the western experience may seem dated, but in the last few years social scientists have proposed findings that question the standard theses that whites moved into the borderland with a set of attitudes inducing them to think negatively of the native *pobladores* and that Anglos have continued to deny Chicanos a modicum of equality. These recent theories suggest that competition in the Southwest—over land, political control, economic opportunities, and demographic supremacy—may have been behind the rise of racist sentiments. This approach posits that Anglos had fairly neutral notions about race and that views about immorality, indolence, and vice emanated from negative relations centered on certain social and economic conditions. Only after Anglos subordinated Mexicans and forced them into exploitative situations did the majority use racism as a rationalization for that debasement. Those looking for a middle ground between these two arguments might advance the plausible thesis that prejudice and exploitation went hand in hand, fueling each other as circumstances dictated.[12]

Chicano history, then, can be quite instructive in understanding the American West. First, it reminds us that settlers came from all directions, not just those areas east of the Mississippi. Indeed, the push north from Mexico was as significant as westward expansion, a point dramatized today as Hispanics have come to compose the majority of citizens in some sections of southwestern states (similarly, immigration from Asia in the last few decades reminds us of still another direction). Since immigrants from Mexico after 1848 have come from diverse backgrounds and have adapted in varying degrees to the U.S. landscape, we now recognize that the West has never been a homogeneous place of Anglo Saxons but includes a rainbow of peoples united by their common commitment to the values of human liberty. The majority of Mexican-descent people, whether previous occupiers of the borderlands or post-1848 immigrants, faced unique limitations to their aspirations: obstacles manifested themselves in Jim Crow traditions, wage differentials, poll taxes, and the white man's primary. The notion of unfettered opportunity in the West thus turns out to be myth; in many ways, Mexicans and other minorities constituted the counterparts of African Americans in the South. We can also appreciate the role that non-elites played in the western saga by taking note of the Mexican-American experience. Chicano bibliographies today consist of monographs and articles on aspects of Mexican-American history that exclude biographies of great women and men. We have come to understand, therefore, that little people can make as indelible an imprint on the history of the West as do elites. Chicano history also gives us a better appreciation of the meaning of regions. Even today, there remain discernible centers of Hispanic concentrations: villages in northern New Mexico, towns in South Texas that reflect a rural ambient, and sprawling barrios in cities such as East Los Angeles, San Antonio, and Houston. Chicano history has made the study of such population nodes a respectable enterprise; previously, scholars regarded such research as provincial. The lessons to be taken from Chicano history seem lengthy.

Mexican-American history, only a bit older than a score of years, has a secure spot in the history of the West, and it will play an important role in the future re-envisioning of the West. The success of symposia that attract Borderlanders, Anglo-American academicians, women scholars, and Chicano historians reaffirms the widespread interest researchers have in this fascinating area of study. The prominent role given to Mexican ethnics in Rodman Paul's *The Far West and the Great Plains in Transition, 1859–1900* (New York: Harper and Row, 1988), written for the "New American Nation" series, is further testimony to scholars' increased awareness of the Mexican-American presence in the West.[13] In the future, the task of furthering Mexican-American history will be carried forth by an energized coterie of up-and-coming Mexican-American historians like David G. Gutiérrez as well as Anglo-American colleagues trained in either Borderlands or the several subfields of western history. This cohort will consider Mexican-descent people to be as significant to Turner's frontier as were the westering Americans whom the Wisconsin mentor had in mind.

Notes

1. Arnoldo De León, "The Tejano Experience in Six Texas Regions," *West Texas Historical Association Yearbook* 65 (1989).

2. Richard L. Nostrand, "The Hispano Homeland in 1900," *Annals of the Association of American Geographers* 70 (September 1980): 382–96; Miles Hansen, "Commentary: The Hispano Homeland in 1900," ibid., 71 (June 1981): 280–82; Richard L. Nostrand, "Comments in Reply," ibid., 282–83; J. M. Blaut and Antonio Ríos-Bustamante, "Commentary on Nostrand's 'Hispanos' and Their 'Homeland,'" ibid., 74 (1984): 157–64; Richard L. Nostrand, "Hispano Cultural Distinctiveness: A Reply," ibid., 164–69; "Rejoinders," ibid., 16–71; Richard L. Nostrand, *The Hispano Homeland* (Norman, 1992); Richard L. Nostrand and Lawrence E. Estaville Jr., "Introduction: The Homeland Concept," *Journal of Cultural Geography* 13 (Spring/Summer 1993): 1–4; Richard L. Nostrand, "The New Mexico–Centered Hispano Homeland," ibid.; Sylvia Rodríguez, *The Hispano Homeland Debate* (Stanford, 1986).

3. Among Arreola's numerous contributions are "Mexican Restaurants in Tuc-

son," *Journal of Cultural Geography* 3 (Spring/Summer 1983): 108–14; "Fences as Landscape Taste: Tucson's *Barrios*," ibid., 2 (Fall/Winter 1981): 96–105; "Mexican American Exterior Murals," *Geographical Review* 74 (October 1984): 409–24; "Mexican American Housescapes," ibid., 78 (July 1988): 299–315; "Plaza Towns of South Texas," ibid., 82 (January 1992): 56–73.

4. David J. Weber, *The Mexican Frontier, 1821–1846: The American Southwest under Mexico* (Albuquerque, 1982), 277–79.

5. Gerald E. Poyo and Gilberto M. Hinojosa, *Tejano Origins in Eighteenth-Century San Antonio* (Austin, 1991); Jesús F. de la Teja, *A Revolution Remembered: The Memoirs and Selected Correspondence of Juan N. Seguín* (Austin, 1991); Ramón A. Gutiérrez, *When Jesus Came, the Corn Mothers Went Away: Marriage, Sexuality, and Power in New Mexico, 1500–1846* (Stanford, 1991); Deena J. González, "The Spanish Mexican Women of Santa Fe: Patterns of Their Resistance and Accommodation, 1820–1880" (Ph.D. diss., University of California, Berkeley, 1986); Douglas Monroy, *Thrown among Strangers: The Making of Mexican Culture in Frontier California* (Berkeley, 1990); Antonia I. Castañeda, "*Presidarias y Pobladoras*: Spanish-Mexican Women in Frontier Monterey, Alta California, 1770–1821" (Ph.D. diss., Stanford University, 1990).

6. James A. Sandos, *Rebellion in the Borderlands: Anarchism and the Plan of San Diego, 1904–1923* (Norman, 1992); Don M. Coerver and Linda B. Hall, *Texas and the Mexican Revolution: A Study in State and National Border Policy* (San Antonio, 1984), 85–108.

7. Carlos Muñoz, *Youth, Identity, Power: The Chicano Movement* (New York, 1989); Mario T. García, *Mexican Americans: Leadership, Ideology, and Identity, 1930–1960* (New Haven, 1989); Juan Gómez-Quiñones, *Chicano Politics: Reality and Promise, 1940–1990* (Albuquerque, 1990).

8. Muñoz, *Youth, Identity, Power;* and García, *Mexican Americans.*

9. Early pieces from that forthcoming monograph are "From Hope to Frustration: Mexican Americans and Lyndon Johnson in 1967," *Western Historical Quarterly* 24 (November 1993): 469–94, and "Lyndon, *La Raza*, and the Paradox of Texas History," in *Lyndon Baines Johnson and the Exercise of Power*, ed. Bernard J. Firestone and Robert D. Vogt (Westport, Conn., 1988).

10. Neil Foley, "The New South in the Southwest: Anglos, Blacks, and Mexicans in Central Texas, 1880–1930" (Ph.D. diss., University of Michigan, 1990); Gutiérrez, *When Jesus Came.*

11. Arnoldo De León, "Our Gringo Amigos: Anglo Americans and the Tejano Experience," *East Texas Historical Journal* 32 (1993): 72–99.

12. Kenneth L. Stewart and Arnoldo De León, *Not Room Enough: Mexicans, Anglos, and Socioeconomic Change in Texas, 1850–1900* (Albuquerque, 1993), 73–74, 82–84.

13. Other works include Richard White, *"It's Your Misfortune and None of My Own": A New History of the American West* (Norman, 1991), and David J. Weber, *The Spanish Frontier in North America* (New Haven, 1992).

Interpreting Voice and Locating Power

Vicki L. Ruiz

The indigenous peoples of California were astute observers as they recorded the movements of the Spanish-speaking strangers who arrived on their shores during the late eighteenth century. With a mixture of fascination and suspicion, they noted the strangers' manners (including the lack thereof), weapons, livestock, and appearance. Certainly they noticed the absence of women. In a memorandum dated 22 June 1774, Junipero Serra wryly commented that the Indians believed the Spaniards to be "the sons of the mules on which they rode."[1] In reviewing Chicano historiography over the past twenty years, one might reach a similar conclusion. With a growing number of exceptions,[2] Chicano history has meant just that—Chicano, with emphasis on the masculine ending. Gender has rarely surfaced as a category of analysis. The next twenty years will be different. Professor David Gutiérrez's brilliant essay moves beyond historiography as he identifies a plethora of issues to be questioned and problematized. He offers possible theoretical directions in a field inhabited by specialized monographs. He challenges us to consider a conceptual sweep of Chicano history drawing on frameworks rooted in philosophy, feminist studies, and literary criticism. I would like to continue this discussion—adding my own modifications through a blend of historiography and primary documents, blending interpretation and voice.

Race, class, and *gender* have become familiar watchwords, maybe even forming a mantra, for social historians, but few such historians have gotten beneath the surface to explore the intersections of these words in a manner that sheds light on power and powerlessness, boundaries and voice, hegemony and agency. In deciphering conceptions of power, one must consider the politics and interplay of gender and sexuality. Drawing on exciting, innovative studies by borderlands and nineteenth-century scholars as well as my own research, I would like to share with you my thoughts on *compadrazgo/comadrazgo*—the ties of godparenthood established through the sacrament of baptism. Refracted through the lens of gender, race, and social location, a case study of *comadrazgo* offers a glimpse into cultural production, class formation, and community building on the Spanish-Mexican frontier.

Few scholars of the Mexican North would deny the pervasive web of patriarchy that shaped relations between women and men. Yet women had their own worlds of influence, rooted in female networks based on ties of consanguine and fictive kinship. The works of Helen Lara Cea, Antonia Castañeda, Angelina Veyna, Ramón Gutiérrez, Douglas Monroy, and James Brooks provide valuable explorations into women's relations across class and ethnicity.[3] Helen Lara Cea, in particular, brings out the "lay ministry" role of women settlers who, as midwives to mission neophytes, baptized sickly or stillborn babies. As godmothers for these infants, they established the bonds of *comadrazgo* between indigenous and Spanish-Mexican women.[4] The importance of the *comadre* relationship lasted well beyond the mission era. In *We Fed Them Cactus*, New Mexico native Fabiola Cabeza de Baca, born in 1894, recalled her grandmother's efforts to control smallpox.

> When she went to live in La Liendre, there were terrible outbreaks of smallpox and she had difficulty convincing the villagers that vaccination was a solution. Not until she had a godchild in every family was she able to control the dreaded disease. In Spanish tradition, a godmother takes the responsibility of a real mother, and in that way, grandmother conquered many superstitions. . . . At least she had the power to decide what should be done to her godchildren.[5]

Acculturation was not a one-way street. Spanish-speaking women adopted many of the herbal remedies used by indigenous peoples. One source claimed that Eulalia Pérez (the healer, teacher, and quartermaster at the San Gabriel mission) had at her disposal every California "herb . . . that was known to possess healing qualities" and that she "had learned of their properties from the Indians."[6] The close contact between Indians and colonists alarmed some sectors of the elite in both California and New Mexico. Governor Pedro Fages, for example, "issued orders to regulate the number of Indians allowed in the pueblo at any given time and to prohibit those who did from staying overnight."[7]

The relationship between Spanish-Mexican and Indian women forms a fascinating and portentous research area. To what extent did a shared "sisterhood" exist and under what conditions? Señora Doña Juana Machado Alipáz de Ridington, in her reminiscence housed at the San Diego Historical Society Research Archives, related the story of how in 1838 Ceseara, an *india* servant, warned her *patróna* (or mistress), Eustaquia López, of an impending attack on Rancho Jamul. "Doña Eustaquia with much prudence went to the room where her daughters were sewing; she told them to leave their work, take their reboso [*sic*] . . . and go for a walk along the edge of the cornfield." And in this way, the family escaped.[8] Conversely, as Antonia Castañeda pointed out, during the Bear Flag Revolt Rosalía Vallejo de Leese, "who was pregnant and herself a prisoner of John C. Fremont," refused to obey Fremont's orders that she turn over her *india* servant for the entertainment of his officers.[9]

Historians like Ramón Gutiérrez, Douglas Monroy, and Antonia Castañeda also acknowledge the exploitation *among* women of differing classes, races, and social position. For women in domestic service, racial and class hierarchies undermined any pretense of a shared sisterhood. In San Antonio, Texas, in 1735, Anttonia Lusgardia Ernandes sued her former *patrón* for custody of their son. Her testimony bears witness to the conditions of servitude and, by inference, the nexus between patriarchy and race-class hegemony.

I, Anttonia Lusgardia Ernandes, a free mulatta residing in the presidio, do hereby appear before your Lordship in the best form according to law and my own interests and state that about eight or nine years ago I entered the home of Don Miguel Nuñes, taking a daughter of mine with me. I entered the said home without any salary whatever and while I was working in the said home of Don Miguel Nuñes Morillo I suffered so much from lack of clothing and from mistreatment of my humble person that I left the said house and went to the home of Alberto Lopez, taking two children with me, one of whom I had when I entered the home of the said Don Miguel and another which I gave birth to in his home. Just for this reason, and because his wife baptized the same creature, he, exercising absolute power, snatched away from me my son—the only man I have and the one who I hope will eventually support me. He took him from the house where I live and carried him to his own, I being but a poor, helpless woman whose only protection is a good administration and a good judicial system. Your Lordship will please demand that the said Don Miguel Nuñes, without the least delay, shall proceed to deliver my son to me without making any excuses. I wish to make use of all the laws in my favor, and of Your Lordship, as a father and protector of the poor and helpless, as well as anything else which might be in my favor.[10]

Admitting paternity, Miguel Nuñes Morillo claimed that his former servant had relinquished the child to his wife. The court, however, remanded custody of the child to Ernandes on the condition that she give her son "a proper home."[11] Under these circumstances, the sacrament of baptism did little to promote women's networks across class and race.

The Ernandes case seemed exceptional in that a servant had challenged her former master in court. Indentured servitude was prevalent on the colonial frontier. Ramón Gutiérrez persuasively argues that captive Indians pressed into bondage by New Mexican colonists formed their own caste. After serving their time, these *genízaros* (or detribalized peoples) created their own communities separate from the colonists.[12]

Bonded labor persisted well into the nineteenth century. California rancher Cave Couts and his wife Ysidora Bandini de Couts regularly appeared before the local courts to secure Indian children from desperate, indigent parents. Doña Ysidora, for example, paid $50 to indenture a six-year-old child named Sasaria for a period of twelve to fifteen years.[13]

Evidence of indenturement appears in both political documents and cultural artifacts. Oral tradition has preserved this legacy. A version of a New Mexican folk song "Una Indita en su Chinante" (An Indian Girl in Her Garden) includes the following verse:

> The Comanche and his wife
> Went to Santa Fe,
> To sell the little Comanches
> For sugar and coffee.[14]

Indenturement and domestic service bring out the fissures marking colonial society. However, women's interactions across race and social location[15] did not necessarily revolve around a mistress-maid relationship. The reminiscence of Señora Doña Jesus Moreno de Soza reveals a lively interchange between a Mexicana and an Apache woman at a fiesta in Tucson. "[The park] used to have a dancing platform. Once it happened that an Apache squaw named Luisa was dancing." According to Moreno de Soza: "When Petrita Santa Cruz . . . came along, and looking at the Apache squaw said, 'That is enough get out, we want to dance.' The Apache squaw replied, 'I am a person, too.'"[16]

Another intriguing piece of evidence, a letter written by Rosita Rodrígues to her father in 1846, offers a glimpse into the relationships among Mexican women and Native Americans: "I remained a prisoner among the Comanche Indians about one year during which time I was obliged to work very hard, but was not otherwise badly treated as I was the property of an Old Squaw who became much attached to me and would not allow me to be ill treated. My little boy Incarnación is still a prisoner among the Comanches. I heard from him a short time ago—he was well and hearty but he is pure Indian now."[17]

Bonded labor cut both ways, but as the above letter indicates, tribal adoption could soften the situation. The work of the historian James Brooks illustrates how "captives" became "cousins" through the exchanges of women and children between Spanish-Mexican colonists and indigenous peoples. Brooks posits that a "community of interests" developed between subsistence mestizo farmers and their Indian neighbors and that the New Mexican elite became increasingly concerned that area villagers were acculturating to native ways.[18] Don Fernando de la Concha, for instance, firmly believed that New Mexican settlers "love distance . . . in order to adopt the liberty and slovenliness they see . . . in their neighbors, the wild Indians."[19]

I would argue that the *comadre* relationship, whether established through the sacrament of baptism or the rite of tribal adoption, could foster ties between mestizo colonists and Native Americans. "Class," as defined by a shared lifestyle, served to bridge differences in culture and social location. This pattern also holds up when examining fictive kinship within the walls of the California missions, where soldier and settler wives baptized indigenous infants. The elites, with the seigneurial worldview, used *compadrazgo* as a venue of social control, whereas mestizos and Indians conferred a more polycratic meaning to baptism and adoption. James Brooks pairs the terms *exploitation* and *negotiation* in his perceptive analysis of intercultural relations on the New Mexican frontier.[20] The critical issue here is power. Indeed, women's histories must be reconceptualized "as a series of dialectical relations among and across races and classes of women representing diverse cultures and unequal power."[21]

For over twenty years, social historians have grappled with the hows and whys of recording histories premised on people. As an outgrowth of their efforts, *integration* has become the buzzword in curriculum reform, a term that suggests the inclusion of gender and/or race. Integration is but a small step toward the goal, not the goal itself. Infusion and intersection across theory and evidence—genderizing, racializing, and signifying class—must be the task at hand. As Ellen DuBois and I profess in the second edition to *Unequal Sisters*: "We do not want to become so engulfed in theoretical abstraction that we lose touch with human action; and yet, we can no longer avoid analyzing the languages, attending to the silences, and decoding the symbols by which people place themselves in history. In the end, situating historical experience and understanding how it has been constructed may help us arrive at a new, more inclusive synthesis."[22] However, in our quest for a representative (dare I say "multicultural"?) history of the U.S. West, we must listen to the voices. Knowledge of cultural studies, deconstruction, and feminist theories can help us become better listeners, but they can never replace the sentiments expressed by the actors themselves.

Notes

I would like to thank Victor Becerra and Clyde Milner for their encouragement and patience and James Brooks, Ellen DuBois, Ramón Gutiérrez, and Angelina Veyna for their insights and friendship.

1. "Memorandum dated June 22, 1774," in Antonine Tibesar, ed., *The Writings of Junipero Serra*, vol. 2 (Washington, D.C., 1955), 87.

2. Historical monographs in which gender takes center stage include the following: Sarah Deutsch, *No Separate Refuge: Culture, Class, and Gender on an Anglo-Hispanic Frontier in the American Southwest, 1880–1940* (New York, 1987); Ramón Gutiérrez, *When Jesus Came, the Corn Mothers Went Away: Marriage, Sexuality, and Power in New Mexico, 1500–1846* (Stanford, 1991); Deena J. González, *Refusing The Favor: The Spanish-Mexican Women of Santa Fe, 1820–1880* (New York, forthcoming); and Vicki L. Ruiz, *Cannery Women, Cannery Lives: Mexican Women, Unionization, and the California Food Processing Industry, 1930–1950* (Albuquerque, 1987). For a focus on the family, see Richard Griswold del Castillo, *La Familia: The Mexican American Family in the Urban Southwest* (Notre Dame, 1984). Pathbreaking collections devoted to Chicana scholarship are Adelaida R. Del Castillo, ed., *Between Borders: Essays on Mexicana/Chicana History* (Los Angeles, 1990), and Beatríz Pesquera and Adela de la Torre, eds., *Building with Our Hands: Directions in Chicana Scholarship* (Berkeley, 1993). In addition, the following historical and interdisciplinary anthologies also incorporate Chicana scholarship: Magdalena Mora and Adelaida R. Del Castillo, eds., *Mexican Women in the United States: Struggles Past and Present* (Los Angeles, 1980); Joan Jensen and Darlis Miller, eds., *New Mexico Women: Intercultural Perspectives* (Albuquerque, 1986); Susan Armitage and Elizabeth Jameson, eds., *The Women's West* (Norman, 1987); Vicki L. Ruiz and Susan Tiano, eds., *Women on the U.S.-Mexico Border: Responses to Change* (1987; reprint, Boulder, 1991); Lillian Schlis-

sel, Vicki L. Ruiz, and Janice Monk, *Western Women: Their Land, Their Lives* (Albuquerque, 1988); Ellen Carol DuBois and Vicki L. Ruiz, *Unequal Sisters: A Multicultural Reader in U.S. Women's History* (New York, 1990); Vicki L. Ruiz and Ellen Carol DuBois, *Unequal Sisters, Second Edition* (New York, 1994); and Susan Armitage and Elizabeth Jameson, *Writing the Range* (Norman, in press). Furthermore, see *Aztlán*'s first-ever volume on gender, "Las obreras: The Politics of Work and Family," *Aztlán* 20 (1991): 1–2 [actual publication date, 1993].

3. Helen Lara Cea, "Notes on the Use of Parish Registers in the Reconstruction of Chicana History in California Prior to 1850," in Del Castillo, *Between Borders*, 131–59; Antonia I. Castañeda, "Presidarias y Pobladoras: Spanish-Mexican Women in Frontier Monterey, Alta California, 1770–1821" (Ph.D. diss., Stanford University, 1990); Antonia I. Castañeda, "Spanish and English Speaking Women on Worldwide Frontiers: A Discussion of the Migration of Women to Alta California and New Zealand," in Schlissel, Ruiz, and Monk, *Western Women*, 283–300; Angelina F. Veyna, "'It Is My Last Wish That . . .': A Look at Nuevo Mexicanas through Their Testaments," in Pesquera and De la Torre, *Building with Our Hands*, 91–108; Gutiérrez, *When Jesus Came;* Douglas Monroy, *Thrown among Strangers: The Making of Mexican Culture in Frontier California* (Berkeley, 1990); and James F. Brooks, "'This Evil Extends Especially to the Feminine Sex': Captivity and Identity in New Mexico, 1700–1847" (seminar paper, University of California, Davis, 1992), forthcoming in Armitage and Jameson, *Writing the Range*.

4. Lara Cea, "Parish Registers," 140–42.

5. Fabiola Cabeza de Baca, *We Fed Them Cactus* (Albuquerque, 1954), 60.

6. Mrs. A. S. C. Forbes, *Mission Tales in the Days of the Dons* (Los Angeles, 1926), 174–75. The narrative of Eulalia Pérez has been preserved at the Bancroft Library. See Eulalia Pérez, "A Vieja y Sus Recuerdos" (1876), Bancroft Library, University of California, Berkeley.

7. Brooks, "This Evil," 5–7; Antonio Ríos-Bustamante and Pedro Castillo, *An Illustrated History of Mexican Los Angeles, 1781–1985* (Los Angeles, 1986), 53.

8. Castañeda, "Spanish and English Speaking Women," 293; Señora Doña Juana Machado Alipáz de Ridington, "Times Gone By in Alta California" (1878), San Diego Historical Society Research Archives.

9. Castañeda, "Spanish and English Speaking Women," 292.

10. "Child Custody, Mulatto Woman" (9 August 1735), Bexar Archives, Barker History Center, University of Texas, Austin.

11. Bexar Archives Inventory, "Child Custody, Mulatto Woman" (9 August 1735).

12. Gutiérrez, *When Jesus Came*, 179–80, 195–97, 305.

13. Monroy, *Thrown among Strangers*, 192–93.

14. John Donald Robb, *Folk Music of New Mexico and the Southwest: A Self-Portrait of a People* (Norman, 1980), 442. The verse in the original Spanish follows:

> El comanche y la comancha
> se fueron para Santa Fe
> a vender los comanchitos
> por azúcar y café.

15. By "social location," I refer to a combination of race and class. A mestiza subsistence farmer, for example, may have shared ethnic and kinship ties with a Pueblo woman, and their standards of living may have been similar, but these women occupied different strata or social locations within colonial life.

16. Señora Doña Jesus Moreno de Soza, "Reminiscences" (1939), Antonio Soza Papers, Arizona Historical Society Library, Tucson. Note: Although suffering their own share of stereotypes, some Mexican women, such as Moreno de Soza, did not hesitate to use the term *squaw* when referring to Native American women. Seemingly unaware of the contradiction, they adopted Anglo stereotypes of Indian women.

17. Rosita Rodrígues, "Letter to Don Miguel Rodrígues" (15 January 1846), Barker History Center.

18. Brooks, "This Evil," 2–7, 8–9, 16. For an elaboration of these issues, see James F. Brooks, "Captives and Cousins: Bondage and Identity in New Mexico, 1700–1837" (Master's thesis, University of California, Davis, 1991).

19. Donald E. Worcester, trans., "Don Fernando de la Concha to Lieutenant Colonial Don Fernando Chacón, Advice on Governing New Mexico, 1794," *New Mexico Historical Review* 24 (1949): 250.

20. Lara Cea, "Parish Registers," 139–42; Brooks, "This Evil," 4.

21. DuBois and Ruiz, *Unequal Sisters: A Multicultural Reader*, xiii.

22. Ruiz and DuBois, *Unequal Sisters, Second Edition*, xv.

Echo Park, Dinosaur National Monument. Courtesy National Archives.

4

A Place of Extremes: Nature, History, and the American West

Susan Rhoades Neel

Not far from the tiny gas-and-go town of Dinosaur, Colorado, a ragged dirt road drops off a high plateau and heads down toward the confluence of the Green and Yampa Rivers. Deep in a desert canyon, the road ends at a place called Echo Park. Here the Green River loops back on its course, carving a long, narrow peninsula from a red sandstone massif. A sheer rock wall, awash with great streaks of desert varnish, rises from the water's edge. The river is not wide—a good arm could send a stone across—nor is it boisterous, as rivers so often are in this canyon country. Like a ribbon of molten glass, the water glides by noiselessly, carrying along the odd bit of cottonwood duff on its glistening surface. There is a profound stillness here, as though the earth had drawn a deep breath and held it. Nature's ordinary chatterings—the persistent flutter of windblown leaves, the scuffle of a rabbit dashing helter-skelter through the scrub—all are rendered inconsequential by the immense, silent stone. Not even the murmuring of children at play on the riverbank breaks the spell of quietude.

I take the road to Echo Park often, sometimes in my Jeep, sometimes only in my dreams. I go there to remind myself that the "nature" in the title of this essay is not merely an academic abstraction and that western history is best, truest, when it keeps nature in sight. I have little interest in a history that would posit places like Echo Park as counterpoints to the supposed depravity of modern life, their beauty and wildness posed as a stinging rebuke to our own "unnaturalness." Such a history does no more than perpetuate our imagined separation from nature. What we need is a history that has at its heart this simple but enduring truth: nature has shaped us as surely as we have it. With every turn of the season, touch of the hand, or gaze into the vast blue sky, nature and culture together have made this place called the West. By attending as much to the workings of the natural world as to the human one, western history can serve to remind us that in being part of nature we are bound by it and that humans alone are not the measure of all things. And that is why, for me, all western history begins at Echo Park—and ends there too.

The New Western Regionalism

Westerners, to paraphrase Wallace Stegner, seem to need a history to match the scenery. We are intent on rooting our region's exceptionalism and significance in the land, in its vastness, its magnificence, even its harshness. Out West, it is said, nature has worked some kind of wonder, transforming the ordinary into the remarkable, the old into the new, molding us into a more audacious and egalitarian people or, depending on who is telling the tale, into a society of extraordinary villainy and rapaciousness. From Frederic Remington to Kevin Costner, from Frederick Jackson Turner to Patricia Nelson Limerick, the western environment has been central to our popular and scholarly envisionings of the West's history. Like the strong, steady current of the Green River, the idea of a distinctive western society shaped by a distinctive nature courses through the canyons of our imagined past. This is no less true of the "new" western historians than the old, for they too have found in nature both means and moral for the West's past. The new western history, for all its theoretical sophistication and attentiveness to the too-long-neglected issues of cultural diversity, race, class, and gender, continues in significant ways to be configured around ideas about nature and its role in shaping western society. My purpose here is to consider why this is so and to critically examine some of the philosophical and historiographical assumptions about the environment present in recent efforts to reconfigure western history.

For the most part, the new western history takes as its starting point the idea that the West is a specific, identifiable place and that western history is properly the story of how that region was formed and reproduced over time through the interaction of diverse cultures with each other and with nature. Regionalism, of course, is nothing new to western history.[1] Walter Prescott Webb made the case for a regional approach in his classic 1931 study *The Great Plains*.[2] Webb began with what he believed any westerner knew—that the West was different. Its customs, institutions, and habits of mind were unlike those in any other part of the nation. He dismissed traditional interpretations of western history because they failed to account for the West's enduring distinctiveness. Much like the plainsmen he so admired, Webb imagined himself breaking trail, abandoning "well-established principles of thinking about the West and the frontier."[3]

Webb found the source of his region's exceptionalism in its environment. Virtually the entire reach of the continental United States west of the ninety-eighth meridian, he noted, is characterized by at least two of three key features—insufficiency of rainfall, lack of trees, and flatness of terrain. With a hubris typical of the young Texan, Webb labeled this vast reach "the Great Plains environment." His argument was simple: the western environment was so different from the humid, forested East that settlers were compelled to abandon old ways of doing things and to innovate new technologies, methods of agriculture, and laws. For Webb, all of western history flowed from the wellspring of environment. "This land," he concluded, "with the unity given it by its three dominant characteristics has from the beginning worked its inexorable effect upon nature's children."[4]

The flaws in Webb's history are manifest. Having claimed the West for his subject, he rarely saw beyond Texas. He overemphasized geographic unity within the West by ignoring what did not fit (the Rocky Mountains, for example), underestimated similarities between East and West, and in some instances, incorrectly attributed western origins to technologies innovated elsewhere. Even as he wrote *The Great Plains,* its environmental essentialism and determinism had fallen into disfavor among geographers and historians alike. Webb also indulged in racial stereotyping, moving Indians, the Spanish, and Mexicans on and off the stage of his historical drama for the sole purpose of demonstrating by comparison the adaptive "genius" of white settlers. As for women, Webb saw the West as "strictly a man's country." Yet for all its egregious faults, Webb's regionalism has had a certain attraction for those seeking a new western history. Never mind that his reading of the West's history was imperfect; his accomplishment was in finding the right vantage point from which to get the best view—the fixed ground of region. The current renewed enthusiasm for region as an organizing concept for western history stems from several historiographical and ideological concerns.

For the latest cadre of historians determined to wrest western history from the vice of Frederick Jackson Turner, regionalism's greatest appeal is as a counterparadigm to the frontier thesis.[5] Turner too put nature at the center of western history. Nature, Turner said, made America out there in those many places called the West. For Turner, nature was a transforming agent, an object of Euro-American desire, a stage for the play and a metaphor for the drama's meaning. On Turner's frontier, nature served as a cornucopia of potential commodities, an abundance of resources, un-

used and free for the taking, beckoning successive waves of frontier arche-
types ever westward. From the act of exploiting nature, capitalizing on its
potential, flowed all the accoutrements of "civilized" society—communities, markets, transportation systems, political institutions, law. Desiring
its resources, Euro-Americans turned what they called "wilderness" into
settled, "civilized" terrain, but in doing so, they were themselves transformed. On the frontier, Turner said, the wildness of unsettled nature initially overwhelmed the newcomers and reduced them to a sort of
"primitiveness." Thus purged of Old World habits, the frontiersman soon
regained his composure and set about his business—furs were taken, trees
felled, cattle fattened. From this contest between nature and colonist
emerged a unique American character and a distinctive political culture—
what Turner saw as those most American of sensibilities: individualism
and democracy.

For more than a half century, scholars have cataloged the defects in
Turner's postulation of history, not least among these being its artificial geography of "civilized" and "savage" space and Turner's wonder-working
nature, deterministic and yet vaguely mystical, always the agent of change
but never the patient.[6] Nationalistic, simplistic, and hopelessly mired in
metaphors of racial and sexual domination, Turner's frontier thesis seems
to tell us more about the ambitions and anxieties of his own age than
about the realities of Euro-American settlement or, more specifically,
about the history of that region we now call the West. Some historians
have argued for a renovation of the frontier thesis by purging it of Turner's
jingoism and social Darwinist assumptions. It is possible to embrace
within the idea of moving frontiers a diversity of cultures and to acknowledge the appalling consequences of expansionism for many of those peoples and much of the land. But other critics insist that such a retooling is
wrongheaded because it overlooks the frontier's most serious conceptual
flaws. Lost in space but stuck in time, the frontier is at once too broad and
too narrow a concept. It has always seemed more mythic than real, not a
place but a process so sweeping in effect and occurring in so many places
that it defies substantive or specific description.

Trying to understand the West from the perspective of the frontier is
like viewing the scenery from a moving car—the passing terrain is blurred
and distorted. Calling the idea of frontier "abstract," "bewildering," and
"unsubtle," the new regionalists insist that it is better to pull the car over,
turn off the engine, and survey the vista in all its stationary detail. Focusing on region seems to give concreteness to western history, a "down-to-
earth clarity," says Limerick.[7] Replacing frontier with region also allows
historians to connect the twentieth-century West with its past. By its very

definition, frontier history comes to an end, thus leaving more than a hundred years of western history without a conceptual mooring. Concentrate on place rather than process, however, and 1890 appears not as an end but as only one of many historical watersheds. "Deemphasize the frontier and its supposed end," Limerick says, "and Western American history has a new look."[8]

This "new look" strikes powerful personal and ideological chords among many new western historians. Underlying this most recent effort to replace the frontier paradigm with regionalism is a sense, forged from the historians' own experiences, that the history of a real place and those who made their lives there has been distorted and obscured by the "vaporous frontier." Of all its failings, it is the frontier's apparent inability to explain the West in which we now live that has most animated the turn to regionalism. "I am from Banning, California, a town on the edge of the desert," says Limerick at the outset of her essay "What on Earth Is the New Western History?" Recalling her childhood experience of that dry place, Limerick questions "standing models of western history [that] simply won't fit Banning regardless of how you trim and stitch, tighten and loosen."[9] Limerick and others have embraced regionalism because it seems to be the explanatory model best able to account for those places that they know as home and those experiences that resonate through their own lives and family stories.[10]

For many new western historians, landscape and personal narrative intertwine into a singular trope, that of a hard life in a hard land, of environmental and social declension witnessed. "I have never been able to think of the West as Turner did, as some process in motion," says Donald Worster. "Instead, I think of it as a distinct place inhabited by distinct people: people like my parents, driven out of western Kansas by dust storms to an even hotter, drier life in Needles, California, working along the way in flyblown cafes, fruit orchards, and on railroad gangs, always feeling dwarfed by the bigness of the land and by the economic power accumulated there." The historian's witness of a life lived out in an identifiably "western" environment serves as emblem for the larger, regional narrative. As it did for Webb, the idea of a western exceptionalism rooted in a distinctive environment fits the new western historians' sense of place. Westerners *are* different, Banning is *not* like Portage, Wisconsin, and at some visceral level it feels right to link that difference to the land. "I know in my bones, if not always through my education, that Webb was right," says Worster.[11]

For Worster and many of his contemporaries, regionalism reflects a particular ideological outlook as well as a personal sense of western place and experience. More than mere geographic space, region can be thought of as a social ideal. Nineteenth-century regionalists such as Josiah Royce argued that regional consciousness or, in his words, "wise provincialism" fostered orderly and moral community life amid an increasingly fragmented and materialistic society. Turner believed that regional societies were free from the exploitative and transitory tendencies of the frontier yet were resistant to the instability and divisiveness of an urban, industrial-based nationalism. For twentieth-century regionalists such as Howard W. Odum and Lewis Mumford, region represented the level of human organization at which diversity was most likely to be balanced into a harmonious unity. These regionalists based their social ideal on what they perceived as the diversity and balance of nature and believed that regional societies were best because they most effectively connect human beings with their natural environment.[12]

This tradition of regionalism has influenced much of the new western history. Rejecting the idea of scholarship as neutral or objective, the new western historians have adopted the stance of social critics and reformers.[13] In the past, they argue, are to be found the roots of a contemporary West rife with racial injustice, economic inequity, and wanton destruction of the environment. An imperfect understanding of the past, however, has too often blinded us to these problems and inhibited efforts to correct them. Only by lifting the veil of old Turnerian mythologies, the western historians argue, can society be reformed. If we are to create a more humane and just society, we must begin by taking a cold, hard look at our flawed past. "We need new kinds of heroes," says Worster, "a new appreciation of nature's powers of recovery, and new sense of purpose in this region—all of which means we need a new past."[14] The purpose of western history ought to be, in Worster's words, to "discover a new regional identity and set of loyalties, more inclusive and open to diversity than we have known, more compatible with a planet-wide sense of ecological responsibility."[15] In such a western history, region serves as the conceptual bridge between interpretation of the past and the historians' reformist agenda.

The new western history, in summary, has headed for the terra firma of region because it constitutes a literal and intellectual landscape especially appealing to the most recent generation of western historians. Concerns about the role of nature in the West's history and about human impact on the environment are central to the historiographical foundation of the new regionalism as well as to its broader philosophical underpinnings. The challenge confronting the new regionalists is to articulate what Michael Malone calls a "genuine regionalism," that is, a paradigm that does more than simply tip its hat to the idea of the West as a distinctive place before dancing off with older interpretive modes.[16] Not surprisingly, in trying to construct such a paradigm, the new regionalists have relied on their own particular reading of western environmental history and of the environment itself in order to define the region and to find for its past a new significance and narrative structure.

Aridity and the Definition of "West"

In his essay "New West, True West," Donald Worster urges historians to ignore the western history path marked out by Turner and to follow instead the road sign reading "To a fixed geographic region."[17] Turner's path, the new regionalists warn, is covered with brambles so thick and thorny that we will never reach our destination. But the road to region, we are assured, is unobstructed, the route straight and true. We won't get lost because the place called the West is set out on the map for all to see. Forget that "vague mythical landscape" of frontier and think region, Worster says, and the West takes on "a clear, concrete shape."[18] Yet for all its promised clarity, the concept of the West as place turns out to be as problematic in its own ways as the idea of frontier. Whatever virtues region may have over frontier, precision and constancy are not among them. Nothing better illustrates this than the role accorded environment in the efforts to define what constitutes the West.

Regionalists have long defined the West by a singular condition of environment—aridity. More than a century ago, John Wesley Powell pointed out the demarcation of the continent's humid and arid regions at the one hundredth meridian. Webb made that observation central to his environmental definition of the West in 1931 and even more directly several decades later when he declared, "The heart of the West is a desert, unqualified and absolute."[19] Over the years regionalists have offered up a fuller, more varied list of cultural as well as environmental map coordinates for the West. Look for that territory with the greatest diversity of racial and ethnic groups, the new regionalists say. Look for the region that, until the early twentieth century, had the highest ratio of urban to rural population and that today has the most public lands and the most unoccupied space. But it is aridity, regionalists continue to insist, that constitutes the region's most fundamental characteristic. A host of features may differentiate the West from other parts of the nation, but aridity serves as the connecting sinew of region, unifying all its disparate aspects like musculature holding a body's many parts into identifiable form. "Aridity, and aridity alone, makes the various Wests one," said Wallace Stegner.[20]

Aridity, it would seem, confers on western regionalism coherence and authority, but beneath the surface elegance are some disturbing flaws. In defining the West by aridity, regionalists acquiesce to the very bias that heretofore has privileged the history of Anglo-American settlement in the region. Although it is true that climate influences the particular configuration of topography, flora, and fauna in any given area, nature assigns no value to these variations. Climate takes on meaning only through the cultures inhabiting a place. The significance attached to the physical reality of average annual rainfall below twenty inches varies among the West's different peoples. We cannot assume, for example, that Ute Indians perceived the sparse annual rainfall in the Great Salt Lake Valley in the same way as did the Mormon colonists who arrived in the mid-nineteenth century, or the ethnic Mexicans who came decades later to work in the valley's mills and smelters, or the Japanese truck farmers who came in the early 1900s, or the Hmong refugees who arrived in the 1970s. The fact that in the dry West rivers are few, erratic, and often surrounded by formidable canyons has an entirely different significance to indigenous agriculturalists, Hispanic pastoralists, and Anglo urban entrepreneurs. From the many meanings climate has had in the West, why select aridity, which reflects a particularly Anglo-American perception of the environment, as the region's defining feature?

Aridity is a concept burdened with ethnocentric connotations. Implicit in the idea of a region that lacks enough water for things to grow and that is dry, barren, lifeless, and dull is a binary vision of a place that is lush, fecund, and productive.[21] An arid region, in this sense, is an aberrant one, a deviation from an environment of adequacy, specifically one suited for European-derived, nonirrigated agriculture. The "arid" West has meaning only in relation to the "normal" East, where the landscape is verdant, the wide rivers are traversable, and all the "customary" ways of making a life from the land are possible. Which environment is called normal and which aberrant depends entirely on who is doing the labeling. It would be just as accurate to point out the abundance of rainfall in the East, but that condition is rarely remarked on by scholars because they assume it as the norm. Only the West's aridity is marked, in much the same way that descriptors denoting otherness are attached to people, as in "the black politician" or "the woman attorney" but never "the white congressman" or "the male lawyer." By singling out aridity as the West's defining characteristic, regionalists position the edifice of western history on an inherently ethnocentric foundation. For those who would reject the idea of frontier as ethnocentric, such a definition of region will hardly do.

The concept of aridity not only is culturally biased but also falsely implies for the region an ecological coherence that does not in reality exist.

Substantial sections of the region west of the one hundredth meridian are not arid. The heaviest rainfall in all the continental United States occurs in the Pacific Northwest, for example. In California, annual precipitation varies from under two inches in the Mojave Desert to more than ninety inches in the Sierra Nevadas. Similar degrees of variation characterize Oregon, Washington, and Idaho. A greater proportion of Texas is humid or subhumid than is arid. Minnesota has more semiarid land than Kansas, but few would consider Minnesota as part of the West. Regionalists rightly insist that some level of generalization must be tolerated in defining the West because no region is entirely homogeneous in its physical characteristics. But such diversity would as easily warrant the conclusion that climate divides the West internally as the assertion that aridity unifies the region. What logic justifies accepting aridity as the appropriate generalization when so many events important to western history occurred in nonarid places—the California and Alaska gold rushes, for example, or the rise of the Pacific-Asia trade, the growth of the timber and fisheries industries, and the creation of America's first national parks and forests?

The danger in accommodating aridity as a generalization is that it obscures what may be a far more salient characteristic of the western environment—extreme variability. Precipitation, which varies dramatically both temporally and spatially, is a good case in point. Consider the examples of Electra and Tamarack, two California towns located just fifty miles apart. Tamarack, at an elevation of 8,000 feet, gets an average of forty-two feet of snow annually. Electra, situated at an elevation of 725 feet above sea level, has less than one inch of snow per year. Throughout the West, precipitation occurs unevenly over the course of widely differing annual cycles. California receives most of its rain in the winter and spring, whereas in Tucson, Arizona, nearly the entire year's precipitation arrives in sudden torrents between July and September, and in parts of the Pacific Northwest it rains on nearly half the days of the year. The West also experiences irregular wet and dry cycles, some extending over many decades. In Los Angeles, for example, the annual average is nearly fifteen inches of rain for a one-hundred-year period, but within that time span were years with as much as forty inches and as little as six. The hallmark of the West's hydrology is unpredictability and variability.[22]

Such extremity typifies many aspects of the western environment.[23] The highest peaks and lowest valleys in the continental United States are to be found in the West, as are the widest seasonal fluctuations in temperature and variations in humidity. Trace on the map virtually any component of the physical environment (type of vegetation, precipitation, temperature, distribution of animal species), and you will find the eastern

part of the continent characterized by broad bands of similarity with gradual change generally according to longitude, whereas in the West there is a
dizzying, swirled pattern corresponding largely to the region's radically
varied topography.[24] It is this environmental eccentricity that has most influenced western life and that accounts in good part for the enduring place
of the West in national mythology. For millennia, peoples have set their
epic tales in extreme places, imagining their gods and cultural heroes as
residents of the darkest forests, the highest peaks, the most desolate
deserts. Americans have done no less, locating their nation-building myths
and secular heroes out West. Nor is it surprising that in our postmodern
tales of anguish and alienation, the heroes drive their cars through vast
western spaces, seeking oblivion at the edge of strange western precipices.
Regional history must begin not with an unjustified assertion of geographic unity but with an acknowledgment that the western experience
has been forged in an environment of profound variability and extremity.

It is important as well for regional history to recognize that the western environment is not immutable. Throughout the region, in the great
forests of the Rockies, the Sierras, and the Pacific Northwest, on the
prairies, along the coastal and inland waterways, even in the southwestern
deserts, the distribution and diversity of plant and animal species is the result, in part, of land use by indigenous and migrant peoples. For as long as
humans have inhabited the West, they have altered the environment. It is
a mistake, as Richard White has argued, to think of region as "something
that has always existed in some neat geographical package"—because the
environment is dynamic, not static.[25] The region is not a fixed entity, says
White, but "a land and people constantly in the midst of reinvention and
reshaping."[26] The West is given character as a singular place not by some
intrinsic quality of environment but by changing relationships forged between western peoples and the land. "It is this sense of historically derived
relationships," says White, "that is central to the regionalism of the New
Western History."[27]

By resisting facile definitions that fix the West in a timeless nature and
by adopting instead a more complex concept of region as a changing mosaic of relationships among different peoples and different environments,
regionalism takes on a new depth and vitality. But this relational West
raises its own set of definitional questions. What, precisely, are the "historically derived relationships" that define the West? Limerick characterizes these relationships as conquest, by which she means "the drawing of
lines on a map, the definition and allocation of ownership (personal,
tribal, corporate, state, federal, and international), and the evolution of
land from matter to property."[28] White says that the West is "a product of

conquest and of the mixing of diverse groups of peoples," a process largely centered on conflicts over possession and use of land and natural resources[29] For Worster, the West "derives its identity primarily from its ecologically adapted modes of production."[30]

Conquest, conflict, modes of production—all certainly are to be found in the West, but how are they unique to the region? How was capitalist exploitation of western water different from experiences in other parts of the nation—in the coal mines of Kentucky, for example, or in the cotton mills of the South or the logging camps of Minnesota? How was conquest in California different from conquest in New England or in the Ohio Valley or in Hawaii? What distinguishes conflicts over land and resources among Europeans, Native Americans, and Anglo Americans in the East or in the Great Lakes region from those in the West? Significant differences do exist, for example in the greater role played by the federal government in the West. But these differences have yet to be fully delineated by the new regionalists, and we are left with nagging doubts about just what it is that makes the West a region. It is entirely possible, as Michael McGerr has suggested, that as different as the western environment is, human interaction with it may not result in a society substantially different from that in other places.[31] Having staked their claim in the "mappable West," albeit one vastly more sophisticated than Webb's old region, the new regionalists still face the challenge of adequately defining the region. Without such a definition, regionalism will be open to the same charges of ethnocentrism, vagueness, and irrelevance leveled at the concept of frontier.

It is worth noting, with some irony, that as the new regionalists chart their way through the relational West, they may well find themselves on that old frontier road once again. If we think of the West not as a fixed entity but as a product of changing relationships, our attention logically shifts from the operation of historical processes in a specific place to those processes that create the region. In other words, the relevant question is, "How and when did the West become a region?" That is precisely the issue that William Cronon and his fellow neo-Turnerians put at the heart of a new *frontier* history. Frontier and region are not "isolated, alternative ways of viewing the American past but rather [are] phases of a single historical process," say Cronon, George Miles, and Jay Gitlin.[32] The process of moving from frontier to region—invasion of a place by a new people, settling new communities there and establishing new economic, political, and social systems—occurred throughout America. The result is regions as varied as New England, the South, and the West, but that difference in outcome should not obscure the fact that all of America shares a common history of making the transition from frontier to region. This characterization of frontier and region is not inconsistent with the new regionalism, which posits much the same relationship between place and process. What does distinguish the two approaches is the differing ideas about the relationship of region to nation or, more specifically, the significance of the West in the nation's history.

Environment and the Significance of the West

Whatever faults are to be found in the frontier thesis, original or neo-Turnerian version, its one undeniable virtue is in claiming a place for the West in the nation's history. By stressing an enduring western exceptionalism, regionalists like Webb relinquished much of the West's place in the bigger story. As Elliott West has noted, Webb gave "specificity and permanence" to western history by linking the region's unique culture to a distinctive environment, but in doing so, he "surrendered western history's special claim—the notion that it provided a unifying vision for all Americans."[33] An unabashed western chauvinist, Webb in the end found little of national significance in the region's history. And therein has been western regionalism's most disaffecting flaw. Beyond those momentous nineteenth-century events that completed the United States as a continental nation, what happened in the West struck many scholars as irrelevant to the main currents of American history. To be sure, western history could be interesting, even lively, and many historians happily retreated into a provincialism that highlighted the colorful and melodramatic aspects of the West's past. Other scholars, however, especially those writing in the 1960s and 1970s, ignored regionalism altogether and chose to place western subjects in interpretive contexts that seemed closer to the center of American history—urbanization, the persistence of ethnic cultures, the divisions of race, class, and gender.

The new regionalists, however, have been dissatisfied equally with localism and with a history that does no more than replay national trends on the regional stage. Central to their construction of a new western history has been the search for a wider significance to the western experience. Although committed to the idea of the West as a distinctive place with its own, intrinsic local meanings, the new regionalism insists that, in important ways, the West accounts for what America has become. The new regionalists point to the crucial role of western resources—minerals, timber, agricultural products—in the development of the national economy. They also note that the demands of bringing the West into the national and, ultimately, the global market system stimulated the expansion of the federal government, profoundly altering the relationship of the central state to all regions of the nation. But as important as these economic and political factors were, the greatest significance of the West, the new regionalists say, is to be found in what Limerick calls the legacy of conquest.

In the western version of conquest, the new regionalism posits, an Anglo-American culture driven by the imperatives of capitalism indulged in an orgy of subjugation and exploitation unlike that experienced anywhere else in America. "Conquest," wrote Limerick, "forms the historical bedrock of the whole nation, and the American West is a preeminent case study in conquest and its consequences."[34] In this tragic tale—and it is as tragedy that the new regionalists see the West's history—nature is no less a victim than those dispossessed and exploited peoples shoved to the peripheries of western society. "The drive for the economic development of the West," says Worster, "was often a ruthless assault on nature, and it has left behind it much death, depletion, and ruin."[35] For the new regionalists, social and ecological disruptions are the interwoven consequences of conquest—they are part of a whole cloth.

The new regionalist version of the West's significance draws heavily on recent work in environmental history, a field that has evolved simultaneously (one might even say symbiotically) with the new western history. Since the 1980s, much of the best scholarship in environmental history has focused on the ecological changes resulting from the expansion of European and Anglo-American systems of land use and on the ideological and institutional mechanisms through which those systems have been perpetuated. Indeed, the great transformation of North America's indigenous landscape into one organized according to what Cronon has called the logic of capital has become the dominating trope of environmental history.[36] Environmental histories of Island County, Washington, of New Mexico's Sangre de Cristo Mountains and Pajarito Plateau, of the badlands of the southern high plains, and of the Calapooia Valley in Oregon, to cite just a few examples, have greatly enhanced our understanding of conflicting systems of land use in the West and of how ecological change—sometimes intentionally but often inadvertently—impoverished some western peoples while enriching others.[37] In addition to these environmental histories, recent studies focusing on landscape art and photography in the West, on the history of science in the region, and on the movement to preserve wilderness and scenic landscapes have suggested that those currents within American society that may once have been seen as being in opposition to the imposition of a market system on the western environment actually served to rationalize that process or to provide new forms of commodifying nature.[38]

Yet for all the valuable insights provided by these studies, the environmental history of the West is not sufficiently extensive or conclusive to warrant the assertions that, in Limerick's words, the national "faith that humans can master the world—of nature and of humans"—was put to its greatest test in the West or, as Worster has suggested, that in its ecological relationships, western society "best exemplifies the modern capitalist state at work."[39] Too many questions about the human interaction with the western environment remain to be answered before the new regionalism can justifiably recast the significance of the West in terms of ecological change. Western environmental history, for example, has yet to fully explore the varieties of human-nature relationships in the region, particularly as they vary by class and gender, or to account for the ways in which the environment has been used to resist Anglo-American expansion. Nor do we have good comparative studies to demonstrate that what occurred in the West was markedly different from the environmental history of other regions.

Nature and a New Western Narrative

Regardless of how the new regionalists reconfigure the West's significance, their histories will have to match the narrative power of that old frontier tale. "The greatest attraction of the frontier thesis," William Cronon argues, "has been its simplicity and its sense of movement, its ability to shape and set in motion so many of the mere *facts* that American historians need to narrate."[40] Turner's narrative structure gave the disparate pieces of the past an order and coherence, connecting America's many places to a national culture through a common story: all places had the same storied past and, therefore, in some sense shared in the nation's fate. This is one of the reasons that the frontier thesis has had, and continues to have, a powerful hold on the popular and scholarly imagination. If regionalism is to break the hold of frontier on western history, it will have to replace not only Turner's interpretation of the western past but also his narrative form. The great challenge for western historians is to find a new way of telling the story of the West, of ordering and signifying the facts, that is at once reflective of the new visions they have of and for America and yet as compelling in its "movement" as Turner's frontier thesis.

Upon what warp can this new story be woven? Nature, say the new western historians, can serve as one of the strong narrative fibers out of which a new western history cloth can be made. By making the interaction of people and the natural world the narrative device, Cronon says, "western history can become what it has always been, the story of human beings working with changing tools to transform the resources of the land, struggling over how that land should be owned and understood, and defining their notions of political and cultural community, all within a context of shifting environmental and economic constraints."[41] Limerick also suggests that in focusing on "the story of human efforts to 'master' nature in the region," western history takes on narrative continuity.

Although western historians may want environment to serve as a narrative thread connecting the full chronological sweep of the region's history, the task so far has proven beyond the methodological capability of environmental history. In practice, whereas the human-nature dialectic has provided narrative focus to nineteenth-century environmental histories of the West, the same has not been generally true of twentieth-century studies. Indeed, environmental historians have treated nature very differently in the frontier and in the postfrontier eras. In their studies of the frontier West, environmental historians have brought the dialectic between nature and culture into focus by concentrating on a singular process—the extension of a Euro-American system of land use across the region. Because the process of imposing Euro-American ways of perceiving, valuing, and using nature was, in the West, largely (although not completely) a nineteenth-century phenomenon, the human-nature dialectic has tended to recede from historical view in the twentieth century. Nature as a concrete reality shaping the lives of western peoples is largely absent from twentieth-century history.

This is not to suggest that nature and culture ceased to be mutually informing in the twentieth century, only that the lens through which historians seem best able to discern the dialogue became irrelevant. The conversation between humans and nature is one carried on between parties so familiar with one another that a knowing nod and a few cryptic words convey meaning. For historians looking in on the parties, it is often difficult to tell that a conversation is even going on, let alone what the discussion is about. The task of finding ways of capturing the human-nature dialectic and tracing its trajectory through time remains the most difficult challenge facing environmental historians. To date, they have accomplished this best by focusing on dislocation, either cultural or ecological, that is, by looking at a moment in time when ecological relations broke down—the dust bowl, the decline of California's coastal fisheries—or when distinct cultures were in conflict.

Nature, it would seem, ill serves the goal of connecting frontier and postfrontier Wests into a single narrative scheme. Writing nature into the western narrative poses another challenge. As western historians seek to tell new stories of the West, they need to be cautious not to mistake the ordering of narrative for simplification. Turner not only gave western history "movement" but also set that movement to epic rhythms. The heroic intonations of the frontier thesis derived from Turner's plotting of events, as well as from his distillation of so much into simplified patterns and of so many into stereotypical characters. Neither people nor nature can be reduced to stock types. Facile dichotomies between "natural" and "unnatural," between "wilderness" and "civilization," and between "harmony" and "disorder" do not reflect the concrete reality of an intricate, changeable natural world. Western history with nature in it must consist of complex, finely textured stories set to subtle, discordant harmonies, not to the strident, heroic cadences Turner chose. In these stories we will find no easy lessons, no exportable heroes. The past will not provide us with a transcendent set of values about nature and how to treat it. Nor can we use past nature as a moral template for our own social relations, judging society by how successfully it mirrors a perceived orderliness or balance in nature.

Yet our histories should be meaningful ones, with significance for our own lives. No one has made a better case for why that is so than William Cronon. "Stories about the past are better," he reminds us, "if they increase our attention to nature and the place of people within it [because] narratives remain our chief moral compass in the world. Because we use them to motivate and explain our actions, the stories we tell change the way we act in the world. We find in such stories our histories and prophecies both, which means they remain our best path to an engaged moral life."[42] Who we are, as individuals and as a society, derives in part from the ways in which we have drawn our physical and spiritual sustenance from the physical world in which we live. All peoples of the West have found in nature sources of delight and of terror, tools of oppression and means of maintaining human dignity. Western history should teach us about the centrality of nature to the human experience, indeed about how that experience is not apart from nature. As problematic as the role of environment remains in recent efforts to construct a new western history, it is the insistence on making nature a part of the story that ensures the field's continuing vitality.

Notes

An earlier version of this essay appeared under the title "A Place of Extremes: Nature, History, and the American West," by Susan Rhoades Neel. Previously published in the *Western Historical Quarterly* 25 (Winter 1994): 489–505. Copyright by Western History Association. Reprinted by permission.

1. For a good survey of regionalism in western history, see Gerald D. Nash, *Creating the West: Historical Interpretations, 1890–1990* (Albuquerque, 1991), 101–58. On regionalism and the new western history, see Patricia Nelson Limerick, "What on Earth Is the New Western History?" and "The Trail to Santa Fe: The Un-

leashing of the Western Public Intellectual," in *Trails: Toward a New Western History,* ed. Patricia Nelson Limerick, Clyde A. Milner II, and Charles E. Rankin (Lawrence, 1991), 59–77, 81–96; Donald Worster, "Beyond the Agrarian Myth," in ibid., 3–25, and "New West, True West," *Under Western Skies: Nature and History in the American West* (New York, 1992), 19–33; Spencer C. Olin Jr., "Toward a Synthesis of the Political and Social History of the American West," *Pacific Historical Review* 55 (November 1986): 599–611; Frederick C. Luebke, "Regionalism and the Great Plains: Problems of Concept and Method," *Western Historical Quarterly* 15 (January 1984): 19–38; Michael C. Steiner, "The Significance of Turner's Sectional Thesis," *Western Historical Quarterly* 10 (October 1979): 437–66; Martin Ridge, "The American West: From Frontier to Region," *New Mexico Historical Review* 64 (April 1989): 125–41; Richard Jensen, "On Modernizing Frederick Jackson Turner: The Historiography of Regionalism," *Western Historical Quarterly* 11 (July 1980): 307–22; and Richard Maxwell Brown, "The New Regionalism in America, 1970–1981," in *Regionalism and the Pacific Northwest,* ed. William G. Robbins, Robert J. Frank, and Richard E. Ross (Corvallis, Oreg., 1983), 37–96. For examples of new western regional histories, see Patricia Nelson Limerick, *Legacy of Conquest: The Unbroken Past of the American West* (New York, 1987); Michael P. Malone and Richard W. Etulain, *The American West: A Twentieth-Century History* (Lincoln, 1989); Richard White, *"It's Your Misfortune and None of My Own": A New History of the American West* (Norman, 1991); and Donald Worster, *Rivers of Empire: Water, Aridity, and the Growth of the American West* (New York, 1985).

2. Walter Prescott Webb, *The Great Plains* (Boston, 1931). On Webb and regionalism, see Gregory M. Tobin, *The Making of a History: Walter Prescott Webb and The Great Plains* (Austin, 1976); Elliott West, "Walter Prescott Webb and the Search for the West," in *Writing Western History: Essays on Major Western Historians,* ed. Richard W. Etulain (Albuquerque, 1991), 167–91; and James C. Malin, "Webb and Regionalism," in *History and Ecology: Studies of the Grassland,* ed. Robert P. Swierenga (Lincoln, 1984), 85–104.

3. Webb, *Great Plains,* vi–vii.

4. Ibid., 8.

5. Turner, of course, devoted as much attention (arguably more) to the idea of region or, as he preferred, section, but the new regionalists have not embraced his sectional thesis because, as Worster has noted in "New West, True West" (256 n. 5), Turner did not see what we now define as the West "as a cohesive whole, fixed in place." Richard White also dismisses the sectional thesis as unconvincing. See Richard White, "Frederick Jackson Turner," in *Historians of the American Frontier: A Bio-Bibliographical Sourcebook,* ed. John R. Wunder (New York, 1988), 671. Other historians have found the sectional thesis a useful if flawed route toward a new regionalism. See Steiner, "Significance of Turner's Sectional Thesis," and his "Frederick Jackson Turner and Western Regionalism," in Etulain, *Writing Western History,* 103–35, and Jensen, "On Modernizing Frederick Jackson Turner."

6. For a useful overview of the critical response to Turner, see Nash, *Creating the West,* 3–99.

7. Limerick, *Legacy of Conquest,* 26.

8. Ibid., 26–27.

9. Limerick, "What on Earth Is the New Western History?" 81, 82.

10. I do not mean to imply that only westerners can write western history, nor do I know of any historians who make such a claim. My point is simply that within the new western history, there is a keenly felt and openly expressed desire by historians from the West to tell a history consistent with their own experience of the region and perceptions of its environment. The new western historians are not unique in this, of course; as Nash has pointed out in *Creating the West* (259), western historians are always writing about themselves. For a discussion of the role of nostalgia and sense of place in Turner's work, see Steiner, "Significance of Turner's Sectional Thesis." But the new western historians have been explicit in connecting personal experience and a sense of the land with their adoption of regionalism. See, for example, Worster, "New West, True West," 24, and White, "*It's Your Misfortune*," xviii–xix.

11. Worster, "New West, True West," 24.

12. J. Nicholas Entrikin, *The Betweenness of Place: Towards a Geography of Modernity* (Baltimore, 1991), 80. On Royce, see Robert V. Hine, "Josiah Royce: The West as Community," in Etulain, *Writing Western History*, 19–41. For Turner's view about region, see Steiner, "The Significance of Turner's Sectional Thesis" and "Turner and Western Regionalism." On Odum and Mumford, see Entrikin, *The Betweenness of Place*, 75–80.

13. Worster and Limerick have been explicit in calling for an activist or reformist western history. The history of the West, says Worster, "cannot be kept isolated from public controversy, struggles over power, the search for new moral standards, or the ongoing human debate over fundamental principles and values." Worster, "Beyond the Agrarian Myth," 16. See also Limerick, "Trail to Santa Fe," 63–67.

14. Donald Worster, "A Country without Secrets," *Under Western Skies,* 253.

15. Worster, "Beyond the Agrarian Myth," 18.

16. Both Worster and Malone have noted the need for a regionalism that does not simply apply the older Turnerian approach to a specific geographic locale. See Michael P. Malone, "The 'New Western History': An Assessment," in Limerick, Milner, and Rankin, *Trails,* 100, and Worster, "New West, True West," 24.

17. Worster, "New West, True West," 22–23.

18. Worster, "Beyond the Agrarian Myth," 11.

19. Walter Prescott Webb, "The American West: Perpetual Mirage," *Harper's* 214 (May 1957), 26.

20. Wallace Stegner, "Living Dry," *The American West as Living Space* (Ann Arbor, 1987), 8.

21. The terms *dry, lifeless, dull,* and *uninteresting* appear in various definitions of *arid.* See, for example, *Webster's Third New International Dictionary of the English Language,* unabridged edition (Springfield, Mass., 1986); *Oxford American Dictionary* (New York, 1980); and Sir Dudley Stamp and Audrey N. Clark, eds., *A Glossary of Geographical Terms* (1961; 3d ed., rev., London, 1979), 34–35. See also the entry for *hydrology* in Douglas M. Considine, ed., *Van Nostrand's Scientific Encyclopedia* (1938; 7th ed., rev., New York, 1989), esp. 1502–3; "Mean Annual Rainfall" in Warren A. Beck and Ynez D. Haase, *Historical Atlas of the American West* (Norman, 1989), 3; and Mohamed T. El-Ashry and Diana C. Gibbons, "The West in Profile," in *Water and Arid Lands of the Western United States,* ed. Mohamed T. El-Ashry and Diana C. Gibbons (Cambridge, England, 1988), 1–19.

22. Norris Hundley makes this point about California: "It is a mistake . . . to think of California in terms of averages and regular cycles of precipitation. . . . [G]reat irregularity characterizes the typical precipitation pattern throughout California." Norris Hundley Jr., *The Great Thirst: Californians and Water, 1770s–1990s* (Berkeley, 1992), 9, 13.

23. William Cronon suggests the idea of extremity in his essay on Kennecott, Alaska: "The thing that initially most strikes one about Kennecott is just how *western* it is. . . . Although [Kennecott] inverts the dryness that characterizes large parts of the arid West, it shares with the rest of the region a more fundamental trait: a climate of extremes. It has too much cold, too much rain and snow, too much and too little sun to be mistaken for anywhere else on the continent." William Cronon, "Kennecott Journey: The Paths out of Town," in *Under an Open Sky: Rethinking America's Western Past*, ed. William Cronon, George Miles, and Jay Gitlin (New York, 1992), 32.

24. For graphic illustrations of this, see National Geographic Society, *Atlas of North America: Space Age Portrait of a Continent* (Washington, D.C., 1985) and *The National Atlas of the United States of America* (Washington, D.C., 1970).

25. White, *"It's Your Misfortune,"* 3.

26. Richard White, "Trashing the Trails," in Limerick, Milner, and Rankin, *Trails*, 39.

27. Ibid.

28. Limerick, *Legacy of Conquest*, 27.

29. White, *"It's Your Misfortune,"* 4, and "Trashing the Trails," 36–38.

30. Worster, "New West, True West," 27.

31. Michael E. McGerr, "Is There a Twentieth-Century West?" in Cronon, Miles, and Gitlin, *Under An Open Sky*, 247.

32. William Cronon, George Miles, and Jay Gitlin, "Becoming West: Toward a New Meaning for Western History," in Cronon, Miles, and Gitlin, *Under An Open Sky*, 7.

33. West, "Walter Prescott Webb," 174.

34. Limerick, *Legacy of Conquest*, 28.

35. Worster, "Beyond the Agrarian Myth," 13.

36. For good historiographical overviews of the field, see Richard White, "American Environmental History: The Development of a New Historical Field," *Pacific Historical Review* 54 (August 1985): 297–335; Donald Worster, "Doing Environmental History," in *The Ends of the Earth: Perspectives on Modern Environmental History*, ed. Donald Worster (Cambridge, England, 1988), 289–307; and "A Round Table: Environmental History," *Journal of American History* 76 (March 1990): 1087–147.

37. See Richard White, *Land Use, Environment, and Social Change: The Shaping of Island County, Washington* (Seattle, 1980); William deBuys, *Enchantment and Exploitation: The Life and Hard Times of a New Mexico Mountain Range* (Albuquerque, 1985); Hal K. Rothman, *On Rims and Ridges: The Los Alamos Area since 1880* (Lincoln, 1992); Dan L. Flores, *Caprock Canyonlands: Journeys into the Heart of the Southern Plains* (Austin, 1990); and Peter G. Boag, *Environment and Experience: Settlement Culture in Nineteenth-Century Oregon* (Berkeley, 1992).

38. See, for example, Nancy K. Anderson, "'The Kiss of Enterprise': The Western Landscape as Symbol and Resource," in *The West as America: Reinterpreting Im-*

ages of the Frontier, 1820–1920, ed. William H. Truettner (Washington, D.C., 1991), 237–83; Michael L. Smith, *Pacific Visions: California Scientists and the Environment, 1850–1915* (New Haven, 1987); Arthur F. McEvoy, *The Fisherman's Problem: Ecology and Law in the California Fisheries, 1850–1980* (Cambridge, England, 1986); and Chris J. Magoc, "'The Selling of Wonderland': Yellowstone National Park, the Northern Pacific Railroad, and the Culture of Consumption, 1872–1903" (Ph.D. diss., University of New Mexico, 1992).

39. Limerick, *Legacy of Conquest,* 29; and Worster, "Beyond the Agrarian Myth," 14.

40. William Cronon, "Revisiting the Vanishing Frontier," *Western Historical Quarterly* 18 (1987): 170.

41. Ibid., 172.

42. Cronon, "Nature, History, and Narrative," *Journal of American History* 78 (March 1992): 1375.

A Mosaic of Different Environments

Robert W. Righter

The major virtue of Professor Susan Neel's essay is that she provides us with a fresh reminder that the American West is a region of environmental or natural extremes. This idea is surely worthy of comment. But first, a definition of the American West is in order. Historians, environmental or otherwise, will continue to debate whether the American West is a geographical place or a cultural process. But let us grant the new western history a victory, relegating the "American frontier" to process and the "American West" to place. If the West is a place, where is it, and what are its characteristics? Eschewing the many geographic spats, let us define the West as the region between the ninety-eighth meridian and the Pacific Ocean, bordered on the north by Canada and on the south by Mexico. What are the region's characteristics? Historians from Walter Prescott Webb to Donald Worster have focused on its most distinguishing feature, its aridity. Admittedly, the parched landscape cannot be denied. When it comes to water, nature has blessed the West here and there but certainly not everywhere. Perhaps, however, historians such as Webb, Worster, W. Eugene Hollon, and Bernard DeVoto have overstressed the "everywhere." Defining the American West as arid is like describing Swiss cheese without the holes. The essence is defined, but not the distinctiveness. According to Susan Neel, the West finds its distinctiveness in its diversity, its extreme environments, of which aridity is only one. Perhaps a more accurate description would be the "mosaic West," reminiscent of the Yellowstone landscape after the spectacular 1988 fires. The fires swept over the lodgepole pine forests, but almost miraculously and surely capriciously, the windblown inferno spared patches of wild, green groves; the result was a fascinating mosaic of different environments.

Susan Neel advocates looking at the West in a similar fashion, as a place of geographic diversity and a region of *extremes*. "A region of extremes" fits nicely into my plethora of definitions. If I can indulge in a brief autobiographical excursion, one can see that my experience and understanding strengthen such a thesis. I was raised near San Francisco, attended college in Salem, Oregon, did graduate work at Santa Barbara, taught in Los Angeles, then accepted a position in Laramie, Wyoming. My present appointment is in El Paso, Texas. I read Professor Neel's paper in the Wind River Mountains. Every one of these locations I consider to be the American West, but they are environmentally different—one might even say extremely different. The California locations are generally temperate, Mediterranean climates, with the aridity of Los Angeles moderated by a massive injection of imported water.

Salem, Oregon, boasts about seventy inches of rainfall each year, the very antithesis of aridity. There one finds a watery deluge rather than a desert. Laramie, Wyoming, is semiarid, but its extremes fall in the arena of altitude and temperature. It is high and dry and cold. The Red Desert of Wyoming, for instance, is indeed a desert, but a lost wanderer is far more likely to die of frostbite than heat exhaustion. Farming is a marginal activity on the northern high plains, but the limits are prescribed not so much by a lack of water as by a short growing season. My present home, El Paso, can occasionally be cold, but in this arid region heat is the enemy. Buy an automobile battery in Wyoming, and the salesperson will tout its "cold cranking power." Buy one in El Paso, and the pitch is the battery's ability to withstand heat.

When Walter Prescott Webb concluded his controversial *Harper's Magazine* article "The American West: Perpetual Mirage," he likened the westerner to a musician "performing on a giant stringed instrument with many of the strings missing."[1] I prefer to replace the "giant stringed instrument" with a twelve-string guitar. The westerner tries to play the guitar, and eventually through compensation and ingenuity he succeeds, although the music is "sometimes odd." Webb implied that almost all of the missing strings are associated with aridity. However, no one can deny that heat, cold, fire, flood, blizzard, wind, hail, and altitude number among the out-of-tune strings with which westerners must contend, making it difficult to live in harmony (i.e., prosperity) with the environment. Neel maintains that defining the West environmentally does not work because there is no unified ecological basis to the West. She is correct. The West has less unity and more diversity than the South, the North, or the Midwest. Environmentally, it is unique. It has the highest mountain (in the lower forty-eight states) and the lowest point in the country. In the nightly television meteorologist's competition to point out the coldest place and the hottest place in the nation, the West often wins both contests hands down. No other region of the nation (New England, the South, the Midwest) can match the variety of climates in the West.

This diversity has been somewhat submerged in our regional history. The preoccupation with aridity may be conditioned by how we approach the West. I do not mean how we think about the West, but how most Anglo Americans have historically *entered* the West, as well as how most Americans have imagined that entrance. Fur trappers, government explorers, miners, cattlemen, and settlers penetrated the West from the east. Until fairly recently these groups set the model for how historians conceptualized western history, ignoring Mexicans who entered from the south or Chinese from the Pacific Rim. If these same Anglo-American groups had entered the West from the west, would our perception be different? I have always thought that when the Lewis and Clark party spent the winter of 1805–6 at Fort Clatsop, near the mouth of the Columbia River, they may have wished, indeed prayed, for some of the West's vaunted aridity. Instead, they bore witness to another extreme.

This diversity enhances rather than diminishes the importance of the western environment. The West is a region where nature dominates and humans accommodate. Neither does environmental diversity deny the West its most distinguishing environmental characteristic. The West has space, vast landscapes with minimal human impact. Any easterner traveling west perceives that somewhere in the middle of Nebraska (or Kansas or South Dakota), the West begins. Just where is speculative, for as the geographer Yi-Fu Tuan notes: "No two persons see the same reality. No two social groups make precisely the same evaluation of the environment."[2] The landscape, however, changes. Towns, houses, and people are fewer, the sky is bluer, humidity flees, and the sense of space becomes an undeniable reality.

This can be a freeing or a fearful experience, depending on the individual. In the category of fearful I recall a Green River, Wyoming, friend who finally persuaded his Brooklyn-based father to come west. After the father's arrival, the two took a day trip south from Green River to Flaming Gorge Reservoir. It was a dramatic drive with vast plains and the snowcapped Uinta Mountains for a backdrop. However, the father didn't see it that way. Increasingly jittery, he finally shouted at his son, "Stop the car!" He insisted that his son return immediately to Green River. Infinite land and sky—endless space—worked on the mind of this urban row-house alien to create scenarios of aloneness, nakedness, and danger.

Of course westerners find such fear inexplicable. It is often a difficult place to live, but a sense of freedom and "the solace of open space," as writer Gretel Erhlich put it, offer compensations unmatched elsewhere. Bernard DeVoto explained that the West's "landscape is dramatic, its climate violent."[3] This striking yet turbulent quality is part of the attraction of the extreme, mosaic West. The region can produce strong feelings of attachment. Yi-Fu Tuan calls this topophilia, and the West in all its varieties induces abundant feelings of connection.

Because the land and its inhabitants are so central to westerners and their history, the region seems to have become a favorite focus for environmental historians. No one can dispute that the leading environmental historians also define themselves as historians of the American West. This region of environmental extremes offers a perfect springboard from which to examine the proper relationship between the anthropocentric and the biocentric. What better place to study people, as Don Worster says, "from the Earth up"? The West offers a vast sagebrush stage from which the environmental historian can project a different, perhaps contrary, view of the American experience.[4]

Worster recently wrote, "Conventional history has been too anthropocentric in outlook, sundering the seamless unity of humankind and the rest of nature."[5] The West—a place where nature and humankind are so intertwined—can help historians resurrect this unity through story and narrative. Susan Neel suggests, "Western history should teach us of the centrality of nature to the human experience." We need to write this history. We need to move the perspective of nature into history. "Martha," the last passenger pigeon, must tell her tale. If Martha, who died on 1 September 1914 in a Cincinnati zoo, could interpret nineteenth-century American history, her saga would be quite different from the anthropocentric one.[6] She would set the nineteenth century upside down. Progress becomes regress. Human wealth becomes nature's impoverishment. And it would be clear that for all the manifest strides of the American nation, some cultures or some species paid the price. The story of the westering American becomes much different. Social historians of the American West have detailed the anthropocentric price in terms of race, class, and gender. Whether Martha's story—and other tales like it—have been heard is problematical. We need to tell them often.

As we rewrite western history we must find the proper balance between the anthropocentric and the biocentric. In the past, people have always been on center stage in the epic of the West; nature has been the backdrop—a dramatic backdrop summoned when necessary to illuminate the human drama. The environmental historian must now move nature onto center stage. However, as stage directors, we have a fine line to follow. We cannot remove humankind from the story. If we do, we face the certain reality that we are shifting from our field of history and the humanities to natural history and science. How many of us can master the intricacies of natural history? How many of us feel comfortable in the field of nature writing? We must, of course, embrace interdisciplinary methods, but we should guard against venturing far afield from our training, lest it taint what we research and write. To return to Neel's thesis, we had best confine our narrative to human sentiments and reactions to the extreme variations of the West rather than to entrap ourselves in unfamiliar arenas. We need to tell and interpret stories illustrating, according to Neel, that "the peoples of the West have found in nature sources of delight and of terror, tools of oppression and means of maintaining human dignity." The interaction of humans and their environment is where we can be most effective.[7]

And environmental historians do want to be effective. Frederick Jackson Turner's insistence that history should enlighten the present continues to have resonance for contemporary scholars. Surely environmental historians head the list of such scholars. We are often presentist, and we do fall victim to treating history, as Richard White cleverly put it, "as a sort of intellectual scavenger hunt from which one returns with useful ideas for our time."[8] We are earnest scholars, and earnest scholars are easily seduced by bias. Caution is advised by Neel, and it should be heeded. In our stories of the American West, "we will find no easy lessons, no exportable heroes. The past will not provide us with a transcendent set of values about nature and how to treat it."

The environmental past may not provide the answers, but Neel recognizes that such an observation will not dissuade environmental historians from crossing the line between scholarship and advocacy. Since "a deep concern over the fate of the earth is what most distinguishes environmental history," we should not be surprised that members of our guild frequently descend the steps of the ivory tower to romp in the rough-and-tumble world of policy-making.[9] Lessons from the extreme environment of the West may offer solutions to try and paths to take to avoid an extreme fate for the earth. Turner's most often quoted axiom that "each age writes the history of the past anew with reference to the conditions uppermost in its own time" seems applicable. Turner did not mean to imply that there are no verities, that there are no lasting principles. Nor did he want to suggest that we must teach and write environmental history only to please the present. But he did recognize that we cull, discard, select, and resurrect—all depending on what society perceives to be significant. Today, the relationship of people and cultures to the environment numbers among the significant, both in the West and in the world.

Notes

1. Walter Prescott Webb, "The American West: Perpetual Mirage," *Harper's Magazine* 214 (May 1957): 31.

2. Yi-Fu Tuan, *Topophilia: A Study of Environmental Perception, Attitudes, and Values* (1974; New York, 1990): 5.

3. Gretel Erhlich, *The Solace of Open Spaces* (New York, 1985); Bernard DeVoto, "The Anxious West," *Harper's Magazine* 193 (December 1946): 481.

4. Both quotations are from Donald Worster, ed., *The Ends of the Earth: Perspectives on Modern Environmental History* (New York, 1988), 289.

5. Ibid., preface.

6. A. W. Schorger, *The Passenger Pigeon: Its Natural History and Extinction* (Norman, 1973): 28–30. Schorger is too much a naturalist and too little a historian to succeed in making this book interpretive rather than factual.

7. There is always an exception. Most recently Dan Flores, in *Caprock Canyonlands* (Austin, 1990), successfully wedded nature writing, mysticism, and a biocentric view with history and a sprinkling of anthropology.

8. Richard White, "American Environmental History: The Development of a New Historical Field," *Pacific Historical Review* 54 (1985): 316.

9. In his presidential address to the American Society for Environmental History conference in Pittsburgh, March 1993, William Cronon addressed at some length the propensity of environmental historians to make their research "useful" to both policymakers and "the earth itself." See William Cronon, "The Uses of Environmental History," *Environmental History Review* 17 (Fall 1993): 1–22.

Place versus Region in Western Environmental History

Dan Flores

As a graduate student, I briefly admired fantasy art and practitioners of it like Frank Frazetta, and twenty years ago I once owned (again, briefly) one of Frazetta's prints. As I was reading Susan Rhoades Neel's essay on environment and western history, this print popped into my head. I recall few of the details of it now. It was blue-green. It was large. Mostly it was aswirl with life, with comings, goings, conquests, and capitulations. A dozen societies were in various processes of emergence and decline in it, and their stages and potential fates were wondrous to contemplate on an idle summer day. But more than all of the *history* represented there, what riveted me most was a pair of tiny figures, near the bottom, which I suspect most viewers of the print missed. For at the edges of this maelstrom of life, here were the obligatory academics, attired in caps and gowns and observing and gesturing and arguing about the meaning of what lay sprawled before them—and, of course, remaining safely detached from it all.

Granted, Professor Neel has gotten most of the canvas spread out before us here: Turner, Webb, Limerick, Worster, White, and Cronon, along with Frontier, Region, Aridity, and Process. And her essay is both stylishly written and a provocative synthesis of a good deal of the modern debate about western history, about the roles of nature and culture in interpreting the history of the vast stretch of country the whole world knows as, simply, "the West." She grapples on the definitional turf too, or at least most of it. The idea that the West is bounded by environmental characteristics gets its due, as does the event-institutional sequence we historians call "process"—although "system" does escape her analysis. The fact that I admired the context she establishes but disagreed with much of what she concludes in no way diminished my stimulation at reading her essay and pondering her ideas.

Neel's evocative opening carries us with her from the wide plateau, where we see but do not understand, down into the kernel of the western earth to watch time and history surge by in a river metaphor. This is a symbolic journey, like participating in a rite of passage in the rock-art caves of southern France, and when the torches are finally lit, spread before us like a panel of pictographs are the images and icons of our modern-day perceptions of the West. Judging from the tone of the presentation, it is clear that our party consists of apprentice shamans whose task it is to deconstruct the existing images and then to decide on what symbols *we* might utilize to give new power and meaning to our own explanations. Neel is our capable guide through this late-twentieth-century dreamtime ceremony, interpreting older symbols for us and pointing out some of the new glyphs and markers that a few of our contemporaries are using to capture the present reality. Here, we apprentices are told, on this wall is everything our ancestors knew, set down by our most far-seeing shamans. The problem is that their marks don't represent our current experiences. Your task is to devise new marks that do.

So far so good. Of course we need the discussion of definitions, not only because you can't talk profitably about what you can't define but also because the definitions put forth by our great historians have come to a strange turn: they don't seem to fit either our time or our view down the river and may actually have been too exclusionary even back when they seemed to explain things very well. Relying on Shaman Frederick Jackson Turner's definition— the symbols signifying a process called the "frontier"—has special problems, of course, and not only because of ethnic marginalizations. There is also, as Neel points out, the problem of trying to figure out what to do with the interpretive symbols (other than to market them) once the so-called frontier process has run its course. And if Shaman Turner's particular glyphs are to be relied on, why designate a "West" upon which to base all our speculations about the process? Frontiering, in fact, is what we humans have been doing at least since the Upper Paleolithic.

Shaman Walter Prescott Webb's symbols, as Neel points out, have been easy to pick apart but difficult to dismiss in the round. And in fact a good many modern historians do embrace his assertion of a set of environmental characteristics that make of the West a real and recognizable place on the map. Who doesn't recognize those characteristics? You know you've arrived in the West when grass and cactus overwhelm trees, when the air carries dust instead of pollen, when the opalescent wool of humidity lifts and transparent light allows the eyes to outrun all the other senses. These are the superficial effects of aridity on a landscape, but to Webb they were only the beginnings of an influence that altered all life under its sway.

Neel guides us through Webb's shamanic symbols gracefully, and she correctly points out some of their flaws. Webb did draw a circle around half the continent and then talk only about a little, and atypical, piece of it. He ignored (if his follower Wordsmith-shaman Wallace Stegner did not) all those many pieces within his circle that are not arid, including the Rocky Mountain West, the area that serves as the core water-source region for the surrounding drylands and within which elevation appears more an influence than aridity. Webb's treatment of aridity was, to substantiate our guide's charge, very much ethnocentric. And yet among our ranks there are many— and I am one—who would suspect a non sequitur in Professor Neel's conclusion that because Indians, Hispanics, Asians, and Anglo Americans all perceived aridity differently, it follows that the effects of aridity are strictly cultural. In simplest terms, what the symbol for aridity means, in fact, is "not much water," and since water is one of the basic requirements for the human organism irrespective of culture, gender, or place of national origin, aridity freely translates in real environmental terms to *limits*. Just how those limits get dealt with does have cultural manifestations, but this does not alter the fact of those limits as biological, hence universal, hence real. A lack of water may well limit human population growth everywhere, eventually. But societies in places like the arid West will face that sobering situation sooner than those everywhere else.

As for the environmental diversity that exists across the western half of America, Neel is quite right to point it out. It is an interpretive difficulty, although not as much a problem as she thinks. Combine all those environmentally distinctive (i.e., unarid) places like the Pacific Northwest and Alaska with those places of political-institutional uniqueness like California and Texas, and the difficulty of defining *where* the West is, based on anything resembling an environmental or institutional baseline, becomes apparent. As our guide toward interpretive regionalism, it might have been worthwhile for Professor Neel to broach the example of another part of the United States that has long been recognized as a distinctive region but that also lacks environmental uniformity. The South, very obviously, does exist as a recognizable region in terms of culture, literature, and sense of itself. But as the geographer Yi-Fu Tuan has instructed us, one of the key elements that goes into the creation of place out of space is a sense of a shared history. This has played a critical role in southern regionalism. The historian David Emmons, in a recent article, similarly argues that at the heart of western self-identity is this sense of a shared history, not so much of interethnic strife (which was common across much of America) or even the presence of cowboys (although that gets us closer) as of a shared history that played out during the time when the global industrial economy had reached a particular level of maturity and reach that was capable of unprecedented rapidity in its transformation of places into cogs in a market system. In this interpretation California, Alaska, Texas—or the Sonoran Desert, the Grand Tetons, and the Columbia Valley—have a tie that binds.

It is in her discussion of regionalism that I think Professor Neel simultaneously holds before us exactly the proper set of symbols for our own shamanic acts yet proceeds to confuse us by asserting that our task is to apply them to the West as a whole. As any monkey wrencher will tell you, you don't cut down a billboard with a speed square, and you don't strip octagonal bolts with a hexagonal wrench. Having made her excellent points about western diversity, she assumes that any western history fundamentally based on environment is thus going to founder on that diversity . . . which leads us back to Turner and process?

I don't think so, although Turner's recognition that adaptation takes place is useful still, if only as a start. Nor do I accept her critique that it is difficult to find environmental histories of the West that address the human-nature dialectic in the twentieth century. Although many of our histories of the West as a whole suffer from the literary dissonance of forcing all those diverse places to hew to a singular interpretive thread, Neel neglects to point out that much western environmental history already exists (and much more is being written) that carries regionalism to the very scale that someone like Lewis Mumford envisioned for it and indeed to the scale that enables us to approach the actual complexity of the way people and nature interact.

This kind of western environmental history is truly place-specific. Although it makes every effort to see its place as part of the larger regional or national, indeed as part of the global, process of environmental integration and transformation, its focus is on what postmodernists would call "particularism." It ricochets off the difficulties, say, of trying to fit Texas—only a third of which *is* arid or semiarid and a state that virtually lacks both public lands and Indians—with the rest of the West, by drawing its boundaries bioregionally and examining the nature-culture dialectic as a thematic manifestation of a particular *place*. The narrative line of such histories is commonly grafted onto sequential cultural inhabitations, and interpretively it could borrow from social scientists like Roy Rappaport and Karl Butzer a sophisticated study of cultural adaptation as being central to human success in place. If this western environmental history has a founding shaman, it is probably the curmudgeonly James Malin of Kansas.

The new western environmental historians who have done such work— and I am thinking of William DeBuys's *Enchantment and Exploitation* (1985, on the Sangre de Cristo range in New Mexico), James Sherow's *Watering the Valley* (1990, on the Arkansas Valley of Colorado and Kansas), Peter Boag's *Environment and Experience* (1992, on the Willamette Valley of Oregon), Hal Rothman's *On Rims and Ridges* (1993, on the Jemez range in New Mexico), and perhaps my *Caprock Canyonlands* (1990, on the southern high plains of Texas and New Mexico)—have consistently had close personal ties with their places. The surprising result has not been regional defensiveness so much as sharp critique. Despite their specificity, not one of these books has so far been considered provincial. Whether they represent historical balkanization of the kind that European historians, especially the Annalists, have been accused may be another matter. But we should seek to embrace a history that can treat one thousand years in the Sangre de Cristo Mountains in something like the manner to which Languedoc is accustomed.

A question worth pondering is whether modern professional historians, of the West or of anywhere else, aren't in some danger of a detachment—like the academics in my fantasy art print—that renders us superfluous to anyone but ourselves. What we may as well acknowledge is that the reason Turner and Webb still dominate our discussions of theory about western history is that their ideas *felt* intuitively right to their readers, many of whom were on the scene and experienced the life these historians described and who in turn granted validity to the frontier and aridity interpretations. In some real sense, and however inaccurately in refinement, Turner and Webb did not so much invent their theories as capture a prevailing folk sense of history.

Therefore, if Professor Neel is right (and I believe she is) that *regional* history—and, maybe more particularly, *bio*regional or *place* history—is emerging as one manifestation of some kind of consciousness shift in western communities, then we historian-shamans might consider the unthinkable: listening, rather than talking among ourselves.

5

Significant Lives: Asia and Asian Americans in the U.S. West

Gail M. Nomura

The dominant, Eurocentric view of U.S. history places European settlers center stage and relegates Asian Americans to the wings. This centrist interpretation became clear to me when one of my colleagues questioned the researching and teaching of Asian American history in the Pacific Northwest.

"Just how many Chinese were there?" he challenged.

I told him numbers didn't necessarily indicate significance. "For example," I said, "Lewis and Clark were only two men, yet volumes are written about them—with little enough reference to the diverse peoples who met or accompanied their Corps of Discovery. And, at times, there were more 'Chinese' in parts of the Pacific Northwest than there were European settlers."

My colleague used the term "Chinese" because that is the generic label employed by those ignorant of the variation of Asian ethnic groups. There was much to tell him. I wanted to emphasize the diversity of Asian Americans, to stress that I do not see significance only in numbers, and to interrogate the term *significance* itself.

It is these considerations, in the context of "justifying" the study of Asian Americans in U.S. history, that I would like to address in this essay. This challenge is best begun by asking a question: Why is significance *ascribed* to European-American settlers, whereas people of color must *achieve* it?

I do not intend to discuss the role that Asian Americans played in U.S. western history by merely recentering the narrative from European-American settlers to Asian American settlers. Rather, I would like to question the meaning of the term *significant,* to reflect on what it indicates when we say a group is "significant," to weigh the criteria used in establishing the "significance" of any group's role in history, and to suggest ways we might better envision a *multi*cultural history of the U.S. West by understanding Asian American history.

The first step in assessing any group is to know what it is. What we call "Asian Americans" is not, as my misguided colleague and many people in the United States seem to think, a unified, homogeneous grouping. The ethnic peoples called Asian Americans include Chinese, Filipino, Japanese, Korean, South Asian (e.g., Asian Indian, Pakistani, Bangladeshi, and Sri Lankan), and Southeast Asian (e.g., Vietnamese, Lao, Hmong, Cambodian, Thai, Indonesian, Malaysian, and Singaporean). The complexity of this term "Asian American" is further illustrated by noting the many ethnicities within the larger subcategories—such as Southeast Asian American—or even within a seemingly homogeneous subcategory such as Japanese American, in which Okinawan Americans compose a distinct grouping.

To the above Asian American grouping we might also add Pacific Islanders (e.g., native Hawaiian, Samoan, Chamoru,[1] Fijian, Tongan, and Taihitian). The U.S. Census Bureau lists Asian and Pacific Islanders together, and many political coalitions have been formed by these groups, who share some common agendas and histories.

All of these peoples possess distinct histories, languages, cultures, religions, and conflicts among and between themselves. What they share is a common history in the United States of exclusion and discrimination. Assessing these diverse populations is problematic, since there are so many different histories to discuss. However, I will suggest ways in which these varied voices help articulate a multicultural history of the U.S. West.

Since I assume no static, exclusive, dominant center of U.S. western history, my discussion is not, and cannot be, the study of margins. I believe in an inclusive history that bespeaks the significance of the lives of all our people. Such a history reveals not only a diverse and complex U.S. West but a variegated and manifold United States.

Borders: The East as West

First of all, in envisioning a multicultural history of the U.S. West, we must question the borders that define this region. Asia is inextricably linked to the U.S. West. At one time a land bridge connected North America to Asia, facilitating the migration of people from Asia to the Americas. Columbus's search for a new maritime route to Asia, and his landing in the

Americas, initiated a process of cultural confrontation and transformation, the consequences of which we are still reaping. The voyages of Columbus set the stage for conquest and colonization, the political foundation of the United States. The mythic China market stimulated explorers to search for direct routes to China. In 1778, Captain Cook, looking for the fabled Northwest Passage connecting Europe to Asia, accidentally "encountered" Hawai`i. The U.S. desire for the China trade propelled expansion in the Pacific. The national fantasy of the U.S. West was tied to expectations about the "Orient" beyond the wilderness, and in many cases, state and national policies were shaped by the lure of trade with Asia.

Americans pushed into the Pacific Northwest, in part to profit from the commodity of furs, so vital for participation in the China trade. Of course, John Jacob Astor and other American entrepreneurs advocated acquisition of the Columbia River, especially its mouth, which would open the gates to Asian trade across the Rockies and down the Missouri River to St. Louis. Competing nations initially supported the independence of the Kingdom of Hawai`i as an international port open to all because of its strategic location as a reprovisioning stop for traders and whalers in the mid-Pacific.

To expansionists, Asia appeared to offer limitless opportunities for commerce. In debates in the 1849 California constitutional convention, one delegate, H. W. Halleck, argued for the most expansive boundaries to be set for California:

> No other portion of the globe will exercise a greater influence upon the civilization and commerce of the world. The people of California will penetrate the hitherto inaccessible portions of Asia, carrying with them not only the arts and sciences, but the refining and purifying influence of civilization and Christianity; they will unlock the vast resources of the East, and, by reversing the commerce of the world, pour the riches of India into the metropolis of the new State.[2]

Expanding trade with Asia continued to fuel state economic policies in the U.S. West into the twentieth century.

With the acquisition of Pacific Basin territory, our stake in Asia and in Pacific affairs rose. Alaska was purchased in 1867, in part to serve as a drawbridge to Asia. The Midway Islands were annexed in the same year, pushing the American presence ever deeper into the Pacific. At the turn of the century we engaged in our first Asian-theater wars: the Spanish-American War in 1898 and the Boxer Rebellion in 1900. Were these wars in fact far western wars? We used some of the same cavalry troops from the Indian wars and sent them across the Pacific into Beijing to aid the foreign legations under siege and to the Philippines to oust the Spaniards and then to suppress the Filipino nationalists. Debate over our imperialist adventure in the Philippines affected the U.S. elections of 1900. Americans were struggling to come to grips with the United States as a colonizer. The newly acquired U.S. territories of Hawai`i, Wake, Guam, and the Philippines, along with Midway, provided a chain of ports and later airports across the Pacific to Asia.[3]

Recognizing the significance of our Pacific and Asian territories forces us to question how we define the boundaries of the U.S. West. Indeed, with the acquisition of the Philippines, Hawai`i, Guam, Wake, and American Samoa at the turn of the century and, after World War II, of American Micronesia, the U.S. West literally moved to the so-called Far East and became ever more entwined in Asian and Pacific affairs. The western border of the U.S. West became Asia itself. The Far East became the Far West.

It is impossible to view Asian American history without understanding this "Far Eastern" context. Asian American history connects the U.S. West to the global experience of the diaspora and the interchange of people and ideas from the colonial and postcolonial era, to transnational labor migration, to international assembly lines in Asia, and to multinational financial and corporate structures in the Pacific Rim. The Pacific Coast states have always been oriented to Asia and the Pacific, an orientation that explains, in part, why the largest West Coast cities are the ports of Seattle, Portland, San Francisco, and Los Angeles. The largest city in Hawai`i, Honolulu, has long functioned as a link between the U.S. mainland and Asia. In envisioning the U.S. West as a vital component of the Pacific Basin, we challenge the Eurocentric focus of both western and national U.S. history. The roots of what is currently called the Pacific Century, with attention focused on the Pacific Basin, took firm hold in the U.S. West of the nineteenth century and have continued to grow throughout the twentieth century.

Asia and the "Core" of America

Exclusionists tie American lineage to Europe and refuse to acknowledge Asian elements in defining the "core" of America. Thus, there exists an overriding sense that Asia is alien to the United States, but the roots of the United States are more global than is usually acknowledged.

Europe and Asia have a long and rich history of contact. Medieval Europe was fascinated with Asia as the source of such marvels as spices, silks, and porcelain—as well as fantastic monsters. Until the sixteenth century, Europe was an area marginal to Asia, and it was only after the development of capitalism that the dominance of the northwestern Atlantic economy emerged. Even then, until the late nineteenth century, China saw Europeans as barbarians with little to offer. Indeed, it was Asia that possessed the civilized treasures Europe longed to acquire.

The impact of Chinese civilization on western European civilization is undeniable. China exerted influence through books, manuscripts, tangible objects like porcelain, and the knowledge of technologies, such as the printing press and gunpowder. Donald Lach has documented much of this impact and points to the elephant in the iconography of European art as a symbol of Asia in the making of Europe.[4] The rediscovery of Asia's high civilization by Renaissance Europe was a significant intellectual factor in the making of early modern Europe. The Enlightenment philosophers, especially Voltaire, admired Confucius as the Noble Sage, the archetypal rationalist philosopher, and viewed the government of China as the rational model of a meritocracy with virtuous leaders chosen through a civil service examination system. H. G. Creel points out that the abolition of hereditary aristocracy in ancient Confucian China, nearly two thousand years earlier, fueled the attack on hereditary privilege in Europe. Creel notes that Confucianism played an important role "in the development of democratic ideals in Europe and in the background of the French Revolution. Through French thought it indirectly influenced the development of democracy in America. It is of interest that Thomas Jefferson proposed, as the 'key-stone of the arch of our government,' an educational system that shows remarkable similarities to the Chinese examination system. . . . The extent to which Confucianism contributed to the development of Western democracy is forgotten."[5] Forgotten or remembered, Asian ideas continued to cross the Atlantic via Europe.

In the United States, Asian religions and philosophies provided alternatives at times when there was doubt about common morals and ethics. The impact of Mahatma Gandhi's teachings on Martin Luther King Jr. and leaders of the antiwar movement is well known, as is the influence of Indian mysticism and the idea of reincarnation and karma on the Transcendentalists (Boston Brahmins).[6] More recently, at the Democratic convention in 1992, Vice President Al Gore quoted Gandhi when he called for Americans to become the change they wanted to see in the future. Buddhism, Zen, Hinduism, Confucianism, and Taoism have had a profound effect on the counterculture of beatniks and hippies. Asian meditation centers abound. The generation of the 1960s extolled Mao's anti-imperialist stance, and the leader's little red book was as much a symbol of protest on college campuses in the U.S. West as was the peace symbol.

The arts and architecture of Asia surround us. Chinoiserie has been a popular decorative style since colonial times. American homeowners in the early 1900s patterned their new craftsman-style homes on Japanese architecture. After Frank Lloyd Wright viewed the Japanese exhibit at the 1893 Chicago World's Columbian Exposition, he incorporated Japanese forms into his own work. Japanese gardens influenced U.S. landscape architecture while Japanese woodblock printing influenced impressionist painters.

American popular culture has also been deeply affected by Asia. Who hasn't heard of (or tasted!) stir fry, instant ramen, soy sauce, tofu, and sushi? Chinese restaurants have sprung up in nearly every town in the nation. Asian martial arts, typified by the *Karate Kid* film series, are embraced as confidence builders. Even the western movie classic the *Magnificent Seven* was modeled after Akira Kurosawa's *Seven Samurai*.

The interaction has not been totally positive. The Vietnam War created a widespread sense of disillusionment and dissent in the United States, ushering in a generation of intense social criticism and social consciousness of global dimensions. The antiwar movement spawned widespread protests, particularly on college campuses. American war efforts in Vietnam and Cambodia highlighted the contradiction between the enormous destructive capabilities of American technology and the very real limits of that power to crush the nationalist resistance of a smaller, poorer, and weaker nation, North Vietnam, and make it conform to American purposes. The Vietnam War led Americans to question the myths of American global, political, cultural, and moral supremacy. Certainly the image of defeat associated with Vietnam has troubled Americans greatly in the last two decades.

This is not to say that the dominant elements in the American core are Asian. The core comprises elements from throughout the world and is in a constant process of change and modification. The concept of the core can be contested at any given time. It cannot be claimed, in other words, that the American core of the Puritan period is the same as the core in the 1990s. An understanding of the multicultural and global dimensions of the core leads to an inclusive definition of "American" and a broad understanding of American society. The question remains: Why is it so important to some to deny links to Asia and other lands? Why do some people fight to defend Eurocentric assertions that Western civilization is purely and uniquely self-invented?

Asian Americans and the Defining of "American"

Asian American history begins in the U.S. West. It is in the West that the peoples, politics, and economies of Asia and the United States met and mixed at the grassroots level. This is particularly true in Hawai`i and along the Pacific Coast, where a large population of Asian/Pacific Americans has resided since the nineteenth century. The large concentration of Asian immigrants in the U.S. West evoked an anti-Asian exclusion movement and racist policies.

Although expansionists were eager to penetrate Asia, they were not eager to confront Asians in their own western mainland territories. Roger Daniels has noted: "Among westerners, particularly Californians, a defensive rather than expansive frontier psychology often developed. Although Californians dreamed of expansion, territorial and commercial, ever westward toward Japan, China, and India, they often felt that their rocky coastline should serve as a bulwark or dike against the human sea of Asian immigration which seemed to threaten their way of life." Daniels calls this the "defensive frontier" psyche, which set a trend that "modified the fundamental American attitudes toward immigration nearly a half-century before the rest of the nation."[7]

This defensive frontier psyche is exemplified by the memorial written in 1921 by the James J. Sexton Post #224 Veterans of Foreign Wars of Aberdeen, Washington, and addressed to the secretary of the interior and U.S. Bureau of Indian Affairs. In advocating the exclusion of Japanese immigrants from leasing rights on the Yakima Indian Reservation, the memorial declared:

> We are rapidly approaching the following condition throughout the West: Either the Jap must leave, or the white man will have to live [sic]. The white man cannot live in competition with the Jap. Are you going to allow the future inhabitant of Our West to be a Mongolian, or a Hybred [sic]. Will you save America for the American; if so we urge you and request you to use all possible influence to put a stop to the leasing of lands to the Japanese either directly or through renegade white men.[8]

Asians became the accepted target of nativist-racist antagonism, which served to unify the increasingly heterogeneous white population in the U.S. West. An American ethnicity could be achieved through the assertion that it was not Asian. Asians were a necessary "Other" in defining who was an American. The idea of assimilability was utilized. Europeans were assimilable. Asians were declared unassimilable. In arguing for the unassimilability of Asians, exclusionists aimed to affirm a racist foundation for the American nation.[9] Overriding all other factors in the construction of this exclusive definition of "American" was the assertion that Asians were unalterably alien, naturally inclined to Oriental despotism, and incapable of assimilating to democratic self-government.

Asian immigrants were seen as the vanguard of the Yellow Peril. The anti-Asian movement culminated in the total exclusion of Asian immigration and the prohibition of naturalization. This movement portrayed the Asian in America as un-American and led to the enactment of anti-Asian laws, which enshrined this assumption of the Asian as alien.

The responses of westerners to Asian immigrants fixed the political psyche of Americans in their dealings with Asia in the twentieth century. American westerners responded to Asian immigrants as if they were an invading army. How Asian immigrants settled in the hostile West and struggled to enjoy rights equal to those of white European Americans is part of the history of a cultural confrontation that extended to diplomatic confrontation: Anti-Asian discrimination was a national as well as local policy. Discriminatory national policies of naturalization and immigration adversely affected diplomatic relations between the United States and Japan before World War II. U.S. historians underestimate the impact of anti-Japanese legislation, particularly the 1924 Immigration Act excluding Japanese immigration. Such acts undermined moderate elements in Japan, leading to a deterioration of U.S.-Japanese relations in the critical decades before the Pacific war.

U.S. naturalization laws kept Asian immigrants foreign. While these immigrants were systematically denied every avenue of legally becoming American, they were consistently faulted for remaining foreign. Exclusionist forces perceived Asian immigrants as incapable of being American. In the eyes of exclusionists, the melting pot of America could never be hot enough to melt Asian immigrants into the national culture. Asian Americans have challenged the exclusive definition of "American" and have, by this search for justice, broadened the inclusiveness of American ideals. Legal challenges by Asian Americans have helped define and refine legal interpretations, and this process has cast new light on the workings of our justice system and our ideals.

Takao Ozawa and Bhagat Singh Thind contested for naturalization rights. In a legal brief for the U.S. Supreme Court, Ozawa argued: "In name, General Benedict Arnold was an American, but at heart he was a traitor. In name, I am not an American, but at heart I am a true American."[10] Naturalization laws stated that "whites" and those of African nativity and descent were allowed to become naturalized. Ozawa, who was of Japanese descent, and Thind, who was of South Asian descent, argued for inclusion in naturalization rights by challenging the category "white." In the 1922 Ozawa decision the Supreme Court judged "white" to mean Caucasian and affirmed a racial prerequisite for naturalization that excluded all those of the Mongolian race. But in the 1923 Thind decision, because South Asians were, by the racial classifications of that time, considered to be Aryan and thus Caucasian, the U.S. Supreme Court refined its exclusionary definition for naturalization by now relying on the "understanding of the common man" rather than on a "scientific" basis of racial classification. Thus, the U.S. Supreme Court affirmed the legality of the useful exclusionary category of "alien ineligible to citizenship." But Asian immigrants continued to fight for naturalization rights.

Asian immigrants persisted as active agents in the making of their own history. They challenged the fluctuating boundaries of who was and was not included in America. They disputed exclusion through legal and diplomatic channels and through creative resistance and organization. By taking a stand, they became a permanent part of the American experience.

Starting with the repeal of the Chinese Exclusion Act in 1943, Asian immigrants chipped at the barriers to citizenship by arguing that anti-Asian discriminatory policies were not "democratic," especially in view of the war effort. Filipinos and South Asians, who were also allies in arms, joined in the challenge. As Trinidad A. Rojo argued: "From the standpoint of biology, color line, history, anthropology, logic, justice, fairness, and world's democracy, your naturalization law is consistently inconsistent toward us. It is a record against you rather than against us."[11] In 1946, Filipinos and South Asians won rights to naturalization and a small immigration quota. In 1952, the United States finally recognized that people of all races had the right to immigrate to the United States and to become naturalized citizens.

Asian Americans persisted and built stable communities through supportive coalitions. For example, the Filipino community in the Yakima Valley in Washington secured leasing rights on the Yakima Indian Reservation by directly contesting classification as "alien."[12] Though Filipinos were U.S. nationals and held U.S. passports, before World War II it was generally held that anti-alien land laws were applicable to them. Therefore, Filipinos were not allowed to directly lease land on the Yakima Indian Reservation before World War II, since the Bureau of Indian Affairs chose to adhere to state law denying this right. Filipinos circumvented the law by arranging to farm through labor agreements with Indian allottees. To Filipinos, farming was a means of creating jobs for themselves during the Great Depression. But as Filipinos left migrant-labor status and became independent reservation farmers, they collided with white farmers, who sought to exclude Filipinos from the privilege of leasing reservation land.

After the passage of the 1937 amended Washington alien land law, which defined "alien" as "noncitizen," there was a crackdown on Filipino reservation farmers. Following a mass arrest of Filipino farmers, the Filipino Community of Yakima Valley, Inc., was organized in August 1937 to "fight for justice" and settle the issue of their legal status and rights. They circulated petitions, sought the support of labor unions and civic groups, wrote to President Franklin D. Roosevelt, to the speaker of the U.S. House of Representatives, to President Manuel Quezon of the Commonwealth of the Philippines, to the resident commissioner of the Philippines, and to other officials, and worked out an agreement with the Yakima Tribal Council. Meanwhile, through the united efforts of Filipinos across Washington, the test case of Pio DeCano, a Filipino leader in Seattle, reached the state supreme court. In February 1941, the court ruled that the 1937 amended Washington alien land law was unconstitutional due to the technicality that the law had been improperly titled. Finally, in 1942, because of the determined efforts of these Asian Americans, who forced the government into the embarrassing position of having to either support or openly discriminate against an ally in arms, the Yakima Valley Filipinos secured leasing rights on the reservation and ensured for themselves a permanent home in Yakima Valley, ironically on Indian land.[13]

Yet exclusionists persisted in viewing Asia and Asian Americans as alien to American culture. They refused to acknowledge non-Western elements in the American core and professed that western Europe alone had created the idea of democracy and freedom. In truth, the idea of freedom and revolution has a long history in Asia. Confucianism carries the seeds of revolution, making it the duty of the people to overthrow a tyrant and to institute a humanistic government working for the benefit and welfare of all. Asian immigrants recognized injustice; they protested and opposed oppression not because they were "Americanized" but because their own traditions had taught them to resist injustice. As one Chinese rhyme from San Francisco's Chinatown goes:

> So, liberty is your national principle;
> Why do you practice autocracy?
> You don't uphold justice, you Americans,
> You detain me in prison, guard me closely.
> Your officials are wolves and tigers,
> All ruthless, all wanting to bite me.
> An innocent man implicated, such an injustice!
> When can I get out of this prison and free my mind?[14]

After the valiant defense of Bataan and Corregidor by Filipino and American troops, as Manuel Buaken wrote, the United States suddenly discovered that Filipinos were "one with . . . freedom-loving 'westerners.' One in courage. One in ideals." But Buaken asserted: "It is not that we have changed, it is only that your knowledge of us is widened now. Knowledge of the fundamental unity of our peoples has been pictured for all the world to know on the great screen of this world catastrophe. Bataan has been a drama of 'American' character reading."[15]

Asian American history teaches us about the continuing process of "inventing" America through interactions of ideas from around the world and across time. As Carlos Bulosan pointed out in his 1946 book *America Is in the Heart*, people throughout time and history have been struggling for and contributing to the formation of "America," which is still an unfinished dream. Despite the dated use of gendered terminology, Bulosan has written one of the best statements about "America":

> It is but fair to say that America is not a land of one race or one class of men. We are all Americans that have toiled and suffered and known oppression and defeat, from the first Indian that offered peace in Manhattan to the last Filipino pea pickers. America is not bound by geographical latitudes. America is not merely a land or an institution. America is in the hearts of men that died for freedom; it is also in the eyes of men that are building a new world. America is a prophecy of a new society of men: of a system that knows no sorrow or strife or suffering. America is a warning to those who would try to falsify the ideals of freemen.
>
> America is also the nameless foreigner, the homeless refugee, the hungry boy begging for a job and the black body dangling on a tree. America is the illiterate immigrant who is ashamed that the world of books and intellectual opportunities is closed to him. We are all that nameless foreigner, that homeless refugee, that hungry boy, that illiterate immigrant and that lynched black body. All of us, from the first Adams to the last Filipino, native born or alien, educated or illiterate—*We are America!* [16]

Asian/Pacific Americans' resistance to injustice challenged the United States to uphold the principles of equality and justice. Their persistence in seeking justice resulted in rectification, even if it took a half century in one instance and a century in another instance. In the first instance, Gordon Hirabayashi's conviction for resisting the internment of Japanese Americans during World War II was overturned in 1987 by the U.S. Court of Appeals, Ninth Circuit, on the basis of recently uncovered evidence that the U.S. government knowingly suppressed, altered, and destroyed evidence proving that there existed no military necessity for the removal and internment of Japanese Americans during World War II. Moreover, after a concerted redress movement by Japanese Americans, Congress passed and the president signed the Civil Liberties Act of 1988, which issued

an apology and paid monetary compensation to redress the unjust relocation and internment of Japanese Americans during World War II.
Hirabayashi's guiding principle for his resistance and half a century of
struggle was that idealism is realism. That is, in confusing times, your
ideals are your only realistic source for your actions.

In the second instance, the persistence of native Hawaiian protest and
resistance to the U.S.-assisted illegal overthrow of the constitutional government of the Kingdom of Hawai`i in 1893 resulted in the passage of the
Akaka Joint Resolution (Public Law 103-150), which was signed into law
on 23 November 1993 and which apologized for the complicity of the
U.S. government in the illegal overthrow of the Kingdom of Hawai`i in
1893, an overthrow that led to the deprivation of native Hawaiian rights
of self-determination, and pledged to acknowledge the ramifications of
the overthrow of the monarchy in order to work toward reconciliation
with the native Hawaiian people. Native Hawaiian resistance to injustice
is expressed in the state motto of Hawai`i: "Ua mau ke ea o ka 'aina i ka
pono" (The life of the land is perpetuated in righteousness).

Two lessons drawn from these long struggles for justice are that "idealism *is* realism" and that "ua mau ke ea o ka 'aina i ka pono"—the life of
the land is perpetuated in righteousness.

Demographic and Economic Significance

In rethinking the role of Asian Americans in the history of the U.S. West,
I am reminded of a *haole* (white) docent who led a tour of missionary
houses in Honolulu, enthusiastically explaining that a *haole* Christian missionary had built Kawaiahao Church by carving coral blocks at Pearl Harbor and dragging the heavy blocks several miles to the Honolulu church
site. This was quite a feat, the docent thought. She spoke only of the missionary and never mentioned that it was native Hawaiians who had carved
the coral blocks, dragged them from Pearl Harbor to Honolulu, constructed the church, and worshipped in it. It is in this way that we see only
the power-holders without seeing the real builders of the edifice of U.S.
history.

In the mid-nineteenth century, Asian immigrants represented a major
segment of the population of the U.S. West. Chinese composed 9.2
percent of the population in California in 1860; in 1870 they were 28.5
percent in Idaho and 9.5 percent in Montana, and in 1880 they were
8.7 percent in Nevada.[17] But anti-Asian immigration exclusion acts distorted the population composition of the U.S. West. We can ask what exactly would have been the racial composition of the U.S. West if Asian

Japanese Americans' persistent protests against internment prompted the U.S. government to overturn the wartime convictions of Gordon Hirabayashi, Fred Korematsu, and Min Yasui, who were arrested for resisting internment. The protests also led to the passage of the 1988 Civil Liberties Act, in which the government apologized to Japanese Americans and paid reparations. Clipping courtesy of Gordon Hirabayashi. Photo courtesy of the *Walla Walla Union-Bulletin,* reprinted with permission.

This photo depicts members of one of the native Hawaiian resistance movements, the Protect Kaho'olawe Ohana, taking part in a 1987 religious procession on the island of Kaho'olawe. In the 1993 Akaka Joint Resolution, the U.S. government issued an official apology for its complicity in the overthrow of the Kingdom of Hawai`i in 1893. Photo courtesy of Franco Salmoiraghi, reprinted with permission.

immigration had been allowed to continue without the imposition of these acts. Yet though immigration restrictions altered and stunted the demographics, significant Asian American populations were concentrated in cities, in certain regions, and within particular occupations.

Asian immigration was vital to the economic growth of the U.S. West, but listing Asian contributions creates misunderstanding because it means that the Anglo is still the focal point. In the context of the U.S. West, when I am asked to discuss the "contributions" of Asian Americans, I feel I am actually being asked, "How much did your group contribute to the Anglo capitalist system of oppression of native peoples and destruction of the environment?" Yet I believe that it is necessary to fully acknowledge the critical role of Asian Americans in the transformation, for good or bad, of the U.S. West. To ignore this Asian American role is to discount or trivialize the role of Asian Americans as builders of our country and to acknowledge, as either villains or heroes, only the elite.

Asians supplied the labor to build the railroads, which provided the transportation infrastructure for commercial growth. In addition to building the western half of the transcontinental railroad, Asian laborers constructed and maintained many of the other railroads in the West. Asian laborers were pivotal to agricultural development in the West. Sucheng Chan has documented the integral role that Chinese immigrants played in developing California agriculture. She asserts, "Working as truck gardeners, vegetable peddlers, commission merchants, farm cooks, tenant farmers, and owner-operators of farms, thousands of Chinese brought new land under cultivation, experimented with various crops, and provided much of the labor needed to plant, harvest, pack, preserve, and sell the crops in almost every major agricultural region of California."[18] Japanese, Filipinos, Koreans, and Asian Indians also furnished the labor needed by West Coast agriculturalists. And Japanese farmers innovated on and dominated in the cultivation of many kinds of vegetable, fruit, and floral crops. Asian labor was indispensable in the sugar and pineapple industry in Hawai`i, in the Alaskan salmon canneries, and in the lumber industry. Asian immigrants helped build U.S-Asian trade and operated small shops serving both ethnic and nonethnic customers.

A striking example of the multicultural nature of the labor force in the West is that of native Hawaiians in the early Pacific Northwest. Hawai`i became an important waystation for the trans-Pacific sea trade soon after its contact with the West in 1778. British and American ships on their way to and from the Pacific Northwest for furs to trade in China would stop for rest and provisions in Hawai`i. Hawaiians were known for their seamanship, and a system of contract labor was developed in which Hawaiians (known variously as Kanakas, Owyhees, Blue Men, or Sandwich Islanders) were employed as sailors. Thus, Hawaiians first came to the Pacific Northwest as sailors, accompanying the early expeditions inland. Later they were recruited as the first skilled and unskilled laborers for the fur trade. Numbering more than a thousand during the first half of the nineteenth century, Hawaiian communities were scattered throughout the Pacific Northwest, including Fort Vancouver and Fort Walla Walla. Many Hawaiians intermarried with Indians, and their descendants still recognize their Hawaiian origins.[19]

Significant Lives, Significant Voices

Asian Americans lived in the West. They shaped the western landscape through cultivation and toil. They were not simply excluded. They were not just passive victims to be conquered and subjugated. They built and they molded and they struggled.

As an Asian American myself, I am particularly aware that the vital role of Asian Americans in the history of the U.S. West goes unrecognized. I believe we need to hear the voices of Asian Americans themselves in order to understand their place in history and gain a full account of the western U.S. experience. For example, Trinidad Rojo presents Filipino-American view of the process of European conquest and colonization of the United States: "When the Europeans came to this continent, they did not take the trouble of applying for naturalization rights to the Indians. We understand, they simply declared themselves the new bosses of the land; and the Indians left by bullets and bayonets were told to preserve themselves in a museum of living species, called INDIAN RESERVATIONS." Rojo went on to point out: "We came here because Americans went to the Philippines. . . . I may say that America invited itself with the gun to the Philippines."[20]

An important alternative perspective to traditional accounts of Japanese-American internment in World War II is provided by the Fair Play Committee (FPC) of the Heart Mountain, Wyoming, concentration camp, which opposed the drafting of Japanese Americans from the camps without restoration of their freedom and civil rights. The Fair Play Committee reasoned:

> Without any hearings, without due process of law as guaranteed by the Constitution and Bill of Rights, without any charges filed against us, without any evidence of wrongdoing on our part, one hundred and ten thousand innocent people were kicked out of their homes, literally up-

rooted from where they have lived for the greater part of their life, and herded like dangerous criminals into concentration camps with barb wire fence and military police guarding it, AND THEN, WITHOUT RECTIFICA-TION OF THE INJUSTICES COMMITTED AGAINST US NOR WITHOUT RESTORATION OF OUR RIGHTS AS GUARANTEED BY THE CONSTITUTION, WE ARE ORDERED TO JOIN THE ARMY THRU *DISCRIMINATORY PROCEDURES* INTO A *SEGREGATED COMBAT UNIT!* Is that the American way? *NO!* The FPC be-lieves that unless such actions are opposed *NOW,* and steps taken to rem-edy such injustices and discriminations *IMMEDIATELY* the future of all minorities and the future of this democratic nation is in danger. . . .

We are not being disloyal. We are not evading the draft. We are all loyal Americans fighting for JUSTICE AND DEMOCRACY RIGHT HERE AT HOME. So, restore our rights as such, rectify the injustices of evacuation, of the concentration, of the detention, and of the pauperization as such. In short, treat us in accordance with the principles of the Constitution.[21]

When interrogated by the government, Frank Emi, a leader of the Fair Play Committee, reiterated, "I believe it is more my duty to try to uphold those supreme laws of the United States which is in the Constitution, and you could say that you are fighting for democracy abroad, but if you lose democracy at home what have you won?"[22] The actions of the Fair Play Committee and Frank Emi are testimony to the ways in which Asian Americans were active agents in the making of U.S. history. Their voices must be heard.

In writing a more inclusive history, one need not rely only on the voices of excluders to hear the experiences of Asian Americans. Traditional sources exist: histories written by Asian communities, as well as documents from the ethnic press, letters, and diaries. These ethnic community histo-ries present an alternative perspective to the usual view espoused by the ex-cluders. Japanese immigrant histories, for example, give us an insight into how the immigrants viewed the anti-Japanese movement. One immigrant history written in 1935 displays a clear understanding of the racist nature of the exclusion movement: "Exclusion of the Japanese was based initially on the same principle concerning colored races such as the blacks and the Chinese." This history analyzed the political usage of assimilation by the exclusionists: "Yet the self-contradiction in the rationale of the American exclusionists is that the Japanese must be excluded since we do not assim-ilate. Rejecting our naturalization rights, excluding the Japanese socially and economically and thereby closing our road to assimilation, the Amer-icans still demand that we assimilate. Such is like tying someone's feet and then ordering him to run, and finally clubbing him to death because he cannot run."[23]

Manuel Buaken's conclusion to his 1948 book *I Have Lived with the American People* contains a message as relevant to the United States entering the twenty-first century as it was to the United States after World War II:

> I have lived with the American people. Here are your lives as we see them, we Filipinos here in the United States, and here are the lives that we must lead, we Filipinos. Your lives, our lives, could all be better, must all be better, or the world cannot stand. Life must be more abundant for all of us, and unless people know that there are no "superior" or "inferior" races, no god-given rights to rule over other races, unless Americans know this there can never be a new order, can never be any realization of the dreams we all hold for peace and prosperity and liberty for all of us.[24]

Oral histories are useful sources of experiences often not recorded in formal documents. Oral histories of Asian immigrant women in particular give a compelling historical perspective on the plight of working mothers. One Korean mother of five recalled her life in Sacramento, California: "I did the laundry for Caucasians and Korean bachelors. I had to wash by hand and iron. I got paid about eighty cents or one dollar per day [in 1916]. . . . I never went to bed before 1:00 a.m. and had to get up at 4:00 a.m. to cook for my husband who had stomach trouble."[25] Child care was a critical issue for working mothers, whose labor was vital as a supplement to the meager incomes of their husbands, who were paid unfairly because of race. A Japanese immigrant woman who had to leave her young children in a plantation nursery while she worked in the sugar fields in Hawai`i remembered: "The younger child was too young to know, but the older one used to cry every day when I left them at the baby home. Even now I can hear her wailing."[26] Some of the most riveting and instructive oral histories are told by Southeast Asian refugees who give us alternative views of the Vietnam War. A South Vietnamese woman now living in Oklahoma recalled the realities of war: "I had seen children without arms and babies who were killed by the land bombs. Sometimes the babies were in their mothers' arms when they were killed. I did not always know who was doing this or why, but after a while it did not seem to matter. Too many friends did not come back [from the war], and I did not want to lose my sons, too."[27]

There are less-recognized sources of the Asian American experience. Poetry, rhymes, and songs give us insights into the inner thoughts of the immigrants and reveal an awareness of injustice, hopes, and visions for the future. For example, these Asian immigrants were young, ambitious, and full of hope as they departed their lands of birth. Their dreams are summed up in the poem "Ode on Leaving My Home Town," by Kenji Abe, a Japanese immigrant who first began working the railroad sections in Washington State in 1906. He wrote:

> Over the horizon of the wide Pacific,
> Entertaining high ambitions,
> I looked for eternal happiness.
> Great love . . .
> Huge efforts . . .
> Large land . . .
> Vast sky . . .
> I survey my future path.
> On my two shoulders I bear a mission;
> In my heart hope swells.
> Goodbye, my home country.
> Farewell![28]

Teiko Tomita, a Japanese immigrant in Washington State, conveyed in a poem the loneliness and monotony felt by most new settlers in the U.S. West. These immigrants missed their families and friends and often found that the only way to distinguish one day from another might be the sun's rising and setting:

> Neighbors are five miles far away
> Many days without seeing anyone
> Today, too,
> Without seeing anyone
> The sun sets[29]

Sasakura Ushu, a Japanese immigrant working on a sugar plantation in Hawai'i, spoke of a connectedness to nature and a longing for a home far away in time and space: "Every evening, touched by the nostalgic sound of chirping insects, I left a stand of sugarcane for them while cutting the rest."[30] A Japanese immigrant satirical poem *(senryu)* by Koyo captures the lament of many westerners:

> . . . and early to rise . . .
> No matter how early, though,
> It don't make me rich![31]

Unusual sources exist, such as Wong Sam and Assistants' *English-Chinese Phrase Book*, published and distributed by Wells, Fargo in 1875 (revised in 1877). The phrase book gives us a stark look at frontier life, listing some 250 ways to die in the U.S. West including:

> He came to his death by homicide.
> He was murdered by a thief.
> He committed suicide.
> He was choked to death with a lasso, by a robber.
> He was starved to death in prison.
> He was frozen to death in the snow.
> ....
> He was killed by an assassin.
> ....
> He was smothered in his room.
> ....
> He was shot dead by his enemy.
> He was poisoned to death by his friend.[32]

Asian immigrants were never silent, though many non-Asians may have wanted them to be. Their voices are proof of the significance, the undeniable significance, of the lives of the people themselves who give life, dignity, and restoration of authenticity to our multicultural western experience.

The Changing Demography of the West

Asian Americans have persisted as a discrete ethnic group despite repeated forecasts that they would disappear or assimilate into oblivion. Moreover, new immigrants from Asia are further changing the composition, especially of the U.S. West. Changes in immigration laws since 1965 resulted in Asians becoming the highest number of non–Western hemisphere immigrants. The number of Asian/Pacific Americans has doubled with each census since 1970. This population growth is reflected in our education system in the U.S. West—with large percentages of Asian Americans in the major universities, particularly in California and Hawai`i. In growing numbers and with increasing participation in electoral politics, Asian/Pacific Americans represent a significant political presence in the U.S. West, particularly in Hawai`i, Washington, and California, the last being a state typically seen as central to the outcome of the presidential election.

In the U.S. West, the majority-minority society is almost a reality. Hawai`i is already a majority-minority population. California will soon be. How the U.S. West handles this new phenomenon will be instructive to the nation as a whole. The 1992 Los Angeles riots clearly illustrate that in the U.S. West, race relations are beyond black-white issues. The national press may have covered the uprising as an African-American reaction to the *Rodney King* verdict, but in truth, the event involved the complex issues and relationships of inner-city Latinos and Korean Americans as well.

What about the future? Certainly the rapidly changing demographics of the West will influence this question. I hope that the U.S. West will be a vital area that recognizes and values diversity. Our diverse American society is a microcosm of the global community. How the United States deals with its own multiculturalism is instructive in how it relates to other nation-states.

I welcome the new western history, which is more inclusive and cognizant of the complexities of the western U.S. experience. But it must be emphasized that there is nothing particularly "new" in the new western history. The recognition of a multicultural, multiethnic U.S. West is not an original idea. Monoculturalism has never had a place in the history of the U.S. West. Asian Americans and other people of color knew that the West was multicultural, no matter what traditional historians wrote. Still, we must be wary of those who are too quick to appropriate research on the histories of people of color, often without acknowledging the pioneering works done by historians of color. We cannot rush to synthesize without thoroughly understanding the diversity.

There are those who oppose an inclusive history. These opponents fear the ungluing of American society—the glue being a Eurocentric cultural hegemony. They advocate a return to Eurocentric "basics" and "standards" in writing "American" history. This battle to bring recognition not only to Asian American history but also to the histories of all U.S. peoples of color and to women's history raises several questions: Who controls the writing of history? Whose representation of whose collective memory gets recorded?

I believe we need to recognize a shared memory of the many diverse groups inhabiting the U.S. West and the nation as a whole. We need to recognize the West as populated by women and men and people of *all* colors. By recognizing and incorporating the views from the "margins," we gain a more inclusive and fuller history and achieve a greater understanding of the multiple centers and, more important, the whole. The changing demographics of the United States will further challenge our writing of U.S. history to better reflect the understanding of an increasingly diverse United States. We need to chart our future with vision and clarity. Rather than resist change, we must welcome innovation and think beyond the limits of our current system. We must rethink, reconceptualize, and re-envision a multicultural history of the U.S. West that recognizes our whole voices.

Notes

I would like to thank Mikiso Hane, Sucheta Mazumdar, and Gary Okihiro for their careful reading of this manuscript and their suggestions. I would also like to thank Stephen Sumida, Davianna McGregor, Gordon Hirabayashi, Tom Fujita-Rony, Richard Kim, Evelyn R. Flores, K. Scott Wong, and Carrie Waara for their help and suggestions.

An earlier version of this essay appeared under the title "Significant Lives: Asia and Asian Americans in the History of the U. S. West," by Gail M. Nomura. Previously published in the *Western Historical Quarterly* 25 (Spring 1994): 69–88. Copyright by Western History Association. Reprinted by permission.

1. Robert Underwood, the current delegate to Congress from Guam, was the chair of the Kumision I Fino' Chamoru (Chamoru Language Commission) in 1983 when it introduced a new orthography that was better reflective of the pronunciation of the indigenous people of Guam. If one followed the rules of the new orthography, the name of the indigenous people and the name of their language would be spelled "Chamoru" (some at first spelled in "Chamorru," but this is no longer used). The commission did allow for the continuation of traditional spellings of proper nouns to avoid confusion. Therefore, people continued to use the traditional "Chamorro" spelling while others began using the "Chamoru" spelling. More than just a spelling issue, the core of this debate as to how to spell the very name of this distinctive people is the issue of the colonized status of Chamoru as symbolized by a spelling of their name by others in a manner not reflective of their own pronunciation. A prominent indigenous activist group calls itself Chamoru Nation. The question remains: who is in charge of a people's language?

2. Reginald Horsman, *Race and Manifest Destiny: The Origins of American Racial Anglo-Saxonism* (Cambridge, Mass., 1981), 287.

3. Hawai`i and Alaska are usually excluded from the history of the West. But Asian American history requires the inclusion and in-depth study of these two states. It is significant that debate over statehood rested not only on arguments of contiguous union but also on questions of common history and culture. John Whitehead argues persuasively for the commonalities of Hawai`i with the more traditional West and points out that Hawai`i was part of "the first maritime Far West" and that "diplomatically, geographically, and historically Hawai`i has long and deep connections to the American West." See John Whitehead, "Hawai`i: The First and Last Far West?" *Western Historical Quarterly* 23 (May 1992): 177.

4. Donald F. Lach, *Asia in the Making of Europe* (Chicago, 1965).

5. H. G. Creel, *Confucius: The Man and the Myth* (New York, 1949), 5. For a fuller discussion, see Creel's chapter "Confucianism and Western Democracy," 254–78.

6. For example, see Sudarshan Kapur, *Raising Up a Prophet: The African-American Encounter with Gandhi* (Boston, 1992).

7. Roger Daniels, *Asian America: Chinese and Japanese in the United States since 1850* (Seattle, 1988), 3–4.

8. Memorial of James J. Sexton, Post #224, Veterans of Foreign Wars, 3 February 1921, RG 75, Seattle Federal Archives and Records Center, Seattle, Wash.

9. For example, see Alexander Saxton, *The Indispensable Enemy: Labor and the Anti-Chinese Movement in California* (Berkeley, 1971).

10. Yuji Ichioka, *The Issei: The World of the First Generation Japanese Immigrants, 1885–924* (New York, 1988), 219.

11. Trinidad Rojo, "An Appeal for U.S. Citizenship," *Philippine Mail*, 26 February 1940, reprinted in Hyung-chan Kim and Cynthia C. Mejia, *The Filipinos in America, 1898–1974: A Chronology and Fact Book* (Dobbs Ferry, N.Y., 1976), 104.

12. The Yakama Nation has revised the spelling of its name from "Yakima" to "Yakama."

13. See Gail M. Nomura, "Within the Law: The Establishment of Filipino Leasing Rights on the Yakima Indian Reservation,"*Amerasia Journal* 13 (1986–87): 99–117.

14. Marlon K. Hom, *Songs of Gold Mountain: Cantonese Rhymes from San Francisco Chinatown* (Berkeley, 1987), 85.

15. Manuel Buaken, *I Have Lived with the American People* (Caldwell, Idaho, 1948), 294.

16. Carlos Bulosan, *America Is in the Heart* (1946; reprint, Seattle, 1973), 189.

17. Daniels, *Asian America*, 70–71.

18. Sucheng Chan, *This Bittersweet Soil: The Chinese in California Agriculture, 1860–1910* (Berkeley, 1986), 403.

19. See E. Momilani Naughton, "Hawaiians in the Fur Trade: Cultural Influence on the Northwest Coast, 1811–1875" (Master's thesis, Western Washington University, Bellingham, 1983); Janice K. Duncan, *Minority without a Champion: Kanakas on the Pacific Coast, 1788–1850* (Portland, 1972).

20. Rojo, "An Appeal for U.S. Citizenship," 103–4.

21. Fair Play Committee Bulletin reprinted in Gail M. Nomura et al., eds., *Frontiers of Asian American Studies* (Pullman, Wash., 1989), 52.

22. Hearing Transcript, 4 April 1944, reprinted in ibid., 67.

23. Yakima Nihonjin-kai, *Yakima Heigen Nihonjin-shi* (The History of the Japanese in the Yakima Valley) (Yakima, Wash., 1935), 154.

24. Buaken, *Have Lived*, 333.

25. Asian Women United of California, eds., *Making Waves: An Anthology of Writings by and about Asian American Women* (Boston, 1989), 59.

26. Gail M. Nomura, "Issei Working Women in Hawaii," in ibid., 144.

27. Paul James Rutledge, *The Vietnamese Experience in America* (Bloomington, 1992), 18. For an excellent collection of Vietnamese oral histories, see James M. Freeman, *Hearts of Sorrow: Vietnamese-American Lives* (Stanford, 1989).

28. Poem cited in Kazuo Ito, *Issei: A History of Japanese Immigrants in North America*, trans. Shinichiro Nakamura and Jean S. Gerard (Seattle, 1973), 34–35.

29. Kazuo Ito, *Hokubei hyakunen zakura* (North American Hundred Years Cherries) (Tokyo, 1969), 519. For a fuller discussion of Tomita, see Gail M. Nomura, "Tsugiki, A Grafting: A History of a Japanese Pioneer Woman in Washington State," in *Women in Pacific Northwest History: An Anthology*, ed. Karen J. Blair (Seattle, 1988).

30. Ushu cited in Franklin Odo and Kazuko Sinoto, A *Pictorial History of the Japanese in Hawaii, 1885–1924* (Honolulu, 1985), 79.

31. Poem cited in Stephen H. Sumida, "Hawaii, the Northwest, and Asia: Localism and Local Literacy Developments in the Creation of an Asian Immigrant's Sensibility," *Seattle Review: Blue Funnel Line* 11 (Spring/Summer 1988): 13.

32. Jeffrey Paul Chan et al., *The Big Aiiieeeee! An Anthology of Chinese American and Japanese American Literature* (New York, 1991), 98.

Through Western Eyes:
Discovering Chinese Women in America

Sucheta Mazumdar

When Union Pacific met Central Pacific at Promontory Point in 1869, Bret Harte had the engine from the West snorting to its counterpart from the East:

> You brag of your East! *You* do?
> Why, I bring the East to *you!*
> All of the Orient, all Cathay,
> Find through me the shortest way.[1]

In this essay I want to explore the ways in which the American West indeed brought the Orient to the East and, in so doing, forged an Anglo-American cultural identity that served to bind the two halves of the nation together.

In our efforts to separate American history from its colonial connections with Europe, it is common to distance American ideological proclivities from those of western Europe. Orientalism, a style of thought based on an episte-mological distinction between "the Orient" and "the Occident"—the East and the West—is seen as a European discourse, specifically an Anglo-French discourse, a product and a legacy of the one-thousand-year contact with the Arab Islamic world and of the more immediate history of nineteenth-century colonialism. Orientalism formed the backdrop against which European na-tion-state identity and culture were formulated and strengthened. What I want to propose is that Orientalism was and is as much a part of the nine-teenth- and twentieth-century American discourse, but with one difference. If the Arab world and Islam, as representations of the Orient, served to set off European-Anglo-French culture and identity, as Edward Said has shown in his classic study, I propose that the Chinese and the Japanese have had the same role in the production of American material culture and national cultural identity and that the American West, with its greater familiarity and proxim-ity to both Asia and the Asian immigrants, has played a crucial role in the shaping of this discourse.

Edward Said has pointed to a specific development in nineteenth-century Orientalism. A distillation of essentialist ideas about the "Orient" focused on its habits of sensuality, depravity, aberrant mentality, lying and cheating, and backwardness; all of these aspects of the "Oriental character" then became part of a coherent explanation of the people and the place.[2] Before the Orientalist discourse came to dominate, American traders for example, even in the early nineteenth century, "of solid Puritan stock for the most part," had had very little to say about issues of polygamy or infanticide, prostitution, or even opium addiction in China.[3] In the late eighteenth and early nineteenth centuries, the differences between American and Chinese styles of clothing, of furniture, and of architecture were noted primarily by the East Coast–based American traders to China. The Chinese and their artifacts, though "curious" and "peculiar," were not considered so "alien" as to be inimitable. The vogue for chinoiseries in eighteenth-century New England is well known; Chinese-style gardens and porcelains were to be found in many wealthy American homes. One American diplomat, after his return from China to Philadelphia, brought over Chinese servants, named his house "China Retreat," and built a pagoda-like dome on his house and lived among entirely Chinese furnishings.[4] But by the mid-nineteenth century, this fascination for the curious and different in one's life was replaced by the notion of the exotic, which could not be imitated; it could only be observed at a distance. On the one hand, there was an increasing disdain for the Chinese "civilization" by East Coast intellectuals, as seen in Ralph Waldo Emerson's famous dismissal: "China, reverend dullness! hoary ideot!, all she can say at the convocation of nations must be—'I made the tea.'"[5] On the other hand, there was also a growing interest in the objectification of the exotic, an integral process of Orientalizing the East. And as I explore below, the discourse on Chinese women helped identify most clearly these fundamental differences.

The first known Chinese woman in the United States was Afong Moy, who was displayed sitting amid Chinese paraphernalia at the American Museum, the Brooklyn Institute, and various other New York locations between 1834 and 1847. In the latter year she shared star billing with Tom Thumb. When Afong Moy left for Boston, Barnum's Chinese Museum catered to the New Yorkers' curiosity about the "Celestial Empire" by producing Pwan-ye-koo and her maidservant in 1850. The small bound feet of both women were a prime feature of the advertisements announcing their displays. In both these cases, the allure of the women was heightened by the suggestion that they were upper-class; the illustrations of the women show them sitting demurely, their contours obscured by brocades and silk clothing. Barnum described Pwan-ye-koo's bound feet as an indication of her high social position, "a choice mark of distingué character."[6] Displays of "Siamese twins," troops of Chinese musicians, and acrobats both preceded and followed the exhibitions of Afong Moy and Pwan-ye-koo on the East Coast. However, it was the West's greater familiarity with Chinese women as prostitutes that was to shape immigration and judicial policies, not to mention popular cultural notions about the Chinese and particularly about their women.

In keeping with the emerging racist discourse on anatomy, a discussion begun as early as 1816 by George Cuvier, who sought to prove that genitalia varied according to race, it was posited that Chinese women had horizontal vaginas in keeping with their slanted eyes.[7] As late as the 1880s, J. W. Buel, accompanied by two friends and a policeman, conducted a "scientific experiment" in San Francisco's Chinatown: "In order to set at rest a question which has been fiercely debated by students of nature . . . our investigation justi-fies the assertion that there are no physical differences between the Chinese and American women, their conformation being identical."[8] That it should have taken Buel up to the 1880s to ascertain the facts is surprising. For as early as 1851, Frank Soule, in his *Annals of San Francisco,* could write that although most of the people in the city were "generally orderly, obedient and useful," the Chinese were an exception. They were "bringing with them a number of their women who were among the filthiest and most abandoned of their sex."[9] At this time there were only seven Chinese women in San Francisco, and at least two of them worked as domestics; there were well over a thousand other prostitutes of various nationalities. But this did not deter a municipal com-mittee from visiting Chinatown in 1854 and declaring that most Chinese women were prostitutes.[10] By midcentury, an iconography of the sexualized woman had developed in Europe, a convention of representation of the pros-titute. Like Manet's *Olympia,* which has been discussed in detail as drawing on a convention of early erotic photography by having the central figure con-front the observer directly, Ah Toy, one of the better known of the Chinese prostitutes in San Francisco, was illustrated in the *San Francisco Chronicle* wearing a tight-fitting outfit and sitting in an Olympia-like pose offering her-self up to the observer.[11] The exotic "Oriental" and the erotic "Oriental" had come together.

Throughout the 1850s and 1860s, Chinese prostitutes were singled out for raids by the Vigilance Committees and were frequently taken to court for keeping "disorderly houses." The viewpoint that all Chinese women were prostitutes gained currency through these and assorted other raids; by 1866 "An Act for the Suppression of Chinese Houses of Ill-Fame" was passed by the California State Legislature.[12] Under the supposition that the Chinese were inclined to use all housing for such illegal purposes, it was now possible for landlords to deny housing to Chinese. The law also made it profitable to give information to officials about these alleged houses of ill fame. This pattern was followed elsewhere in the American West. In Colorado, Wyoming, Utah, and Nevada the furor over Chinese prostitutes in the 1870s would have sug-gested that there were thousands of them; the reality was closer to what was found in Denver: out of 360 identified Denver prostitutes, 204 were white, 44 were black, 2 were Mexican, and 3 were "Oriental."[13] The Page Act, intro-duced in California in 1870 and passed by Congress in 1875, was entitled "An Act to Prevent the Kidnapping and Importation of Mongolian, Chinese, and Japanese Females for Demoralizing Purposes." It assumed, in effect, that all Asian women coming into the country were doing so for "criminal and de-moralizing purposes" unless proven otherwise.[14] In addition to the immigra-tion officials, the American Consul in Hong Kong also was to ascertain that the Chinese women were not coming for "lewd and immoral purposes." The women had to have their photographs taken and "swear to a certain state of facts" before they were allowed to board the ship.[15] Given that William Sanger found that one-fourth of the male population of most American cities visited prostitutes and that there were prostitutes of every race and nationality in every city, the special attention given to Chinese prostitution is a reflection of the prurient interest in "Oriental depravity," which was to occupy the American media for decades to come.[16]

Nothing denoted the dangers of Chinese depravity quite as effectively as the use of opium and "the dens of infamy" in Chinatowns. The Opium War (1839–42) had captured the American imagination, and it was almost as if there could be no discussion of the Chinese without a mention of opium; editorials and newspaper articles usually discussed the negative effects of Chinese immigration and Chinese vices in the same sentence. Even a description of violence against the Chinese brought in a mention of opium; the reporter of the *Rocky Mountain News* covering the aftermath of the 1880 riot in Denver, in which hundreds of Chinese had been beaten up and at least one killed and the Chinese residential area burned to the ground, found, "There was nothing left whole . . . and the rooms so recently the abode of ignorance, vice, and shame, contained nothing beyond the horrid stench emitted by the little wads of opium."[17] Perhaps the fear and fascination with opium had less to do with the Chinese than with the emerging Christian temperance movement, particularly in the West.[18] What if, in addition to alcohol, the masses turned to opium? For on Denver's Arapahoe Street, the opium joints had been found to be catering to Caucasian women.[19] As has been discussed by several scholars, including Barbara Epstein, the Christian Temperance Union was a central organ of the Victorian women's cult of culture and domesticity.[20] And all excesses, whether alcohol or opium, were a threat to this paradigm of domesticity.

The Chinese prostitute embodied the sexualized woman who threatened the domestic ideal and symbolized both disease and depravity. As early as the 1850s in California, General Mariano Vallejo had noted that Chinese immigration was "very harmful to the moral and material development of the country, to the spread of the white race and the healthfulness of San Francisco, the spot in which were congregated most of the Chinese women, who . . . had made it a duty to keep the hospitals always filled with syphilitics."[21] By 1876, the president of the American Medical Association declared Chinese syphilis more deadly than any other form; it was but one step to the argument that the Chinese women were poisoning the Anglo-Saxon blood.[22] Fears of Oriental pederasty and disease came together in Denver, where the presence of an estimated 450 Chinese out of a total population of 40,000 in 1880 had nevertheless made the issue of Chinese labor immigration a major election-year issue. A letter to the editor, supporting Chinese exclusion, declaimed, "Chinese harlots have diseased small boys of ten years of age and upwards, of some of the most respected citizens."[23] Never mind the question of what boys of ten were doing visiting Chinese prostitutes, even as all Chinese women were being criminalized as prostitutes, Anglo-Saxon prostitutes were redeeming themselves by protecting ill-fated Chinese men from the fury of lynch mobs.

An unlikely emulator of Thomas Nast's famous depiction of Columbia defending Chinese men cowering at her feet was Liz Preston, a madam of a Denver brothel. Preston was said to have protected "four cowering Chinese" with a shotgun during the anti-Chinese riot of 31 October 1880. "Ten Amazonian beauties" apparently backed her up and managed to save some thirty-four Chinese men. As William Roberts, a Denver fireman and deputy sheriff, noted in his journal, "That day the pariahs, the outcasts of society, the denizens of Holladay Street, the center of the red light district, put themselves in the hall of fame. . . . And perhaps the recording angel gave them one white mark."[24] And that may not have been all that white women gained from the emerging American discourse on the Chinese.

Issues such as the exclusion of the Chinese have been understood primarily in terms of the particularities of American settlement of the West, the opposition to cheap Chinese labor by organized white workers, the fear of being inundated by millions of Chinese immigrants, the American missionaries, the American racist discourse, and the "indispensable enemy" that enabled white workers' unionization.[25] Yet these propositions alone do not explain the Orientalizing of the Chinese and the simultaneous outpouring of interest in the conditions of Chinese immigrant women. I propose that the answers lie very much in an examination of the conditions of American women in the American West and their own struggles for equality within the family and in society.

As historians of women have pointed out, "One of the ironies of Jacksonian democracy was the simultaneous development of the 'true cult of womanhood' and rhetoric celebrating the equality of men."[26] As white women's political demands that too closely approached the prerogatives of men met with resistance, ideas about womanhood and separate spheres evolved. Middle-class women were caught up in the cult of domesticity, Christian marriage, and motherhood in rapidly urbanizing America. Women found it possible to continue to participate in politics and public action only through the resurgence of revival religion and through the claims for their "higher moral nature" that permitted activism in organizations seeking to correct injustices toward women and children. Others extended "motherhood" to include all of society, an argument that stressed women's role as "social housekeepers."[27] The catalogue of horrors experienced by Chinese women underlined the subversion of utilitarian positions of authors such as John Stuart Mill, who had argued that the condition of women in society was a barometer of its progress and level of civilization; it was now argued that countries that treated women poorly were further down on the evolutionary scale. The Anglo-Saxon races were superior because they treated their women better. As one 1835 editorial in *Atkinson's Casket* stated: "The fairest and weakest of the human race: mothers, sisters, daughters, names which thrill to the sensorium of Europeans . . . is in the case of the Chinese females a sorrowful task; pity in its extreme feeling is awakened. . . . In childhood slighted—in maidenhood sold—in mature womenhood shackled."[28] A longer and louder litany of the conditions of Chinese women may also have subverted more radical tendencies in the emerging women's movement in America by reiterating the message that American women already enjoyed an enviable position of freedom and equality.

In the post–Civil War period as American women struggled to reclaim lost political and public space, China became an example of the social decay and the immorality that must result when women are removed from the public sphere. American women, as missionaries and as wives of missionaries, had begun arriving in China in increasing numbers from the midcentury onward. Many focused on the status of women in China and the Chinese family as their particular realm of work. The resultant "evangelical enthnography," as Joan Jacobs Brumberg has labeled it, published in American women's magazines such as the *Ladies Repository* and then the *Ladies' Home Journal*, energetically took up issues of polygamy, female infanticide, and foot-binding. Popularization of the list of heathen atrocities committed against women in China was furthered by the foreign mission crusade, "a powerful and multifaceted sisterhood of agencies."[29] Between 1868 and 1873, women separated from the "parent boards" of male directors in each of the major American Protestant evangelical denominations and generated their own foreign mission organizations under exclusively female leadership. These missionaries focused on women's issues both at home and abroad. Through talks by China-returned missionaries to women's groups and through articles on Chinese, Indian, and other unfortunate women in the *Ladies' Home Journal* and scores of other women's magazines, the average urban American woman became intimately familiar with foot-binding, the tyranny of concubinage, harems, the seclusion of Chinese women, their illiterate status, and child marriages.[30] Moved by the sad tales narrated by a Mrs. John Gullik, a Presbyterian missionary to China in 1873, a group of women came together in San Francisco to form the California branch of the Women's Foreign Missionary Society. But enthusiasm for rescuing women in distant China soon waned. The officers of the organization decided that they needed "something tangible right here at home, to create a greater interest." And what better focus than Chinese prostitution, which threatened both Christian marriage and the health of Christian men? As Peggy Pascoe has written, "Protestant women quickly came to see Chinese immigrant prostitution as symbolic of the abuse of women that flourished in western cities."[31]

Additionally, Protestant culture had other challenges that had to be met in the American West. Women like Angie Newman, who was to leave her mark on the home mission field, found "the substitution of the Harem for the Home in all our western borders" a matter of grave concern.[32] The non-Mormon attacks on the degradations of polygamy for women had been going on for decades. And though Mormons in Utah struggled to retain the practice and leaders such as Franklin D. Richards and Brigham Young stressed the importance of religious duty and companionate marriage in Mormon marriages, the hostility toward polygamy was not readily deflected. Mormons abandoned the practice under federal pressure in 1890.[33] Polygamy in the West, therefore, had a particular resonance, and Chinese polygamy challenged the Protestant woman's faith in monogamy and companionate marriage; chastity was the bedrock upon which this marriage was to be built. Polygamous Chinese were seen as the very antithesis of these beliefs and had to be excluded. The men were declared physically and morally unclean; Chinese women were labeled both victims and breeders of "moral and physical pestilence" in the American West.[34]

The institution of bride-price in China, rather than dowry, with which the English and Euro-Americans were far more familiar in their own society, also led to the widespread discussion of all Chinese marriage as a form of slavery. This, coming on the heels of the Civil War, added particular fuel to the anti-Chinese movement. By extension, since all women, whether prostitutes or wives, were "purchased" and all men, as "coolies," were also enslaved, the Chinese came to be portrayed in some instances as no different from African Americans. Cartoons and drawings published on both coasts depicted the Chinese with African-American features. Fatness was associated in contemporary Britain and America with lax morals; as one commentator noted, "The grossest and stoutest of these women are to be found among the lowest and most disgusting classes of prostitutes."[35] In many cartoons Chinese women were shown not only with African-American features but also as rather fat. *Hutching's Illustrated California Magazine* of 1857 elaborated on one such illustration: "Unlike other Oriental nations, the Chinese have sent hither swarms of their females, a large part of whom are a depraved class; and though with complexions in some instances approaching to fair, their whole physiognomy but a slight removal from the African race."[36] It has been suggested that this was a "Negroization" of the Chinese on the West Coast, where there were very few African Americans and where the Chinese came to occupy the lowest rank in the racial hierarchies of the day.[37] I would take the argument further. Illustrating the malleability of racial phenotype, I suggest that the Chinese conveniently "became black" in this equation of Chinese as slaves. In the post–Civil War period, some used Chinese slavery to suggest that the situation of the antebellum African-American had not been that bad. An article in the *Californian* argued, for instance, "There exists in this country, wherever the Chinese have obtained a foothold, a slavery so vile and debasing that all the horrors of negro American slavery do not begin to compare with it." The author, focusing on the sale of Chinese women and children, continued, "The negro of antebellum days was a prince in fortune to the luckless Chinese slave: the former was sold to work, while the latter is selected, bought and handed over for a use compared to which death would be a happy release."[38] For many who had never set eyes on a Chinese man or woman, the issue of slavery among the Chinese became the primary argument for exclusion.

In these and dozens of other ways, a new "Orient" was created during the course of the nineteenth century: the supine, backward, degenerate "East," the backdrop against which energetic Americans could take their measure; the "other," which reiterated the hierarchies of the races, of superior and inferior cultures, and which reassured Americans of their dominant place under the sun. Repulsive yet attractive, like a magic crystal ball, opium-sodden polygamous nineteenth-century China gave Americans a glimpse of their own degenerate tendencies. Americans formulated hundreds of ways that set "us" apart from "them"—why "they" could not be assimilated and become part of "America." The contrast with the Chinese also reiterated a racial connection with the new masses of immigrants from Europe swarming to American shores in the 1870s and 1880s. After reading extensively about dirt, disease, and decadence in California's Chinatowns in 1870, James Gordon Bennet of the *New York Herald* concluded, "Compared with these base Chinese, the vilest dregs that come into New York from the vilest holes in Europe are refined and attractive people."[39]

In 1882 the Chinese Exclusion Act was passed, followed by a string of other legislation that terminated Chinese immigration to the United States; the Chinese population declined from an overall high of 107,488 in 1890 to 89,863 within a decade and continued declining until the 1920s. Firmly relegated to the margins of American society, Chinese women lapsed back into the realm of the exotic, their souls and bodies in need of rescue. There was little discussion in the American press of the women's rights and anti-foot-binding movements not only in China but also in the Chinatowns of San Francisco and Los Angeles. The arrival in 1902 of sixteen-year-old Xue Jinqin as a student at the University of California, Berkeley, and her lecture to an audience numbering around a thousand in San Francisco's Chinatown on women's education and on "women's obligations to break the old Chinese practices" passed unnoticed by the East Coast media.[40] So too did Mrs. Joe Wing's half-hour speech in Los Angeles in 1905; she discussed the persecution of women in China and demanded that women learn to read and write so that "men wouldn't bully them."[41] But dozens of photographs were taken when there were raids on houses of "ill repute"—such as attempts to rescue Chinese women by Donaldina Cameron of the Chinese Mission Home in San Francisco.

By the twentieth century, exotic Chinese women and evil Chinatowns had become an integral part of the American West; they were perceived as "different," and their difference had to be preserved, even under duress. Donaldina Cameron in the 1920s insisted on keeping "her [Chinese] girls in native costume, deploring their preference for leather shoes over their own gay embroidered ones [and only] regretfully indulging them in a change from their own style of hairdressing."[42] San Francisco's Chinatown came to represent the "Orient" in America; New York's rowdy Irish-Italian-Chinese neighborhood was perhaps not as evocative. Ernest Peixotto and Robert Fletcher collaborated on an expensive portfolio of drawings of San Francisco's Chinatown in 1898. The accompanying text effused: "The streets of Chinatown fairly swarm with its silent-footed inhabitants. They do not come and go, they appear and disappear. From dark door-ways and alleys, and from the gloomy interior of shops, these pallid-faced figures with shaven heads and dangling cues clothed in voluminous black or blue blouses and short straight trousers, their ankles swathed in white linen and their feet mounted on padded slippers, they pass and repass in spectral procession.[43]

When Hollywood emerged in the 1920s with Dr. Fu Manchu, the depraved Chinese man with "terror in each split-second of his slanted eyes," and with movies of "tong wars" in shady Chinatowns with dark alleyways peopled with "inscrutable Orientals," Americans all over the country simply had their notions of the "Orient" reconfirmed. From Ah Toy to Suzy Wong, American Orientalism and its many faces had come full circle.

Notes

I would like to thank colleagues at the Center for Studies of Ethnicity and Race in America (CSERA), University of Colorado, Boulder, for their comments on an earlier draft of this essay. A Rockefeller Fellowship at CSERA in the fall of 1994 enabled me to carry out the research for this essay.

1. Cited in Howard Lamar, ed., *The Reader's Encyclopedia of the American West* (New York, 1977), 203.

2. Edward Said, *Orientalism* (New York, 1978), 205. Space and other considerations have encouraged me to limit my discussion to the Chinese experience in this essay.

3. Stuart Creighton Miller, *The Unwelcome Immigrant* (Berkeley, 1969), 32–33.

4. Many such examples are discussed by Harold Isaacs, *Images of Asia* (New York, 1958), 69–71, 93–96, and by Miller, *Unwelcome Immigrant*, 16–37.

5. Ralph Waldo Emerson, *The Journal and Miscellaneous Notebooks of Ralph Waldo Emerson*, ed. William H. Gillman et al., vol. 2 (Cambridge, Mass., 1961), 224.

6. *Morning Courier* and *New York Enquirer*, 10 April 1850.

7. Jerome Ch'en, *China and the West: Society and Culture* (London, 1979), 224–25; Sander Gilman, "Black Bodies, White Bodies," in *Race, Writing, and Difference,* ed. Henry Louis Gates (Chicago, 1986), 232–37.

8. Curt Gentry, *The Madams of San Francisco* (Sausalito, Calif., 1964), 57.

9. Cited in ibid., 62.

10. *Alta California*, 22 August 1854.

11. George Needham, "Manet, Olympia, and Pornographic Photography," in *Woman as Sex Object,* ed. Thomas Hess and Linda Nochlin (New York, 1972), 81–89. The illustration of Ah Toy is reproduced in Judy Yung, *Chinese Women of America* (Seattle, 1986), 17.

12. Brenda E. Pillors, "The Criminalization of Prostitution in the United States: The Case of San Francisco, 1854–1919" (Ph.D. diss., University of California, Berkeley, 1982); *Statutes of California (2865–66),* 81–82.

13. Anne Butler, *Daughters of Joy, Sisters of Misery* (Urbana, 1985), 6–7. The remaining 107, whose ethnicity was not accounted for, were probably French, for there was a direct importation of French prostitutes to Denver.

14. *California Statutes, 1870,* 330.

15. Letter of Giles H. Gray, cited by Sucheng Chan, "The Exclusion of Chinese Women, 1870–1943," in *Entry Denied,* ed. Sucheng Chan (Philadelphia, 1991), 103–4.

16. William Sanger, *History of Prostitution* (New York, 1858).

17. *Rocky Mountain News,* 1 November 1880, 8.

18. The Colorado Women's Christian Temperance Union, for example, was founded in 1878.

19. Roy Wortman, "Denver's Anti-Chinese Riot, 1880," *Colorado Magazine Western History* 42 (1965): 279.

20. Barbara Epstein, *The Politics of Domesticity: Women, Evangelism, and Temperance in Nineteenth Century America* (Middletown, Conn., 1981); Peggy Pascoe, *Relations of Rescue* (New York, 1990).

21. Cited in Gentry, *Madams of San Francisco,* 62.

22. *Transactions of the American Medical Association* 27 (1876): 106–7, cited in Miller, *Unwelcome Immigrant,* 163 (see also p. 171).

23. *Rocky Mountain News,* 27 October 1880, 2.

24. Cited in Wortman, "Denver's Anti-Chinese Riot," 283.

25. These interpretations have been forwarded by numerous scholars, including Roger Daniels, *Asian America* (Seattle, 1988), and Alexander Saxton, *The Indispensable Enemy* (Berkeley, 1971).

26. Paula Baker, "The Domestication of Politics: Women and American Political Society, 1790–1920," *American Historical Review* 89 (1984): 630.

27. In addition to Baker, this section has drawn on Mary Ryan, *Womanhood in America: From Colonial Times to the Present* (New York, 1975).

28. Miller, *Unwelcome Immigrant,* 88.

29. Joan Jacobs Brumberg, "The Ethnological Mirror: American Evangelical Women and Their Heathen Sisters, 1870–1910," in *Women and the Structure of Society,* ed. Barbara J. Harris and JoAnn K. McNamara (Durham, N.C., 1984), 110.

30. E.g., *Ladies' Home Journal* 16 (1899).

31. Pascoe, *Relations of Rescue,* 13–14.

32. Ibid., 24.

33. Lawrence Foster, "Polygamy and the Frontier: Mormon Women in Early Utah," *Utah Historical Quarterly* 50 (1982): 268–89.

34. Miller, *Unwelcome Immigrant,* 163.

35. Gilman, "Black Bodies, White Bodies," 242.

36. *Hutching's Illustrated California Magazine* 1 (March 1857), illustration reproduced in Robert Heizer and Alan Almquist, *The Other Californians* (Berkeley, 1971).

37. Dan Caldwell, "The Negroization of the Chinese Stereotype in California," *Southern California Quarterly* 53 (June 1971).

38. M. G. C. Edholm, "A Stain on the Flag," *Californian (California Illustrated Magazine)* 1 (February 1892): 159.

39. Cited in Miller, *Unwelcome Immigrant,* 182–83.

40. Judy Yung, "The Social Awakening of Chinese American Women as Reported in Chung Sai Yat Po, 1900–1911," *Chinese America: History and Perspectives* (San Francisco, 1988).

41. Sucheta Mazumdar, "In the Family," in *Linking Our Lives: Chinese American Women of Los Angeles,* UCLA Chinese American Oral History Project (Los Angeles, 1984), 36.

42. Cited in Pascoe, *Relations of Rescue,* 118.

43. Robert Howe Fletcher, *Ten Drawings in Chinatown* (San Francisco, 1898), Bancroft Manuscript Collection, University of California, Berkeley.

Extending Democracy's Reach

Gary Y. Okihiro

Over two decades ago, Stanford M. Lyman published an essay titled "The Significance of Asians in American Society," a much overlooked, though brilliant work.[1] Although Lyman failed, in my estimation, to prove his thesis, he pointed the way toward a new understanding of U.S. race relations.[2] The dominant paradigm, argued Lyman, was based on black-white relations and ignored the trajectories of other groups, including Asians. The black-white model, he continued, derived largely from the plantation South, characterized by the master-slave relationship. Asians, he offered, stimulated a new stage of race relations, one that represented a move away from the rural South toward the urban West and away from racism within total institutions toward racism in modern institutional settings. Although the argument is flawed, Lyman's search for a more inclusive paradigm of U.S. race relations remains a valid endeavor, and like Lyman and some among the new western historians, I believe the West holds the key to that problematic.

But locating the significance of Asians within U.S. race relations and anti-Asianism is a revival of the moribund literature of the past that focused on the excluders and not the excluded. Multiculturalism has all too often meant depicting Asians as victims, most prominently within U.S. history texts, as objects of exclusion in the nineteenth-century anti-Chinese movement and as "Americans betrayed" in the twentieth-century mass detention of Japanese Americans. But multiculturalism has also meant a "contributions" approach that asks, oblivious to the wider social relations and institutions, about the roles played by women and various ethnic and minority groups in the building of the nation. Asians are herein celebrated for their labor, foremost in the construction of the transcontinental railroad and in the development of western agriculture and Hawaiian sugar plantations.

The contributions approach, it seems to me, slights the true significance of Asians in the American West and elsewhere. Helping to bind the nation with bands of steel, however masculine and heroic, and laying the foundations for California's orchard and vegetable economy, however important, and planting and reaping Hawaiian sugar, however profitable, pale in comparison with the centrality of the Founding Fathers, the framers of the constitution, the shapers of letters and science of the American core. I would, however, hasten to add that the core deliberately and systematically built the republic for itself, for those it defined as members of the American community, and just as deliberately and systematically marginalized the efforts of nonmembers of that community. How, then, could the contributions of the latter equal those of the former?

Instead, what I would like to suggest is that the deeper significance of Asians, and indeed of all minorities, in the West and in America as a whole rests in their opposition to the dominant paradigm, in their contestation at the borders, at the gates that admitted members and barred nonmembers. What I contend, albeit in summary fashion, is that racial minorities, specifically Asian Americans, have in the past repeatedly sought inclusion within American society, within the promise of American democracy, within the ideals of equality and human dignity and have, just as regularly, been rebuffed and excluded from that company and ideal. What I will suggest further is that racial minorities, in their struggles for inclusion and equality, helped to preserve and advance the very privileges that were denied to them and thereby democratized America for the benefit of all Americans.

Hawaiian planters thought of imported Asian workers as mere commodities necessary for the production of sugar. "I can see little difference between the importation of foreign laborers and the importation of jute bags from India," declared Richard A. Cooke, president of the Hawaiian Sugar Planters' Association (HSPA). Theo. H. Davies, a Honolulu mercantile house, confirmed in a letter to C. McLennan, manager of Laupahoehoe Plantation, on 2 July 1890 that the company had received his requisition for "bonemeal, canvas, Japanese laborers, macaroni, Chinamen."[3] In testimony before the U.S. Congress in 1910, HSPA Secretary Royal D. Mead reported:

"The Asiatic has had only an economic value in the social equation. So far as the institutions, laws, customs, and language of the permanent population go, his presence is no more felt than is that of the cattle on the ranges."[4]

When no longer useful as laborers, Asians were denied entry into America, "repatriated," and displaced or marginalized. Those goals were achieved by the Chinese Exclusion Act of 1882, the Gentlemen's Agreement of 1908, the 1917 and 1924 Immigration Acts, and the Tydings-McDuffie Act of 1934, by which Chinese, Japanese, Korean, Asian-Indian, and Filipino exclusion was affected. The exclusion of Asian women, California's (and other states') antimiscegenation statute(s), and the 1922 Cable Act that stripped U.S. citizenship from women who married Asian migrants ("aliens ineligible to citizenship") restricted the ability of Asians to reproduce and create stable communities, and the 1922 *Ozawa* ruling by the U.S. Supreme Court affirmed earlier decisions that the naturalization laws did not apply to Asians. "The widespread animosity toward the California Chinese," observed several students of California's anti-Asian movement, "was translated into a broad range of discriminatory legislation designed to drive out those already here and to discourage the immigration of others."[5]

Despite the dissonance between the rhetoric and the practice of American democracy, its promise of equality held out much hope to Asians. During the 1909 sugar plantation strike on the island of Oahu involving about seven thousand workers, Japanese strikers argued against the racial hierarchies created by the planters: "Is it not a matter of simple justice, and moral duty to give [the] same wages and same treatment to laborers of equal efficiency, irrespective of race, color, creed, nationality, or previous condition of servitude?" And in 1903, in Oxnard, California, over thirteen hundred Japanese and Mexican sugar-beet field hands joined together in a historic union, the Japanese-Mexican Labor Association (JMLA). When the American Federation of Labor (AFL) offered to charter the JMLA, but only after the union had been purged of all of its Japanese members, the union's secretary, J. M. Lizarras, a Mexican, responded to the AFL's Samuel Gompers, "We would be false [to the Japanese] and to ourselves and to the cause of Unionism, if we . . . accept privileges for ourselves which are not according to them [Asians]." Workers should unite, Lizarras concluded, "without regard to their color or race."[6]

The Chinese contested, early on, inequities in the education of their children. In 1884, eight-year-old Mamie Tape, the American-born daughter of Chinese migrants Joseph and Mary McGladery Tape, was denied admittance to California's Spring Valley Primary School by the principal, Jennie Hurley. The Tapes challenged Hurley's decision, and in January 1885, the court decided in favor of the petitioners, citing the equal protection clause of the Fourteenth Amendment. "To deny a child, born of Chinese parents in this State, entrance to the public schools," wrote the superior court judge, "would be a violation of the law of the state and the Constitution of the United States."[7] The *Tape* decision was affirmed by the state supreme court, but neither ruling challenged the "separate but equal" doctrine that would be established eleven years later in the landmark 1896 U.S. Supreme Court decision of *Plessy v. Ferguson*.

The state responded by enacting legislation designed to skirt the court rulings by enabling school boards to establish separate schools for Asians; as was mandated by the 1885 amendment to Section 1662 of the 1880 Political Code: "Trustees shall have power to exclude children of filthy or vicious habits, or children suffering from contagious or infectious diseases, and also to establish separate schools for children of Mongolian or Chinese descent. When such separate schools are established Chinese or Mongolian children must not be admitted to any other schools." The legislation was praised by San Francisco's school superintendent as "not a question of race prejudice" but "a question of demoralization of one high race by a lower," and on 13 April 1885, Mamie Tape, described by the *San Francisco Evening Bulletin* as neatly dressed, with her hair in "the traditional braid of American children hanging down her back and tied with a ribbon," joined her brother Frank and four other "bright Chinese lads" at Rose Thayer's Chinese Primary School on Jackson and Powell Streets in San Francisco.[8]

Mary McGladery Tape, unconvinced that the exclusion of her daughter was "not a question of race prejudice," wrote a letter to the board of education dated 8 April 1885. "I see that you are going to make all sorts of excuses to keep my child out of the Public Schools," she began. "Dear sirs, Will you please tell me! Is it a disgrace to be born a Chinese? Didn't God make us all!!! What right! have you to bar my children out of the school because she is a chinese Descend." Tape concluded: "I will let the world see sir What justice there is When it is govern by the Race prejudice men! Just because she is of the Chinese descend. not because she don't dress like you because she does. Just because she is decended [*sic*] of Chinese parents I guess she is more of a American then a good many of you that is going to prewent [*sic*] her being Educated."[9]

In 1920, the Hawaiian legislature passed Act 30, which authorized the Department of Public Instruction to issue and revoke operating permits to foreign-language schools, to test and certify language-school teachers, who were required to have knowledge of the "ideals of democracy, American history and institutions and the English language," and to regulate the curricula, textbooks, and hours of operation of those schools. Despite the regulatory intent of the act, the department applied its provisions toward eliminating the territory's 143 Japanese-language schools, and on 28 December 1922, a group of 87 language schools joined in a petition testing the constitutionality of Act 30. As the litigation moved from territorial circuit court to the U.S. District Court, to the Ninth Court of Appeals in San Francisco, and finally to the U.S. Supreme Court, the Hawaiian legislature tightened controls over the language schools by passing Act 171 in 1923 and Act 152 in 1925.[10]

On 21 February 1927, the Supreme Court rendered a unanimous decision in favor of the Japanese-language school petitioners, arguing that despite the "grave problems" of a "large alien population in the Hawaiian Islands," parents had the right to determine the education of their children and the state had limits in curtailing the rights and powers of individuals.[11] At a mass meeting held the following month, five thousand supporters of the successful constitutional challenge passed a series of resolutions: "We re-affirm our confidence in the friendship and good-will of the American people, and reassert our pride in the fact that our children are American citizens." They added, "We emphatically reaffirm our continued loyalty to America and our desire to rear our children as loyal, patriotic and useful citizens of the United States." Kinzaburo Makino, a test-case leader, told the gathered throng that the litigation was "the right of a people living in a free democracy to seek legal clarification regarding constitutionality of their laws." But he cautioned, "We must never forget that we have to stand up for our rights as guaranteed under the Constitution."[12]

Exploited and seen to have no more effect than "cattle on the ranges," Asian-American laborers went on strike for equality "irrespective of race, color, creed, nationality, or previous condition of servitude" and organized themselves into unions "without regard to their color or race." Relegated to "Oriental" schools, Asian Americans challenged segregation and, to paraphrase Mary McGladery Tape, declared themselves to be more American than those who would deny a child equal education on the basis of race. The language-school challenge of the 1920s, which taught Asian Americans to stand up for their "rights as guaranteed under the Constitution," presaged the successful fight for bilingual language rights some five decades later, resulting in the 1974 Supreme Court decision of *Lau v. Nichols*.[13] The struggle for nonracism in the workplace, equality in education, and linguistic and cultural rights helped to extend democracy's reach and significantly advanced the fundamental freedoms of all Americans. That, I maintain, is the true significance of Asians in America.

Notes

1. Stanford M. Lyman, *The Asian in the West* (Reno, 1970), 3–8.

2. For another conceptualization of U.S. race relations, see Michael Omi and Howard Winant, *Racial Formation in the United States: From the 1960s to the 1980s* (New York, 1986).

3. Cooke and Davies cited in Ronald Takaki, *Pau Hana: Plantation Life and Labor in Hawaii, 1835–1920* (Honolulu, 1983), 23.

4. Quoted in Gary Y. Okihiro, *Cane Fires: The Anti-Japanese Movement in Hawaii, 1865–1945* (Philadelphia, 1991), 16–17.

5. Jacobus tenBroek, Edward N. Barnhart, and Floyd W. Matson, *Prejudice, War, and the Constitution* (Berkeley, 1954), 17.

6. Both quotations in Yuji Ichioka, *The Issei: The World of the First Generation Japanese Immigrants, 1885–1924* (New York, 1988), 96–99.

7. Victor Low, *The Unimpressible Race: A Century of Educational Struggle by the Chinese in San Francisco* (San Francisco, 1982), 62.

8. Ibid., 59–73.

9. Ibid., Appendix D.

10. Okihiro, *Cane Fires,* 136–38, 153–54.

11. Kenneth B. O'Brien Jr., "Education, Americanization, and the Supreme Court: The 1920s," *American Quarterly* 13 (Summer 1961): 170–71.

12. Okihiro, *Cane Fires,* 154–55.

13. See L. Ling-chi Wang, "Lau v. Nichols: History of a Struggle for Equal and Quality Education," in *Counterpoint: Perspectives on Asian America,* ed. Emma Gee (Los Angeles, 1976), 240–63.

6

Cultural Filters: The Significance of Perception

Anne F. Hyde

The geographic region of the American West has done much to shape the culture and character of the United States. Conversely, the culture and character of the United States has reshaped much of the western landscape. Frederick Jackson Turner told us as much in 1893. He argued that the West molded American culture because it was a frontier, a meeting ground between savagery and civilization. Because frontier, for Turner, did not mean a specific place, the geographic realities of the Far West played no important role in his thinking.

I argue instead that the West has shaping power because of its unique geography and not necessarily because it was or is a frontier. Its significance comes from the fact that in a certain part of the American continent, particularly the lands west of the one hundredth meridian, Anglo Americans came up against a series of landscapes that defied their notions about utility and beauty. The region's strange appearance, combined with national expectations about its uses, created a volatile mixture of geography and culture.

Distinctive and unfamiliar landscapes presented explorers, travelers, and settlers with perceptual challenges. What was the West? What did it look like? How could it be first understood, then lived upon, made profitable, or consumed? Meeting this challenge with new methods of interpretation forced Americans to make sense of their surroundings and, at times, distort the landscape. These shifting perceptions reflected the ways in which American culture defined itself—and this is the significance of perception in the history of the American West.

Other historians have made observations along these lines. Walter Prescott Webb devoted a career to the distinctive characteristics of the Great Plains, arguing that geography determined the culture that developed there. Donald Worster, in his work on the use and misuse of land and water in the West, has shown us the folly of ignoring geographic realities. Henry Nash Smith and, more recently, Annette Kolodny have looked at the way in which the West, both the real West and the West that Americans imagined, affected American culture in the nineteenth century. William Goetzmann has surveyed the history of western exploration as a vehicle of empire building and argued that explorers were the point men of American culture, bringing it west as they carried images of the West east.[1]

Few historians have looked systematically at the history of perceiving the West. However, this history of perception is crucial in understanding how the region has been used. I see two basic problems in understanding Anglo-American perceptions of the region. First, what does *perception* mean? It denotes both firsthand observations of Americans who viewed the West for the first time in the nineteenth and early twentieth centuries and the responses of readers or viewers to those firsthand accounts or images. What did both groups expect to see? How did their expectations color their perceptions of the Far West? Working like filters on a camera lens, cultural expectations, biases, and ideology affected what people saw and what they recorded for others. Second, we must remember that the perceptions of Anglo observers do not represent the entire spectrum of vision, though in the nineteenth century their views, however limited, had tremendous impact on the region.

This essay explores the role of culture in the history of perception in the American West. In particular, I want to look at the filters that altered and shaped this perception. Because of the enormous interest in the West and because of its distance from eastern population centers, the perceptions of early interpreters shaped American ideas about the West. How Americans gained their knowledge about the West resembled a game of telephone throughout most of the nineteenth century. Most Americans got their information about the West after it had been filtered through several observers and recorders. Certainly the views of Anglo Americans vary enormously. How did different peoples' or groups' perceptions shape the West, and how did the West shape these perceptions?[2]

Because I want to look at the role of perception as a cultural shaper, it is important to look at what might influence such perceptions. Modes of transportation provide a significant filter on what people see. The earliest American explorers viewed the West in terms very different from those used by tourists on Interstate 80 two centuries later. Another important filter is gender. When women and men looked at the landscape, they often saw very different things. Another sort of filter is the medium upon which firsthand responses are recorded. Because most people saw the West through words and pictures made by others, the medium of exchange becomes important in understanding national conceptions about the region. Words, pictures, buildings, and more recently, films have all recorded perceptions. What happens in the translation between viewer and image? How does the medium change the perception?

Working underneath all of these filters is the crucial lens of cultural preparation or expectation. If the eye acts as a camera body, culture works as a lens providing focus. In large part, the history of Anglo-American perception in the West is one of willful misperception. To counter this view, one could examine the perceptions of nonwhite westerners. What did they see when they looked at the landscape? How did they filter their views? Because Native Americans and Hispanic colonizers had little interest in remodeling the landscape on a large scale, they seemed more likely to accept far western geography at face value. Culturally, the landscape seemed useful to them.[3] White Americans, using their own culture, focused their cameras and saw a highly mutable West—a place that could be remade into anything they wanted as they twisted and adjusted that cultural focus.

Describing the West:
Explorers and Their Words

The concept of cultural preparation and its impact on perceptions of the West is vital. A quick trip through the history of western exploration should demonstrate the significance of expectation. In general, people see what they are looking for. If you have been told that a place is beautiful, generally when you see it, the spot will appear beautiful. And in general, landscape that is familiar is pleasing.[4] Navajo, Paiute, or Apache Indians, for example, would have been stunned to know that nineteenth-century white observers found the western deserts hideous and threatening. Because native peoples knew how to find water, food, and shelter, the desert seemed a comfortable place to them. Similarly, what white Americans expected and what was familiar had great impact on what they found in the Far West in the early nineteenth century.

Geographical knowledge of the American West did not begin with a blank slate. Myths and assumptions long preceded and shaped knowledge. A useful way to characterize nineteenth-century exploration is as a series of "reality checks" that had relatively little effect on a durable myth. For example, we often assume that Thomas Jefferson sent Meriwether Lewis and William Clark into a great void when they headed up the Missouri River in 1804 to inspect the newly acquired Louisiana Purchase.

Jefferson, however, had devised the expedition based on several clear geographic assumptions. He believed, with the weight of science and history behind him, that a waterway existed connecting the Atlantic and Pacific Oceans. Reality, in this case, came in the guise of reports from fur traders and fur company explorers and chipped away at this belief, reducing the waterway to a western-flowing river and an eastern-flowing river that were interrupted by an insignificant portage over a small mountain range. As Bernard DeVoto put it: "This basic conception, this irreducible minimum, left no room for the Rocky Mountains. Geographical thinking had been unable to imagine them."[5] Perhaps even more significant was Jefferson's assumption that the West, like most of the territory east of the Mississippi, would provide climate and land suitable for American farming. In his message to Congress justifying the expedition, Jefferson explained that "the Missouri, traversing a moderate climate," would provide passage through a rich and fertile agricultural region.[6] Jefferson's instructions to Lewis and Clark, exhorting them to pay careful attention to climate, soil, mineral production, and navigational possibilities of various rivers, reflect these assumptions.

Lewis and Clark's report describing the torturous 220-mile portage through the deep snows of Montana's Bitterroot Mountains seriously damaged the concept of a Northwest Passage. However, their report did nothing to erode the notion of the West as an agricultural wonderland destined for American use. Despite the fact that Lewis and Clark described great treeless expanses, unnavigable rivers, and an array of native peoples, Anglo Americans continued to believe that the Far West could be readily molded to fit their economy, society, and culture. Lewis and Clark found a garden, perhaps a rocky and cold one, but a garden nevertheless—because they were expected to find one.[7]

Nearly fifteen years later, another official expedition ventured into the supposed "Garden of the West." Led by Stephen Harriman Long of the U.S. Topographical Engineers, this group headed into the heart of the continent, along the Platte, Arkansas, and Canadian Rivers. Perhaps because Long and his men expected to find a fertile region much like the Mississippi Valley just to the east, the arid, treeless plains seemed especially bleak. The report they brought back was not optimistic. The Long expedition found only hostile Indians, towering mountains, and sandy wastes, a region that, according to Long, was "almost wholly unfit for cultivation, and of course uninhabitable by a people depending upon agriculture for their subsistence."[8] As a result of Long's judgment, the center of the American West was designated the "Great American Desert."[9]

Such a dismal appellation did little to slow the conquest of the West, nor did it put much of a dent in American assumptions about the region. As the United States made moves toward acquiring Texas, Oregon, California, and the rest of the Great Basin, few Americans considered the geographic realities of the land they coveted. Throughout the nineteenth century, Americans seemed to be looking for two things in the West. One was a scenic West, a place that represented the power and beauty of the American nation and that could be compared to the most sublime scenes in Europe. The other West offered a locus of opportunity and a testing ground for American ingenuity, a notion that had been present long before Thomas Jefferson. However, these two Wests seem mutually exclusive. How could Americans perceive the landscape as sublime Eden and at the same time build farms and mines on top of it? Even more poignant, both of these western visions clashed with the facts of the landscape. And this clash, because of the powerful ideology about the role of the West, could not be reconciled by nineteenth-century Americans.

Although some people worried that the nation was growing too fast and that expansion would destroy the union, no one seemed to question the notion that the land could meet aesthetic standards and the needs of traditional American farming and industry. Even if deserts did mar the landscape, they presented a challenge to be met, not a barrier to development or understanding. The perception of the Far West as a potential wonderland was far too strong.

John Charles Frémont set off on a series of expeditions in 1842 to prove that such a wonderland did exist. His own ambitions and the expansionist fervor of his patrons dictated what he saw. The Great American Desert became the Great Plains, home to nutritious grasses, innumerable buffalo and antelope, and picturesque Indians. The Rocky Mountains contained scenes of grandeur and sublimity that rivaled the famed Alps of Europe. Oregon and California cried out for the plows of industrious American farmers to make the valleys into fertile oases. Certain parts of the Far West could not be described in such glowing terms, but Frémont tended to ignore these unfortunate areas, which included the huge expanses of the Great Basin and the plains. He simply explained them away: "In America, such things are new and strange, unknown and unsuspected," implying that once known, these regions could be made more appealing.[10]

The news in Frémont's *Report of the Exploring Expedition to the Rocky Mountains in the Year 1842 and to Oregon and North California in the Years 1843–1844* captivated Americans. The report read like an adventure story, but it also provided clear descriptions of the landscape. Frémont used familiar language and analogy to make the Far West comprehensible

Central Chain of the Wind River Range, Charles Preuss, 1842. Lithograph in John Charles Frémont, *Report of the Exploring Expedition to the Rocky Mountains in the Year 1842 and to Oregon and North California in the Years 1843–1844* (Washington, D.C., 1845).

to his readers. Because of the publicity surrounding his expedition and the astounding popularity of his *Report,* the words Frémont selected had great impact on American perceptions of the region.[11]

Remodeling the West:
Promoters and Settlers

Frémont simply echoed what white Americans had assumed all along— that the West was a place of opportunity where American enterprise could spread its wings. However, by the middle of the nineteenth century, geographical knowledge had placed question marks on this opportunity. The Great Plains looked fertile with all of those buffalo chewing grass, but where were the trees and the rain? The Rockies and the Sierra Nevada could be crossed and they had spots of undeniable beauty, but could they ever be anything but a barrier to development? The Great Basin and the desert Southwest provided another cipher. Indians had lived there for thousands of years and Mormons had recently established a toehold using irrigation, but could mainstream Americans establish profitable enterprises in those regions? How could the Far West be made into America? These areas presented perceptual challenges that would take another fifty years to solve.

In general, Anglo Americans chose two strategies to deal with the geography of the Far West. Both of these reflected the power of the cultural filter Americans used to view the region. The first method involved denying the facts of the landscape and insisting that the entire region would support traditional American patterns of living. The semiarid plains could be made into agricultural bonanzas while the deserts and mountains could flower with irrigation and mining. The ingrained American belief in Manifest Destiny made geographical barriers impossible. One could argue that this is a history of stubborn misperception.

Confidence and determination could even alter geography. For example, as settlement in the Mississippi Valley pushed people farther west and as the promises of promoters enticed them, Americans began to reevaluate the Great American Desert. Driven by optimism and faith, folk wisdom and science put forth the notion that if the region was settled, more rain would fall. Boosters, settlers, and railroad builders insisted that if Americans dug up the plains and planted crops and trees, annual rainfall would increase. In 1867, Ferdinand V. Hayden, the eminent and politically astute director of the U.S. Geological and Geographical Survey of the Territories, announced, "The planting of ten or fifteen acres of forest-trees on each quarter-section will have a most important effect on the climate, equalizing and increasing the moisture." Thus rain would indeed follow the plow.[12] Others insisted that the electricity created by trains on railroad tracks and by telegraph wires would stimulate cloud formation.[13] Such fanciful claims evolved out of the perception that the West could be made into whatever Americans wanted it to be, despite geographic realities.

A second way to deal with unpleasant geographical truths was to search for regions of the West that did fit American perceptions of what the West should be and to pretend nothing else existed. The strenuous effort by promoters to make the West attractive to wealthy American tourists by making it into a version of Europe exemplifies this strategy. The practice of imposing European standards on American landscape had a long history. This tendency developed out of Americans' insecurities about their culture, doubts that had been present since the nation's beginnings. Europe provided the standards that determined what was beautiful, what was historical, and what was civilized. And, much to the discomfort of culturally conscious Americans, most of the eastern half of the nation simply did not measure up.[14]

When railroad travel made tourism possible in 1869, Americans were eager to find the scenery they craved, and promoters were just as eager to provide it. Unpleasant or inconvenient deserts and plains could be ignored or simply slept through. Instead, promoters advised visitors to focus on California and Colorado, the two places easiest to describe in European terms.[15]

The resort town of Colorado Springs offers a clear illustration. The Rockies provided an alpine setting that promoters were quick to exploit. A pamphlet produced by the Denver and Rio Grande Railroad promised, "All the sublimest glories of the Swiss and Italian Alps, all the picturesque savagery of the Tyrol, and all the softer beauties of Killarny and Como and Naples dwindle to insignificance by comparison with the stupendous scenes that meet the gaze at every turn in Colorado."[16] The president of the Denver and Rio Grande, General William Palmer, added an English resort to this alpine splendor in hopes of attracting wealthy tourists to his railroad and community. Because the dry, windblown sage plains covering the site that Palmer chose for his new town did not fit American percep-

Distant View of the Rocky Mountains, Samuel Seymour, 1823. Courtesy Harry Ransom Humanities Research Center, University of Texas at Austin.

tions of what a "Europeanized" West should be, Palmer simply changed the landscape. He planted trees, built casinos and hotels, designed Queen Anne houses, and held "fox hunts" in which coyotes, who did not understand the sport, were chased through the sagebrush. Because American tourists perceived European scenery as being proper scenery, they sought it and encouraged its cultivation in the Far West, even though few parts of the region could be construed as looking the least bit European.

These perceptions of what the West should be, ideas created by a century of cultural preparation, prevented Americans from accepting the facts of the far western landscape. The result was an unprecedented series of failures. The cultural determination to re-create the West to suit the needs of white American left a legacy of environmental destruction and abandoned farms, resort areas, and mines. In spite of this, we have insisted on representing the history of the nineteenth-century American West as a heroic success story, though the new western history has made a few inroads on this monolith.[17] Nevertheless, the lens of cultural expectation is still carefully focused.

An important variant on this lens is the filter of gender. Women saw the West very differently from men, particularly in the nineteenth century. In general, they saw much less economic opportunity and exciting adventure. As they looked at the great expanses stretching west and at the mountains looming overhead, they saw danger and real limits to stable agricultural and family existence.[18] Tamsen Donner voiced her concerns in her diary as her party wandered from the main trail onto the infamous Hastings Cutoff. Caroline Kirkland warned other women of the dangers and discomforts of the Michigan frontier and of the lies presented in promotional literature written by men. On the Dakota plains of Ole Rölvaag's novel *Giants in the Earth,* Beret sees misfortune lurking in the endless prairie grasses while her husband, Per Hansa, can see only endless profits. Although men mocked them for being frightened, these women held perceptions far more accurate than the optimistic ones of their brave husbands. The places they attempted to settle and conquer often proved to be disastrous for the maintenance of family life.[19]

Such impressionistic accounts suggest that gender may be crucial in determining perception. Particularly in the case of nineteenth-century women who rooted their lives so entirely in the health and safety of their families, gender may have prevented other cultural filters from acting so strongly. The struggle to keep up domestic standards under primitive frontier conditions and the fear of losing the network of family and friends that gave life meaning made the West less appealing to many women.[20] In fact, women may have held the advantage in looking at the West because ambition and Manifest Destiny did not color their perceptions so strongly.

Travel, Technology, and Vision

Certainly most white American men perceived the West through a cultural filter of optimism, Manifest Destiny, and pure stubbornness, but other filters acted on nearly everyone's impressions of the Far West. Perception often depends largely on mode of transportation. Speed, distance, safety, and comfort have enormous impact on any observer. Whether one travels across the landscape on foot, on horseback, by stagecoach, by train, or by airplane affects what one sees. Someone being chased by an angry buffalo or being jolted through wagon ruts sees a different West than someone enjoying a game of whist in a parlor car or sipping a cocktail at thirty thousand feet.

The first explorers, travelers, and settlers who ventured into the new world of the Far West did so on foot or horseback. They moved slowly across the great distances and depended on the landscape for much of their food, water, and fuel. In addition, most of these early sojourners were headed for Oregon or California and had little interest in the plains and the mountains of the western interior.[21] Their concerns about safety and the difficulties of everyday travel colored their perceptions of the region.[22] The plains, deserts, and mountains stood, for most people, as obstacles rather than objects to admire. One can hardly blame the members of the Donner Party, for example, for not being thrilled by the sight of the magnificent Sierra Nevada rising over them as they stumbled out of the Carson sink.

Though many travelers did comment on certain sights as being particularly beautiful, their perceptions of beauty depended a great deal on cultural preparation and the realities of traveling across the plains, mountains, and deserts. For people who came from an agriculturally based culture and who were accustomed to well-watered, wooded areas, the plains were a shock. Americans and Europeans used trees to determine an area's fertility, and the plains did not measure up. A generation of overland emigrants who moved out across the plains with the intention of making their fortunes in Oregon or California found the region strange and unsettling. The lack of wood made building fires and repairing wagons difficult, and the flat unchanging landscape made distances impossible to judge. Traveling in a wagon over rough roads, swallowing alkali dust, drinking muddy water, and worrying about the possibility of Indian attacks did little to improve the travelers' perceptions of the landscape.[23]

When the influential newspaper editor Horace Greeley, who had urged Americans to head west, finally took his own advice in 1859, he traveled in a slightly more comfortable way. Ensconced in a coach that had rudimentary springs and reassured with the promise of stage stations to provide meals and a place to sleep, Greeley had different concerns. Monotony and boredom replaced physical hardship and actual danger. Even so, he was shocked by the landscape, particularly the lack of trees. In Greeley's view, land had no value if it could not be used for farming or for growing trees to build stout farmhouses or produce railroad ties. By the time he reached Utah, his shock had turned into depression. He disconsolately remarked, "I have not seen the raw material of a decent axe-helve growing in all my last thousand miles of travel."[24]

Despite his initial disgust with the region, Greeley found much to celebrate. He had seen oases of trees and rivers at the base of the Rockies and in California, and he fervently believed that what nature had left out of the West, industrious Americans could provide. All they needed was a railroad to get them quickly and comfortably to the more amenable parts of the landscape and to bring the materials necessary to make the West into a properly productive part of the United States.

Travel by train forever changed the experience of crossing the continent. Safety, comfort, and speed not only made the trip more pleasant and faster but also changed the perceptions of travelers. The far western landscape looked different from a train than it had from a horse, a wagon, or a stagecoach. Gazing out a window while seated in the plush luxury of a Pullman car and hurtling along the track at twenty-five miles an hour affected the way Americans saw the West. Mark Twain explained the significance of comfort while traveling when he observed, "Nothing helps scenery like ham and eggs."[25] Such luxuries took the threat out of the wilderness and made it something to enjoy.

Speed and luxury, however, altered what people actually saw. Perceptive travelers had long noted that the swiftness of the train made the scenery a rapidly moving blur. The historian Wolfgang Schivelbusch explains that railroad travel required a new kind of perception. All details near the train disappeared into a haze of speed, and the traveler could see only the general outline of the far distance. Schivelbusch calls this "panoramic perception."[26] The scenery, which from a slow and bumpy coach had provided the only entertainment available, became a boring fog from the window of a train.

The speed of train travel not only affected what people saw from the window but also changed their perceptions of the space covered by the train. Many nineteenth-century observers noted the phenomenon of the annihilation of space. The railroad linked places together as its speed destroyed the distance between them.[27] In the American West, however, the new experience of train travel did not conquer space. In a sense, the railroad created new spaces as it initiated large numbers of people to vast tracts of land. Because few towns interrupted the expanse and because travelers now spent days in what seemed like a gigantic void, space seemed to expand. The region's lack of recognizable landmarks often disoriented passengers, who could find no way to tell how far they had traveled. Subtle geographic changes noted by earlier overland travelers disappeared with the train's rapid movement. Many observers shared the feelings of an 1881 tourist who commented in her journal one morning, "We wake up in the morning and find ourselves speeding along the great American desert, a wide expanse [where] all is blank and bare."[28] Vast monotony challenged the idea that Americans had controlled their landscape.[29]

Paradoxically, the comfort and power of the train also changed national perceptions about the utility and conquerability of the region. The space might be vast and alien, but if Americans could build a railroad across it, the Far West could be mastered by American ingenuity as well. Railroad promoters assured travelers and settlers that the railroad had changed the landscape forever. "Once the home of the savage and the wild beast," an early Union Pacific guidebook noted, "the deep gulches and gloomy canyons are alive with the sounds of labor, the ring of pick, shovel, and drill."[30] Evidence of such material progress helped to convince Americans of both the economic potential of the region and the safety of travel.

Railroad builders had a vested interest in making sure that Americans perceived the West as fertile, safe, and readily developed. The huge tracts of land granted to them by the federal government in recompense for building track needed to be bought by settlers and speculators if the railroads were to be profitable. The Union Pacific Railroad alone had more than twelve million acres of land to sell, most of it in the arid parts of the West. As a result, an entire industry developed around making the West attractive to potential settlers.[31] This meant, of course, making it familiar—green and fertile.

Beginning in the 1850s with the promotional department of the Illinois Central, railroad boosters littered the nation with circulars, pamphlets, and newspaper advertisements. Hordes of paid agents visited farming regions all over the eastern half of the nation and traveled throughout northern Europe looking for land-hungry and ambitious potential settlers. Would-be farmers were lured to Illinois and Iowa and then to Kansas and Nebraska "because it is the garden spot of the world . . . because it rains here more than in any other place, and just at the right time."[32]

Even the undeniably dry plains of Colorado, Wyoming, and western Kansas became arcadias. Promotional materials designated these regions as "semiarid" but insisted, "Successful crops can be raised every year without irrigation."[33] Anyone who suggested that inadequate rainfall might be a problem on the plains west of the one hundredth meridian was laughed at and reminded that a nation that could bring iron rails west of the Mississippi could surely bring some rain. The presence of the railroad alerted Americans to the enormous space in the center of the nation and convinced them that this land could be made into a familiar and profitable version of America.

If the train encouraged Americans to look at the vast spaces of the Far West and to perceive them as potential homes, scenic wonderlands, and moneymakers, the automobile allowed them to envision the complete remodeling of the region. The appearance of the automobile in the early twentieth century had two contradictory effects on perceptions of the West. It reintroduced the idea of adventure into travel, and it allowed a mass penetration of the West in areas Anglo Americans had never seen before. Now that trains crisscrossed the landscape, now that the Great Plains, the mountains, and the deserts had burgeoning communities, and now that most of the Indians were herded onto isolated tracts of land, many Americans felt confident that the region was safe enough for an "adventure." The car allowed them to have it.

The car gave the illusion of freedom by taking travelers out of trains and placing them in control of individual vehicles. The automobile liberated the traveler from the restriction of railroad schedules and tracks. The artist James Montgomery Flagg expressed a common feeling when he wrote that there was "a freedom about motoring across the continent" as opposed to what he described as "the galling monotony of the stifling Pullmans."[34] Even though the earliest motorists spent most of their time pushing their vehicles out of the mud, changing tires, or cranking engines, they saw themselves as freed by their machines.[35] The driver of the car controlled where it went, when it traveled, and how quickly it covered a certain distance, giving motorists a sense of personal choice. The availability and quality of roads, automobiles, and motoring supplies placed obvious limitations on this choice but did not change the perception that from the car, Americans could see the "real" West.

However, like the wagon, the stagecoach, or the train, the automobile itself affected how people viewed the landscape. Like the train, the car had speed and power that heightened the perception of control over the landscape, but the relatively small size of the car and the ability to stop and start it at will increased the sense of intimacy. The experience of driving created an illusion of knowing the landscape even while whizzing past it at high speeds. Speed itself interfered with actual vision. Because moving fast was lulling and addictive, few drivers could resist the urge to cover ground as quickly as possible. Only the grandest natural or human-made objects could lure the motorist to stop before the need for gas, food, or sleep forced a break. The intimate knowledge made possible by the car was often overwhelmed by the rush to cover distance.

Beginning in the early decades of the twentieth century, many Americans could claim firsthand knowledge of the West. The automobile and the large numbers of travelers it carried across the region produced new perceptions of the West. The automobile provided a filter of safety and control, making the Far West a place of comfortable adventure. It also became a region of great distance, but a distance that could be conquered by an individual in three days. The West presented challenging geographical variety, challenges that could be met with different grades of gas, types of tires, and styles of dress. Deserts and mountains held no terrors as long as the motorist had reliable sources of gas, food, and water. Roads and cars made the West "knowable," but in the most superficial sense; this too increased the perception that the region could be anything that Americans desired.

The airplane also added to the complexity of the perception question. In some ways, the airplane provides a very accurate view. When you fly over the western landscape, you are struck with how little of the land is settled. Lights are few and far between, and green circles or squares of farmland appear like tiny grafts on a vast expanse of brown skin. Mark Reisner describes what we have achieved in the West as a beachhead against wilderness and aridity, and his description is borne out in the view from thirty thousand feet.[36] Though we pass over the region in comfort, we are reminded of the inaccuracy of our perceptions and of how little control we have actually achieved.

The View from Afar

A century before Americans could climb in their cars and speed across the western expanses and see the West for themselves, they believed they knew what the region looked like. Beginning early in the nineteenth century, the views of these armchair travelers determined much about perceptions of the Far West. What Americans read and saw and how they interpreted this information are complex issues but important ones to consider. Images of the West in a variety of media provided another critical filter through which Americans perceived the West. Though written descriptions played a crucial role in forming ideas about the West, pictorial material had special impact.

For example, many tourists who ventured West in the late nineteenth century expected to see a version of the Alps in Colorado and California because of the enormously popular work of Albert Bierstadt.[37] A few years later the photographs of William Henry Jackson and the paintings of Thomas Moran played a role in popularizing Yellowstone as the first national park.[38] Similarly, later in the century, the drawings, paintings, and sculptures of Frederic Remington created an image of American enterprise in the West, a place of vibrant soldiers, cowboys, Indians, and horses, now indelibly etched in national culture. Remington's visions have particular import because they depict the West as a blank place where white Americans make exciting things happen, not as a geographic region where the people and the climate have the power to limit what happens.[39]

Given the significance of these pictures in creating American perceptions about the West, we need to look at them more carefully. Stunned by both the beauty and the sterility of the region, artists groped for adequate ways to depict it. Professionally trained artists had a particularly difficult time because far western scenery bore little resemblance to the landscape they considered artistically significant. The artists who traveled west and drew, painted, or photographed the region carried cultural expectations with them, and many had specific goals in creating their art. Often the works they sent back to eastern audiences were reflections of personal ambitions or national expectations about the West rather than depictions of actual sights.

The first artists to travel west in the early nineteenth century had a clear mission. Hoping to preserve the pristine grandeur of western landscapes and peoples on canvas, painters like Karl Bodmer and George Catlin perceived an exotic world of color and action. They did more than document the appearance and customs of Native Americans; they extended and glamorized the idea of the noble savage in the American mind.[40]

Similarly, the artists who traveled with the geographical surveys of the mid-nineteenth century did more than provide illustrations for the scientific treatises produced by the surveyors. Recognizing the midcentury appetite for sublimity and heroic images, many artists made the western landscape bigger, better, and more fertile than it was. They created an image of the West as a compendium of fantastic landforms, plants, and animals that reflected the variety and wealth Americans hoped they would find.[41]

John Mix Stanley, for example, who accompanied Colonel Stephen

Chain of Spires Along the Gila River, John Mix Stanley, 1855. Oil on canvas (31" x 42"). Courtesy Phoenix Art Museum. Purchased with funds provided by the estate of Carolann Smurthwaite.

Watts Kearny on his march across the Southwest in 1846, was hired to make accurate depictions of the landscape for military use. Instead, his delight in the color and shapes of the region drove him to combine plants, animals, and geological forms in impossible ways. In *Chain of Spires Along the Gila River* (1855), cacti, ferns, spires of rock, rushing water, deer, and horned toads all crowd the same painting. Stanley's perception of the Southwest seemed to be a bizarre cornucopia—desert forms in lush surroundings.[42]

Later in the century, artists' different purposes in going west affected their perceptions in equally important ways. By the 1860s, some painters could see the commercial possibilities of the western landscape. Albert Bierstadt, for example, saw the potential for making a name for himself in the West. Determined to find scenery in America that could be heralded in Europe, he latched onto the Rockies and the Sierra Nevada. In paintings like *The Rocky Mountains, Lander's Peak* (1863), Bierstadt produced a vision that thrilled Americans—towering Alps with American flourishes. Sharply pointed granite peaks and fantastically illuminated clouds float above a tranquil, wooded genre scene. Bierstadt painted the West as Americans hoped it would be, making his paintings vastly popular and reinforcing the perception of the West as either Europe or sublime Eden.[43]

A similar shaping of reality appeared in other media. Photography provides a useful example because of the illusion that it captures truth. This illusion made photography especially effective in convincing Americans that the West could be what they wanted it to be. In 1851, the first photographs of the West to reach a large audience appeared in New York with the claim, "These views are no exaggerated and high-colored sketches, got up to produce effect, but are . . . the stereotyped impression of the real thing itself."[44]

Such a claim denies the significant control the photographer has over

Among the Sierra Nevada Mountains, California, Albert Bierstadt, 1868. Oil on canvas (72" x 120"). Courtesy National Museum of American Art, Smithsonian Institution, bequest of Helen Huntington Hull, granddaughter of William Brown Dinsmore, who acquired the painting in 1873 for "The Locusts," the family estate in Dutchess County, New York.

the creation of an image. Carleton Watkins, one of the earliest successful landscape photographers, understood the art involved in photography. He used a combination of painterly aesthetics and photographic truth to make the western landscape appealing to American audiences. His compositions included careful framing and sharp contrasts between light and dark. He used trees to frame a single monolithic object, which provided a picturesque introduction to the scenery in a style not unlike the paintings of Claude Lorrain and his American followers in the Hudson River school. These images presented an ideal version of the landscape—carefully balanced, silent, and grand.[45]

The photographers who accompanied government surveys, ostensibly with scientific intentions, demonstrated the considerable manipulation possible in the medium of photography. Because Rick Dingus has "rephotographed" the work done by Timothy O'Sullivan, who accompanied George Montague Wheeler and Clarence King on parts of their surveys

The Castle Geyser, Upper Geyser Basin, Yellowstone National Park, Thomas Moran, 1873. Chromolithograph by Louis Prang. Courtesy Bancroft Library.

The Three Brothers, Carleton Watkins, 1868. Courtesy Bancroft Library.

into the Great Basin, we know "how much the choice of positioning, lighting, lens, and framing alters a subject."[46] O'Sullivan clearly heightened the drama of the landscape in shaping his images, sometimes holding his camera at odd angles to tilt the horizon or masking the background to make a rock or a tree stand out. Much like the scientists themselves, O'Sullivan "was willing to subdue or enhance certain features of the environment. . . . so he could thereby convey the truth as he saw it."[47] And this truth, of course, had more to do with cultural expectation than with geographic fact. The most important filters O'Sullivan and other photographers placed on their cameras were their own notions about what the West should or could be.

The work of these photographers reinforced a powerful perceptual tradition that had been present since the first explorations of the region. The perception of the West depended largely on national ideology.

"Conglomerate Column
[Witches Rock #1],"
Timothy O'Sullivan, 1869.
In Clarence King, *U.S.
Geological Survey of the
Fortieth Parallel*, vol. 2
(Washington, D.C., 1878).

"Conglomerate Column
[Witches Rock #1]," Rick
Dingus, 1978. In Rick
Dingus, *The Photographic
Artifacts of Timothy
O'Sullivan* (Albuquerque,
1982).

Americans had invested so much hope in the West of their dreams that they would not even consider the possibility that the geographic West would not fulfill their expectations. For much of the nineteenth century, most Americans were dependent on the perceptions of others—artists, writers, promoters, and scientists—for their information about the Far West. This gave nineteenth-century observers the awesome responsibility of producing a West that Americans wanted to see. Amazingly enough, they did manufacture this miraculous West, despite the "reality checks" of failed farms and ghost towns. Deserts became gardens and Rockies became Alps and, at least in national mythology, the West continued to be the land of opportunity.

New Perceptions, Stubborn Legacies

Finally, I want to explore the significance of the history of perception in the twentieth century. Americans could now see the West for themselves, but the perceptual legacy of the nineteenth century certainly colored their view. As Patricia Nelson Limerick has argued, the nineteenth and twentieth centuries are not easily separated in western history.[48] The perceptions of the West constructed in the nineteenth century continue to affect our ideas and behavior. The tension between wanting to expand and develop agriculture and industry and wanting to enjoy splendid scenery has not been resolved. We still perceive the West as the setting for limitless opportunity and indestructible wilderness, despite the realities that surface daily. The persistence of successive droughts in the Great Plains, of failing dams and irrigated lands destroyed by salt, and of deserted mining towns and overgrazed ranges seems to have had little impact on national mythology. Because few Americans have been able to disengage the cultural filters that affect their vision of the region, the twentieth-century West is the result of the West we perceived in the nineteenth century.

The interpretation of the West has changed as Americans have integrated the region into their culture. Because the landscape of the Far West now represents a distinctive national culture, cacti, Indians, and rock monoliths have become tourist attractions. However, few of the cultural filters that affected perceptions in the nineteenth century have been removed. Some, in fact, have been enhanced. New developments in communication and technological skill heighten the perception that the West can be molded in any way its inhabitants see fit. Cellular phones shrink frightening distance into a momentary crackle, and great dams can turn any desert into a garden.

In some ways, the twentieth century brought a new set of mispercep-

A Dash for the Timber, Frederic Remington, 1889. Oil on canvas (no. 1961.381).
Courtesy Amon Carter Museum, Fort Worth, Texas.

tions, but in other ways it brought a new understanding of what the West
could mean for American culture. As non-Anglo Americans have begun to
challenge mainstream views of what the West was, is, or should be, our
perceptions of the region have grown increasingly complex. Americans
discovered that the parts of the West they had been avoiding or ignoring
were invested with unique cultural and economic value. Some artists
looked beyond European models and reveled in the distinctive shapes and
colors of the Southwest. Georgia O'Keeffe's abstract landscapes challenged
Frederic Remington's men of action in the category of most popular western art.[49] Ethnologists and anthropologists learned to appreciate the rich
history and culture of Indian peoples. The former wastelands of the Great
Basin and the Southwest have become convenient testing grounds and
waste dumps.

These discoveries, however, also continued the old role of the West:
providing what the nation needed. By the early twentieth century, the nation needed a distinctive history and personality—one that distinguished
it from Europe—and the West provided this. The areas that did not meet
economic needs could be turned into quaint "frontierlands," places where
scenery and native peoples combined to give white Americans a sense of

history. Early in the century, for example, the Santa Fe Railroad recognized the growing perception of the unique landscape of the Southwest as the "real America" and cleverly packaged it for Americans to consume.[50]

Many of us now perceive the West as original, distinctive, and quintessentially American. The irony is that much of the West that seems so important to our self-perception either never existed or has disappeared, but we have re-created it as we imagine it must have been. The perceptual West of glorious mountains, verdant grazing land, and noble Indians now decorates T-shirts and motel rooms because the landscape has been molded to fit our perceptions of what Anglo Americans thought the West should be; in the process, the landscape was eaten by cattle, blasted by miners, and blurred by smog. We need to reexamine our perceptual legacies and take some cues from other cultures about using adaptation rather than remodeling as our approach to the West. Perhaps then we will take off some of the filters and look at the western landscape with a clearer view.

Notes

An earlier version of this essay appeared under the title "Cultural Filters: The Significance of Perception in the History of the American West," by Anne F. Hyde. Previously published in the *Western Historical Quarterly* 24 (August 1993): 351–74. Copyright by Western History Association. Reprinted by permission.

1. Walter Prescott Webb, *The Great Plains* (Boston, 1931); Donald Worster, *Dust Bowl: The Southern Plains in the 1930s* (New York, 1979) and *Rivers of Empire: Water, Aridity, and the Growth of the American West* (New York, 1985); Henry Nash Smith, *Virgin Land: The American West as Symbol and Myth* (Cambridge, Mass., 1950); Annette Kolodny, *The Land before Her: Fantasy and Experience of the American Frontiers, 1630–1860* (Chapel Hill, 1984); William H. Goetzmann, *Exploration and Empire: The Explorer and the Scientist in the Winning of the American West* (New York, 1966).

2. This gets into sticky issues involving "reader response theory" and understanding why people read texts or view images; it is at least worth considering the relationship between eyewitnesses and armchair observers. For a clear description of the basics of such ideas, see Terry Eagleton, *Literary Theory: An Introduction* (Minneapolis, 1983), 74–88, or John Berger, *About Looking* (New York, 1980).

3. Little work has been done on Native Americans' or non-Anglo colonizers' perceptions of landscape. See Douglas Monroy, *Thrown among Strangers: The Making of Mexican Culture in Frontier California* (Berkeley, 1990), 10–50, 134–62, for examples of peoples who accepted the limitations of landscape. See Richard White, *The Roots of Dependency: Subsistence, Environment, and Social Change among the Choctaws, Pawnees, and Navajos* (Lincoln, 1983), and Ramón A. Gutiérrez, *When Jesus Came, the Corn Mothers Went Away: Marriage, Sexuality, and Power in New Mex-*

ico, 1500–1846 (Stanford, 1991), for discussions of the impact of conquest on perception and use of land. For a discussion of Asian views of the region, particularly of Japanese-American internees, see Patricia Nelson Limerick, "Disorientation and Reorientation: The American Landscape Discovered from the West," *Journal of American History* 79 (December 1992): 1021–49.

4. For a more detailed discussion of these points, see Yi-Fu Tuan, *Topophilia: A Study of Environmental Perception, Attitudes, and Values* (Englewood Cliffs, N.J., 1974) and *Space and Place: The Perspective of Experience* (Minneapolis, 1977), and John A. Jakle, *The Visual Elements of Landscape* (Amherst, Mass., 1987). For a general discussion on the cultural role of perception, see John Brinckerhoff Jackson, *Discovering the Vernacular Landscape* (New Haven, 1984).

5. Bernard DeVoto, ed., *The Journals of Lewis and Clark* (Cambridge, Mass., 1953), xl–xli. See also Donald Jackson, *Thomas Jefferson and the Stony Mountains: Exploring the West from Monticello* (Urbana, 1981).

6. Thomas Jefferson, Message to Congress, 18 January 1803, in *Letters of the Lewis and Clark Expedition,* ed. Donald Jackson, 2 vols. (1962; reprint, Urbana, 1978), 1:12.

7. For a more detailed discussion of the impact of Lewis and Clark on national ideology, see John Logan Allen, *Passage through the Garden: Lewis and Clark and the Image of the American Northwest* (Urbana, 1975).

8. Edwin James, "Account of an Expedition from Pittsburgh to the Rocky Mountains, Performed in the Years 1819, 1820," in *Early Western Travels, 1748–1846,* ed. Reuben Gold Thwaites, 32 vols. (Cleveland, 1905), 17:147.

9. Lieutenant Zebulon Pike may have been the first to designate the region as useless deserts, but his report was not well known during the early nineteenth century. For discussions about the origins and ramifications of the "Great American Desert" idea, see W. Eugene Hollon, *The Great American Desert: Then and Now* (1966; reprint, Lincoln, 1974); Goetzmann, *Exploration and Empire,* 49–64; and Martyn J. Bowden, "The Great American Desert in the American Mind: The Historiography of a Geographical Notion," in *Geographies of the Mind: Essays in Historical Geography,* ed. David Lowenthal and Martyn J. Bowden (New York, 1976), 119–47.

10. Donald Jackson and Mary Lee Spence, eds., *The Expeditions of John Charles Frémont,* 3 vols. (Urbana, 1970), 2:702.

11. For an analysis of Frémont's language in the *Report,* see Anne Farrar Hyde, *An American Vision: Far Western Landscape and National Culture, 1820–1920* (New York, 1990), 1–6. For descriptions of the popularity and impact of the *Report,* see Allan Nevins, *Frémont: Pathmarker of the West* (1939; reprint, New York, 1955), or Ferol Egan, *Frémont: Explorer for a Restless Nation* (New York, 1977).

12. Quoted in Smith, *Virgin Land,* 180. See also David M. Emmons, *Garden in the Grasslands: Boomer Literature of the Central Great Plains* (Lincoln, 1971), 128–61.

13. Webb, *Great Plains,* 376–82.

14. For discussions about American cultural insecurities, see Barbara Novak, *Nature and Culture: American Landscape and Painting, 1825–1875* (New York, 1980); Elizabeth McKinsey, *Niagara Falls: Icon of the American Sublime* (Cambridge, England, 1985); and Christopher Mulvey, *Anglo-American Landscapes: A Study of Nineteenth-Century Anglo-American Travel Literature* (Cambridge, England, 1983).

15. Hyde, *American Vision*, 107–46.

16. Passenger Department, Chicago, Burlington, and Quincy Railroad, *The Heart of the Continent: An Historical and Descriptive Treatise…of the Advantages, Resources, and Scenery of the Great West* (Chicago, 1882), 29.

17. See, for example, Patricia Nelson Limerick, *The Legacy of Conquest: The Unbroken Past of the American West* (New York, 1987); Donald Worster, *Under Western Skies: Nature and History in the American West* (New York, 1992); and Richard White, *"It's Your Misfortune and None of My Own": A New History of the American West* (Norman, 1991).

18. For a clear definition of these gender differences, see Glenda Riley, *The Female Frontier: A Comparative View of Women on the Prairie and the Plains* (Lawrence, 1988), 195–97. Kolodny, in *The Land before Her,* provides a provocative discussion of the real differences in the ways that women imagined and perceived aspects of the frontier.

19. George R. Stewart, *Ordeal by Hunger: The Story of the Donner Party* (1960; reprint, Boston, 1964), 5; Caroline S. Kirkland [Mrs. Mary Clavers], *A New Home—Who'll Follow? Or, Glimpses of Western Life* (Boston, 1839); O. E. Rölvaag, *Giants in the Earth* (New York, 1927).

20. For a discussion of the powerful impact of women's sphere on frontier life, see Julie Roy Jeffrey, *Frontier Women: The Trans-Mississippi West, 1840–1880* (New York, 1979). For the ambivalent feelings about leaving settled areas and the difficulty of maintaining standards on the frontier, see John Mack Faragher, *Women and Men on the Overland Trail* (New Haven, 1979), 66–109, and Joanna L. Stratton, *Pioneer Women: Voices from the Kansas Frontier* (New York, 1981), 34–106.

21. The exceptions to this would be travelers like Francis Parkman, Bayard Taylor, and Edwin Bryant, who took the trip into the West for pleasure.

22. Much attention has been given to the Overland Trail experience, but little work has been done on the overlanders' perceptions of the landscape. John D. Unruh Jr., *The Plains Across: The Overland Emigrants and the Trans-Mississippi West, 1840–60* (Urbana, 1979), and Faragher, *Women and Men*, both devote some discussion to this issue but are more concerned with the mechanics of travel and social relationships.

23. For examples of overlanders' reactions to the environment, see William Swain's account in J. S. Holliday, *The World Rushed In: The California Gold Rush Experience* (New York, 1981), 150–71, or Phoebe Goodell Judson, *A Pioneer's Search for an Ideal Home* (1925; reprint, Lincoln, 1984), 31–38. For a more general discussion of the difficulties of travel, see Faragher, *Women and Men*, 66–87.

24. Horace Greeley, *An Overland Journey from New York to San Francisco in the Summer of 1859* (New York, 1860), 205.

25. Samuel Clemens [Mark Twain], *Roughing It* (1872; reprint, New York, 1980), 114. See also Patricia Nelson Limerick, *Desert Passages: Encounters with the American Deserts* (Albuquerque, 1985), 75.

26. Wolfgang Schivelbusch, *The Railway Journey: Trains and Travel in the Nineteenth Century* (New York, 1977), 65–66. See also Geoffrey Hindley, *Tourists, Travellers, and Pilgrims* (London, 1983), 198–205.

27. Stephen Kern, *The Culture of Time and Space, 1880–1918* (Cambridge,

Mass., 1983), 10–64; John R. Stilgoe, *Metropolitan Corridor: Railroads and the American Scene* (New Haven, 1983), 249–56.

28. Lady Duffus Hardy, *Through Cities and Prairie Lands: Sketches of an American Tour* (New York, 1881), 134–35.

29. Hyde, *American Vision*, 117–20.

30. Thomas Nelson, *The Union Pacific Railroad: A Trip across the Continent from Omaha to Ogden* (New York, 1870), 15. For a discussion of Americans' fascination with the technology of railroads, see Stilgoe, *Metropolitan Corridor*, 137–45.

31. Emmons, *Garden in the Grasslands*, 25–46; Robert G. Athearn, *Union Pacific Country* (Chicago, 1971), 147–97.

32. Paul Wallace Gates, *The Illinois Central Railroad and Its Colonization Work* (Cambridge, Mass., 1934), 171–99; 1873 pamphlet quoted in Emmons, *Garden in the Grasslands*, 35–36.

33. George S. Clason, *Free Homestead Lands of Colorado Described: A Handbook for Settlers* (Denver, 1915), 97.

34. James Montgomery Flagg, *Boulevards All the Way—Maybe!* (New York, 1925), 138. For discussions of the perceived freedom created by the automobile, see Warren James Belasco, *Americans on the Road: From Autocamp to Motel, 1910–1945* (Cambridge, Mass., 1979), 18–22; James J. Flink, *The Automobile Age* (Cambridge, Mass., 1988), 129–31; or John A. Jakle, *The Tourist: Travel in Twentieth-Century North America* (Lincoln, 1985), 146–52.

35. See Flink, *Automobile Age*, 169–71, for a description of early travel. See also Vernon McGill, *Diary of a Motor Journey from Chicago to Los Angeles* (Los Angeles, 1922).

36. Marc Reisner, *Cadillac Desert: The American West and Its Disappearing Water* (New York, 1986), 3.

37. For the impact of Bierstadt on national conceptions of the West, see William H. Goetzmann and William N. Goetzmann, *The West of the Imagination* (New York, 1986), 149–51; Hyde, *American Vision*, 77–80; and Nancy K. Anderson and Linda S. Ferber, *Albert Bierstadt: Art and Enterprise* (New York, 1990), 24–34.

38. Peter B. Hales, *William Henry Jackson and the Transformation of the American Landscape* (Philadelphia, 1988); Carol Clark, *Thomas Moran: Watercolors of the American West* (Austin, 1980).

39. Ben Merchant Vorpahl, *Frederic Remington and the West: With the Eye of the Mind* (Austin, 1978), 38–47, has a perceptive discussion of Remington and the Far Western landscape.

40. Many tourists were disappointed because they did not see Indians that resembled Catlin's noble figures or the heroic characters of James Fenimore Cooper's novels. See Hyde, *American Vision*, 27–31, 140–42. For more detailed discussions of George Catlin, see William H. Truettner, *The Natural Man Observed: A Study of Catlin's Indian Gallery* (Washington, D.C., 1979); for Karl Bodmer, see John C. Ewers et al., *Views of a Vanishing Frontier* (Omaha, 1984).

41. Hyde, *American Vision*, 54–62.

42. Goetzmann and Goetzmann, *West of the Imagination*, 38–40.

43. Gordon Hendricks, *Albert Bierstadt: Painter of the American West* (New York, 1974), 51–58, 149–50; Anderson and Ferber, *Albert Bierstadt*, 74–77.

44. *Catalogue of the Daguerreotype Panoramic Views in California, by R. H. Vance* (New York, 1851).

45. Hyde, *American Vision,* 81–85; Peter E. Palmquist, *Carleton E. Watkins: Photographer of the American West* (Albuquerque, 1983), 18–26.

46. Rick Dingus, *The Photographic Artifacts of Timothy O'Sullivan* (Albuquerque, 1982), xiii.

47. Ibid., 55.

48. Limerick, *Legacy of Conquest.*

49. See Patricia Janis Broder, *The American West: The Modern Vision* (Boston, 1984), for a perceptive discussion of the change in western art from narrative realism to symbolic abstraction.

50. T. C. McLuhan, *Dream Tracks: The Railroad and the American Indian, 1890–1930* (New York, 1985), 13–29; see also Hyde, *American Vision,* 229–44.

COMMENTARIES
Looking West from Here and There

Martha A. Sandweiss

It is ironic that so much of our enduring national myth about the West should have been created by nineteenth-century explorers, artists, and writers who never really lived there. These chroniclers could propose hypotheses they would never have to test. After a season in the West they could return to the comfort of home, never worrying about whether winter would prove as felicitous as spring or whether technology would make the desert bloom. To an eastern audience hungry for news of the sparsely settled West, they left behind a mixed legacy of spare facts and complex ideas that ranged from useful maps and geological sketches to culturally loaded ideas about the region's native peoples and the utility of the western landscape. And, as Anne Hyde suggests, their reports and photographs, books and paintings, not only shaped a national myth but also helped set the stage for more than a century and a half of federal policy toward the West. The constraints or "filters" that conditioned the perceptions of these early western chroniclers are thus worth examining in some detail.

The idea of "perception" that frames Hyde's essay is used in several different ways that might be useful to distinguish. First, it denotes personal, firsthand observation of the West, such as the perceptions formed by Major Stephen H. Long and his companions on their trek across the plains in 1819–21. It also refers to the response of readers or viewers of the firsthand accounts produced by eyewitness observers like Long or Albert Bierstadt. Finally, it describes the more generalized cultural beliefs of countless Americans with little exposure to either the West or the many visual and literary accounts produced to describe the region. This is the sense of the word that Hyde uses when she refers to our continuing cultural "perception" of the West as a place of limitless opportunity.

Each use of the word *perception* raises different conceptual problems, for in each case the perceiver is developing an understanding of the West based on a different sort of information or experience. Because most dictionary definitions of the word *perception* invoke the concept of direct visual cognition or apprehension, it seems most appropriate to apply the word only to the activities of eyewitness observers of the West and to clarify that second- and third-hand consumers of information or ideas gathered knowledge in a different way.

As Hyde suggests, even firsthand observations are conditioned by cultural filters, and she argues for the importance of gender and comfort as important mediating factors. To these, we might also add the health and age of the observer and even the local weather. Calling for a cross-cultural perspective, Hyde also proposes that we look at the perceptions of early Hispanic travelers and settlers as well as those of Native American peoples. This is an important idea that suggests yet another category for analysis. We might also consider the differences in the perceptions formed by western residents and western travelers, even within the same ethnic group; an unfamiliar terrain is always very different from the familiar landscape of home.

But any discussion of western literary or visual images must begin with the acknowledgment that visual or literary renderings of firsthand experiences do not necessarily reflect the creator's "perceptions" of the West. That is, they do not always convey the feelings experienced by the artist at the time he or she observed a particular scene. The creative process is much more complicated than that. Artists are not necessarily reporters, and they have no moral obligation either to tell the truth or to reveal their own feelings. Indeed, nineteenth-century artists and writers often served particular patrons who had very specific goals for their work. If Alfred Jacob Miller painted Indian odalisques, it was not necessarily because they fairly represented either the women he found at the fur traders' rendezvous of 1837 or his own longings. It may also have been because he was in the employ of the Scottish nobleman William Drummond Stewart, who wanted romantic paintings of the West to take home to Murthley Castle. Likewise, whereas Carleton E. Watkins's landscape photographs of the West are often, as Hyde argues, "balanced, silent and grand," it is important to note that many were done for commercial clients who wanted to promote a particular popular understanding of their steam navigation company, mining operation, or large industrial farm. The worlds of western art and western commerce often intermingled.

As businessmen or entrepreneurs with complicated agendas for their work, most chroniclers of the nineteenth-century West worked with a public audience in mind. Thus to Hyde's list of factors motivating artists, a list that includes "personal ambitions" and "national expectations," we must add economic considerations, embracing everything from the very specific demands of patrons to the more nebulous demands of public audiences. Consider, for example, the John Mix Stanley painting that she cites, *Chain of Spires Along the Gila* (1855). We should not necessarily conclude from the image itself that Stanley "perceived"—that is, saw, experienced, and understood—the Southwest as a "bizarre cornucopia." The image, after all, was painted some nine years after his trip to the region. We must thus ask whether he painted it as a record of a particular site or as a kind of typical landscape, specific to none, that would recapitulate a wide range of experiences. Perhaps he intended to convey an impression or idea rather than an actual perception of a particular place. Perhaps he merely wanted to work out a formal painting problem. We must be wary of the ways in which we use images as primary source evidence of either the physical appearance of a place or the actual beliefs or intentions of its creator.

The worlds of firsthand observers and secondhand viewers are inextricably intertwined. Western travelers' eyewitness accounts sent back east could inform and shape Americans' understanding of the West. But the needs, demands, and desires of a distant audience could also dictate the form of a work created in the field.

These distant readers and viewers who encountered eyewitness accounts and images of the West in public ways—through published works or exhibitions—form the second category of "perceivers" that Hyde addresses in her essay. To distinguish their means of learning from those of firsthand observers, let us say that these secondhand observers "understood" or "imagined" the West rather than "perceiving" it for themselves.

How did they receive their firsthand accounts of the West? And what relationship did the message they receive have to the one that firsthand observers sought to create? I pose this last question because so much of what was initially written about the West, or drawn or photographed there, passed through a sort of translation process before it reached a wide audience. Hyde's metaphor of a game of "telephone" is apt. Letters to a hometown newspaper might become a published book. A photograph might be distributed with descriptive captions written by a publisher or might be reproduced as a wood engraving. A painting might become a hand-colored engraving marketed to a mass public. Changes in content (and often in meaning) would inevitably occur, for firsthand observers could not always control the message their work conveyed to distant viewers.

The consumers of western literature or western imagery might not discriminate between the descriptive material produced by an eyewitness observer and that produced by someone else. Among Currier and Ives's most popular western prints, playing on numerous widely held beliefs about the West, were those created by Frances Palmer, an Englishwoman who never ventured west herself. Likewise popular were the paintings and prints of the hunting and wildlife artist Arthur Fitzwilliam Tait, who never ventured west of the Adirondacks and who based his western scenes on earlier works by the artists Karl Bodmer and George Catlin, works that he looked up at the New York Public Library.

Hyde's interesting questions about the filters through which eyewitness observers viewed the western landscape might also be applied to the vast American audience that encountered the West in other forms, through books, pictures, and films. Did gender, class, and age influence the image of the West these consumers formed from their reading of the texts and viewing of the images? Did women read Charles Frémont's report differently than men did? Did they draw different lessons from Bierstadt's paintings? Did youths take away from dime novels different ideas than did their parents? What filters, we might usefully ask, were in operation back in eastern America?

The third and final sense in which Hyde uses the concept of perception is to apply to broad, generally held cultural beliefs, as when she discusses the perceptions of the West constructed in the nineteenth century as opposed to twentieth-century beliefs, or the nineteenth-century "perception that the West could be made into whatever Americans wanted it to be, despite geographic realities." Again, because "perception" connotes mental apprehension or personal observation, it seems more useful to introduce another term that more clearly suggests that broadly held beliefs are shaped by a wide variety of political, cultural, and economic forces that may or may not reflect visual or literary information about the western landscape or the experience of being in the West. What we're really talking about here is a mode of thought shaped by popular culture in its most broadly construed form, a form of thought that reflects the zeitgeist of the age.

Many questions might be asked about the ways in which specific information is translated into general beliefs, personal visions into popular myth. But again, Hyde's essay suggests a useful approach. We might ask, as we did with eyewitness observers and the viewers or readers of their work, what cultural filters operated on the vast number of Americans who had no personal experience of the West but who nonetheless formed certain beliefs about it. However popular certain ideas might have been, they were not universally held. Were popular beliefs about the West conditioned by gender, class, geographical location, or political persuasion? This is a rhetorical question, for of course they were.

Hyde asserts, "Few historians have looked systematically at the history of perceiving the West." Such a statement is true only in the narrowest definition of the historical profession, for the field has long been of interest to western literary historians, western art historians, and students of popular culture. Nonetheless, one of the significant virtues of Hyde's essay is its suggestion that cultural history deserves greater pride of place in the academic study of the West. The complicated history of western literary and visual images—from their creation through their publication and popular reception—is a history intertwined with the history of exploration and settlement, political decision making, and economic development. It is, as Hyde argues, a history that is fundamental to a deeper understanding of the questions that are central to the field of western historical studies.

The Shadow of Pikes Peak

Elliott West

Nathan C. Meeker loved three things above all. He loved his wife, the long-suffering Arvilla. He loved the Prohibitionist cause. And he loved the idea of how agricultural reform might improve society and elevate the spirits of those who worked the soil. In 1869 Meeker left love number one to pursue numbers two and three in the great West. He went to Colorado, hurrying to a place that was, to him, symbolic of the West's glorious, uplifting possibilities: Pikes Peak. One story has it that Meeker arrived late at night near the mountain's base and that, after a few hours of tossing in bed in anticipation, he arose at the first of false dawn and looked out of his tent at the magnificent shape that towered in the dark. Overwhelmed with emotion, he wrote an ode on the "awful majesty" of such a masterpiece of God's handiwork. By the time he finished, it was full light. Stepping from his tent for another view of the peak, he looked up and saw—a haystack.[1]

Anne Hyde, a young historian who works near the foot of that mountain that Meeker didn't see, has written a provocative essay on the importance of perception—or rather misperception—in understanding western history, and she raises important issues to which we have paid too little attention. Historians have not ignored perceptions of the West, of course. There is an enormous, sprawling scholarship on the mythic West and on western literary and artistic images. But Hyde is stressing a couple of points that have not been taken seriously enough. First, she is arguing that we need to identify and define the many variables of perception—the "cultural filters," to use her phrase, through which actualities are bent into what is finally perceived by individuals. These filters might be cultural expectations rooted in historical experience or might be distorting mechanisms arising from changing technology. In the case of the latter, I found especially fascinating her insights into how modes of travel influence how we see the land and our relationship to it and what we anticipate from it.

Second, and more fundamentally, Hyde is arguing that perception is an integral part of studying everything else, from the topics laid out in traditional texts, such as ranching, politics, military campaigns, and town building, to the subjects of contemporary concern, such as gender and ethnic relations. The premise is simple. A prominent Yale alumnus has put it well. "How I see the world," he wrote, "is the only way I know to react to the world." These words are from William F. Buckley in his most recent book, *WindFall*, but the principle holds, whether we are talking about mining and native-white relations or about sailing and Tory politics.[2]

The role of perception in human action has long been a part of western historiography. There are the well-known works by William Goetzmann and John Logan Allen on expectations and exploration, for instance, and works by David Emmons and Donald Worster on fantasies of the Great Plains and their disastrous consequences.[3] But we need to think more broadly and complexly about the dynamic relationship between perception and action. In a recent essay on the continuing process of discovery in North America, for instance, Richard White wrote that European Americans' mental encounters with the West have been a kind of conversation, with each exchange building on the ones before it. People act on the land according to particular imagined constructions of "nature"; what they do changes the actual environment; the modified environment inspires new mental constructions, which lead people to make different sorts of changes.[4] Considered this way, as a component of every human's dialogue with his surroundings, perception is not just another significant topic; it is an essential element in understanding all other significant topics.

That means, among other things, that we have to be very careful in defining and using the term *perception*. In the other commentary on Hyde's essay, Martha Sandweiss considers some of the various meanings of this flexible word and some of their implications. Instead I would like to expand on what Hyde has said and to suggest a few ways that this perceptual approach, however we define it, might be applied other than the ways she has emphasized.

For example, Hyde stresses the promise and possibilities newcomers saw in the land itself. But perceptions of the West were never limited to the landscape per se and to what it would give pioneers and let them do. There was always a social dimension to the vision. Easterners looked westward and pictured who was and would be living there. These perceptions were often as bizarrely wrongheaded as those of the physical potential of the land, and when pioneers acted on them, the results were similarly calamitous.

Hyde tells us about William Jackson Palmer, who, like Nathan Meeker, stood at the base of Pikes Peak and had a vision, in his case of a place of surpassing beauty, European-style, that would become a lounging ground for the well-to-do from both sides of the Atlantic. But that was not all he saw. A few months after Meeker's encounter with the haystack, Palmer sat at about the same spot and wrote his wife of rising early in the morning, gazing at Pikes Peak, and envisioning what might be: his own castle, surrounded by prosperous farmhouses and round about a vast deer park with buffalo, antelope, "and with them a few Indians to recall more vividly the wild prairie life—which the Americans of a few years hence will only know from the pages of storybooks." Two years later, with plans for Colorado Springs well under way, he wrote more specifically of his social vision: "We shall have a new and better civilization in the far West; only may the people never get to be as thick as on the eastern seaboard. We will surrender the briny border as a sort of extensive Castle Garden to receive and filter the foreign swarms and prepare them by a gradual process for coming to the inner temple of Americanism out in Colorado. . . . Isn't that a logical as well as a unique notion?"[5]

Well, it was not so logical and, alas, certainly not unique. At the time Palmer was writing, the percentage of foreign-born in Colorado was more than twice that in his native state of Delaware, half again that of Maryland, and greater than that in Pennsylvania. The state along the eastern "briny border" with the highest portion of aliens was New York, with about 26 percent. Wyoming and Montana each had more than 38 percent, whereas Idaho had 52 percent, twice that of New York, and these figures do not include most Hispanics, who were counted as native-born, or Indians, who stubbornly refused to vanish into the storybooks.[6] In short, if Palmer had wanted to escape the "foreign swarms," he should have headed back east, because the West was then, as it is now, the most ethnically diverse part of America.

The Palmers of that time perceived the West not just as a wilderness of sublime scenery; they saw it also as a kind of social void waiting to be filled with people of their choosing. Just as they looked at deserts and saw gardens and looked at the plains and saw European resorts, so they looked at human diversity and saw uniformity or saw nobody at all. They then projected westward a society of blue-eyed sons of Albion.

This perceptual approach should also be applied to all groups involved in the story. For all of the new ideas in Hyde's essay, her approach is in one way traditional. Her emphasis is on the cultural misperceptions of Anglo Americans moving west. We should also consider the perceptions of the many other ethnic groups that accompanied the Anglo invasion, of the earlier Hispanic intruders who would in turn be intruded on, and of the Asians for whom eastward expansion was another distinct experience.

Yet another cultural variable must be included. Early in her essay Hyde stated, "In . . . he lands west of the one hundredth meridian, Anglo Americans came up against a series of landscapes that defied their notions about utility and beauty." She might just as well have written, "In . . . he lands west of the one hundredth meridian, Americans came up against thousands of eastern interlopers who acted very oddly and who had very strange ideas about the land." These Americans—the Native Americans—brought their own cultural biases to events. Reconstructing the Indian perception of contact, exchange, and conflict is one of the most challenging, and essential, tasks before us. The obstacles are formidable, beginning with the fact that most of what we know of native perceptions comes from white observers, so the voices are doubly and triply filtered, like the electronically altered accents of a witness testifying against the Mafia. And yet, keeping in mind the Buckley principle, we cannot possibly understand what happened, the changing hows and whys of Indian history, without some conception of what natives saw and what reality had become by the time it arrived in the native consciousness.

Interestingly, most work so far has focused on the time most difficult to recapture—the earliest contact between Europeans and Indians. From the eastern United States there is the work of James Merrell, James Axtell, Mary Helms, and George Sabo. Investigations in the West have lagged a little behind, but the work that has been done shows that the effort is clearly worth it. Ramón Gutiérrez's *When Jesus Came, the Corn Mothers Went Away* shows how wonderfully, deliciously complicated the story gets when we bring to it the native cultural perceptions.[7]

Finally, as Hyde notes briefly, we ought to carry this perceptual approach forward into the present era. Certainly the perceptions Hyde discusses have survived. The two insistent images she stresses—the West as economic opportunity and the scenic West of "frontierlands"—in a way have converged in what is arguably the region's leading industry: tourism. In the West of today, the search for the scenic *is* opportunity. But this seeming reconciliation actually represents a new set of contradictions, as millions of vacationers leave the crowded, polluted cities of the East and flee to litter-choked, bumper-to-bumper, smog-shrouded Yosemite and Jackson Hole. As Hyde notes, the earlier, nineteenth-century versions of these nagging national psychic needs had a profound impact on western lands. How much, much greater, then, are the ecological consequences today, given the numbers of people involved? Pikes Peak draws rather larger crowds than in the days of Meeker and Palmer; in 1981, 253,000 persons drove to the top. In 1955, the last year before limits were set on river traffic through the Grand Canyon, about as many people floated through the canyon by raft as emigrated to Oregon by wagon between 1840 and 1850. There is not the slightest hint that the situation is changing. I suggest a simple measurement, which might be called the "turnstile test." The perception of the West as sublime wilderness will remain among the preeminent factors in its history as long as the number of annual visits to the four most popular western national parks (Grand Canyon, Yosemite, Yellowstone, and Olympic) is greater than the population of New England.

Just as surely, the misperception of the blue-eyed West remains an important part of contemporary life. William Jackson Palmer's vision survives in extreme form in places like northern Idaho, pockets of the dream of the West as Aryan America's last line of defense against ethnic and racial degeneration. Far more widespread is resentment and alarm over the most recent immigration from across our southern border and across the Pacific. The confusion of perception and reality results in the strangest contortions in the current debate. Critics of the new immigration sometimes invoke the principles of conservatism, even as they promote what would be a profoundly radical innovation (ethnic uniformity) and as they resist the West's oldest process (immigration and adaptation) and work to undo its most ancient condition (cultural diversity).

Less can be said about bringing into the present century the perceptions of other cultural groups, for the good reason that, except in Hispanic studies, relatively little attention has been given to the subject. There *are* a growing number of works on recent Indian history, but their emphasis has not been on the perceptual world—how Native Americans have seen themselves and their place in the changes around them. Enough has been done to be provocative: David Baird's recent presidential address before the Western History Association; John Farella's study of Navajo philosophy, *The Main Stalk;* and a few tribal studies that raise the issue, such as Morris Foster's recent *Being Comanche.*[8] Nonetheless, the history of Native American self-perception in the twentieth century is one of the great understudied topics before us.

We can learn more, in fact, by turning from shelves of history to those of literature, specifically to the large and growing number of fictional works by Native American authors, established stars like James Welch, Louise Erdrich, and Leslie Marmon Silko and slightly lesser known writers like Diane Glancy.

When we integrate their writing into western literature, it is impossible to miss what seems to me a revealing irony. Among even our best white writers, the descendants of those supposedly practical and pragmatic and realistic and forward-looking pioneers, we are far more likely to find stories that look *backward* to a lost, magnificent West free of restraints or to a place of Old Testament wrestlings with God and the devil, a land of Little Big Men and Blood Meridians and Buffalo Girls. Yet among Indian novelists, grandchildren of those supposedly tradition-bound peoples who, as the cliché goes, "watched their way of life disappear," the stories are almost without exception in the *present*, or rather the present is bound seamlessly to the past, usually through rich weavings of family and kin, as in Erdrich's trilogy.

This is not to say that Indians have not misperceived and suffered the consequences. Obviously they have. But the themes of this new native literature—of return and reconciliation, of beliefs both evolved and enduring, of many peoples and traditions tangled beyond any thought of unraveling—suggest at the very least a different perceptual experience, in particular one that has been fairly successful at negotiating the changes of the past century and a half and at keeping today and yesterday connected.

So as we mark the centennial of a thesis that celebrated adjustment to changing circumstances, it seems especially timely to study more closely how Native Americans have taken in the reality of events since the Europeans' arrival in the West. We may find that they have a stronger claim as masters of adaptation than do the white pioneers Turner celebrated, because it may be that Native Americans have had a more accurate perception of what the West was and is, what it can and cannot do, and who has been here. Telling that story will certainly enrich and nicely complicate western history; it might also offer hints about how to cope with the present, about how to look at a haystack and see a haystack, or to use Hyde's words, how to "reexamine our perceptual legacies and . . . look at the western landscape with a clearer view."

Notes

1. Marshall Sprague, *Massacre: The Tragedy at White River* (Boston, 1957), 16–17.

2. William F. Buckley Jr., *WindFall: The End of the Affair* (New York: 1992), xii.

3. William H. Goetzmann, *Exploration and Empire: The Explorer and the Scientist in the Winning of the American West* (New York, 1966) and *New Lands, New Men: America and the Second Great Age of Discovery* (New York, 1986); John Logan Allen, *Passage through the Garden: Lewis and Clark and the Image of the American Northwest* (Urbana, 1975); David M. Emmons, *Garden in the Grasslands: Boomer Literature of the Central Great Plains* (Lincoln, 1971); Donald Worster, *Dust Bowl: The Southern Plains in the 1930s* (New York, 1979).

4. Richard White, "Discovering Nature in North America," *Journal of American History* 79 (December 1992): 877.

5. John S. Fisher, *A Builder of the West: The Life of General William Jackson Palmer* (Caldwell, Idaho, 1939), 163–64, 202–3.

6. U.S. Office of the Census, Ninth Census, Volume I, *Statistics of the Population of the United States* . . . (Washington, D.C., 1872), 299.

7. James Merrell, *The Indians' New World: Catawbas and Their Neighbors from European Contact through the Era of Removal* (Chapel Hill, 1989); James Axtell, "Through Another Glass Darkly: Early Indian Views of Europeans," *After Columbus: Essays in the Ethnohistory of Colonial America* (New York, 1988), 125–43, and *Imagining the Other: First Encounters in North America* (Washington, D.C., 1991); Mary Helms, *Ulysses' Sail: The Ethnographic Odyssey of Power, Knowledge, and Geographical Distance* (Princeton, 1988); George Sabo III, "Reordering Their World: A Caddoan Ethnohistory," in *Visions and Revisions: Ethnohistorical Perspectives on Southern Cultures*, ed. George Sabo III and William M. Schneider (Athens, 1989), 25–47; Ramón Gutiérrez, *When Jesus Came, the Corn Mothers Went Away: Marriage, Sexuality, and Power in New Mexico, 1500–1846* (Stanford, 1991).

8. David Baird, "Are the Five Tribes of Oklahoma 'Real Indians'?" *Western Historical Quarterly* 21 (1990): 5–18; John R. Farella, *The Main Stalk: A Synthesis of Navajo Philosophy* (Tucson, 1984); Morris W. Foster, *Being Comanche: A Social History of an American Indian Community* (Tucson, 1991).

7

Still Native:
The Significance of Native Americans
in the History of the Twentieth-Century
American West

David Rich Lewis

When Frederick Jackson Turner reimagined American history in 1893, he considered Native Americans to be of little significance. He demonstrated more interest in the process of heroic, white yeomen hewing out a corridor of civilization in an environment that all but overwhelmed them, transforming them from immigrants into Americans. Indians were Indians, part of that wild frontier environment. They posed "a common danger" and served as "a consolidating agent in our history," faceless obstacles to be overcome and subdued in the process of westering.[1]

Common wisdom and events of the day seemed to justify Turner's perspective. After all, Indian populations were at their low ebb, a vanishing vestige of the frontier experience. Turner's contemporaries saw the breakup of Indian reservations and the "final promise" of assimilation through allotment and agrarian settlement as an eventuality—the ultimate realization of the Euro-American belief in the unilinear progress of peoples from savagism to civility. Why should he have written differently?[2]

Yet one hundred years later, there are those who voice essentially the same attitudes: that modern Indians are unimportant in the larger picture; that they are obstacles in the development of the American West; that they must assimilate or disappear; and that the answer to the "Indian Problem" again lies in abrogating their special relationship with the federal government. James Watt, secretary of the interior during Ronald Reagan's presidency, was only the most visible of those lamenting reservations and Indians as examples of the "failure of socialism," as stumbling blocks in the development of the West. Whereas Turner tried to sell a theory and Watt

This cartoon by Oliphant appeared in 1983. Copyright 1983 Universal Press Syndicate, reprinted with permission.

tried to sell everything, both tried to sell the idea that this was an Indian rather than a non-Indian problem, one fueled by persistent misperceptions and political agendas dismissive of contemporary Native American cultures and realities.[3]

In the following pages, let me suggest six broad areas of significance for Native Americans in the history of the twentieth-century American West and, by extension, the history of the nation. The first four areas of significance—persistence, land, economic development, and political sovereignty—are overlapping and interdependent. The fifth and sixth areas address larger cultural issues: the persistent symbolic value of native peoples, and the contributions emerging from Native American history and literature. There are many other areas of significance that could be discussed. I offer these as suggestions to stimulate discussion and focus attention on issues of importance for Indian peoples.

Persistence

The first significance of Native Americans in the twentieth-century American West is their physical and cultural persistence as identifiable ethnic individuals and communities in the face of overwhelming odds—the odds by which Turner's contemporaries viewed them as increasingly insignificant. Five hundred years of disease and conquest, removal and reservation, reduced the native population of the continental United States from a conservatively estimated 2 to 5 million people to only 228,000 survivors by 1890. Such wholesale depopulation had repercussions across the spectrum of cultural knowledge and practice. Entire groups disappeared or withdrew and regrouped in unwanted corners of the country. They persisted by selectively resisting, adopting, and adapting to meet ever-changing circumstances. Federal officials pushed Indians to respond to policy and directed change at a pace and on a scale unexpected of any other group. When Indians failed to acculturate rapidly enough, reformers and bureaucrats abandoned them on the periphery of American society.[4]

But Native Americans did not disappear and, in fact, staged an impressive comeback, demonstrating cultural resilience and experimentation in the face of the policy pendulum of allotment, reorganization, termination, self-determination, and the recent threat of fiscal termination disguised as Reagan's "New Federalism."[5] Revitalization movements and pan-Indian organizations emerged in the early twentieth century to counter the hopelessness of allotted reservation life, to transcend tribal politics, and to sustain a native identity—one that not only recognized diversity within the Indian population but also acknowledged a shared experience distinct from that of nonnative Americans.[6] In the 1930s, Native Americans variably used or rejected the Indian Reorganization Act (IRA) of 1934 to create tribal governments to protect their identity and sovereignty.[7] Tribes began to renew group ceremonialism and re-create homelands where Indians and Indianness could continue. What emerged from the IRA process was a more unified ethnic identity, voice, and story than had previously existed—a truly "Indian" history as opposed to the greater diversity of native group histories, but native nonetheless.

In the post–World War II era, growing Indian populations, limited reservation opportunities, and federal relocation programs sparked a migration from reservation to city. The urbanization of Indian peoples parallels the urbanization of the West. In 1980, 77 percent of all American Indians lived west of the Mississippi River, and over half lived in urban areas—Los Angeles, Tulsa, Phoenix, and a host of other cities, all with their own recognizable Indian communities and cultural centers. In 1990, one hundred years after their population nadir, there were almost 2 million American Indians (0.8 percent of the total U.S. population), representing 314 recognized tribes, 197 Alaskan native villages, and many more groups awaiting federal recognition. More than half lived in just six states—Oklahoma, California, Arizona, New Mexico, Alaska, and Washington—all in the West. Native Americans are a youthful population, and their numbers continue to grow at an astounding rate, leading to projections of 4.6 million Indians by 2050. Navajos alone are expected to double their population of 219,198 in the next twenty years—both a benefit and a potential threat to their future.[8]

This physical and cultural survival has not been without costs—the loss of diversity, cultural knowledge, land, and identity. Intermarriage and the emergence of mixed-blood groups have generated and will continue to generate social and political factionalism within tribes, necessitating the periodic and painful redefinition of tribal identity and Indianness. Rapid population growth, underdevelopment, health issues, and migrations between city and reservation feed the outward appearances of a growing culture of poverty. In 1989, 27 percent of all Indian families were living in poverty, nearly three times the national average. Media images of American consumerism bombard Indians, intensifying the cultural and generational disjunctures in value and expectation, needs and wants. Tribes find themselves balancing the modern rights and resources that make their identity possible against periodic disunity, divergent pan-Indian agendas, and challenges by outsiders intent on abridging their sovereignty.[9]

That the people demonstrated a genius for enduring, for surviving the descendants of Columbus, is undeniable. Whether or not they continue to do so is up to the next generation. Many suggest Indian persistence depends on educating young people in their own language and customs while training them to meet the needs of the tribal group in an increasingly technological world. Most tribes are working with state school districts to add cultural heritage units to the curricula while others are creating their own schools. Today there are twenty-nine tribally controlled colleges serving over ten thousand students in twelve states. Leaders like Wilma Mankiller of the Cherokee Nation recognize the need for more effective educational opportunities for Indian children, to instill hope and produce "a cadre of well-trained young people to help us enter the twenty-first century on our own terms."[10]

Land

A second significance of Native Americans in the twentieth-century West is their control of land and valuable natural resources. Placed on unwanted and apparently worthless reservations in the nineteenth century, Indians and neighboring whites later discovered that these lands were often resource rich. Today, the land provides not only a place but also a way for In-

This Ed Stein cartoon appeared in the *Rocky Mountain News* in 1979 (reprinted with permission of Newspaper Enterprise Association, Inc.).

dian peoples to live in the modern, industrial world. Landownership and resource rights give tribes power and the ability to exercise political sovereignty but also subject them to conflicting forces from both within and outside their groups.

Land holds several levels of value for Indian peoples. First, most Indian oral traditions posit the earth and its occupants as animate, sentient, and connected through the power of creation. Nineteenth-century treaty negotiators heard native orators express this unity between people and earth in their refusal to part with the land or cut it with the plow. Those same messages resonate today among Western Shoshones who refuse to recognize federal abrogation of their treaty rights and oppose the use of their land as a nuclear test range. "The earth is our mother," stated Carrie Dann. "It is not for sale."[11]

Second, Native Americans recognize the importance of land as a place for community and continuity in the twentieth century. Their land base holds them together physically and culturally as identifiable groups, separate and safe from a national mainstream that has swept along other ethnic groups. "Everything is tied to our homeland," said the Flathead writer and historian D'Arcy McNickle. "Our language, religion, songs, beliefs—everything. Without our homeland, we are nothing."[12] The land holds Native American ancestors and gives place to their cosmologies. The land gives them identity. Hupas of northern California call themselves *Natinook-wa,* "the people of *Natinook,* the place by the river to which the trails lead back." Natinook or Hoopa Valley is the center of creation on "This Earth." In their geopolitical name, Hupas linguistically demonstrate the connection of people with place with earth. No matter where they go in life, eventually all trails return them to the center, to the valley, to the people.[13]

Finally, the land provides native groups a means of support. Removed from extensive territories to limited reservations in the nineteenth century, Indian groups altered their subsistence strategies. Dependency increased as herding replaced hunting and as warriors became farmers. Western development swept around reservations and then backtracked in the early twentieth century. Suddenly reservations became attractive because they contained natural resources absent or overexploited in other parts of the West. Where tribes retained control of their lands, they exerted some influence over the nature of development and gained some socioeconomic benefits. In other cases they watched their land, resources, and power slip away.[14]

Herein lies the problem: that control of Indian homelands has been anything but consistent. Allotment resulted in the alienation of more than 80 percent of reservation lands by 1930. Of the Indians receiving title to individual allotments, 90 percent sold or lost those lands. Under the 1934 IRA, Indian Bureau plans to repurchase 25.6 million acres to help tribes achieve "the modest standard of living of rural white people" fell woefully short because of budget constraints and the antagonism of western members of Congress. That kind of opposition continued to plague tribes in the 1950s as they began to rebuild their landed estates using royalty and claims-case money. Politicians and special-interest groups renewed their attacks on Indian lands, resources, and rights by terminating federal trust responsibilities and supervising the division of collective assets for twelve tribes.[15]

As the promise of Indian self-determination emerged in the 1960s and 1970s, tribes reasserted their treaty rights to alienated lands and resources. The Passamaquoddy and Penobscot Indians sued Maine for 58 percent of that state and $25 billion in damages, and they surprised everyone by winning. Indian groups in the Pacific Northwest and Great Lakes regions have been able to reestablish their aboriginal hunting and fishing rights.[16] But failures and stalemates in the process continue to offset the gains. In the 1980s, Northern Utes regained legal jurisdiction to 4 million acres that had composed their preallotment reservations in Utah, only to lose the land again in 1994. Even legislative action such as the 1971 Alaska Native Claims Settlement Act, which looked good initially, is proving a mixed blessing. Such money settlements have rarely been as worthwhile as control of the land. Less blatant and more insidious attacks on Indian lands continue as ill-advised development plans drain off much-needed capital and as off-reservation sources contaminate reservation soil, air, and water.[17]

Today American Indians control over 90 million acres in the United States (including 56.2 million acres in federal trust)—a sizable chunk but still less than 3 percent of their aboriginal estate. From the 16-million-acre Navajo Reservation, which bridges three states, to the tiny California mission *rancherias* like Jamul Village, with 6.03 acres, Indian-controlled lands provide modern Indian peoples a source for identity and the ability to practice meaningful self-determination. This landed estate and the control of natural resources set them apart, affording them an economic and political significance beyond that of other ethnic groups in shaping the present and future history of the American West.[18]

Economic Development

A third and related significance of Native Americans is the nature of reservation economic development and its impact on local and regional economies in the American West. Before European contact, native groups maintained diversified subsistence economies based on cultural preferences and the natural or periodic abundances in their environments. Contact, coupled with the devastating effects of epidemic disease and of an extractive market economy based on fur, hides, and ultimately land, slowly drew natives into a dependent state.[19]

During the nineteenth and early twentieth centuries, federal officials attempted to transform Indians into yeomen farm families, individualizing Indian landholders at the very time that white farmers and corporate capitalists were consolidating operations in response to environmental and competitive market realities. Indian farming and ranching may have reinforced a kind of rural lifestyle identity among Indians, but it never generated the kind of self-sufficient agrarian market economy officials hoped for. Local Indian subsistence economies mixing farming, ranching, wage work, and more traditional native resource use suffered during the national depression and environmental nightmare of the 1930s. Direct federal relief and job programs like the Indian Division of the Civilian Conservation Corps buoyed reservation economies through the 1930s until World War II created military service and war industry jobs in the West.[20]

In the post–World War II era, Native Americans looked for new economic opportunities. Indian agricultural operations persisted but employed relatively few and produced meager profits in comparison with other economic opportunities, including leasing reservation lands to non-Indians. More and more Indians turned to off-reservation wage work or moved to nearby cities to earn a living. Indians took up jobs in the auto industry of Detroit, in the high steel construction industry of the urban East, in the mines of the Southwest, and in the forests and fisheries of the Pacific Northwest. The Tohono O'odham, for example, left their cattle and floodplain farms to serve as domestic servants and wage laborers in nearby Tucson, as agricultural laborers in the booming cotton industry of southern Arizona, and as Indian extras for Hollywood Westerns.[21] Others followed suit. From the late 1930s, when John Ford and Hollywood discovered Monument Valley, Navajos played Apaches, Navajos played Comanches, and Navajos and other Indians played the extras, the cannon fodder for John Wayne and the cavalry. The landscape and Indians of Arizona became our cinematic projection of a savage West, the "real" West, but Indians rarely played a film lead when a white actor or actress was available.[22]

To provide jobs and economic opportunities for growing reservation populations, western tribes turned to their greatest asset—land and natural resources. This shift parallels that of the larger American West; it marks a retreat from small-scale agriculture and a move toward growing dependence on natural resources and the boom-and-bust cycles of extractive industries. Currently, Indians control approximately 30 percent of the coal west of the Mississippi River, over 40 percent of uranium sources, 4 percent of known oil and gas reserves, and other mineral resources of indeterminate value. They own millions of acres of forest land and the rights to an unquantified amount of water, which is becoming as precious as life itself in the arid West. Mineral, oil, and gas leases, timber contracts with multinational corporations, and plants to process or transport those resources have generated reservation jobs and billions of dollars in royalties, severance taxes, and direct revenues. Of all these resources, water—

the control, quantification, and marketing of Indian water and water rights—is central to the future of reservation economies and western development.[23]

Despite this seeming abundance, only a small number of reservations contain readily exploitable resources. Tribes with little to offer beyond open land and a large, low-wage labor force have had to explore other development options. Subsidized training programs and the creation of tribal enterprise zones with less restrictive regulations have attracted some outside corporations.[24] In the last thirty years, tribes have initiated a variety of small businesses and joint-venture corporations: the Paiutes of Utah produced safety clothing for industry and government; in Arizona the Hopi Electronics Enterprise produced and sold equipment to IBM, Motorola, and Hughes Aircraft; Wisconsin Winnebagos started their own pharmaceuticals company; the Eastern Band of Cherokees built the largest mirror company in the United States; the Siletz Indians of Oregon launched their own salmon smokehouse and native plant nursery; and the Sioux Manufacturing Corporation on the Devil's Lake Reservation produced radar-absorbing tank camouflage for Operation Desert Storm.[25]

This 1991 cartoon from the *Navajo Times* was originated by Tom Arviso Jr. and illustrated by Jack Ahasteen. Reprinted with permission by Tom Arviso Jr.

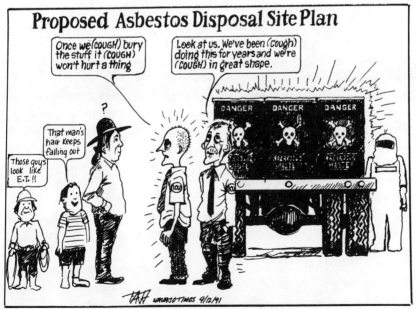

NAVAJO TIMES. Originated by Tom Arviso, Jr. and illustrated by Jack Ahasteen. Reprinted with permission.

Perennial hard times have forced others—like the Turtle Mountain Chippewas, Rosebud Sioux, Kaibab Paiutes, Skull Valley Goshutes, and Mescalero Apaches—to explore the ramifications of locating national landfills, toxic waste incinerators, or nuclear waste repositories on their lands, that is, of becoming national dumping grounds as a means of economic development for their people.[26]

Economic alternatives do exist. In 1938, the anthropologist Ruth M. Underhill observed, "Anyone writing a book on Indian economics might do worse than start with the subject of games; for all games included betting, whether they were athletic contests for the young men or games of chance for which the old people squatted on the sand throwing dice to the accompaniment of solemn song."[27] Gambling as a modern development strategy surfaced when Florida Seminoles opened a bingo parlor in 1979 and weathered legal challenges by the state. Other tribes followed suit in this cultural-economic discovery, pressing their sovereignty by opening full-scale casinos. In 1988, Congress clamped down on tribal operations with the Indian Gaming Regulatory Act, which established three classes of operations and made tribes negotiate compacts with state governments.

Despite regulation and the threat of new gambling taxes that many Native Americans claim abridge tribal sovereignty, tribes have made a fortune from their gaming halls and tax-free smoke shops. Hotel-casino complexes are popping up on reservations across the country to cash in on area residents and a growing tourist trade. As of June 1993, tribes operated 209 legal gaming establishments, an estimated $6 billion annual industry creating needed jobs and cash flow for both Indian and non-Indian communities. Tribes have used gaming revenues to fund a variety of development projects including housing, health and education facilities, land acquisition, and reservation industries, as well as to replace lost federal dollars for services and entitlement programs. Indian gaming promises to be the economic bonanza that tribes need to combat underdevelopment, but it suffers near constant attack by politicians and citizens as immoral, counterproductive, and (perhaps most important) threatening to existing non-Indian gaming operations. Although gambling is not without its own inherent socioeconomic problems, when compared with other development strategies such as resource mining or with the lack of alternatives for meaningful development, Indian gaming offers a reasonable chance for the economic self-sufficiency necessary to ensure native self-determination.[28]

Rapid economic development through resource management and business or gaming enterprises benefits Indian communities but also forces them to confront and balance economic needs against cultural values. Their decisions about how or if to develop certain areas or pursue certain strategies can have unpredicted costs. Extractive industries tie native groups to international fluctuations in resource price and demand, deplete nonrenewable resources, and leave reservations with long-term environmental and health problems. On the Navajo and Spokane reservations, uranium tailings contaminate soil and water, sickening humans and animals. Oil wells, strip mines, timber clear-cuts, power plants, and industrial wastes pollute the physical environment and threaten sacred sites. Corporations have been quick to realize the benefits of doing business on reservations, but few have established long-term operations or understood the needs and cultural norms of their native employees. In the end these industries create their own type of dependency.

The Bureau of Indian Affairs (BIA), in balancing its trust responsibilities with Indian self-determination, has both squandered tribal resources and saved tribes from shortsighted expediency and greed. Management and mismanagement of tribal resources and businesses are ongoing problems, evidenced by the erosion of Indian fishing rights in the Pacific Northwest and Great Lakes regions, by failed sustained-yield timber programs on the Hupa, Yakima, Colville, Fort Apache, and other reservations throughout the West, and most recently by the dramatic revelations about financial improprieties with the Utah Navajo oil trust fund and Utah Navajo Industries. Overall, tribal councils themselves have a poor record of managing and reinvesting windfall resource royalties into reservation development because of the serious need for immediate per capita distributions and entitlement programs. Long-term economic planning is made more difficult by the reversal of federal programs, by rapidly changing tribal needs, and by the politics of personality and faction that contribute to a high turnover rate in tribal governments.[29]

Although Indian economic advances are heartening, perhaps more significant is the fact that, overall, reservation economies remain insignificant, existing on the edge of American market capitalism. Reservations remain what some have called internal colonies or dependent incorporated peripheries. They show up on high-altitude mapping photographs as places where development stops. Isolation, unemployment, and poverty breed a host of social problems. Indians have had more experience with poverty than any other group in the country—poverty that has become a way of life, "a fine art" for some. A paternalistic government has virtually ensured this situation through years of inconsistent policy, financial mismanagement, and direct relief, encouraging a cycle of dependence and a perceived lack of alternatives. Future options will have to be weighed by each generation as it balances cultural identity with development.[30]

Political Sovereignty

A fourth significance of Native Americans in the history of the twentieth-century West is their political sovereignty and emerging voice in regional politics. During the nineteenth century, Indian groups constituted domestic dependent nations, subject to the will of the federal government. What little political power they had came from their military and diplomatic skills, their economic and cultural stability, and their freedom from state jurisdiction. Too often that power existed at the sufferance of federal officials and white advocates with "good intentions" who championed Indian causes but offered their own, rather than Indian, solutions to issues. Indian political influence reached a low point in 1903 when the Supreme Court affirmed the plenary authority of Congress to alter treaty provisions without Indian consent.[31] Over the next thirty years, pan-Indian organizations, successful U.S. Court of Claims suits, citizenship, and the reorganization of tribal governments slowly began to increase the political profile, if not the actual power, of Native Americans.

A measurable leap in Indian political significance came after passage of the 1946 Indian Claims Commission Act. The act, intended to vacate federal responsibility for past wrongs, allowed tribes to sue the government. Its result was to awaken tribes to the enduring power of the 370 treaties signed between 1789 and 1868. Once a vehicle for alienating Indian title, treaties became the basis for claiming land and just compensation and for establishing tribes' distinct relationship with the federal government. Tribes prevailed in 58 percent of the 852 suits (consolidated into 370 dockets) filed with the commission between 1946 and 1978. They won small cash trust settlements instead of land, but the victories, more moral than equitable, showed Indians a powerful alternative to the legislative and policy process that seldom favored them.

That point became very clear in 1953 when Congress and the BIA followed up with two tribal-hostile policies. House Concurrent Resolution No. 108 called for the termination of Indian treaty rights and federal trust responsibilities as soon as possible. A companion bill, Public Law 280, allowed certain states limited civil and criminal jurisdiction on Indian reservations, abridging Indian sovereignty and immunity from state control. Congress intended to get out of the Indian business, to break up tribal governments and individualize tribal holdings, and to reduce Indian political and economic power. Between 1953 and 1962, federal officials targeted more than sixty groups for termination. In the end the process claimed twelve victims—most notably the Klamaths, the Menominees, and the Mixed-Blood Northern Utes—by exploiting tribal factionalism and short-term economic interests. As the failures of termination became evident, the government reestablished its trust relationship with a number of the groups, but the damage to Indian resources and sovereignty remained.[32]

The claims-case process, Public Law 280, and the threat of termination contributed to a growing political sophistication among tribes. A number of educated, articulate, and thoughtful leaders began to emerge, people who understood the needs and cultural desires of their communities, the nature of American politics and law, and the political power inherent in tribal land and resources. Pan-Indian organizations like the National Tribal Chairmen's Association, the Native American Rights Fund, the Council of Energy Resource Tribes, and the American Indian Movement arose to shape Indian policy and political debate through collective action.

But the reality of modern tribal and pan-Indian unity is as elusive as any idea of absolute aboriginal unity. Inter- and intratribal factionalism keeps groups divided, making coherent tribal administration and long-term planning difficult. The push and pull of personalities and band politics, the shifting tribal agendas, and the largely semantic battle pitting "traditionalists" against "progressives" further limit cooperation and true power in the arena of modern, interest-group politics. Although the rhetoric, if not the reality, of Indian political power increased with the self-determination and "government-to-government" policy agendas of the 1970s and 1980s, the problem of finding an acceptable balance between federal trust and true tribal autonomy remains.[33]

Indian peoples continue to be targets of racial and economic discrimination; they struggle for full political recognition and equality, but their political clout is increasing and cannot be ignored forever. Tribal populations continue to grow, and their ability to manipulate local political structures through the ballot box is becoming more evident. Even though only a handful of native people have been elected nationally, an increasing number are running for and winning state and local offices. For example, in 1990, the Mormon power elite of San Juan County, Utah, "turned white" when Navajos, led by county commissioner Mark Maryboy, threatened to capture Republican-controlled county offices and command their fair share of public services. The last-minute record turnout by white Republicans ensured the defeat of all Navajo Democrats except Maryboy but forced both state parties into a greater awareness of the potential of organized Indian voters. Few others have joined together to challenge the system so directly, but the potential of bloc voting has not escaped Indian organizers and white incumbents. Tribes are already shaping national policy debates on issues ranging from skeletal and artifact repatriation to the location of toxic waste dumps and national wilderness areas and will continue to expand their lobbying and policy influence over time.[34]

Perhaps the greatest source of political clout western tribes have today is water, which gives them a powerful voice in the politics and development of the West. Although Indians were unable to halt the damming of the Columbia and Missouri Rivers in the first half of the twentieth century—damming that had disastrous effects on tribal communities and economies—they have played a more prominent role in determining the nature and construction of new water projects. Today along the Columbia River, the Skokomish, Skagit, Snoqualmie, and Kootenai peoples are re-asserting treaty rights to dictate stream flows and initiate the destruction of several dams. In both Utah and Arizona, native groups are key players in supplying and receiving water from the controversial Central Utah and Central Arizona projects. Indians have run into problems with environmental groups and each other over the control of western waters. The Animas-LaPlata dam and irrigation project currently pits Southern and Ute Mountain Utes against Navajos and sets non-Indian environmentalists against both groups.[35]

The significance of tribal politics and Indian political power will continue to increase in the American West. Already state and national governments, corporations, and individuals can no longer run roughshod over Indian rights and desires without at least a protracted fight, and the record of Indian litigation in the courts is becoming more impressive. Among the most successful are the Zunis, who in the last decade have won landmark cases for land, water, and religious access rights and for the return of sacred artifacts.[36] On the other hand, this legal wrangling between tribes and governments over issues of land and resources, services and taxation, jurisdiction and politics, is a hindrance to tribal self-determination and a drain on limited tribal funds. It has also raised the specter that Congress might exercise its plenary powers to abrogate treaty rights and end federal trust responsibilities—the political equivalent of the budget-cutting New Federalism that already threatens an economic termination of tribes.

Symbols

Fifth, there is the less tangible, but no less real, significance of Native Americans in the twentieth-century West: their symbolic presence. From first contact, Euro-Americans clad Indians in robes of myth and symbol and adjusted Indian policies to fit those misperceptions. Indians were Caliban—half human, half monster. They were children of nature, noble savages, and bloodthirsty heathens. By the beginning of the twentieth century they were the disappearing Indians, fit for Wild West pageants or, like Ishi, last of the Yahi, for exhibition in the California Museum of Anthropology. Native Americans were Edward S. Curtis's "Vanishing Race" and James Fraser's "End of the Trail." But soon they were forgotten, moved to the periphery of public place and attention. They became the subjects of salvage anthropologists more interested in their past than future. Yet their symbolic value persisted, and images emerged as needed.[37]

In twentieth-century history, literature, art, movies, and advertising—in the images Americans create for ourselves and for export—mythic cowboys and Indians continue to symbolize the frontier experience, the romantic images that recall a simpler though nonexistent American West. Stereotypical Indians, often feathered or in full plains regalia, adorned decorative objects and the visual arts, played supporting roles in American and European literature, and sold products from tobacco to medicines to firearms to cooking oil. Movies and television programs perpetuated images of Indians as savage mounted warriors by focusing on a handful of plains and southwestern tribes—Apaches, Comanches, Cheyennes, Lakotas—rather than on the settled agriculturalists such as the Hopis. More sympathetic portrayals and messages appeared in post–World War II films like *Fort Apache* (1948) and *Broken Arrow* (1950), but even then non-Indians acted the stereotypical Indian leads. As kids, many of us played "Cowboys and Indians" and knew that Indians spoke broken English, used signs, wore feathers, and scalped their enemies. In time we graduated to sports teams with Indian mascots and to anecdotes, jokes, songs, and proverbs with Indian objects.[38]

"Indian memory," wrote Richard Rodriguez, "has become the measure against which America gauges corrupting history when it suits us." During the last thirty years, whites have embraced Indians, or their cherished image, as symbols for the counterculture, American environmentalism, and New Age spirituality and mysticism—symbols for a way of life in opposition to urban, white, Christian, techno-industrial society. In the 1960s the children of American excess made Indians the romantic symbol of their revolt. Indians were tribal, spiritual, drug-using, and wronged, holdouts against conformity and an American political system gone mad with war. Hollywood reflected those images in movies like *Soldier Blue* (1970) and *Little Big Man* (1971)—films that told us more about ourselves, our countercultural desires, and the nightmare of Vietnam than about Native Americans. Even movies like *A Man Called Horse* (1970),

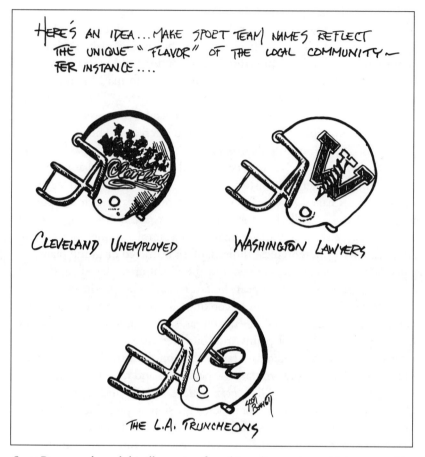

Scott Bennett adapted this illustration from his earlier version, which appeared in the *Lakota Times*, 1 April 1992.

which purported to capture authentic native patterns, remained shallow and lacked cultural acuity. In the end, most movies used stereotypical nineteenth-century natives to address modern, white social issues rather than Indian ones.[39]

Native Americans influenced the thinking of early American conservationists, but later conservationists perpetuated many of the grosser stereotypes. Modern whites embraced the image of Indians as the ultimate environmentalists, beings who lived at peace with each other, who utilized everything they took from the land, and who left no mark of their passing. In so doing, these whites essentially denied native peoples their humanity, culture, history, and modernity. An apocryphal speech written as a film script and attributed to Chief Seattle, together with the image of Iron Eyes

Cody crying over a polluted landscape, made Indians "the mascot of an international ecology movement." Even Indians fostered this facile view for its positive effects. The images offered more a justified critique of industrial society than any critical understanding of Indian peoples' complex interactions with the environment and each other. The trend continues today. Even the highly touted movie *Dances with Wolves* (1990) is a sensitive if misleading dance with mythology, using Indians and animals as environmental symbols to attack twentieth-century human-nature relationships.[40]

New Age philosophy has brought a greater appreciation of things Indian but also has entailed new forms of commercialism, racism, and cultural attacks as born-again Indian "wanna-bes" commandeer native crafts, artifacts, rituals, and places. How-to books, seminars on Indian mysticism, sweat lodges, pipe ceremonies, sun dances, and vision quests taken out of cultural context and conducted by both native and nonnative people for paying customers have become big business. As an increasing number of wanna-bes discover or invent distant Indian blood, they appropriate the Indian public voice and message, emphasizing the mythic and ignoring the realities of modern Indian life.[41]

In the search for escape and a sense of authenticity in a manufactured world, Euro-Americans have placed American Indians outside history, relegating them to an idealized past that never existed, refusing to allow them to be or become modern—the art of historic Gitchigoomism. In the end all stereotypical images, even those deemed temporally functional and used by Indians themselves, persist to the detriment of Native American peoples. They continue to misdirect non-Indian society's relationships with and responses to modern Native Americans. The significance of stereotypes is in how much they hide and in how much they tell us about ourselves rather than about others.[42]

The Field of Study

Finally, the study of Native American history itself has become increasingly significant for academics and for Indian peoples. From its methodological emergence in the 1950s to its popular boom in the 1960s, Native American history has established itself as a dynamic field of study. Donald Parman and Catherine Price assessed the field in 1988, documenting its growth and activity over the previous forty years. Surveys of recent dissertations and articles indicate how productive the field remains. The number of journals devoted specifically to Native American history, culture, law, literature, art, archaeology, or education is truly impressive, as is the larger number of journals that regularly publish on native topics. Monograph series with university presses and the ongoing bibliography and historiographical series sponsored by the D'Arcy McNickle Center for the History of the American Indian demonstrate the depth and breadth of current research, as well as areas for opportunity.[43]

This overall boom in Native American history has given rise to an increasing number of university courses and faculty positions in different disciplines. Native American Studies programs from Berkeley to Minnesota to Dartmouth are creating integrated, interdisciplinary approaches to the subject. Meanwhile, an increasing number of professional organizations ranging from the American Indian Historians Association to the American Society for Ethnohistory provide a community for scholars working in the field. Research libraries and museums with collections emphasizing native history have become increasingly important for both scholars and native peoples. Specialized research centers like the McNickle Center and the University of Utah's American West Center serve as important repositories of information, agencies for collecting oral histories and printed materials, and environments for mentoring and training tribal historians. They help tribes create their own histories and educational materials and assist in preparing scholarly texts and exhibits for tribal litigation.[44]

Perhaps the greatest significance of Indian history for the study of the American West has been in method and theory. Beginning in the 1950s, Native American history moved beyond other areas of American history in theoretical sophistication. The nature of ethnohistory and ethnohistorical research—"the use of historical and ethnological methods and materials to gain knowledge of the nature and causes of change in a culture defined by ethnological concepts and categories"—pushed historians beyond standard printed texts and patterns of analysis. The combination of history, anthropology, and archaeology strengthened the contributions of all three fields. Since then ethnohistorians have incorporated the perspectives of linguistics, literature, folklore, sociology, economics, political science, geography, demography, ecology, and the natural sciences, making ethnohistory a true extension of the interdisciplinary approach that Frederick Jackson Turner endorsed for the study of American history and the American West.[45]

Such research has a significance for native peoples as well as academics. On a practical level, early ethnohistorians provided the documentation that tribes needed to win their twentieth-century claims cases. Ethnohistorians continue to provide expert testimony and written briefs for tribes involved in litigation over land, resources, religious practices and access, reburial, and artifact repatriation. Scholars, both Indian and non-Indian, help tribes define their own past and present identity for future generations by capturing oral histories and creating educational materials that serve Indian community needs. And as more native researchers and teachers emerge from university and tribal college programs, they will contribute to a much-needed dialogue within the scholarly community and create a stronger Indian voice in the production of academic Indian history.[46]

I make this distinction of "academic" history because native peoples always have and always will create and pass down their own oral traditions, their own histories. Folklorists have been responsible for capturing most of that material for non-Indian audiences, but increasingly, native peoples are recording and presenting it themselves, especially in the form of autobiography and modern literature. "I believe stories are encoded in the DNA spiral," wrote Joy Harjo, "and call each cell into perfect position." Early-twentieth-century writers like Gertrude Bonnin, Mourning Dove, Charles Eastman, D'Arcy McNickle, and others set the stage in their writings of Indian experience. An explosion in Indian literature and autobiography followed the publication of N. Scott Momaday's Pulitzer Prize–winning *House Made of Dawn* (1968). Across the country, native authors emerged to voice their experiences: James Welch, Leslie Marmon Silko, Simon Ortiz, Paula Gunn Allen, Gerald Vizenor, Tom King, Louis Owens, Louise Erdrich, Michael Dorris, Anna Lee Walters, Ray Young Bear, and others. Their stories are frequently about the modern world, are pan-Indian in message, and re-create the Native American experience as lived with feeling and insight. These stories are a continuation of native histories and are part of the history of the American West.[47]

Significance and the People

To tell the history of the twentieth-century American West without including Native Americans is like looking through a stereoscope with one eye closed—the image remains but the depth disappears. Indians did not disappear or remain static nineteenth-century caricatures but grew in numbers, in political and economic power, and in the diversity of their experiences. Increasingly urban and increasingly sophisticated in their approach to the larger world, Native Americans command serious attention. Yet for all the changes in their relationships with American society and the federal government, Indians mirror the larger reality of the American West as federal colony. They find themselves in the same Catch-22 situation that many westerners lament: they want and need federal funding but resent the supervision; they depend on their trust relationship yet espouse total sovereignty; they are rebellious and defiant but in the end still dependent. Perhaps their real significance—and the significance of native and colonial peoples around the world—is in this ongoing struggle for recognition, sovereignty, and the opportunity and ability to decide the means to a culturally desired end.

Whatever significance I have described for Native Americans in the history of the twentieth-century American West, they remain people, not some analytical subject or homogeneous unit awaiting definition. They define themselves, their experience and significance, every day in hundreds of variations. They are Tlingit, Natinook-wa, Newe, O'odham, Siwi, Diné, Núciu, Ndee, Nimipu, Apsálooke, Lakota, Tse-tsehes-staestse, Anishinaabeg, and Mesquakie. They remain "The People."

Notes

I would like to thank Peter Iverson, Barre Toelken, Tom King, Peggy Pascoe, Clyde Milner, and Jane Reilly for their comments and help on this essay.

An earlier version of this essay appeared under the title "Still Native: The Significance of Native Americans in the History of the Twentieth-Century American West," by David Rich Lewis. Previously published in the *Western Historical Quarterly* 24 (May 1993): 203–27. Copyright by Western History Association. Reprinted by permission.

1. Frederick Jackson Turner, "The Significance of the Frontier in American History," *The Frontier in American History* (1920; reprint, Huntington, N.Y., 1976), 15; David A. Nichols, "Civilization over Savage: Frederick Jackson Turner and the Indian," *South Dakota History* 2 (Fall 1972): 383–405; Gerald D. Nash, *Creating the West: Historical Interpretations, 1890–1990* (Albuquerque, 1991), 79–83.

2. Frederick E. Hoxie, *A Final Promise: The Campaign to Assimilate the Indians, 1880–1920* (Lincoln, 1984).

3. "Indians Rap Watt's Socialism Remark," *Wisconsin State Journal* (20 January 1983), A1. See also *New York Times,* 19 January 1983, A19, and 25 January 1983, A16. President Ronald Reagan made similar comments about Indians while in the Soviet Union in 1988. See Marjane Ambler, *Breaking the Iron Bonds: Indian Control of Energy Development* (Lawrence, 1990), 3–5, 8.

4. C. Matthew Snipp, *American Indians: The First of This Land* (New York, 1989), 9–11, 63–66; Hoxie, *Final Promise,* x–xi, 240–44.

5. On twentieth-century American Indian policy, see Francis Paul Prucha, *The Great Father: The United States Government and the American Indians,* 2 vols. (Lincoln, 1984); Donald L. Parman, *Indians and the American West in the Twentieth Century* (Bloomington, 1994); James S. Olson and Raymond Wilson, *Native Americans in the Twentieth Century* (Urbana, 1984); and Vine Deloria Jr., ed., *American Indian Policy in the Twentieth Century* (Norman, 1985). For the latest policies, see Presiden-

tial Commission on Indian Reservation Economies, *Report and Recommendations to the President of the United States, Presidential Commission on Indian Reservation Economies, November 1984* (Washington, D.C., 1984); U.S. Congress, Senate, *A New Federalism for American Indians: Final Report and Legislative Recommendations,* 101st Cong., 1st sess., Senate Report 216 (Washington, D.C., 1989); Joseph G. Jorgensen, "Federal Policies, American Indian Policies and the 'New Federalism,'" *American Indian Culture and Research Journal* 10 (1986): 1–14; and C. Patrick Morris, "Termination by Accountants: The Reagan Indian Policy," in *Native Americans and Public Policy,* ed. Fremont J. Lyden and Lyman H. Legters (Pittsburgh, 1992), 63–84.

6. Anthony F. C. Wallace, "Revitalization Movements: Some Theoretical Considerations for Their Comparative Study,"*American Anthropologist* 58 (April 1956): 264–81; Frederick E. Hoxie, "Exploring a Cultural Borderland: Native American Journeys of Discovery in the Early Twentieth Century," *Journal of American History,* 79 (December 1992): 969–95; Hazel W. Hertzberg, *The Search for an American Indian Identity: Modern Pan-Indian Movements* (Syracuse, 1971); D'Arcy McNickle, *Native American Tribalism: Indian Survivals and Renewals* (New York, 1973); Francis Paul Prucha, "American Indian Policy in the Twentieth Century," *Western Historical Quarterly* 15 (January 1984): 13.

7. See Kenneth R. Philp, ed., *Indian Self-Rule: First-Hand Accounts of Indian-White Relations from Roosevelt to Reagan* (Salt Lake City, 1986).

8. Snipp, *American Indians,* 73–88; U.S. Department of Commerce, Bureau of the Census, *We the . . . First Americans* (Washington, D.C., 1993), 2–3; Felicity Barringer, "Census Shows Profound Change in Racial Makeup of the Nation," *New York Times,* 11 March 1991, A1; Jack O. Waddell and O. Michael Watson, eds., *The American Indian in Urban Society* (Lantham, Md., 1984); Bunty Anquoe, "Unrecognized Tribes Finally Get Governmental Attention," *Indian Country Today* (Plains Edition, Rapid City, S.D.), 16 November 1994, A1; Prucha, *Great Father* 2:1191–208, 2:1218–26. Census figures for 1990 (1,959,234) include American Indians, Eskimos, and Aleuts but may be inflated by as much as 9.2 percent (180,874) because more individuals self-identify as "Indian" on the census form than can be accounted for. David Harris, "The 1990 Census Count of American Indians: What Do the Numbers Really Mean?" *Social Science Quarterly* 75 (September 1994): 580–93.

9. Alvin M. Josephy Jr., *Now That the Buffalo's Gone: A Study of Today's American Indians* (1982; reprint, Norman, 1984), 129–30; Prucha, "American Indian Policy," 13–14; Robert F. Berkhofer Jr., "Native Americans," in *Ethnic Leadership in America,* ed. John Higham (Baltimore, 1978), 119–49; U.S. Department of Commerce, *We the . . . First Americans,* 5–6. Nationally, 10 percent of American families lived in poverty in 1989.

10. Wilma Mankiller, "Education and Native Americans: Entering the Twenty-First Century on Our Own Terms," *National Forum* 71 (Spring 1991): 6; William G. Tierney and Clara Sue Kidwell, eds., "American Indian Voices in Higher Education," *Change: The Magazine of Higher Learning* 23 (March/April 1991): 4–46; Olson and Wilson, *Native Americans,* 202–4; Michel Marriott, "Indians Turning to Tribal Colleges for Opportunity and Cultural Values," *New York Times,* 26 February 1992, B6; "AICF Gains Two New Member Colleges," *Indian Country Today,* 22 December 1993, A3.

11. Christopher Vecsey, "American Indian Environmental Religions," in *American Indian Environments: Ecological Issues in Native American History,* ed. Christopher Vecsey and Robert W. Venables (Syracuse, 1980), 1–37; David H. Getches, "A Philosophy of Permanence: The Indians' Legacy for the West," *Journal of the West* 29 (July 1990): 54–68; Olson and Wilson, *Native Americans,* 215–19; Jon Christensen, "The Western Shoshones Look Homeward," *High Country News* (Paonia, Colo.), 31 December 1990, 1; Dann quoted from "Shoshone Sisters Say Ruling Won't End Grazing Battle," *Salt Lake Tribune,* 9 June 1991, A18.

12. Quoted in Josephy, *Now That the Buffalo's Gone,* 132.

13. Lee Davis, "On This Earth: Hupa Land Domains, Images, and Ecology on 'Deddeh Ninnisan'" (Ph.D. diss, University of California, Berkeley, 1988), 2–12; David Rich Lewis, "Changing Subsistence, Changing Reservation Environments: The Hupa, 1850–1980s," *Agricultural History* 66 (Spring 1992): 36–38.

14. Ambler, *Breaking the Iron Bonds,* 6–8; Janet A. McDonnell, *The Dispossession of the American Indian, 1887–1934* (Bloomington, 1991).

15. Donald L. Parman, "Indians of the Modern West," in *The Twentieth-Century West: Historical Interpretations,* ed. Gerald D. Nash and Richard W. Etulain (Albuquerque, 1989), 147–58; Lawrence C. Kelly, "The Indian Reorganization Act: The Dream and the Reality," in *The American Indian: Past and Present,* ed. Roger L. Nichols, 3d ed. (New York, 1986), 252 (quotation); Olson and Wilson, *Native Americans,* 107–56; Josephy, *Now That the Buffalo's Gone,* 32; Arrell M. Gibson, "Indian Land Transfers," in *Handbook of North American Indians,* vol. 4, *History of Indian-White Relations,* ed. Wilcomb E. Washburn (Washington, D.C., 1988), 211–29.

16. Paul Brodeur, *Restitution: The Land Claims of the Mashpee, Passamaquoddy, and Penobscot Indians of New England* (Boston, 1985); Robert Doherty, *Disputed Waters: Native Americans and the Great Lakes Fishery* (Lexington, 1990); James H. Schlender, "Treaty Rights in Wisconsin: A Review," *Northeast Indian Quarterly* 8 (Spring 1991): 4–22; Fay Cohen, *Treaties on Trial: The Continuing Controversy over Northwest Indian Fishing Rights* (Seattle, 1986); Josephy, *Now That the Buffalo's Gone,* 177–211.

17. C. Matthew Snipp, "The Indian Wars, Again," *Rural Sociologist* 11 (Winter 1991): 11–15; Steve Hinchman, "An Indian Tribe Regains Its Sovereign Rights over 3 Million Acres," *High Country News,* 30 March 1987, 10; Tony Semerad, "Ute Tribe Loses Big in Court Battle, but Insists the Turf War Isn't Over," *Salt Lake Tribune,* 24 February 1994, A1; Gary C. Anders, "The Alaska Native Experience with the Alaska Native Claims Settlement Act," in *The Struggle for the Land: Indigenous Insight and Industrial Empire in the Semiarid World,* ed. Paul A. Olson (Lincoln, 1990), 127–45; Keith Scheider, "Washington Nuclear Plant Poses Risk for Indians," *New York Times,* 3 September 1990, 9; Chandler C. Smith, "Optimizing Development Impacts on Indian Reservations," in *Indian SIA: The Social Impact Assessment of Rapid Resource Development on Native Peoples,* ed. Charles C. Geisler et al. (Ann Arbor, 1982), 41–42.

18. Josephy, *Now That the Buffalo's Gone,* 129; Florence Connolly Shipek, *Pushed into the Rocks: Southern California Indian Land Tenure, 1769–1986* (Lincoln, 1987), 103–5.

19. William Cronon and Richard White, "Indians in the Land," *American Heritage* 37 (August-September 1986): 19–25; Richard White, *The Roots of Dependency:*

Subsistence, Environment, and Social Change among the Choctaws, Pawnees, and Navajos (Lincoln, 1983).

20. David Rich Lewis, *Neither Wolf Nor Dog: American Indians, Environment, and Agrarian Change* (New York, 1994); Donald L. Parman, "The Indian and the Civilian Conservation Corps," *Pacific Historical Review* 53 (May 1971): 39–56; Richard Lowitt, *The New Deal and the West* (Bloomington, 1984), 122–37; Olson and Wilson, *Native Americans*, 107–30; Alison R. Bernstein, *American Indians and World War II: Toward a New Era in Indian Affairs* (Norman, 1991). An excellent study with a more positive view of Indian ranching is Peter Iverson, *When Indians Became Cowboys: Native Peoples and Cattle Ranching in the American West* (Norman, 1994). For an overview of economic issues, see D'Arcy McNickle Center for the History of the American Indian, *Overcoming Economic Dependency*, D'Arcy McNickle Center for the History of the American Indian, Occasional Papers in Curriculum Series, No. 9 (Chicago, 1988).

21. Alan L. Sorkin, *American Indians and Federal Aid* (Washington, D.C., 1971), 18, 66–96; William A. Brophy and Sophie D. Aberle, comps., *The Indian: America's Unfinished Business* (Norman, 1966), 63–102; Parman, *Indians and the American West*, 107–24; Kathryn L. MacKay, "Warrior into Welder: A History of Federal Employment Programs for American Indians, 1878–1972" (Ph.D. diss., University of Utah, 1987); Jack O. Waddell, *Papago Indians at Work*, Anthropological Papers of the University of Arizona, No. 12 (Tucson, 1969).

22. Ralph Friar and Natasha Friar, *The Only Good Indian: The Hollywood Gospel* (New York, 1972), 170, 247–58; John A. Price, "The Stereotyping of North American Indians in Motion Pictures," *Ethnohistory* 20 (Spring 1973): 164–66; David Daly and Joel Persky, "The West and the Western," *Journal of the West* 29 (April 1990): 35.

23. Ambler, *Breaking the Iron Bonds*, 29; Robert H. White, *Tribal Assets: The Rebirth of Native America* (New York, 1990), 6; Josephy, *Now That the Buffalo's Gone*, 259; Joseph G. Jorgensen, ed., *Native Americans and Energy Development II* (Cambridge, Mass., 1984); Joseph G. Jorgensen, *Oil Age Eskimos* (Berkeley, 1990); Donald L. Fixico, "Tribal Leaders and the Demand for Natural Energy Resources on Reservation Lands," in *The Plains Indians of the Twentieth Century*, ed. Peter Iverson (Norman, 1985), 219–35; C. Matthew Snipp, "American Indians and Natural Resource Development," *American Journal of Economics and Sociology* 45 (October 1986): 457–74; Thomas R. McGuire, William B. Lord, and Mary G. Wallace, eds., *Indian Water in the New West* (Tucson, 1993); Steven J. Shupe, "Indian Tribes in the Water Marketing Arena," *American Indian Law Review* 15 (1990): 185–205.

24. "Tribes Urged to Entice Industry via Deregulated Business Zones," *Arizona Republic* (Phoenix), 12 December 1986, 3; "Making The Reservations 'Free-Enterprise Zones,'" *North Country, Prout Journal* 1 (April 1985); Alan L. Sorkin, "Business and Industrial Development on American Indian Reservations," *Annals of Regional Science* 7 (December 1973): 115–29.

25. "Paiute Tribe Awarded $75,000 SBA Contract," *Deseret News* (Salt Lake City), 8 June 1987, 1; Dick Beveridge, "Indians Go 'High-Tech' with Jewelry Expertise," *Deseret News*, 25 December 1986, D8; "Winnebago Pharmaceuticals, Inc., Opens in Wisconsin," *Choctaw Community News* (Philadelphia, Miss.) 21 (June

1991): 8; Robert H. White, "Indians' New Harvest," *New York Times*, 22 November 1990, A27. See also Larry Burt, "Western Tribes and Balance Sheets: Business Development Programs in the 1960s and 1970s," *Western Historical Quarterly* 23 (November 1992): 475–95; Sam Stanley, ed., *American Indian Economic Development* (The Hague, 1978); and Stephen Cornell and Joseph P. Kalt, "Pathways from Poverty: Economic Development and Institution-Building on American Indian Reservations," *American Indian Culture and Research Journal* 14 (1990): 89–125.

26. Avis Little Eagle, "Turtle Mountain Members File Suit on Dump Issue," *Lakota Times*, 13 May 1992; Peter Carrels, "South Dakota's Sioux Debate Huge National Garbage Dump," *High Country News*, 17 June 1991, 4; "Tribes OK Incinerator," *High Country News*, 5 November 1990, 4; Tony Davis, "Apaches Split over Nuclear Waste," *High Country News*, 27 January 1992, 12; Melinda Merriam, "Waste Project Lures Hard-Luck Areas," *High Country News*, 27 January 1992, 15; Bunty Anquoe, "Mescalero Apache Sign Agreement to Establish Facility for Nuclear Waste," *Indian Country Today*, 10 February 1994, A1; Mike Gorrell, "Leavitt to Tribe: Don't Waste Utah," *Salt Lake Tribune*, 12 November 1994, A1; Caroline Byrd, "Radioactive Dollars Draw Tribes," *High Country News*, 21 September 1992, 6; Robert Allen Warrior, "Forget 1492, What about 1992?" *Progressive* 56 (March 1992): 18; Jon D. Erickson and Duane Chapman, "Sovereignty for Sale: Nuclear Waste in Indian Country," *Akwe:kon Journal* 10 (Fall 1993): 3–10.

27. Ruth M. Underhill, *Singing for Power: The Song Magic of the Papago Indians of Southern Arizona* (Berkeley, 1938), 151.

28. "Indian Gaming: Law and Legislation," NARF *Legal Review* 10 (Fall 1985): 1–5; Pauline Yoshihashi, "Indian Tribes Put Their Bets on Casinos," *Wall Street Journal* (5 August 1991), B1; Jerry Reynolds, "Yankton Casino Rings Up Positive Change," *Lakota Times*, 1 April 1992, B4; Bunty Anquoe, "Lujan Reverses Gaming Support: Calling for Control," *Lakota Times*, 6 May 1992, A1; "IG Says 209 Gaming Halls—106 are Casinos," *Indian News, Week in Review* (U.S. Department of the Interior, Bureau of Indian Affairs) 18 (7 January 1994): 4–5; Bunty Anquoe, "Proposed Gaming Tax May Affect Tribes," *Indian Country Today*, 30 March 1994, A1. See also "Winner's Circle," *Indian Country Today*, special issue, 10 November 1993; Henry Tatum, "With Casinos, Native Americans Get Revenge," *Salt Lake Tribune*, 30 October 1994, D1; Gary Sokolow, "The Future of Gambling in Indian Country," *American Indian Law Review* 15 (1990): 151–83; and Eduardo E. Cordiero, "The Economics of Bingo: Factors Influencing the Success of Bingo Operations on American Indian Reservations," in *What Can Tribes Do? Strategies and Institutions in American Indian Economic Development*, ed. Stephen Cornell and Joseph P. Kalt (Los Angeles, 1992), 206–38.

29. Smith, "Optimizing Development Impacts," 41–42; Donald L. Parman, "Inconstant Advocacy: The Erosion of Indian Fishing Rights in the Pacific Northwest, 1933–1956," in Nichols, *American Indian*, 256–71; Josephy, *Now That the Buffalo's Gone*, 177–211; Alan S. Newell, Richmond Clow, and Richard N. Ellis, *A Forest in Trust: Three-Quarters of a Century of Indian Forestry, 1910–1986* (Washington, D.C., 1986), chap. 6: 1–12, and passim; Jerry Spangler, "Trust-Fund Crisis Has Deep Roots in Navajo History," *Deseret News*, 17 November 1991, A1; Dan Harrie, "Words Belie Fate of Navajo Firm," *Salt Lake Tribune*, 17 November 1991, B1; Rus-

sell Lawrence Barsh and James Youngblood Henderson, "Tribal Administration of Natural Resource Development," *North Dakota Law Review* 52 (Winter 1975): 307–47; Ronald E. Johnny, "Can Indian Tribes Afford to Let the Bureau of Indian Affairs Continue to Negotiate Permits and Leases of Their Resources?" *American Indian Law Review* 16 (1991): 203–12.

30. Thomas D. Hall, "Native Americans and Incorporation: Patterns and Problems," *American Indian Culture and Research Journal* 11 (1987): 1–30; Rob Schultheis, *The Hidden West: Journeys in the American Outback* (1978; reprint, San Francisco, 1983), 88; White, *Tribal Assets*, 5; Ambler, *Breaking the Iron Bonds*, 5; Getches, "Philosophy of Permanence," 59; Vine Deloria Jr., "The Reservation Conditions," *National Forum* 71 (Spring 1991): 10–12; Patrick C. West, "Tribal Control and the Identity-Poverty Dilemma," in Geisler et al., *Indian SIA*, 80; C. Matthew Snipp and Gene F. Summers, "American Indians and Economic Poverty," in *Rural Poverty in America*, ed. Cynthia M. Duncan (New York, 1992), 155–76; Olson and Wilson, *Native Americans*, 184–87.

31. *Lone Wolf v. Hitchcock* (1903), 187 *U.S. Reports* 553–68; C. Blue Clark, *Lone Wolf v. Hitchcock: Treaty Rights and Indian Law at the End of the Nineteenth Century* (Lincoln, 1994).

32. Imre Sutton, ed., *Irredeemable America: The Indians' Estate and Land Claims* (Albuquerque, 1985); H. D. Rosenthal, *Their Day in Court: A History of the Indian Claims Commission* (New York, 1990); Philp, *Indian Self-Rule*, 114–90; Larry Burt, *Tribalism in Crisis: Federal Indian Policy, 1953–1961* (Albuquerque, 1982); Parman, *Indians and the American West*, 123–47; Olson and Wilson, *Native Americans*, 131–53.

33. Frederick E. Hoxie, ed., *The Struggle for Political Autonomy*, D'Arcy McNickle Center for the History of the American Indian, Occasional Papers in Curriculum Series, No. 11 (Chicago, 1989); Russell Lawrence Barsh and James Youngblood Henderson, *The Road: Indian Tribes and Political Liberty* (Berkeley, 1980); Vine Deloria Jr., *Behind the Trail of Broken Treaties: An Indian Declaration of Independence* (New York, 1974); Prucha, "American Indian Policy," 11–18; Olson and Wilson, *Native Americans*, 157–77; James J. Lopach, Margery Hunter Brown, and Richmond L. Clow, *Tribal Governments Today: Politics on Montana Indian Reservations* (Boulder, 1990).

34. Mark N. Trahant, "Indians Find Success by Going to the Polls," *Salt Lake Tribune*, 2 October 1994, A2; Florence Williams, "Revolution at Utah's Grassroots: Navajos Seek Political Power," *High Country News*, 30 July 1990, 1; Carol Sisco, "Seeds of Change Could Grow in Navajo Vote," *Salt Lake Tribune*, 4 November 1990, B1; Lisa Jones, "Utah's Navajos Build a Political Base for the Future," *High Country News*, 3 December 1991, 7. See also John E. Peterson II, "Dance of the Dead: A Legal Tango for Control of Native American Skeletal Remains," *American Indian Law Review* 15 (1990): 115–50; Devon A. Mihesuah, "Despoiling and Desecration of Indian Property and Possessions," *National Forum* 71 (Spring 1991): 15–17; "Menominees Protest Nuke-Waste Dump," *Wisconsin State Journal* 24 (March 1986), sec. II, 2; and Keith Schneider, "Idaho Tribe Stops Nuclear Waste Truck," *New York Times*, 17 October 1991, A18.

35. Brian Collins, "The Public Gets a Chance to Revamp Dams Built Fifty

Years Ago," *High Country News,* 2 December 1991, 1; Daniel McCool, "The Northern Utes' Long Water Ordeal," *High Country News,* 15 July 1991, 8; James Bishop Jr., "Tribe Wins Back Stolen Water," *High Country News,* 15 June 1992, 1; Lisa Jones, "Navajos Pull Plug on Animas–LaPlata Water Project," *High Country News,* 22 April 1991, 3; Dirk Johnson, "Indians' Water Quest Creates New Foe: Environmentalists," *New York Times,* 28 December 1991, 7; O. Douglas Schwartz, "Indian Rights and Environmental Ethics: Changing Perspectives and a Modest Proposal," *Environmental Ethics* 9 (Winter 1987): 291–302. See also Lloyd Burton, *American Indian Water Rights and the Limits of Law* (Lawrence, 1991), 87–123; Lee F. Brown and Helen M. Ingram, *Water and Poverty in the Southwest* (Tucson, 1987); Josephy, *Now That the Buffalo's Gone,* 151–211; Michael L. Lawson, *Dammed Indians: The Pick-Sloan Plan and the Missouri River Sioux, 1944–1980* (Norman, 1982); Daniel McCool, *Command of the Waters: Iron Triangles, Federal Water Development, and Indian Water* (Berkeley, 1987); and William H. Veeder, *Indian Water Rights in the Concluding Years of the Twentieth Century,* Center for the History of the American Indian, Occasional Papers Series, No. 5 (Chicago, 1982).

36. Institute of the North American West, *Zuni History: Victories in the 1990s* (Seattle, 1991); "Zunis Win Court Battle," *High Country News,* 9 April 1990, 3; Roberto Suro, "Effort to Regain Idols May Alter Views of Indian Art," *New York Times,* 13 August 1990, A1.

37. Robert F. Berkhofer Jr., *The White Man's Indian: Images of the American Indian from Columbus to the Present* (New York, 1978); Robert F. Berkhofer, "White Conceptions of Indians," in *Handbook* 4:522–47; Brian W. Dippie, *The Vanishing American: White Attitudes and U.S. Indian Policy* (Middletown, Conn., 1982).

38. Michael Hilger, *The American Indian in Film* (Metuchen, N.J., 1986); Jon Tuska, *The American West in Film: Critical Approaches to the Western* (Lincoln, 1988), 237–60; Price, "Stereotyping," 166–68; Avis Little Eagle, "Mascots: A History of Cultural Insensitivity," *Lakota Times,* 29 July 1992, B1. See also *Handbook:* Michael T. Marsden and Jack Nachbar, "The Indian in the Movies," 4:607–16; Rayna D. Green, "The Indian in Popular American Culture," 4:587–606; Leslie A. Fiedler, "The Indian in Literature in English," 4:573–81; and Christian F. Feest, "The Indian in Non-English Literature," 4:582–86.

39. Richard Rodriguez, "Mixed Blood, Columbus's Legacy: A World Made *Mestizo,*" *Harper's Magazine* 283 (November 1991): 49; Vine Deloria Jr., *God Is Red* (New York, 1973), 23–74; Stewart Brand, "Indians and the Counterculture, 1960s–1970s," 4:570–72, and Marsden and Nachbar, "The Indian in the Movies," 4:607–8, 4:613–15, in *Handbook.*

40. Rodriguez, "Mixed Blood," 49; Rudolf Kaiser, "Chief Seattle's Speech(es): American Origins and European Reception," in *Recovering the Word: Essays on Native American Literature,* ed. Brian Swann and Arnold Krupat (Berkeley, 1987), 497–536; J. Baird Callicott, "American Indian Land Wisdom," in Olson, *Struggle for the Land,* 255–72; Cronon and White, "Indians in the Land," 19–25; Richard White, "Native Americans and the Environment," in *Scholars and the Indian Experience: Critical Reviews of Recent Writing in the Social Sciences,* ed. W. R. Swagerty (Bloomington, 1984), 180; Richard White, review of *Dances with Wolves,* in *Gateway Heritage* 11 (Spring 1991): 80; Paul W. Valentine, "Film Version of Noble Indian Portrays

Dances with Myths," *Salt Lake Tribune*, 7 April 1991, A19; David Rich Lewis, "Environmental Issues," in *Native America in the Twentieth Century: An Encyclopedia*, ed. Mary B. Davis (New York, 1994), 187–90.

41. Dirk Johnson, "Census Finds Many Claiming New Identity: Indian," *New York Times*, 5 March 1991, A1; William K. Powers, "The Indian Hobbyist Movement in North American," in *Handbook* 4:557–61; David Seals, "Strange Tales along the Powwow Highway," *High Country News*, 10 September 1990, 14; Robert Allen Warrior, "Vine Deloria Jr.: 'It's about Time to Be Interested in Indians Again,'" *Progressive* 54 (April 1990): 26; Rudy Martin, "Medicine War," *Ute Bulletin* (Fort Duchesne, Utah), 26 November 1991, 9; Avis Little Eagle, "Elder Blames Death of Environment on Denial," *Lakota Times*, 26 August 1992, A7; Anthony Eaglestaff, "Wooden Wannabe Drives Wedges among People," *Indian Country Today*, 6 October 1993, A5; David Johnston, "Spiritual Seekers Borrow Indian' Ways," *New York Times*, 27 December 1993, A1; Kirsten Sorenson, "New Age Use of Indian Rituals Draws Fire," *Deseret News*, 4 June 1994, A1; Ed McGaa (Eagle Man), *Rainbow Tribe: Ordinary People Journeying on the Red Road* (New York, 1992).

42. Deloria, *God Is Red*, 50, 64–66; Rodriguez, "Mixed Blood," 49; Michael Dorris, "Indians on the Shelf," in *The American Indian and the Problem of History*, ed. Calvin Martin (New York, 1987), 98–105.

43. Donald L. Parman and Catherine Price, "A 'Work in Progress': The Emergence of Indian History as a Professional Field," *Western Historical Quarterly* 20 (May 1989): 185–96. For McNickle Center publications, see Swagerty, *Scholars and the Indian Experience;* Colin G. Calloway, ed., *New Directions in Native American History* (Norman, 1988); Francis Paul Prucha, *A Bibliographical Guide to the History of Indian-White Relations in the United States* (Chicago, 1977); and Francis Paul Prucha, *Indian-White Relations in the United States: A Bibliography of Works Published, 1975–1980* (Lincoln, 1982). Indiana University Press produced a series of twenty-nine specific bibliographies for the center, and the bibliography series continues with projected volumes covering works since 1980. Although American history textbooks have failed to keep pace with cutting-edge developments in the field (see Frederick E. Hoxie, "The Indians versus the Textbooks: Is There Any Way Out?" *Perspectives* 23 [April 1985]: 18–22), they are improving given the recent trend toward multiculturalism. Perhaps the greatest historiographical gap remains in the development of the history of twentieth-century Native Americans, especially that of the last fifty years. See James Riding In, "Scholars and Twentieth-Century Indians: Reassessing the Recent Past," in Calloway, *New Directions*, 127–49.

44. Special thanks go to Dr. Floyd A. O'Neil, director emeritus of the American West Center, and Dr. Frederick E. Hoxie, former director of the D'Arcy McNickle Center, for assisting me in my research.

45. James Axtell, *The European and the Indian: Essays in the Ethnohistory of Colonial North America* (New York, 1981), 5 (quotation), 3–15; William C. Sturtevant, "Anthropology, History, and Ethnohistory," *Ethnohistory* 13 (Winter-Spring 1966): 1–51.

46. Chris Raymond, "Growth of Scholarship on American Indians Brings New Insights about Native Cultures," *Chronicle of Higher Education* 15 (January 1992): A8; Hoxie, "Exploring a Cultural Borderland," 969–95.

47. Joy Harjo, "Family Album," *Progressive* 56 (March 1992): 23. For more information on American Indian authors, see A. LaVonne Brown Ruoff, "Western American Indian Writers, 1854–1960," and Paula Gunn Allen, "American Indian Fiction, 1968–1983," in *A Literary History of the American West*, ed. Thomas J. Lyon (Fort Worth, 1987), 1038–66; Walter C. Fleming, "Native American Literature Comes of Age," *Montana The Magazine of Western History* 42 (Spring 1992): 73–76; Hoxie, "Exploring a Cultural Borderland," 969–95; Tom Colonnese and Louis Owens, *American Indian Novelists: An Annotated Critical Bibliography* (New York, 1985); Laura Coltelli, ed., *Winged Words: American Indian Writers Speak* (Lincoln, 1990); and James R. Kincaid, "Who Gets to Tell Their Stories?" *New York Times Book Review*, 3 May 1992, 1.

We Are Restored

Peter Iverson

A generation ago, most prospective students of Indian history came to their subject through prior training in the history of the American West. Given the long shadow of Frederick Jackson Turner and the tradition of teaching about the West as movement and as frontier, Indians usually became important only in the context of their relationships with whites and in the era before 1890. This context limited the questions historians tended to ask and usually produced images of Indians as people who responded to white actions. What passed for Indian history, more often than not, placed an emphasis on conflict over coexistence and featured a concern for military engagements. Just as 1890 marked the end of the frontier and the Old West, it also appeared to signal the tragic conclusion of native autonomy—in the snows of December at Wounded Knee. Dee Brown's *Bury My Heart at Wounded Knee,* an "Indian History of the West" published in 1970, epitomized that perspective.[1]

As historians began to turn their attention to the past century, they did so with observable hesitation and tentativeness. When Robert Berkhofer Jr. argued in 1971 for an Indian-centered history, it sounded like a good idea.[2] But how to do it? Did such a focus require new methods? Did it—gasp—mean moving beyond archival research? Did it mean going to Indian country and actually talking and listening to the people themselves? Such a prospect smacked of anthropology or, worse, journalism. Even in the 1990s it doesn't appeal to many. During the era in which we have had the best opportunities for obtaining Indian voices and more fully reflecting the realities of native choices—the period since the Second World War—few historians have ventured. Those that have snuck in have been as likely as not to emphasize traditional concerns of policy rather than ponder the dynamics of self-determination and sovereignty.

One can hardly ignore the workings (or lack thereof) of the federal government in Indian life any more than one can disregard their importance in other spheres. John Collier mattered; Dillon Myer did too. The rapid retreat from federal assistance in the 1980s forced Indian communities to examine other alternatives to economic development. Give Ronald Reagan and James Watt some of the credit for slot machines at Fort McDowell. However, we need to recall that ill-conceived federal policies do not always yield bad results. The so-called Americanization era, which featured the Dawes Act, imposed schooling, and denied the legitimacy of the Sun Dance, also prompted the Native American Church, the Society of American Indians, and other developments that attested to Indian adaptation. The so-called termination era, which sought to end federal trusteeship, also sparked the growth of the National Congress of American Indians and the evolution of tribal institutions.

In a related sense, historians and other chroniclers of Indian life in this or any other century have been tempted to use the handy approach of victimization. From Columbus to the present, there is ample evidence to allow writers to stress prejudice, bigotry, discrimination, hostility, and persecution. Again, one does not want to deny the importance of racism. But a zealous portrayal of the Indian as victim is all too reminiscent of "Son of Bury My Heart at Wounded Knee." It ignores successful forms of persistence, transformation, and creativity that are at the center, one is tempted to say at the heart, of Indian life in this century—or any other.

David Lewis's essay recognizes this important point. He uses appropriate categories to speak to the ongoing nature of the Indian experience. His generous notes demonstrate a sure command of a healthy variety of sources. "Still Native" shows how much distance we have traveled since 1970. And, as I am sure David would agree, it also reveals how far we still need to go. To his discussion of persistence, land, economic development, political power, symbolic value, and scholarly contributions, let me add six overlapping categories of my own: the definition of the Indian West, women and the family, leadership, farming and ranching, migration and urbanization, and community and identity. Perhaps that's ten, but one has to do the best one can in a brief essay.

The Indian West

The Indian West ends neither at the forty-ninth parallel nor at the Rio Grande. The Blackfeet and the Tohono O'odham have known this fact for some time. Inclusion of western Canada, Alaska, and northern Mexico not only verifies the transnational status of a number of native communities but also recognizes the historical connections among Athapaskan-speaking peoples and others who are linked through time and territory across thousands of miles. Catharine McClellan, my tutor in cultural anthropology at the University of Wisconsin, helped me to begin to understand this matter some time ago. Reading her work and, more recently, the work of Canadian and Alaskan writers such as Thomas Berger, Ken Coates, Stephen Haycox, Robin Riddington, and Victoria Wyatt—just to name a few—has broadened my understanding of the Indian past. To the south, Edward Spicer recognized over three decades ago the futility of a Southwest without Mexico; *Cycles of Conquest* offered an early model that contemporary journals such as *Journal of the Southwest* continue to use. Just as the Western History Association now considers its terrain the North American West, Indian historians of the West should as well.[3]

Women and the Family

Although women and the family are not always tied together, the two are examples of subjects we must understand more completely. Women are obviously central to the workings of families and cultures. There have been more women anthropologists than women historians, so anthropologists seem to have figured this out a lot more quickly, but that doesn't allow us much excuse. The important studies over the past generation in western women's history should continue to inspire us to consider how women and men, how families, and how elders have helped shape daily native life, choices, values, and priorities.

Families matter. For those of us whose choices and opportunities have taken us far from relatives, it is useful to recall the words of an Indian woman who defined wealth as being able to see her grandchildren every day. Janine Pease Pretty on Top, the president of Little Bighorn College, understands. She and other Crows have decided to stay or return home. They may make less money and live in less fancy houses, but family, community, and the land more than compensate.

The Navajo poet Luci Tapahonso understands too. Now teaching at the University of Kansas, she recently gave a quietly moving and eloquent reading of her work at Arizona State University. A niece, a student at the university, introduced Tapahonso and spoke of how her aunt's work helped her struggle against homesickness. And in Tapahonso's lines, particularly in the new collection *Sáanii Dahataal: The Women Are Singing*, she testifies to the distance between the Kaw and the San Juan as well as echoes the workings of a family going in to town in Farmington, New Mexico: "My oldest brother always went because he drove, my other brother went because he helped carry laundry, my father went because he was the father, and my mother went because she had the money and knew where to go and what to buy."[4]

Leadership

Anyone who has heard Janine Pease Pretty on Top speak recognizes that she is a leader. I hope she will write her own biography some day. But there are many other significant women leaders who merit such attention. Gretchen Harvey is completing a biography of Ruth Muskrat Bronson, the Cherokee activist. Wilma Mankiller, as David notes, is one of dozens of contemporary native politicians, attorneys, educators, and others whose lives and careers tell us much about the Indian past and present. As one who has written about Peter MacDonald, I can attest to the challenges of the perils of such portraits. The fact remains that we must take on the assignment. Dorothy R. Parker's new biography of D'Arcy McNickle, *Singing an Indian Song*, is another step in the right direction. David's essay on William Wash also offers a sophisticated exploration.[5] The list remains stunningly short. The ranks of the Native American Church, the Society of American Indians, native newspapers, Indian colleges, the National Congress of American Indians, the American Indian Movement, tribal governments, and a host of other institutions and organizations should prompt us to add to the meager total. In so doing, we speak directly to the challenges and questions that have confronted Indian individuals and communities and the varied ways in which people have come forward to deal with these issues.

Farming and Ranching

The subject of David's article in *Ethnohistory,* William Wash, was a Ute rancher. Farming and ranching have been important dimensions within the overall workings of many Indian economies. Few historians, however, have studied the subject. Economists such as Leonard Carlson and Ron Trosper have done significant work. Sarah Carter has completed a useful study of Indian farming in western Canada. Douglas Hurt, Tom Wessel, and I have been among the few to investigate the subject in the United States.[6]

David spoke of symbols. My research about Indian cowboys and ranchers has taught me that the old symbols of cowboys and Indians are misleading at best. Non-Indian cattle ranchers in this century have become increasingly like the Indians of old, surrounded by a society that does not understand them and has other priorities for their land. Indians on many western reservations turned to cattle ranching not only as an appropriate economic activity but also as an activity that could reinforce priorities within Indian society. As these activities did for others, Indian farming and ranching over time contributed to heritage.

In recent times, farmers and ranchers in the West, be they Navajo or Norwegian, have struggled to make a go of it. They are, as Gilbert Fite has put it, a new minority.[7] And although the experiences of Indian and non-Indian farmers and ranchers have not been identical, there is enough commonality to remind us that Indians are westerners, in many instances rural people who have confronted the same dilemmas of a larger economy, even before New Jersey professors and Santa Monica migrants to Montana started giving them unsolicited advice. Those experiences remind us that western history is a story of loss as well as gain, of failure as well as success.

Migration and Urbanization

Even if they stay within the general contours of the reservation, many rural Indians have moved to town in the past generation. That urban movement within Indian country is one of the most crucial and most ignored components of the recent past. It is an understandable movement. The location of schools and jobs has altered how families work. Many people have also moved to reservation bordertown communities or to the city itself. Indians have not migrated to Gallup in order to enjoy the absence of cultural pluralism; they have not moved to Denver to root for failure in football or even to see the air they breathe. Like other westerners, they have been driven by economic reasons. And even so, they have often made the move temporary or have located in the nearest place to a reservation. There are major consequences of urbanization in terms of language, marriage, and identity.

Yet we need to be careful about the trap of urbanization equaling acculturation. As George Horse Capture showed a few years ago in his fine film *I'd Rather Be Powwowing*, you can work as a Xerox repairman during the week and still go to powwows on the weekends. Indeed, one can develop a different kind of Indian identity in opposition to the bigotry and foolishness one may well encounter in town or city. Again, Indians are more than victims, and migration can yield pluses as well as minuses.

Community and Identity

Here symbols come into play as well. As Loretta Fowler has observed, symbols of identity tell us a great deal about the nature of Indian communities.[8] Powwows and language are two cases in point. There are others. We look not only to the writing of Indian people but as well to their weaving, their basketry, their silverwork, their music, and their painting. The work of Daisy Tauglechee, Kenneth Begay, Brent Michael Davids, and T. C. Cannon reveals a lot. Rodeos, giveaways, tribal fairs, and other gatherings are also revealing. As a one-time participant in the seventh annual Sheep Herders Classic, I can't omit basketball tournaments from such a list.

In Arizona and elsewhere there has been a movement to repatriate sacred objects and human remains. This has been a vital source of cultural revitalization. The recovery of objects and remains, of course, yields other symbols, reinforcing community and identity.

And as David Lewis, Edward Spicer, and others have said, the ultimate symbol for many Indians is the land itself, invested with sacred and social meaning. This is where we belong, the stories say. This is where we will be. "Anything that matters is here," wrote Joy Harjo in *Secrets from the Center of the World.* "Anything that will continue to matter in the next several thousand years will continue to be here."[9]

In "The Motion of Songs Rising," Luci Tapahonso tells of an October night and a Yeibicheii ceremony that links the people and the holy people, the Diné and the land:

> We are standing on a small hill and in all directions,
> around us, the flat land listens to the songs rising.
> The holy ones are here dancing.
> The Yeis are here.
>
> In the west, Shiprock looms above the desert.
> Tse bit'a'i, old bird-shaped rock. She watches us.
> Tse bit'a'i, our mother who brought the people here on her
> back. Our refuge from the floods long ago. It was worlds

and centuries ago, yet she remains here. Nihima, our
mother. . . .

The Yeis are dancing again, each step, our strong bodies.
They are dancing the same dance, thousands of years old.
They are here for us now, grateful for another harvest and
our own good health. . . .

They are dancing and in the motion of songs rising,
our breathing becomes the morning moonlit air.
The fires are burning below as always.
We are restored.
We are restored.[10]

Notes

1. Dee Brown, *Bury My Heart at Wounded Knee: An Indian History of the American West* (New York, 1970).

2. Robert F. Berkhofer Jr., "The Political Context of a New Indian History," *Pacific Historical Review* 40 (August 1971): 357–82.

3. Catharine McClellan, *My Old People Say: An Ethnographic Survey of Southern Yukon Territory,* 2 vols. (Ottawa, 1975); Thomas Berger, *Village Journey* (New York, 1985); Kenneth S. Coates, *Best Left as Indians: Native-White Relations in the Yukon Territory, 1840–1973* (Montreal, 1991); Stephen W. Haycox, "Economic Development and Indian Land Rights in Modern Alaska: The 1947 Tongass Timber Act," *Western Historical Quarterly* 31 (February 1990): 20–46; Robin Riddington, *Trail to Heaven: Knowledge and Narrative in a Northern Native Community* (Iowa City, 1988); Victoria Wyatt, "Alaskan Native Wage Earners in the Nineteenth Century: Economic Choices and Economic Identity on Southeast Alaska's Frontier," *Pacific Northwest Quarterly* 78 (1987): 43–49; Edward H. Spicer, *Cycles of Conquest: The Impact of Spain, Mexico, and the United States on the Indians of the Southwest* (Tucson, 1962).

4. Luci Tapahonso, "It Was a Special Treat," *Sáanii Dahataal: The Women Are Singing* (Tucson, 1993), 15.

5. Dorothy R. Parker, *Singing an Indian Song: A Biography of D'Arcy McNickle* (Lincoln, 1992); David Rich Lewis, "Reservation Leadership and the Progressive-Traditional Dichotomy: William Wash and the Northern Utes, 1865–1928," *Ethnohistory* 38 (Spring 1991): 124–42.

6. Leonard A. Carlson, Indians, *Bureaucrats, and Land: The Dawes Act and the Decline of Indian Farming* (Westport, Conn., 1981); Ronald L. Trosper, "American Indian Relative Ranching Efficiency," *American Economic Review* 68 (1978): 503–16; Sarah Carter, *Lost Harvests: Prairie Indian Reserve Farmers and Government Policy* (Montreal, 1990); R. Douglas Hurt, *Indian Agriculture in America: Prehistory to the Present* (Lawrence, 1987); Thomas R. Wessel, "Agent of Acculturation: Farming on the Northern Plains Reservations, 1880–1910," *Agricultural History* 60 (Spring

1986): 233–45; Peter Iverson, *When Indians Became Cowboys: Native Peoples and Cattle Ranching in the American* West (Norman, 1994).

7. Gilbert C. Fite, *American Farmers: The New Minority* (Bloomington, 1981).

8. Loretta Fowler, *Arapahoe Politics, 1851–1978: Symbols in Crises of Authority* (Lincoln, 1982).

9. Joy Harjo, *Secrets from the Center of the World* (Tucson, 1992), 32.

10. Luci Tapahonso, "The Motion of Songs Rising," *Sáanii Dahataal: The Women Are Singing* (Tucson, 1993), 67–68.

New Awareness for an Old Significance

Barre Toelken

David Lewis's essay, "Still Native," is a thorough and generous consideration of Native American persistence in America played off against Frederick Jackson Turner's nonchalant assumption that the Vanishing American was an organic and inevitable feature of the frontier's dynamism. Lewis is thorough in his delineation of those many arenas in which Native Americans not only have persisted but have flourished, often creating new situations and possibilities never dreamed of by that young historian of the 1890s; and Lewis is generous in not attacking Turner for racism or other narrow thinking but rather suggesting there are important dimensions of Native American life and reality that were simply not apparent to Turner. To be sure, even with inflation, hindsight is still cheap; and it does indeed seem more fair for us to acknowledge that for all scholars there have been blank areas, missed opportunities for observation, narrow-minded misinterpretations, and cultural assumptions that have affected all our work. Railing at Turner for his omissions accomplishes little except perhaps to convince ourselves that we are now in a position to see clearly and judge wisely.

Going beyond Turner to point out themes and processes not yet fully appreciated is Lewis's way of addressing the real question, which is not "Where was Turner when the lights went on?" but "Where are we now that *we* have better lights?" A serious consideration of this subject should help us to understand more fully our own position with respect to the limitations and blind spots in the "frontier idea," that wonderful construct that once seemed to articulate our most passionate sense of ourselves. For it is significant that one hundred years after Turner's manifesto, after years of debate, after tons of books about the Native Americans, we are still so generally unaware of Native American issues that the topic can be put forward as a major part of a national conference, in a fully researched essay by an active young scholar. Clearly, the topic has not yet become everyday knowledge.

Using the Indian as a "miner's canary," as has been done so often in the past, we may suspect that these areas of neglect or blindness not only reveal cracks in the frontier plaster but also very likely indicate some shared and deep-seated assumptions about the way we think about our cultural history even now, a long century after the important action was thought to have been concluded. My remarks will parallel those of Lewis; though I have nothing to add to his observations, I want to move his considerations to a level beyond the physical, economic, and social. For equal in significance to the persistence of the Native Americans themselves is the force of their intellectual heritage—which, though massively injured in the European invasion, provides us with some exciting grounds for rethinking the history of the country. Although I am not a practicing deconstructionist, I find one of the basic tenets in that approach to be very serviceable to our discussion; simply phrased, the premise is that *all knowledge is socially and culturally constructed.* If this is so (at least for the sake of argument), and if our histories are thus made up of what elements we choose to include and how we choose to evaluate them—as Professor Lewis has so nicely demonstrated in the case of Turner's comments on Indians—then we might ask further into the meaning of the evidence that Turner and most of his contemporaries, and most of his followers down to the present, have chosen *not* to treat: Native American intellectual activity, worldview, philosophy, and discovery. Of course, all the examples that could be brought forward under these headings would be too many and too complex for a brief response to encompass, so I will concentrate on five topics for which we have ample evidence but precious little appreciation.

Literature

One of the most powerful stories ever to reach print in America is Charles Cultee's "Sun Myth," collected by Franz Boas in 1890. At the time, Cultee was one of the last three people alive who could speak the Kathlamet Chinook language, and by the turn of the century there was no one left who could have told or listened to the story. The text languished in the Bureau of American Ethnology (BAE) reports until the folklorist and linguist Dell Hymes brought it into understandable English and published it in the *Journal of American Folklore* in 1975. Although it can be put beside any worldwide classic, it remains generally unknown and unread in the country of its origin. And in addition to the vast supply of fine literature still lurking in the BAE reports and other repositories (some of them recent in publication), we now have many excellent Native American writers of contemporary literature, as Professor Lewis has noted, and several of them—Louise Erdrich, Simon Ortiz, Leslie Marmon Silko, N. Scott Momaday, James Welch, and Gerald Vizenor—are among the best writers in the country. Silko's *Ceremony* (1977) is arguably among the best novels ever written in North America, but in an odd parallel to the eastern notion of "regional literature" (anything written west of the Hudson River), *Ceremony* is dismissed as narrowly ethnic. The reader needs to know a lot about Indians to understand it, and though this consideration is referred to as critical scholarship when it comes to Shakespeare or Chaucer, it is apparently seen as an unfair burden regarding Native American fields of reference. Turner's "blindness" now seems to recede into a more general cultural unwillingness to take Indian expressions seriously.

Exploration and Discovery

Since much of the excitement of the frontier image relates to the movement across the land, the discovery of new territories, and the basic "drive" to explore the unknown, it is a wonder to me that we have not considered the movements of the Indians and other peoples as an inseparable part of the picture. After all, the Navajos are now thought to have arrived in the Southwest about five hundred years ago, having traveled in a lengthy migration from the Athabascan homeland in what is now Alaska and western Canada. Lacking a precise date, I find it tempting to imagine that they arrived in the southwestern deserts in 1492, at about the same time that some European was lost in the "Indies" (a Native American friend of mine used to say, "Lucky for us he wasn't looking for Turkey!"). And before the Europeans arrived in the Midwest, the Sioux had already obtained horses from the south and had started moving westward out of the forests and onto the plains, just as the Kiowas were moving out of the Yellowstone country and eastward onto the plains— both of them to develop newer, dynamic cultures that had never existed before and that were made possible by this new "Sacred Dog" that made lengthy travel on the plains possible. By the 1900s, the Yaquis were moving northward out of Mexico and into Arizona. Where, then, was the frontier really—and whose frontier was it?

For the Navajos, the long move resulted in an almost totally transformed culture, indeed far more thoroughly altered than that of the Europeans on the frontier, for the Northern Athabascan hunter-fisher culture (based on the death of relatives who supply their bodies for food) changed to an agricultural mode (in which life and fertility dominate as images), and their mostly patriarchal system changed to a matriarchal, matrilocal, matrilineal society while their primary animals (wolf, bear, coyote, mountain lion) changed from food and clothing suppliers to religious emblems of power and witchcraft. Surely, if the frontier is affective for its cultural dynamism, we have not been paying attention to more dramatic examples than our own. And if we add the movement of other cultures into the region (and why not?), we notice that the Hispanic movement is northward and that the Asian movement is eastward. In fact, the West was a cauldron of cultural activity. Does it not seem that the reason we pay attention primarily to our own (European) movement onto a frontier rests not on any objective view of what was going on but rather on the fact that our group became dominant? This is no news, of course, but it requires us to decide whether we are talking about history or about ethnic aggrandizement.

One other example of Native American exploration begs to be mentioned: the first "westerner" to enter Japan during its closed era was not Commodore Matthew C. Perry but Ranald MacDonald, a half-Chinook from Oregon who had himself put off a whaling ship and purposely stranded himself on the Japanese shore. Because he looked Asian and because the Chinook language has a number of words and sounds similar to Japanese, MacDonald escaped the usual penalty (death) for entering the country. Instead, he was kept under house arrest for a number of years, and it was he who taught the English language to three of the four Japanese scholars who became the interpreters when Commodore Perry arrived so aggressively. MacDonald later traveled around Asia and Australia and eventually came home to the United States; he is buried in a well-marked but generally unknown grave on the Northern Colville Indian Reservation in Washington. His remarkable adventure and his intellectual achievement are known to scholars of Japanese political history (and there is a film about him in Japan), but he is essentially an unknown in America.

Language

We have no way of knowing exactly how many languages existed in the Americas before the European invasions, but the figure would certainly be in the several hundreds. The current estimate is that about 150 Native American languages (not dialects) are in *daily use* today in North America alone. It is interesting to note that most of the earliest students of these languages were Germans and German Jews who, like Franz Boas, Leo Frachtenberg, and Melville Jacobs, had been raised in families where languages and language study were a part of one's cultural sophistication. Today, it is Rik Pinnxten, a Belgian, who argues for the use of Navajo as the natural language for mathematics (especially topology and space navigation) because it has precise concepts and terminologies for shapes and movements—terms not found in most of the European languages.

When we consider that each of the Native American languages is based on a distinctive worldview that encourages certain kinds of observations, we must realize that the wide array of languages available to us offers an incredible set of new perspectives from which we could benefit in philosophical and practical ways. The Navajo language, for example, focuses on movement (it has more than 300,000 conjugations for the single verb "to go"); the Siouan languages feature qualities of things, so that adjectives predominate (the term *wakan tanka*, literally "gigantic sacred," has to be translated into English with the addition of a noun, "The Great Spirit," which takes the focus away from the abstract qualities central to the original idea of a god so profoundly beyond us that precision is impossible); the Hopi language focuses on space and time; the Mohave stresses dream imagery; the Tlingit features relationships, genealogy, and ownership. Just as the burning of the jungles continues to rob us of plant species we do not yet know about (along with all their possible medicinal features), so the destruction and erosion of Native American languages has deprived us of a tremendous intellectual treasure (along with all the useful applications that could have been available to us). Yet there are twice as many Zunis today as there were when the Spanish encountered them; there are more Navajo speakers alive today than there have ever been at any other time (of the estimated 250,000 Navajos, more than half speak Navajo every day; more than 50 percent of the schoolchildren speak the language, which is routinely used in the Headstart Program—a far cry from the Bureau of Indian Affairs goal of the 1950s: language extermination). Indeed, the realities of life years ago led many adults of all tribes to be multilingual. Most tribes practiced exogamy; most traded for items, food, and even rituals with other tribes; most encouraged a kind of intertribal diplomacy that necessitated the command of several languages by leaders. Language sophistication and language sharing, in other words, are familiar themes to Native Americans. Why is it that learning a Native American language has not become part of our normal intellectual achievement rather than the passionate hobby of a few anthropologists?

Science

As Virgil Vogel has documented so well in *American Indian Medicine* (published by the University of Oklahoma Press in 1970), more than two hundred Native American medicines—including the contraceptive pill, insulin, digitalis, and vitamin C—are used daily by pharmacologists and are controlled by pharmacological regulations. And there are several hundred other teas, herbs, and salves that are available through oral tradition in folk medicine. Less clear are the facts of how these medicines were first discovered and how the details of their effects and their dosages have been passed along through time without the agency of laboratories, weights and measures, and writing. Obviously, there are other methods of discovery, analysis, and transmission of knowledge than those developed by our own culture. After all, when Jacques Cartier and his men were cured of scurvy by Indians along the Saint Lawrence River in 1535, there was no word for "vitamin C," but the Indians recognized symptoms and prescribed dosages that countered those symptoms in a consistent way. Two hundred years later, James Lind, the Scottish naval surgeon who was looking for a cure for scurvy, encountered Cartier's logs and did some research that eventually led to the issuing of citrus juices to sailors (and to the nickname of "Limey"). We now make pills of vitamin C, but no one knows how many years the Indians of North America had been using the substance consistently before Cartier came along. Incidentally, Cartier did not record in what language he and the Native Americans conversed on that occasion. Did Cartier know some Indian languages, or (more likely) had some of the Indians already become acquainted with French from earlier explorers—as Squanto and Samoset had learned English long before the arrival of the Pilgrims?

Though modern examples of scientific discovery on the basis of Native American worldviews are many, they are generally unrecognized; for convenience two Navajo instances will suffice. Tacheeni Scott, now teaching biology at California State University at Northridge, was able to classify a previously unrecognized organism by showing that two separate animals were sharing a single cell wall. Noting under an electron microscope that the organism made two distinctly different movements that could be described only by two totally separate Navajo verbs, he was able to articulate the existence of two entities before he had actually found a way to separate them (he eventually liberated the two from their common cell wall using a principle he had learned from butchering young sheep). Fred Begay, a nuclear physicist at Los Alamos Laboratories, uses the terminology of Navajo mythology for his work in laser bombardment of heavy water. In the Navajo Emergence Myth, twin sons of the sun are given spears with which to resolve problems on earth: one is a spear of jagged light, like a lightning bolt, which is to be used for destroying monsters; the other is a spear of straight, pure light, which is to be used for healing. Quite aside from the precociousness of the imagery, Begay has found that the complex Navajo verb system provides him with precise terminology for the movement of light beams—something he cannot get from English resources. These are only two examples of the way in which Native American languages have provided our culture with insight we did not already have.

Ecology

Although the subject has now been flayed to death by New Age guru-seekers, the fact remains that Native Americans' attitudes and assumptions about nature are quite different from those supplied by European and Middle Eastern worldviews. Whether these attitudes are qualitatively better than our own will depend on which view one applies to which current dilemma, so I mention the subject only to suggest that the profusion of different models for *thinking of* the environment provides us with a range of insights similar to the variety of perspectives offered by the myriad of Native American languages. If it can be argued that for something as complex as ecological balance, one single answer will never be enough, then it would seem that the more "answers" we have access to, the more likely we will be to develop the kind of new perspectives we need.

In general, though each tribal area has developed different considerations, the basic philosophy in Native American thought about the natural world is that the elements of nature (plants and animals, chiefly) are relatives and that the processes of nature are sacred. Animals and plants "act" like relatives; that is, it is their obligation to supply their relatives (ourselves) with food, and it is our obligation to promote the relationship through reverence, prayers, offerings, and rituals. Whether every Native American "believes in" this equation or not is as pointless a consideration as whether every Anglo American "believes" that trees are a manageable commodity; the key factor is how the cultures *act* according to the model provided. European Americans tend to see the elements of nature as secular and manageable, either as resources to be exploited or as resources to be protected. Native Americans generally see nature as made up of sacred entities or relatives that are not under human control but may be available to humans through appropriate negotiation. Obviously, a discussion of whether to exploit timber resources, sell or divide water, protect an owl, or restrict access to a fragile environment will be different in quality and connotation from a discussion of whether to exploit, sell, divide, protect, and restrict your relatives or religious treasures.

It is possible to forgive Turner his neglect of Indian intellectuality in large part because he—like us—was operating out of a widely accepted set of cultural attitudes with which people had constructed the logic and the sense of that era. After all, the leading cultural studies profession of his time, the American Folklore Society (formed by anthropologists and antiquarians in the 1880s), had listed the collecting of Native American traditions as one of its central concerns, based on the argument that the cultures were quickly vanishing. Edward Curtis was able to get the support of Theodore Roosevelt and others for his project to photograph Native Americans and collect their stories because they and their cultures would soon be gone from the land. The leading folklorist of the time, Alexander Haggerty Krappe, wrote of North American Indians that their tales "give one the impression that their narrators were incapable even of preserving a good tale, to say nothing of inventing a new one" (*The Science of Folklore* [New York: Norton, 1929], 3). It was simple good sense and conventional wisdom for Turner to look elsewhere than the Indians for lasting features of the frontier's effects. But we are in a position to know more than Turner did, so we do not get off so easily.

For all our focus on the "westering" of whites in America, it seems we have overlooked the fact that our intellectual bearings have remained in the East, in Europe, in the Middle East. In other words, while our bodies moved west our spirits clung to old moorings. We European Americans have continued to look *backward* philosophically while moving *forward* physically and politically. Given the potential riches—intellectual, cultural, artistic—that we have rejected or ignored in our encounters with Native Americans (to say nothing of Asians and Hispanics), we become a living demonstration of what Henry David Thoreau called a "dead set"—we made it through a knothole in the fence of life but could not get our sledload of furniture through after us. Perhaps we have flattered ourselves as conquerors and tamers of the wild frontier (like cultural teenagers playing king-of-the-royal-mountain), rather than letting ourselves consider the comparatively shabby alternatives: that as Americans we were not even in a position to achieve intellectual and cultural maturity *until* we engaged the West and its multicultural dynamics and that we have not yet risen to the intellectual demands of that situation. The frontier has been mythically useful to us because it ends in *resolution*, allowing us to have our story and to claim physical success and achievement of economic and social power. This has made it more comfortable to ignore our intellectual failure at coming to grips with the potential insights and perspectives attendant to dynamic cultural diversity, and this failure has plagued us on all fronts ever since.

If the Native Americans have persisted and have set new boundaries or established new themes in American society, perhaps it is time to regard and study them not as relics of *our* frontier adventure but as ineluctable participants in a grander set of cultural dynamics. Their survival, in spite of the years of decimation and plunder, is only a part of that picture; their intellectual impact on the nature of U.S. history and culture has never been peripheral but has been central from the start. The realities of social history, not the demands of political correctness, require us to reconstruct a fuller account, based on our newer awareness of significant factors that have been there all along.

8

"A Memory Sweet to Soldiers": The Significance of Gender

Susan Lee Johnson

Of all the regions people have imagined within the boundaries of what is now the United States, no place has been so consistently identified with maleness—particularly white maleness—as the region imagined as the American West. There is something odd about attending to gender in such a historical place—a place where the dominant popular culture suggests that white women were civilizers, women of color were temptresses or drudges, and men of color were foils for the inevitable white male hero, who is, after all, the true subject of the history of the "American West." Studying women there is like enlisting in the frontier regulars; when you do so, you commit yourself to a battle-ready stance that wearies all but the strongest of heart. Studying men there is like playing with fire; when you do so, you face the engulfing flames of western-history-as-usual, which naturalizes and universalizes white manhood as quickly as you can strike a match to a lodgepole pine.

Yet these same perils mean that we can learn something new about gender from studying an imagined place like the American West—a place where customary gender relations were disrupted for many years by unusual sex ratios and a place around which cultural meanings have collected until it has become a sort of preserve for white masculinity. We can also learn something new about gender from studying a process like the conquest of the West, the consolidation of Anglo-American dominance, and the constant realignment of relations of domination in a multiracial and multiethnic social world. Conversely, if we attend relentlessly to racialized notions of gender, we are bound to learn something new about the West itself—not just the "American West," which too often is shorthand for an Anglo-American West, but all of the regions people have imagined in the western half of the North American continent.

I will not engage in all aspects of this larger project here but will take up those aspects that reflect my particular intellectual and political positioning. As a student, I came to western history first and women's history and women's studies second, and my training in these fields centered disproportionately on Anglo-American experience. I gained what limited knowledge I have of ethnic studies and feminist theory late and largely on my own in the formal sense, though informally, especially in ethnic studies, I have benefited from the training provided by patient and committed friends, colleagues, and students. In time these emphases congealed into a broader concern with questions of region, race, and gender. Ultimately, however, to engage in this larger project of mapping racialized notions of gender onto the field of western history, we will need a set of tools developed in a number of interconnected areas of inquiry: feminist theory, ethnic studies, women's and labor history, lesbian and gay studies, postcolonial and minority discourse, cultural studies, and queer theory, to name a few. I will take on just a piece of that project here, drawing from my own background in the study of region, race, and gender, to ask some questions about the "subject" of the history of the "American West." I see this, then, as a specific intervention in the rewriting of western history, one that is self-conscious of its historical and historiographical moment, rather than as the statement-of-the-century implied by the essay's subtitle, which commemorates, for better or worse, the centenary of Frederick Jackson Turner's frontier thesis.

In recent years, this "subject" has been jostled by the emergence of a small mountain of scholarship on women in the West, indicating deep and active fault lines in the terrain of western history as a whole. Review essays by Joan Jensen and Darlis Miller in 1980 and by Elizabeth Jameson in 1988 surveyed that new terrain as it emerged, and special sections and issues of *Montana The Magazine of Western History* and the *Pacific Historical Review* have brought the issues and concerns of western women's history up to date in the 1990s.[1] Despite this outpouring of scholarship, the truly earth-shattering potential of studying western women has not been realized; only a few groundbreaking works that are not women's history per se try to make gender a central category of analysis.[2] Books and articles about women proliferate; anthologies now include a requisite women's history chapter; and scholarly conferences feature separate panels on women's experiences. Most mainstream scholars, however, leave questions of gender to women's historians, who are also usually women historians. Although this turn of events is hardly unique to western history, it does have its peculiar "western" dimensions and may require peculiarly "western" efforts to change its course.

This is because the relationship between what is western and what is male is overdetermined.[3] That relationship, though it reaches back over the centuries of Anglo-American westward expansion on the North American continent, tightened into an almost impermeable bond by the end of the nineteenth century. The American West as a conceptual region, then, did not become such a stubbornly, almost belligerently, male preserve until, however ironically, as a demographic region it was ceasing to be disproportionately male. The construction of a masculine West was part of a larger late-nineteenth-century "crisis of manliness" in the United States—a crisis in which older definitions of white, middle-class manhood that emphasized restraint and respectability (manly men) gave way to newer meanings that focused on vigor and raw virility (masculine men).[4] That transformation was closely linked both to U.S. imperialism in the Pacific, the Caribbean, and Latin America and to stateside developments such as the rise of organized labor, the shifting tactics of African-American leaders from the late nineteenth to the early twentieth centuries, and the broadening and consolidation of the woman movement in the same period. It was perhaps most evident in the cultural resonance of such turn-of-the-century phenomena as the fiction of Owen Wister, Theodore Roosevelt's advocacy of "the strenuous life," Buffalo Bill's Wild West Show, the art of Frederic Remington, and Frederick Jackson Turner's appeal to the western man of action.

For a hundred years now, many have struggled with the all-too-material legacy of that crisis—that is, the discursive decline of manliness and the concomitant rise of masculinity. This new, hegemonic masculinity has been contested, and in some cases transformed, by a number of twentieth-century social practices: western women's labor force participation during World War II; the growth of lesbian and gay communities in the urban West; and the continuing evolution of competing styles of gender relations among western American Indians, Mexican Americans, Asian Americans, and African Americans. But the discursive apparatus of white masculinity has not been dismantled, and the "American West" still exists as a sort of happy hunting ground for Anglo virility.

Nor, in the academic arena, have the practices of western women's history proved equal to the task; mainstream historians respectfully acknowledge the new scholarship without incorporating its imperatives into their own work.[5] Then too, the field of western women's history has developed with western-history-as-usual as its reference point, deriving part of the legitimacy it *has* achieved from its oppositional relation to the presumed white male subject of the history of the "American West." For this reason, despite constant calls for multicultural approaches, western women's his-

tory is slow to incorporate into *its* purview the imperatives of ethnic studies scholarship, as historian Antonia Castañeda so eloquently explains in
her essay "Women of Color and the Rewriting of Western History."[6] As
long as the close identification between the categories "white men" and the
"American West" continues both in popular culture and in mainstream
scholarship, the relationships among western-history-as-usual, (white)
western women's history, western ethnic history, and the history of western women of color will remain brittle at best.

On the other hand, if we can problematize men and what is "masculine" or "manly" in the history of the American West, and if we can see
such gendered imaginings in all their racial, ethnic, and economic dimensions, we stand to gain even more than an understanding of how various
women and men lived the western past. It is a commonplace of women's
and ethnic studies that, in the United States, women of all races and ethnicities and peoples of color, both women and men, constitute "marked"
and white men "unmarked" categories of human experience—the unmarked category serving as the normative, the more inclusive, the less "interested" and particular. As historians, then, we must both illuminate
female and non-Anglo-American lives and mark the category of white,
male experience—show it to be as historically and culturally contingent,
as deeply linked to conceptions of gender and race, and as limited in its
ability to explain the past as that of any other group of westerners. Only
then can we begin to deflate the overblown rhetoric of white masculinity
that has long been associated with the "American West." That rhetoric not
only has obscured the vast diversity and stubborn inequities of western life
but also has informed configurations of power and politics from Hollywood to Washington, D.C., and has been exported by U.S. media to far
corners of the globe.

My argument, then, runs like this: gender is a relation of difference
and domination constructed such that it appears "natural" in day-to-day
life. The West is historically a place of disrupted gender relations and stunning racial and ethnic diversity, a diversity structured by inequality and injustice. So, studying gender in the West holds promise for the project of
denaturalizing gender and dislodging it from its comfortable moorings in
other relations of domination—from small-town racism to worldwide imperialism. In short, we need to ask what studying gender can do for the
history of the West *and* what studying the West can do for the politics of
gender.

But where to begin? One place to start is with some of the work western historians know best, reading it anew with eyes trained to recognize
the ways in which racialized notions of gender have created meaning and

reinforced power relations in the Wests of academia and popular culture. Indeed, in the West as many scholars have represented it, gender *has* been among the great invisible creators of meaning, perhaps more invisible than race itself, which even in the most predictable, problematic winning-of-the-West narratives has been an explicit, if deeply offensive, analytical theme. To demonstrate this, I have chosen two texts for critical rereading: Henry Nash Smith's *Virgin Land* (1950) and Richard Slotkin's *The Fatal Environment* (1985). These works represent mainstream western intellectual history at its most sophisticated and provocative and are texts that I assume most students of the West have encountered in their academic careers.[7]

There are worlds of difference between *Virgin Land* and *The Fatal Environment,* differences that reflect not only scholarly developments during the thirty-five years that separate their publication dates but changes in the politics of gender as well. Nevertheless, they share the habit of bracketing gendered concerns and associating them primarily with things female, particularly with white women and, sometimes less consciously, with unconventionally gendered white men. As a result, female gender remains the marked category in the texts, a category unmarked by race. Men of color—primarily American Indians—are marked by race but not by gender, whereas women of color are nearly absent altogether. In these texts, white male gender, in all its anxious self-absorption, remains the unspoken but obstreperous subject of the history of the "American West."

First I turn to *Virgin Land*—a gendered appellation if ever there was one. In her appropriately titled book *The Lay of the Land* (1975), Annette Kolodny laid bare a crucial thesis of any feminist critique of Smith.[8] But my critique is not only this critique—that Smith repeats, indeed, takes problematic pleasure in, the land-as-woman metaphor that characterized white men's encounter with the frontier, particularly as earlier images of the land-as-mother gave way to later images of the land-as-virgin. As important as such an indignant slap at male presumption can be, it does not go as far as it might in confounding what historian Regina Kunzel has identified, in a different context, as the "old, old story" of male sexual aggression and female sexual passivity.[9] The gender trouble in *Virgin Land* is at once simpler *and* more complicated than its metaphoric association of the frontier experience with rape culture, at worst, or virgin fetish, at best.

It is simpler because it is not just the monotonous hierarchy of conventional heterosexual relations that *Virgin Land* obscures (indeed, Smith naturalizes more than he obscures that hierarchy). What Smith obscures is that his account of the "impact of the West . . . on the consciousness of Americans" and of the "consequences of this impact in literature and social thought" is mostly concerned with the impact of the West on white men and the consequences of that impact on white male literary and scholarly production. I say "mostly" because Smith includes respectful, if ultimately depreciatory, readings of authors such as Caroline Kirkland and Alice Cary, whom he describes as clever if dowdy literary foremothers of the bright young men who established the frontier realist genre (Hamlin Garland, for example, and, tellingly, Kirkland's biological son, Joseph Kirkland). These nods to matronly white women writers aside, *Virgin Land* is by and large a paean to the extraordinarily rich, elastic, and complex set of meanings that white men have attached to what Smith calls "the vacant continent beyond the frontier." That definition of the West is itself telling, for if the "virgin land" was repeopled by Mexicans and American Indians, it would become clear not only *what* but *who* was unwillingly to play "woman" to westward movement. If Smith had been able to mark the experience that most enthralled him as white, as male, and as heterosexually oriented (but shot through with what Eve Kosofsky Sedgwick calls male homosocial desire), we would have read a quite different book.[10]

Still, the gender trouble in *Virgin Land* is more complicated than a lay-of-the-land thesis suggests, because of the brief, curiously situated chapter that Smith includes at the end of what he calls "Book Two: The *Sons* of Leatherstocking."[11] The final chapter in that "book" is entitled "The Dime Novel Heroine," and so from the start these gun-toting girls are making trouble under a sign that is clearly gendered white male. The "Dime Novel Heroine" is not only conceptually but physically central to *Virgin Land;* the text as a whole roughly straddles it. It is conceptually central because it marks a turning point in Smith's analysis from an earlier emphasis on the West as wilderness to a later emphasis on the West as garden.

For Smith, the emergence in late-nineteenth-century dime novels of the wild western heroine—cross-dressing hunk of a girl who could shoot from the hip like a man—marked the inevitable decline of the wilderness metaphor and its ability to produce a hero suitable to a growing, civilized, democratic nation. From James Fenimore Cooper's Leatherstocking, a man of nature with a perfect moral compass and deep respect for women of culture, Smith traces the "progressive deterioration" of the western hero to "a self-reliant two-gun man who behaved . . . the same . . . whether he were outlaw or peace officer." That deterioration reached its nadir when the heroine too, "freed from the trammels of gentility, developed at last into an Amazon who was distinguished from the hero solely by the physical fact of her sex."[12]

In this, then, gender becomes a distinction without a difference, as

Smith all but dismisses the physicality of the dime-novel heroine in a move that prefigures feminist debates over the meanings of "sex" and "gender," albeit for quite different rhetorical purposes. For Smith, once the wilderness was peopled with similarly gendered toughs, whatever their genitalia, the fate of the frontier hero was sealed. As the representative of his (white) race, the hero had no meaning in a world with one gender, for a world with one gender was a world without gender. In the absence of difference, who would birth the frontier hero? Who would domesticate his increasingly savage soul?

The threat of race suicide, brought about by the collapsing of white womanhood into white manhood, is also reflected in the illustrations for the book, of which there are a dozen.[13] They begin with a beneficent image of the goddess of agriculture in the Mississippi Valley, but they end ominously with a dime-novel cover that features a phallic rendering of Calamity Jane in buckskin, leveling not one but *two* guns (or, as the caption puts it, "a pair of cocked revolvers") at a frightened male foe. Her enemy's name is Gardner (*gardener?*—anyway, Ralph, to his friends), and his only weapon, a fairly good-sized knife, is withdrawn from battle, pointed away from Jane and toward his male companions. The image is complicated further by the dime-novel title that runs in bold letters above it: *Deadwood Dick in Leadville; Or, A Strange Stroke for Liberty.*

Who *is* the subject of this pastiche? Why is Deadwood Dick absent from the cover illustration, and why is Calamity Jane foregrounded? What *will* happen to Deadwood Dick in Leadville, that rough-and-tumble mining camp in Colorado? What "strange stroke for liberty" will he take? The possibilities for Dick and Jane, deadwood and calamity, are multiple. But evidence for a race-and-gender panic reading appears in the figure of the well-dressed, dark-skinned cardplayer in the lower righthand corner of the illustration. The gambler (the text reveals that this is "straight and honest" Carlos Cordova, who carries no gun) looks as if he stands to gain the most when Jane enacts this particular calamity; he sits waiting while the white men rise to meet their challenger.[14]

A full analysis of the fear of race suicide represented in such images and in such texts would require a thorough rereading of the genre, but even this brief glance at the dime-novel hero(in)es who bring up the rear for the sons of Leatherstocking reveals something more than a "progressive deterioration" of the western tale. Smith complains that after the 1880s, dime novels lost whatever literary merit they had once possessed and became locked into formulas that eventually came to characterize most western films and radio shows in the first half of the twentieth cen-

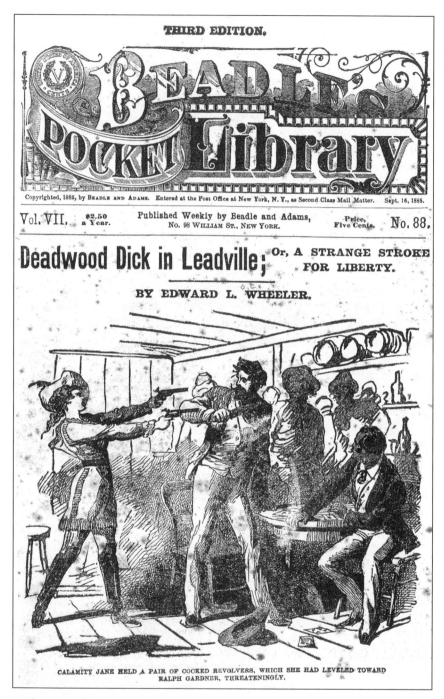

THIRD EDITION.

BEADLE'S POCKET LIBRARY

Copyrighted, 1885, by Beadle and Adams. Entered at the Post Office at New York, N. Y., as Second Class Mail Matter. Sept. 16, 1885.

Vol. VII. $2.50 a Year. Published Weekly by Beadle and Adams, No. 98 William St., New York. Price, Five Cents. No. 88.

Deadwood Dick in Leadville; Or, A STRANGE STROKE FOR LIBERTY.

BY EDWARD L. WHEELER.

CALAMITY JANE HELD A PAIR OF COCKED REVOLVERS, WHICH SHE HAD LEVELED TOWARD RALPH GARDNER, THREATENINGLY.

The cover of the dime novel *Deadwood Dick in Leadville; Or, A Strange Stroke for Liberty*, vol. VII, no. 88 (Sept. 1885) of Beadle's Pocket Library. Courtesy Special Collections, New York Public Library.

tury as well. He thus forecloses analysis of such narratives at this curious moment in their evolving representations of gender and race, turning his attention from the seemingly bankrupt metaphor of the wilderness to the more promising metaphor of the garden. For myself, I would like to have lingered in the "wild" West a little bit longer.

Then again, if rough-and-tumble captures your fancy, there is always the work of Richard Slotkin. Despite the recent publication of *Gunfighter Nation* (1992), the third volume of Slotkin's "frontier myth" trilogy, I will focus on the second volume here, in part because it covers much of the same nineteenth-century ground as *Virgin Land*.[15] Written with the benefit of two decades of feminist ferment, *The Fatal Environment* is more self-conscious than *Virgin Land* about the maleness of the frontier myth it seeks to explicate, but only modestly so. It is a book concerned instead with how "the Myth of the Frontier" developed even as the "real frontier" passed away and the United States became increasingly urban, industrial, and class stratified.

Indeed, Slotkin capitalizes both "myth" and "frontier" and precedes these terms with "the," thereby hypostatizing "the Frontier Myth" as singular and univocal, a kind of pillar of stone that becomes an easy target for patricidal critique. This approach has its benefits; fortified with structuralist tools, Slotkin skillfully historicizes the frontier myth, leaning back as far as the Puritan wars with native peoples and forward to the 1876 Battle of the Little Bighorn, which, in its retelling as "Custer's Last Stand," takes its place as the centerpiece of *The Fatal Environment* (the title itself comes from a poem Walt Whitman first published as "Death-Sonnet for Custer"). Slotkin's purpose is to show how U.S. history was mythologized as an "Indian war" writ large even as mythmakers fretted over the closing of the frontier. The Last Stand story, Slotkin claims, fused these two processes (mythologizing the frontier and fretting over its passing) and thus became the "central fable" of the new, industrial "Myth of the Frontier."[16]

Slotkin shows how "Indian war"—especially the fight-to-the-last of the soldier so white he can dress like an Indian and still stand for his race—became a metaphor for a variety of social conflicts plaguing a newly industrialized nation that was also recovering from a catastrophic civil war. He argues that by the time of Little Bighorn, journalists had already developed the habit of juxtaposing stories of American Indian resistance in the West with articles on the problems of emancipated African Americans in the South and the struggles of organized white workers in the North. Newspapermen not only set these stories side by side but also used common verbal or thematic cues (such as "savage" or "race" or "war") to link the articles to one another, and they occasionally wrote editorials that made the analogies explicit.[17]

So when George Armstrong Custer and his troops met their fate at the hands of two thousand Lakota, Cheyenne, and Arapaho warriors amassed at the Little Bighorn River in June 1876, journalists soon began to see soldiers of civilization making last stands against all manner of savagery, not only in the West but in the North and the South as well. The Great Strike of 1877, in which railroad laborers resisted a nationwide rollback of their wages, is Slotkin's major case in point. As workingmen walked off their jobs and violence ensued, editors rushed in to announce, "The Great Railroad Strike Becomes a Savage War," and headlines about the "fighting strikers" ran cheek-to-cheek with those about "murderous reds" (here meaning Nez Percé Indians but recalling the Paris Communards as well).[18] Slotkin deftly demonstrates how white newspapermen saw class in racial terms during the nineteenth century and how Indian-white conflict, in particular, came to stand for battles between labor and capital.

The analysis falters, though, when Slotkin tries to juggle gender along with his concern for race and class.[19] When gender does trip onto the stage in *The Fatal Environment,* it often does so in the person of female characters in novels.[20] In fact, gender is *always* self-consciously at issue when Slotkin writes about women, and the presence of women, historical or fictional, often prompts him to think of the men he has put on stage as gendered beings too. But when women are nowhere to be found (and in the nineteenth-century West, this state of affairs was not rare), Slotkin's men often revert to their customary status as normative humans, unmarked by gender.

Still, there are exceptions. Slotkin's descriptions of Custer, for example, are probably more deeply gendered than they are racialized; Custer's race seems not at issue until he meets up with racialized "others"—American Indians, in particular—whereas his gender is at issue from childhood, as he seeks to accommodate motherly and fatherly influences. But when it came to Custer and gender, there was trouble afoot, trouble that Slotkin finds symbolized best in how the officer wore his hair: Custer would clip it short for a time, Slotkin observes, and then grow it out and "let his curls swing below his shoulders perfumed with cinnamon oil." Slotkin suggests that the long hair somehow reflected Custer's father's "flamboyance," but it also, the author acknowledges, made Custer "appear 'feminine.'" Furthermore, Custer apparently took sensual pleasure in this "feminine" appearance.[21]

Slotkin makes much of the ways that Custer used his seeming

youth—he was, after all, regarded as America's own "boy general"—to court the favor of older, more powerful men, be they military superiors, New York financial magnates, or Washington politicians.[22] But the author hesitates to explore the ways that Custer's variable gender performances worked to the officer's advantage. This is not to say that Slotkin ignores the evidence. He is quick to include an assessment of Custer by an aide to General Phil Sheridan, Custer's commanding officer. The aide character-ized the relationship between Sheridan and Custer as grounded in differ-ence: "While Sheridan was always cool, Custer was aflame." Custer's flaming tendencies, the aide went on to explain, were not hard to tolerate: "We all liked Custer and did not mind his little freaks . . . any more than we would have minded temper in a woman."[23]

For Slotkin, this characterization is an instance of Custer as a "liminal hero, the boy-man whose sexual character is on the border between mas-culine adulthood and the passionate nature of woman." As such, Custer embodies for Slotkin the key trait of a mythic hero, that is, the "incarna-tion of . . . polar oppositions." Moving swiftly from Custer's "little freaks" to his inevitable rise from the grave as the ultimate American hero, Slotkin concludes: "Custer is presented as the meeting point of the posi-tive and negative forces in American culture—masculinity and femininity, adulthood and childhood, civilization and savagery, sanity and madness, order and disorder."[24] Never mind that each of these oppositions had very specific (and changing) meanings during the nineteenth century. Never mind that the masculine-feminine dichotomy in particular—which I see more as a twentieth-century construction—might be more usefully char-acterized as one between manliness and womanliness in this period. Never mind that these binaries were hotly contested not only within the white, Protestant, middle-class, male-dominated cultural ethos but also from the margins by people not privileged by race, religion, class, or gender.

I could put these critiques aside for a moment. I could even, grudg-ingly and temporarily, grant Custer the central place in U.S. history for which he so longed. But I would also want to linger a little longer than Slotkin does over how Custer inhabited a gender and how his way of do-ing gender (and how much of that way) was mapped onto a whole region and ultimately onto the imagined community of the nation.[25] In addi-tion, I would want to consider, in the context of western history, what gender has to do with race wars and how it inflects class conflict as well. And I would want to think about how the scholarly impulse to find One Big Myth and to identify its One True Hero relates to the dominant cul-tural impulses that, by the twentieth century, turned the "American West" into a mirror for a particular white male subjectivity. This impulse more recently has led Slotkin to argue that a new, less politically problematic national myth "will have to respond to the demographic transformation of the United States and speak to and for a polyglot nationality," as if the old myth spoke for an actual past, before the fabled "demographic transformation," when the United States and its colonial predecessors were not troubled by the presence of women, peoples of color, and unmanly men.[26]

Much is held in abeyance when this impulse to find One Big Myth and to identify its One True Hero is indulged. There is the dime-novel heroine, whose brazen perversion of the heroic suggests that western heroism itself is a parody for which there is no original, only better and worse performances.[27] Recall that Smith's search for the ultimate American hero led him to abandon dime novels just as the she-man came into her pistol-packing own. Also held in abeyance are Custer's "little freaks," which Slotkin quickly positions in a larger symbolic universe of all the grand binary oppositions of modern Anglo-American culture. I am *still* curious, even after 532 pages of *The Fatal Environment,* to learn how a white man who took sensual pleasure in his cinnamon-scented locks and who seemed aflame in relation to more conventionally gendered men came to stand as the great tragic hero of Anglo America in the age of industrialization.

Not only is there little in *The Fatal Environment* to help me make sense of this, there is little in the whole of western historiography to which I can turn in beginning such a project. Even western women's historians have not offered much grist for this mill, except for a delightful disdain for Big Myths and True Heroes and a dogged devotion to the heroics of everyday life.[28] So although I might begin my inquiry into the gendering of the "American West" with the *attitude* of recent western women's history, for *analysis* I am more inclined to turn to current shifts in thinking about gender in the larger field of women's studies. Curiously enough, these two contemporaneous scholarly developments have proceeded relatively independent of one another.

The new work on western women that began to appear in the late 1970s opened up whole social and political worlds to view that had long been obscured by the stultifying maleness of the West as it had been represented in both academia and popular culture. *Frontier Women, Westering Women, The Women's West, Western Women: Their Land, Their Lives*—the book titles were bold and defiant, crafted as if to say: "The game's over, boys. It's my ball and I'm going home." The trouble was that the boys had balls too, and so instead of stopping the contest, the feminist retreat simply started a new, largely white, women's league—a sort of "our books, ourselves" approach to the game of historical scholarship.[29]

Meanwhile, back at the women's studies ranch, scholars in a variety of disciplines were busy lassoing the very category of "women" itself, tying it up in quotation marks, showing it to be not a transparent, self-evident de- notation of people sexed female but, as Denise Riley puts it, a category "historically, discursively constructed . . . a volatile collectivity in which female persons can be very differently positioned, so that the apparent continuity of the subject of 'women' isn't to be relied on."[30] That is, whereas western women's historians took for granted that the subjects of their research and analysis were, in a word, "women," other women's stud- ies scholars (a few of them historians) marveled at how we have come to see "women" and "men" at every academic turn. So while the "women" of western women's history trudged matter-of-factly across the Overland Trail gathering buffalo dung for fuel, the "women" of women's studies got all dressed up and stepped out on the town to a dizzying gender-bender ball, where anything could—and did—happen.

Though inconsistently acknowledged by women's studies scholars privileged by race, ethnicity, class background, or sexuality, the original in- vitations to try out these new dance steps came disproportionately from scholars, writers, and activists marginalized by those very same social con- structions.[31] As Evelyn Brooks Higginbotham has recently argued, white feminist theorists, in particular, have nodded curtly at the overtures of feminists of color while going on "to analyze their own experience in ever more sophisticated forms." Similarly, Norma Alarcón and Chela Sandoval have demonstrated the difficulties that hegemonic feminism has had in incorporating the insights of U.S. Third World feminist theories— insights that necessarily undermine understandings of gender as a binary opposition isolated from other social and discursive categories such as race and culture.[32] To me, this conversation about gender and politics among differently situated feminists, a heated conversation characterized by in- equalities of power among speakers, holds as much promise for thinking about what gender might mean in the history of the West as does the lit- erature that seems to formulate such questions most explicitly—the histo- riography of western women. For my purposes here, then, I will step back from that place called the "Women's West" and survey instead the terrain of gender itself. What *is* gender, anyway, and how can attending to it trans- form our thinking about western history?

One clear trajectory in feminist theory—if I may collapse a series of complex and often contradictory moves into a general, unidirectional trend—has been from structuralist to poststructuralist thinking, from sin- gular to multiple explanations for gender difference and gender hierarchy, and from a self-evident, self-confident agreement on social construction- ism to an increasingly complicated inquiry into just what it *means* to say that gender is socially (or culturally or historically) constructed.[33] An original insight of women's studies in the 1970s was the distinction between sex and gender, with "sex" standing for the biological givens that distinguish female from male and "gender" the cultural elaborations based on the givens of biological sex. Anthropologist Gayle Rubin developed the most stunning explication of this distinction in her essay "The Traffic in Women: Notes on the 'Political Economy' of Sex," which set a high standard for both rigor *and* wit in feminist scholarship.

Poking fun at how fast and loose some had been with the term *patriarchy*, for example, Rubin reminded feminists to maintain a sense of historical specificity. "*Abraham* was a Patriarch," she quipped, "one old man whose absolute power over wives, children, herds and dependents was an aspect of the institution of fatherhood."[34] Substituting the term "sex/gender system" for obfuscating terms like "patriarchy" or "mode of reproduction," Rubin wove together insights from Marx and Engels, Freud and Lacan, and Lévi-Strauss to postulate systematic ties among the creation of two dichotomous genders from the givens of sex, the ubiquity of sexual divisions of labor, and obligatory heterosexuality. Explaining that gender presumes not only identification with one sex but also sexual desire for the other, she invoked the book of Genesis once again: "The sexual division of labor is implicated in both aspects of gender—male and female it creates them, and it creates them heterosexual."[35] If this set of insights alone became commonplace in studies of western places and peoples—insights that refuse to take male-female differences, couplings, and divisions of labor for granted—the field would take a great leap forward.

But there is more. In the last decade, the feminist credo of the distinction between sex and gender has fallen on hard times as some scholars have argued that no real substance of biological sex necessarily lies beneath the cultural elaborations of gender. Thus whereas Smith describes the devolution of the dime-novel heroine into an "Amazon who was distinguished from the hero solely by the physical fact of her sex," some feminist theorists would dispute the "physical fact" itself. As Riley puts it, "Nothing is assumed about an underlying continuity of real women, above whose constant bodies changing aerial descriptions dance."[36] The work of Judith Butler has been particularly revealing on this point. She suggests, first, that even if we assume the stability of male and female bodies, there is no reason that the construction "men" will always follow from male bodies and the construction "women" from female bodies. Nor is there any reason that the seeming binariness of sex (its splitting into two dichotomous categories) will necessarily lead to two, and only two, genders. Second, Butler argues that the duality of sex, far from being an immutable "fact of life," is itself historically constructed through various scientific and other discourses that have worked together to make us see natural male and female bodies even if we are skeptical about "natural women" and "natural men." In this reading, sex was "always already gender," masked as biology's last stand—and sex will presumably go the way of Custer when faced with the warrior wisdom of feminist theory.[37]

For some scholars of the last decade, then, gender is not so much a noun as it is a verb. Butler argues that "gender is always a doing," and Riley speaks of the act of inhabiting a gender, notions I used earlier in my reading of Slotkin's Custer. In this vein, Butler suggests that gender is performative—again, an analysis I drew on in thinking about Custer. Thus, "gender is the repeated stylization of the body, a set of repeated acts . . . that congeal over time to produce the appearance of substance, of a natural sort of being."[38] (And if that still seems abstract, just think of how it worked for John Wayne or how it works for you.) Other scholars, Joan Scott among them, have looked beyond the ways in which people "do" gender to analyze how sexual difference creates meaning in situations in which individual human bodies and their stylization are less at issue.[39] The nineteenth-century creation of the working class on male terms is one case in point; so too, I would contend, is the consolidation of the "American West" as a masculine preserve.

Yet these scholars are among those to whom Higginbotham refers when she notes that the "new wave of feminist theorists finds little to say about race."[40] To the extent that this is true, this "new wave" will prove of limited use to western historians, for whom analysis of racial difference and racial domination must be a key mode of inquiry. And indeed, although most white feminist scholars acknowledge the importance of race somewhere in their work, few follow through with a thoroughgoing analysis of how gender is racialized and race is gendered, even in relationship to white women. In fact, race is perhaps *least* often invoked as a category of analysis when white experience is at issue. This has prompted historian Elsa Barkley Brown to argue, "We have yet to accept the fact that one cannot write adequately about the lives of white women in the United States *in any context* without acknowledging the way in which race shaped their lives."[41]

Nevertheless, it is work by and about women of color that routinely recognizes, as bell hooks puts it, that "none of us experiences ourselves solely as gendered subjects."[42] Higginbotham, in particular, has explored race as a metalanguage that obscures other social relations such as gender and class. Such insights resonate with Slotkin's work on the racializing of class tensions in the nineteenth century but are largely absent in his attempts to analyze gender.[43] Alarcón has gone further to examine the differences between the theoretical subject of Anglo-American feminisms and that of women-of-color feminisms. The Anglo subject of knowledge is "autonomous, self-making, self-determining"; she pursues her own identity largely in opposition to Anglo men. This should sound familiar because it is work like Alarcón's that has informed my thinking not only about the presumed white male subject of the history of the "American West" but also about how western women's history has suffered from its overidentification, in oppositional terms, with western-history-as-usual.

Third World feminisms have developed more diffuse and complex notions of identity and subjectivity, acknowledging multiple referents for consciousness that explode the neat dichotomies of Anglo feminist theories of gender. As Alarcón points out, for example, the existence of class and racial hierarchies often means that one may "'become a woman' in opposition to other women." Such notions of multiple consciousness derive from the historically and culturally specific struggles of U.S. women of color. Gloria Anzaldúa's borderlands consciousness, "*la conciencia de la mestiza,*" is a case in point especially relevant to western historians, arising as it does in part out of Anzaldúa's South Texas roots. Her consciousness of the borderlands encompasses a sense of self and a politics antithetical to binary thinking that opposes Indian to Mexican, Mexican to Anglo, female to male, gay to straight, and south-of-the-border to north-of-the-border.[44]

From these historical and cultural specificities and their resulting notions of consciousness, Sandoval has developed a synergetic theory of "differential consciousness," one that emphasizes the importance of shifting tactics, which enables political coalitions to resist relations of domination in their myriad incarnations. In what is easily one of the most visionary sentences in any recent work of feminist theory, Sandoval explains the grace, flexibility, and strength required of those who would practice this differential consciousness: "enough strength to confidently commit to a well-defined structure of identity for one hour, day, week, month, year; enough flexibility to self-consciously transform that identity according to the requisites of another oppositional ideological tactic if readings of power's formation require it; enough grace to recognize alliance with others committed to egalitarian social relations and race, gender, and class justice, when their readings of power call for alternative oppositional stands."[45]

This is a program for political change on a grand scale, but its implications, I think, are relevant on the relatively smaller scale of transforming the field of western history. It *will* require grace, flexibility, and strength, and it *will* require working in alliance with those whose training and commitments differ from our own, to recognize and refuse the ways that racialized notions of gender have created meaning and reinforced relations of domination in the American West as constructed by both scholarship and popular culture.

This much we have learned: first, gender is what one does rather than what one is. That is, it is not so much that boys will be boys as it is in that being boyish, one becomes a boy in a given context. Second, gender creates meaning quite apart from the practices by which individuals become gendered. That is, political cultures, presidential administrations, social classes, and regions themselves, at certain historical moments, will seem to some to be saturated with womanliness or manliness, femininity or masculinity. Third, gender never exists as a simple binary that can be disaggregated from other constructed relations of difference and domination such as race. As Brown puts it, "All women do not have the same gender."[46] Neither do all men, as suggested by soldiers' perceptions of Custer and Sheridan and by the competing styles of manhood represented in the dime-novel cover for *Deadwood Dick in Leadville*.

What happens when we take these insights back to the land of Big Myths and True Heroes? We do not necessarily stop studying myths, or cultural memories, and their heroes. As a region historically in a colonial relationship with the dominant Northeast, the West, like the South, has produced more than its share of larger-than-life legends who tell us a great deal not only about gender and race relations within particular regions but also about how regions themselves become imagined as gendered and racialized places. Hopefully, though, we can learn to attend to legends less celebrated than Custer and to see the ways in which cultural memory and cultural amnesia among the dominant and the nondominant have helped to create all of the regions people have imagined in western North America.

As a California historian, I am reminded of particular examples. What of Joaquín Murrieta, the supposed scourge of the Southern Mines, who has been remembered by Chicano scholars and activists alike as symbolizing a history of resistance to Anglo domination but who is mostly forgotten in mainstream accounts of the Gold Rush? What of Babe Bean (later known as Jack Garland), who was heralded in the turn-of-the-century press as the "trousered puzzle" of Stockton? This passing woman has been reclaimed by lesbian and gay historians, who discovered that s/he had been born in 1870 as Elvira Virginia Mugarrieta, of Mexican and Anglo parentage. But Babe Bean and many other westerners who engaged in gender and ethnic passing have been largely ignored by western-history-as-usual.

BABE BEAN.
[From a Photograph Taken for the Mail.]

Illustration of Babe Bean (Elvira Virginia Mugarrieta). This appeared in the Stockton, California, *Evening Mail,* 9 October 1897. Courtesy Stockton Public Library.

Attending to such characters will not advance the study of One Big Myth and its One True Hero, but it will represent an attempt to listen in on a many-voiced conversation about cultural memory of a multiracial, once disproportionately male historical place—in this case, California.[47]

Yet even if we turn back to Big Myths and True Heroes from time to time, we need to stop privileging aspects of those myths and characteristics of those heroes that fit most comfortably with dominant cultural notions of how white manhood is embodied in the "American West." I am struck, for example, by the lines of Walt Whitman's "Death-Sonnet for Custer" from which Slotkin chose the title of *The Fatal Environment.*[48] They are bellicose lines that fight to the last until Custer and his entourage finally fall:

> The battle-bulletin,
> The Indian ambuscade, the craft, the fatal
>   environment,
> The cavalry companies fighting to the last in
>   sternest heroism,
> In the midst of their little circle, with their
>   slaughter'd horses for breastworks,
> The fall of Custer and all his officers and men.

My own eyes, though, are drawn to Whitman's last stanza, where an interestingly gendered and unambiguously sexualized Custer, now an object of desire for his officers and men, relinquishes symbols of his power and rests in the sweetness of defeat. Imagine, then, a different title for a book about the myth of the frontier in the age of industrialization, a title drawn instead from these lines of Whitman's:

> Thou of the tawny flowing hair in battle,
> I erewhile saw, with erect head, pressing ever
>   in front, bearing a bright sword in thy hand,
> Now ending well in death the splendid fever of
>   thy deeds,
> (I bring no dirge for thee, I bring a glad
>   triumphal sonnet,)
> Desperate and glorious, aye in defeat most
>   desperate, most glorious,
> After thy many battles in which never yielding up
>   a gun or a color,
> Leaving behind thee a memory sweet to soldiers,
> Thou yieldest up thyself.

I imagine that many of us want to say and do something new about the significance of gender in western history and to say and do it without assuming old postures of domination—without striking a pose, if you will.[49] If that is what we want, then some among us will have to yield up guns and colors, quietly, without trying to become anybody's heroes.

Notes

Many people have read various drafts of this essay and given me suggestions for revision or otherwise offered encouragement, including Nancy Cott, William Cronon, Laura Downs, Yvette Huginnie, Albert Hurtado, Kali Israel, Regina Kunzel, Howard

Lamar, Karen Merrill, Clyde Milner, Kathryn Oberdeck, Peggy Pascoe, Mary Renda, Vicki Ruiz, Barbara Savage, and colleagues in the women's junior faculty reading group of the University of Michigan's history department. Five friends and colleagues have been particularly unstinting with their time, their criticism, and their warm support: Deena González, Camille Guerin-Gonzales, David Gutiérrez, Yukiko Hanawa, and Katherine Morrissey.

An earlier version of this essay appeared under the title "'A Memory Sweet to Soldiers': The Significance of Gender in the History of the 'American West,'" by Susan Lee Johnson. Previously published in the *Western Historical Quarterly* 24 (November 1993): 495–517. Copyright by Western History Association. Reprinted by permission.

1.   Joan M. Jensen and Darlis A. Miller, "The Gentle Tamers Revisited: New Approaches to the History of Women in the American West," *Pacific Historical Review* 49 (May 1980): 173–213; Elizabeth Jameson, "Toward a Multicultural History of Women in the Western United States," *Signs* 13 (Summer 1988): 761–91; "The Contributions and Challenges of Western Women's History: Four Essays by Sarah Deutsch, Virginia Scharff, Glenda Riley, and John Mack Faragher," *Montana The Magazine of Western History* 41 (Spring 1991): 58–73; "Western Women's History Revisited," *Pacific Historical Review* 61, special issue (November 1992).

2.   I am thinking here of Ramón A. Gutiérrez, *When Jesus Came, the Corn Mothers Went Away: Marriage, Sexuality, and Power in New Mexico, 1500–1846* (Stanford, 1991); Albert L. Hurtado, *Indian Survival on the California Frontier* (New Haven, 1988); John Mack Faragher, *Women and Men on the Overland Trail* (New Haven, 1979) and *Sugar Creek: Life on the Illinois Prairie* (New Haven, 1986).

3.   For related arguments, see Katherine G. Morrissey, "Engendering the West," in *Under an Open Sky: Rethinking America's Western Past,* ed. William Cronon, George Miles, and Jay Gitlin (New York, 1992).

4.   Despite its North-South definition of regionalism, the provocative session entitled "Region, Race, and Gender: The 'Masculinity Crisis' and Realignments of Power in Late-Nineteenth-Century America" at the Eighth Berkshire Conference on the History of Women, Douglass College, 10 June 1990, has most influenced my thinking here. Respondents Henry Abelove and Drew Gilpin Faust commented on Nina Silber, "The Romance of Reunion: Northern Conciliation with the South and the Metaphor of Gender," and Gail Bederman, "Ida B. Wells-Barnett's Anti-Lynching Campaign and the Northern Middle Class's 'Crisis of Masculinity.'" Bederman's essay has since been published as "'Civilization,' the Decline of Middle-Class Manliness, and Ida B. Wells's Antilynching Campaign (1892–94)," *Radical History Review* 52 (Winter 1992): 5–30, and Silber's arguments appear in *The Romance of Reunion: Northerners and the South, 1865–1900* (Chapel Hill, 1993). See also Clyde Griffen, "Reconstructing Masculinity from the Evangelical Revival to the Waning of Progressivism: A Speculative Synthesis," in *Meanings for Manhood: Constructions of Masculinity in Victorian America,* ed. Mark C. Carnes and Clyde Griffen (Chicago, 1990).

5.   Sadly, the most exciting and engaging work on the American West to appear in decades represents this tendency: Patricia Nelson Limerick, *Legacy of Conquest: The Unbroken Past of the American West* (New York, 1987). For a recent textbook that tries harder to incorporate the insights of western women's history, see Richard White, *"It's*

Your Misfortune and None of My Own": A New History of the American West (Norman, 1991). The special-chapter approach is represented by Michael P. Malone, ed., *Historians and the American West* (Lincoln, 1983), and Gerald D. Nash and Richard W. Etulain, eds., *The Twentieth-Century West: Historical Interpretations* (Albuquerque, 1989).

6. Antonia I. Castañeda, "Women of Color and the Rewriting of Western History: The Discourse, Politics, and Decolonization of History," *Pacific Historical Review* 61 (November 1992): 501–33. On the calls for multiculturalism, see Jensen and Miller, "The Gentle Tamers," and Jameson, "Toward a Multicultural History." A good example of a multicultural approach is Peggy Pascoe, *Relations of Rescue: The Search for Female Moral Authority in the American West, 1874–1939* (New York, 1990).

7. Henry Nash Smith, *Virgin Land: The American West as Symbol and Myth* (1950; reprint, Cambridge, Mass., 1970); Richard Slotkin, *The Fatal Environment: The Myth of the Frontier in the Age of Industrialization, 1800–1890* (New York, 1985). See also Richard Slotkin, *Regeneration through Violence: The Mythology of the American Frontier, 1600–1860* (Middletown, Conn., 1973) and *Gunfighter Nation: The Myth of the Frontier in Twentieth-Century America* (New York, 1992).

8. Annette Kolodny, *The Lay of the Land: Metaphor as Experience and History in American Life and Letters* (Chapel Hill, 1975).

9. Regina G. Kunzel, *Fallen Women, Problem Girls: Unmarried Mothers and the Professionalization of Social Work, 1890–1945* (New Haven, 1993).

10. Smith, *Virgin Land,* 4, 224–49. Compare Smith's reading of Kirkland and Cary to Annette Kolodny's in *The Land before Her: Fantasy and Experience of the American Frontiers, 1630–1860* (Chapel Hill, 1984), 130–58, 178–90. See also Eve Kosofsky Sedgwick, *Between Men: English Literature and Male Homosocial Desire* (New York, 1985).

11. Smith, *Virgin Land,* 112–20 (emphasis mine).

12. Ibid., 119. As for the physical positioning of the "Dime Novel Heroine" chapter, although the text is divided into a prologue and three "books," the prologue and the first two books constitute the first half, and the third book forms the second half of the volume. The chapter in question appears at the end of the second book.

13. Ibid., see illustrations following p. 98.

14. See Edward L. Wheeler, *Deadwood Dick in Leadville; Or, A Strange Stroke for Liberty* (New York, 1879).

15. Slotkin, *Fatal Environment,* and Slotkin, *Gunfighter Nation.*

16. Slotkin, *Fatal Environment,* 32.

17. Ibid., 336. For an especially satisfying account of related themes, particularly of the construction of western heroes, see Alexander Saxton, *The Rise and Fall of the White Republic: Class Politics and Mass Culture in Nineteenth-Century America* (London, 1990).

18. Ibid., 477–98, quotations on 484.

19. Although I invoke the "race, class, gender" trinity here, there are, of course, other recent claimants to the status of central categories of historical analysis; in the academic circles in which I move, sexuality and the environment are big contenders. I remain ambivalent about the latter, especially until environmental history begins to

take race, class, and gender more (and "nature" less) seriously. Though we no doubt differ on what "more" and "less" would look like in scholarly practice, William Cronon has made a related call in his "Modes of Prophecy and Production: Placing Nature in History," *Journal of American History* 76 (March 1990): 1122–31, esp. 1130–31. I am even more taken with the notion of considering sexuality a separate category of analysis, though where gender leaves off and sexuality begins is always a hard call for me. For an earlier argument, see Gayle Rubin, "Thinking Sex: Notes for a Radical Theory of the Politics of Sexuality," in *Pleasure and Danger: Exploring Female Sexuality*, ed. Carole S. Vance (Boston, 1984). See also John D'Emilio and Estelle B. Freedman, *Intimate Matters: A History of Sexuality in America* (New York, 1988); and new work in lesbian and gay studies represented by Martin Bauml Duberman, Martha Vicinius, and George Chauncey Jr., eds., *Hidden from History: Reclaiming the Gay and Lesbian Past* (New York, 1989); Diana Fuss, ed., *Inside/Out: Lesbian Theories, Gay Theories* (New York, 1991); and Teresa de Lauretis, ed., "Queer Theory: Lesbian and Gay Sexualities" *Differences* 3, special issue (Summer 1991).

20. The other way women routinely appear in Slotkin's *Fatal Environment* is in their proximity to dominant nineteenth-century notions of savagery and disorder. In this, women occupy the same conceptual ground as people of color and the working class in Slotkin's analysis. Slotkin, *Fatal Environment*, 336, 342–43, 348, 478.

21. Ibid., 375.

22. Ibid., 381, 385–87, 390, 405–6. For analysis of such male homosocial ties and their links to homoeroticism and homophobia, see Sedgwick *Between Men*, and Michael Moon, "'The Gentle Boy from the Dangerous Classes': Pederasty, Domesticity, and Capitalism in Horatio Alger," *Representations* 19 (Summer 1987): 87–110.

23. Quoted in Slotkin, *Fatal Environment*, 454.

24. Ibid., 454–55.

25. See Benedict Anderson, *Imagined Communities: Reflections on the Origin and Spread of Nationalism* (1983; 2d ed., rev., London, 1991).

26. Slotkin, *Gunfighter Nation*, 655. Slotkin goes on to say, "Historical memory will have to be revised, not to invent an imaginary role for supposedly marginal minorities, but to register the fact that our history . . . was shaped from the beginning by the meeting, conversation, and mutual adaptation of different cultures." To me, this indicates an unresolved tension in Slotkin's work over the relationship between dominant and nondominant myths, histories, and peoples.

27. See Judith Butler, *Gender Trouble: Feminism and the Subversion of Identity* (New York, 1990), 31.

28. See, for example, Susan Armitage, "Women and Men in Western History: A Stereoptical Vision," *Western Historical Quarterly* 16 (October 1985): 381–95.

29. For a thorough review, see Jameson, "Toward a Multicultural History." Major titles include Julie Roy Jeffrey, *Frontier Women: The Trans-Mississippi West, 1840–1880* (New York, 1979); Sandra L. Myres, *Westering Women and the Frontier Experience, 1800–1915* (Albuquerque, 1982); Susan Armitage and Elizabeth Jameson, eds., *The Women's West* (Norman, 1987); and Lillian Schlissel, Vicki L. Ruiz, and Janice Monk, eds., *Western Women: Their Land, Their Lives* (Albuquerque, 1988). (Sandra Myres disavowed a "radical" feminist approach in her work, though what was

"radical" about contemporaneous scholarship is open to question.) The "our books, ourselves" phrase is a play on *Our Bodies, Ourselves,* the title of the many-editioned bible of the women's health movement. The most recent edition is Boston Women's Health Book Collective, *The New Our Bodies, Ourselves* (New York, 1992).

30. Denise Riley, *"Am I That Name?" Feminism and the Category of "Women" in History* (Minneapolis, 1988), 1–2.

31. I'm thinking here of earlier works such as Cherríe Moraga and Gloria Anzaldúa, eds., *This Bridge Called My Back: Writings by Radical Women of Color* (1981; 2d ed., rev., New York, 1983); Gloria T. Hull, Patricia Bell Scott, and Barbara Smith, eds., *All the Women Are White, All the Blacks Are Men, but Some of Us Are Brave: Black Women's Studies* (Old Westbury, N.Y., 1982); Evelyn Torton Beck, ed., *Nice Jewish Girls: A Lesbian Anthology* (1982; 2d ed., rev., Boston, 1989); Barbara Smith, ed., *Home Girls: A Black Feminist Anthology* (New York, 1983). Another key set of readings came out of the feminist sex wars of the late 1970s and early 1980s, one major skirmish of which took place at the "Towards a Politics of Sexuality" conference at Barnard College, New York, N.Y., on 24 April 1982, the proceedings of which were eventually published in Vance, *Pleasure and Danger.* See also Estelle B. Freedman and Barrie Thorne, eds., "The Feminist Sexuality Debates," *Signs* 10 (Autumn 1984): 102–35. Katie King usefully ties together some of the sex war literature with earlier women-of-color publications in "Producing Sex, Theory, and Culture: Gay/Straight Remappings in Contemporary Feminism," in *Conflicts in Feminism,* ed. Marianne Hirsch and Evelyn Fox Keller (New York, 1990).

32. Evelyn Brooks Higginbotham, "African-American Women's History and the Metalanguage of Race," *Signs* 17 (Winter 1992): 251–74, esp. 252; Norma Alarcón, "The Theoretical Subject(s) of This Bridge Called My Back and Anglo-American Feminism," in *Making Face, Making Soul/Haciendo Caras: Creative and Critical Perspectives by Feminists of Color,* ed. Gloria Anzaldúa (San Francisco, 1990); Chela Sandoval, "U.S. Third World Feminism: The Theory and Method of Oppositional Consciousness in the Postmodern World," *Genders* 10 (Spring 1991): 1–24.

33. The following survey is not intended to serve as a comprehensive guide to recent feminist theory. It neglects key thinkers, texts, and points of view. It is intended to suggest a few feminist avenues of inquiry that I think would be especially useful to western historians.

34. Gayle Rubin, "The Traffic in Women: Notes on the 'Political Economy' of Sex," in *Toward an Anthropology of Women,* ed. Rayna R. Reiter (New York, 1975), 168 (emphasis mine). I rarely use the word *patriarchy,* for the reasons Rubin suggests, but am sympathetic to other ways of thinking about the term. As Mary Childers says: "For a lot of people who know what it is to have a daddy who beats everybody in the family, patriarchy is a great word. . . . And for all of us who work in institutions where there are inaccessible, controlling men at the top, patriarchy is a damn good word." See Mary Childers and bell hooks, "A Conversation about Race and Class," in Hirsch and Keller, *Conflicts in Feminism,* 68.

35. Rubin, "Traffic in Women," 180. See Gen. 1:27, "So God created man in his own image, in the image of God he created him; male and female he created them."

36. Riley, *"Am I That Name?"* 7.

37. Butler, *Gender Trouble*, 6–7. Just as this essay was going to print, Butler's response to critics of *Gender Trouble* appeared: *Bodies That Matter: On the Discursive Limits of "Sex"* (New York, 1993).

38. Butler, *Gender Trouble*, 24–25, 33; Riley, *"Am I That Name?"* 6.

39. Joan Wallach Scott, *Gender and the Politics of History* (New York, 1988).

40. Higginbotham, "African-American Women's History," 251.

41. Elsa Barkley Brown, "Polyrhythms and Improvisation: Lessons for Women's History," *History Workshop Journal* 31–32 (1991): 85–90, esp. 88. See also Hazel V. Carby, *Reconstructing Womanhood: The Emergence of the Afro-American Woman Novelist* (New York, 1987), 18.

42. Childers and hooks, "A Conversation about Race and Class," 68.

43. Higginbotham, "African-American Women's History," 255.

44. Alarcón, "The Theoretical Subject(s) of This Bridge," 357, 360, 361; Gloria Anzaldúa, *Borderlands/La Frontera: The New Mestiza* (San Francisco, 1987). Chandra Talpade Mohanty, "Introduction, Cartographies of Struggle: Third World Women and the Politics of Feminism," and Lourdes Torres, "The Construction of Self in U.S. Latina Autobiographies," both in *Third World Women and the Politics of Feminism,* ed. Chandra Talpade Mohanty, Ann Russo, and Lourdes Torres (Bloomington, 1991), 1–47, 271–87. For excellent historical overviews of some of these struggles, which stress the relational nature of differences among women, see Brown, "Polyrhythms and Improvisation," and Evelyn Nakano Glenn, "From Servitude to Service Work: Historical Continuities in the Racial Division of Paid Reproductive Labor," *Signs* 18 (Autumn 1992): 1–43.

45. Sandoval, "U.S. Third World Feminism," 15.

46. Brown, "Polyrhythms and Improvisation," 88.

47. On Murrieta, see Pedro Castillo and Albert Camarillo, eds., *Furia y Muerte: Los Bandidos Chicanos* (Los Angeles, 1973), esp. 32–51, and Rodolfo Gonzáles, *I am Joaquín/Yo soy Joaquín: An Epic Poem* (1967; reprint, New York, 1972). I have written on the historical memory of Murrieta in "'The Gold She Gathered': Difference and Domination in the California Gold Rush, 1848–1853" (Ph.D. diss., Yale University, 1993). On Babe Bean, see San Francisco Lesbian and Gay History Project, "'She Even Chewed Tobacco': A Pictorial Narrative of Passing Women in America," in *Hidden from History*, ed. Duberman, Vicinius, and Chauncey, which is based on the video by Liz Stevens and Estelle B. Freedman titled *"She Even Chewed Tobacco"* (1983), produced by the History Project and distributed by Women Make Movies (225 Lafayette St., New York, NY 10012); and Louis Sullivan, *From Female to Male: The Life of Jack Bee Garland* (Boston, 1990).

48 Whitman's "Death-Sonnet for Custer" was first published in the *New York Tribune* days after the Battle of the Little Bighorn. It is reproduced in Slotkin, *Fatal Environment,* 10–11; it also appears in later editions of *Leaves of Grass* under the title "Far from Dakota's Cañons." See Walt Whitman, *Complete Poetry and Collected Prose* (New York, 1982), 592–93.

49. The phrase "striking a pose" is derived from Madonna, "Vogue," *The Immaculate Collection,* compact sound disk (New York, 1990).

Staring at the Sun

Albert L. Hurtado

Twenty years ago the historian Richard A. Bartlett wrote that no one had ever questioned or analyzed the masculinity of frontier society. Since maleness was "as obvious as the sun in the daytime," he argued, discussion hardly seemed necessary. The federal censuses made it plain for all to see: in the West there were far more men than women, and this demographic characteristic seemed a likely place to begin a description of western men, women, and families.[1] Since the publication of Bartlett's book, women's history has become a vibrant part of western historiography as scholars have added the voices and images of women to those of cowboys, mountain men, miners, troopers, and other male heroes of the frontier era.[2]

Now Susan Johnson has thrown a few more clouds across the sunny, masculine face of the American West. Although she does not argue with the censuses, she challenges the common assumption that the West "naturally" took on a male character simply because there were a lot of men there. Nor does she argue merely that since there were women in the West, historians should give them due attention. Instead, armed with new theories, she argues that scholars should use gender as a way to analyze the relations of domination and the conquest of the West. It will look like a different place after they have done so. She contends that gender is a constructed identity and that culture and circumstances—not nature—are the builders. When men and women ventured west, Professor Johnson argues, they entered a domain where new gendered identities became possible, perhaps even desirable, at least if people were willing to shed their customary relations and accept alternative ideas about gender.

I am sympathetic with the general idea that gender is a construction, but I hasten to add that the matter is far from settled. Scientists are studying the biological origins of sexual orientation, and some argue that maleness, femaleness, and homosexuality are biologically embedded in the individual.[3] Still, it is difficult to argue against the proposition that society acts strongly on people to produce particular behaviors for each gender. The American West with its large Indian, Hispanic, Anglo, and Asian populations—each with distinctive ideas about gender—seems a particularly fruitful place to study gender and the relations of power.

However, because Johnson has devoted much of her essay to a critique of Henry Nash Smith and Richard Slotkin, some readers will understand that gender analysis is only a method of literary criticism. The writings of Smith and Slotkin are important and fair game for critics, but their intellectual approach to history is limited and too easily dismissed by those who analyze the past with a different set of tools. Thus, despite Professor Johnson's intentions, her essay establishes gender analysis as a specialists' method that has little relevance in other fields of western study. That is not the case. Once we begin to look for "gender happening" in history, we find it everywhere. From the first encounter of the Old World with the New, gender has been an issue in the West.

When Europeans and Euro-Americans explored the continent, they found native people with challenging ideas about gender. A brief survey of America's native cultures turns up women farmers, berdaches (transvestite men), polygyny, sexual acts in religious rites, unembarrassed nudity, female political leaders, free and easy divorce, and complicated kinship arrangements that defined the roles of men, women, and others. I say "others" because evidently some tribes believed that there was a sex-gender continuum with men at one pole, women at the other, and berdaches somewhere in between. When soldiers, missionaries, and traders confronted this brave new world of sex and gender, they were often confounded and sometimes delighted by the possibilities.[4]

Europeans were more often repelled than inspired by the expanded possibilities of native gender roles and relations. Most newcomers were not looking for new genders to inhabit, although some of them soon discovered that in the West their customary gendered identities had become problematic. The main problem for missionaries, soldiers, government officials, and ordinary civilians was to get people to behave according to the norms of European and Anglo-American societies.

Whereas some men were willing to take advantage of the seemingly free sexual attitudes of Indian women, many others were repelled. Whatever the stance of the individual observer, one thing is clear: gender differences were of immediate interest to Europeans. This interest, which amounted to a kind of hobby for some writers, explorers, and chroniclers, was clearly expressed. In 1500 the Spanish novelist Garcí Ordoñez de Montalvo expressed his ideas about the gender possibilities of the New World. "Know that on the right hand of the Indies there is an island called California, very close to . . . the Terrestrial Paradise; and it was peopled by black women, without any man among them, for they lived in the fashion of Amazons."[5] Montalvo went on to relate that these remarkable women rode griffins into battle, captured men, used them for breeding, and then killed them. Welcome to the gender-bender ball. Of course, the tale had a moral ending. A Spanish man subdued the queen of the Amazons, who became a good Catholic. I do not know what became of the griffins.

Montalvo's novel and other fabulous tales informed the gender expectations of Spanish conquistadors who reconnoitered the Southwest.[6] They found no griffin-riding Amazons, but near Arizona's Gila River, Indians told one Spaniard that there was a nearby tribe whose men had penises so long that they had to wrap them four times around their waists to keep from tripping.[7]

One wonders what questions elicited such a response. In any event, Spanish explorers never found these remarkably equipped fellows; perhaps they had eloped with the griffins.

Although the most bizarrely gendered creatures of the Spanish imagination did not materialize, Spaniards found the realities of Indian social life startling enough. Throughout the Southwest the berdache tradition was ubiquitous, and missionaries and soldiers alike agreed that homosexuality had to be eradicated. Everywhere, the berdaches were persecuted and driven underground. Neither were priests tolerant of customary Indian heterosexual behavior, which was far more liberal than Catholic precepts permitted. Soldiers, however, were more open-minded on this matter and were pleased to find that in some Indian societies, the sexual services of women were available. There was a dark side to interracial sex too. Missionaries frequently reported that soldiers and civilians raped Indian women, which suggests one clear implication of the intersection of cultures, genders, and conquest.[8] When missionaries were not complaining about consensual and coerced sex, they were working hard to reorganize the gender relations of western Indians according to Catholic teachings and Spanish customs, which suggests another implication of the relationship of power and gender.

Spanish priests and soldiers were not the only people who were concerned with gender in North America. Fur traders and trappers, who are sometimes seen as cultural brokers because they took Indian wives, occasionally expressed disapproval of Indian gender roles and sexual behavior. Moreover, some fur traders tried to make over Indian wives so that they more closely resembled their white counterparts.[9] Alexander Henry the Younger, a Northwest Company fur trader, was disdainful of Indian genders and sexual practices that he regarded as unconventional. For example, in 1806 Henry characterized the Hidatsa villagers as "loose and licentious"; the men took "pride in displaying their nudities." Henry added, "I am also informed that they are much given to unnatural lusts and prefer a young man to a woman."[10] He was contemptuous of Hidatsa women because they would sleep with a stranger "if he had any property" and also because they stretched their labia to a length of several inches. Henry claimed to have personally observed Hidatsa genitalia while the women were bathing, but he sternly refused to have sex with them because he was 'too much disgusted with them and their long tubes to wish to become more intimately acquainted."[11] Perhaps, but however intimately acquainted Henry may have been with the Hidatsa women, he surely wanted his readers to know that his views on sex and gender were orthodox.

And what about Custer, the boy-general with the cinnamon-perfumed locks? Whatever his physical appearance may have implied, his letters and those of his wife, Elizabeth, indicate that his erotic tastes were unambiguously heterosexual. There is some evidence that suggests that Colonel Custer had extramarital affairs with an officer's wife and perhaps other women as well. His best-documented liaison was with Monahsetah, a young Cheyenne woman captured during the Battle of the Washita in November 1868. Custer and some of his officers shared their blankets with Cheyenne women during the winter campaign that followed the fight at Washita. Some of those Cheyenne women inhabited the "fatal environment" of the Little Bighorn Valley when Custer arrived in 1876. They remembered him. After the battle they prevented others from mutilating his corpse, and they inserted sewing awls in his ears "to improve his hearing," according to Kate Big Head.[12] Is this distinctly Cheyenne women's act an example of the intersection of gender, the relations of power, and conquest in the American West? I think so.

The gendered history of the West was not relegated to acts of violent conquest. Federal Indian agents were eager to thrust Indian women and men into new gender roles that the dominant society approved. Indian men should give up hunting and fighting and should become farmers—women's work in many native societies. And women must learn the homemaking skills that were so highly valued in the cult of domesticity if they were to become a part of the new western society that was abuilding.[13]

As Professor Johnson urges, historians should give increased attention to gender in the history of the American West. The examples cited here suggest that frontier encounters prompted most participants to interpret new experiences through the gendered lenses of their own time and culture. Insofar as the customs of Indians and others posed a challenge, the new masters of the West sought to regender its people along familiar lines that reinforced the status of victor and vanquished alike.

Notes

1. Richard A. Bartlett, *The New Country: A Social History of the American Frontier, 1776–1890* (New York, 1974), 343.

2. The following titles are merely suggestive of the breadth and depth of recent literature on western women. Susan Armitage and Elizabeth Jameson, eds., *The Women's West* (Norman, 1987); Anne M. Butler, *Daughters of Joy, Sisters of Misery: Prostitutes in the American West, 1865–90* (Urbana, 1985); Joan M. Jensen and Darlis A. Miller, eds., *New Mexico Women: Intercultural Perspectives* (Albuquerque, 1986); Polly Welts Kaufman, *Women Teachers on the Frontier* (New Haven, 1984); Peggy Pascoe, *Relations of Rescue: The Search for Female Moral Authority in the American West, 1874–1939* (New York, 1990); Sarah Deutsch, *No Separate Refuge: Culture, Class, and Gender on an Anglo-Hispanic Frontier in the American Southwest, 1880–1940* (New York, 1987); Glenda Riley, *A Place to Grow: Women in the American West* (Arlington Heights, Ill., 1992); Glenda Riley, *The Female Frontier: A Comparative View of Women on the Prairie and the Plains* (Lawrence, 1988).

3. Chandler Burr, "Homosexuality and Biology," *Atlantic Monthly* 271 (March 1993): 47–65.

4. Several recent works examine the berdache tradition in North America. See Walter L. Williams, *The Spirit and the Flesh: Sexual Diversity in American Indian Culture* (Boston, 1986), 17–127; Will Roscoe, *The Zuni Man Woman* (Albuquerque,

1991), 123–46 and passim; and Ramón A. Gutiérrez, *When Jesus Came, the Corn Mothers Went Away: Marriage, Sexuality, and Power in New Mexico, 1500–1846* (Stanford, 1991), 33–35. See also Ramón A. Gutiérrez, "Must We Deracinate Indians to Find Gay Roots?" *Out/Look* (Winter 1989), 61–67.

5. Montalvo quoted in Herbert E. Bolton, *The Spanish Borderlands: A Chronicle of Old Florida and the Southwest* (New Haven, 1921), 105.

6. George P. Hammond, "The Search for the Fabulous in the Settlement of the Southwest," in *New Spain's Far Northern Frontier: Essays on Spain in the American West*, ed. David J. Weber (Albuquerque, 1979), 17–33.

7. Herbert E. Bolton, ed. and trans., "Father Escobar's Relation of the Oñate Expedition to California in 1605," *Catholic Historical Review* 5 (April 1919): 37.

8. Albert L. Hurtado, "Sexuality in California's Franciscan Missions," *California History* 71 (Fall 1992): 370–85, 451–53; Gutiérrez, *When Jesus Came*, 123, 184.

9. Jennifer S. H. Brown, *Strangers in Blood: Fur Trade Company Families in Indian Country* (Vancouver, B.C., 1980); Sylvia Van Kirk, *Many Tender Ties: Women in Fur-Trade Society, 1670–1870* (Norman, 1980). William Swagerty points up the bicultural role of fur traders in "Marriage and Settlement Patterns of Rocky Mountain Trappers and Traders," *Western Historical Quarterly* 11 (April 1980): 159–80.

10. Elliott Coues, ed., *New Light on the Early History of the Greater Northwest: The Manuscript Journals of Alexander Henry and David Thompson, 1799–1814*, 3 vols. (New York, 1897), 1:347–48.

11. Ibid., 357.

12. Robert M. Utley, *Cavalier in Buckskin: George Armstrong Custer and the Western Military Frontier* (Norman, 1988), 107, 110. Kate Big Head is quoted on 193.

13. See, for example, Robert A. Trennert, "Educating Indian Girls at Nonreservation Boarding Schools, 1878–1920," *Western Historical Quarterly* 13 (July 1982): 271–90; R. Douglas Hurt, *Indian Agriculture in America: Prehistory to the Present* (Lawrence, 1987), 96–112; and Albert L. Hurtado, "California Indians and the Workaday West: Labor, Assimilation and Survival," *California History* 69 (Spring 1990): 2–11, 77–79.

A Regendered, Reracialized, Resituated West

Deena J. González

A recent radio program broadcast out of Phoenix, Arizona, asked listeners to describe the "old" West; phone lines were flooded with messages from old-timers decrying the new history they heard was being promoted by "politically correct," "left-wing" and "feminist-female" academics. One caller wanted to know why these "fanatics" did not leave well enough alone; another asked why the "females" were so interested in destroying "our birthright, our heritage, our one natural resource—the old, Wild West."

A local historian answered some of their questions, and as I listened, I could not help but think of the importance of the work of the new historians featured in this collection. We heard a few years ago of the fallout trailing the articles, interviews, and conference discussions of Patricia Nelson Limerick, Richard White, William Cronon, and Peggy Pascoe. Revisionist western history was attacked or defended, but many of the older practitioners of western U.S. history appeared to be caught unaware, just as audiences in Phoenix registered opinions but qualified them with statements like, "I never knew this was going on in western history too; I thought it was restricted to things like blacks and whites."

Susan Johnson's essay will necessarily raise eyebrows and cause consternation of a similar sort, because she negotiates the suspicious terrain of "the" West and dislodges it even further from comfortable "gendered" moorings; by launching the field into interdisciplinary waters—gender studies, women's-feminist studies, labor history, queer theory—she destabilizes the West as male preserve, a historiographical process actually several decades old. But she goes beyond this by suggesting that when regendered, reracialized, and resexualized, this newly reconstructed "West" acquires different meanings, some of them dangerous to audiences who would have their West remain what movies, dime novels, and ex-presidents confirm. Johnson's task, then, requires considerable courage, especially when confronted by a self-consciously styled national mythology, of the Wild West variety, and by the accompanying political agenda it regenerates, of the electoral variety.

Johnson's work breaks new ground, but it also follows an older path. Ever since the Henry Nash Smiths and their students—Annette Kolodny comes to mind but, in general, the new "American Studies" schools of thinking—began probing the meanings of the West in the American imagination and as a global phenomenon, scholars have busily attended to excavations of underexplored topics to emerge with enriching details. Gay forty-niners (not the football players), women tilling the land, cowgirls, Native American sculptors, and postcard art with its racially charged messages form the richness dominating "western" history. Similarly, feminist scholars began over two decades ago to unravel the situations, positions, and contradictory poses of the many groups of women who settled, conquered, and resettled the U.S. "West." Conferences especially exploded the popular assumptions about women's roles and women's lives, sometimes recasting in their place equally restrictive depictions, but new ones nevertheless. Chicano/a scholars have for twenty-five years defaced the racially embedded mythologies surrounding Mexican-ness in the "classic" texts of U.S. western history.

One important point of departure for Chicano/a scholars—a result of our training in Mexican Studies, Southwestern/Borderlands history, and Ethnic Studies—resided in the simple, if still overlooked, fact that long before the

United States was conceived, the region now hegemonized as *the* West was territory and land controlled first by native residents, second by the Spanish Empire, and third by Mexicans. In *Legacy of Conquest,* Patricia Nelson Limerick reframed the story, with the notion of cycles of conquest traced across the centuries, and this popularized an important contribution that in turn helped alter the questions that historians (dubbed the revisionists' brigade or the "new western" historians) seek to answer. Researching topics on the "American" "West" requires much patience, as all of these quotation marks attest, but the thick qualification of each topic, from race to racism, sex to gender, and so on, is indeed a symbol of a revamping. The curriculum of the "West" today tests stereotypes as much as it is grounded in them, assesses origins (the myth of the cowboy, the "vanquished" Indians) as much as it is inheritor of them. If these newer trends document confusion or yield new theories, so be it, scholars like Johnson suggest. Conferences, papers, talks, and museums (new ones like the Women of the West Museum, which will open in Denver, or the Gene Autry Museum in Los Angeles) all become forums for disrupting wagon-train history—sometimes gently, sometimes not. Naturally, the dislocations and encirclements that follow are difficult for many, particularly those who spend less time reading the new ethnography, cultural studies, feminist-gender-queer theory, and literary criticism—all prerequisites for any revisionist.

The newer work is not without its difficulties. Partly, the richness or obtuseness in vocabularies embedded in the recent scholarship generates disdain or enchantment. Either way, we are stuck in what Limerick suggested over and over again in *Legacy*: we fear modernity and yet can't wait to get past it. Beyond lies postmodern fractionalism, possibly a new "frontier," but certainly a dilemma that every good "westerner" has faced: to go or stay? Clearly, Johnson's work, grounded as it is as well in the new feminist theory, makes the case for the necessity of "wider" readings. Wide-ranging bibliographies that question sex and gender as categories of analysis do not, however, imply that we forget Marx (in this case, both Karl and Leo) but that we have a familiarity with the classics of many varieties and with the work challenging constructions on all levels. This is hardly new in western history, for borderlands historians throughout this century questioned geography in refuting Frederick Jackson Turner and, by example, depicted migration as a south-to-north phenomenon. This is hardly new to readers of Smith, Marx, Kolodny, and Richard Slotkin and, more recently, Limerick, White, and Cronon. What is new—with Johnson—is the attention paid to the work by women of color, not women of color as subject categories *for* analysis but as actual theoreticians with an analysis situated historically and marked by difference and differing inquiries. If you have not read Gloria Anzaldúa, Norma Alarcón, Alicia Gaspar de Alba, Ana Castillo, Sandra Cisneros, Emma Pérez, or Chela Sandoval for the new writings on and from the Chicana borderlands, Johnson's essay suggests, your homework awaits you. If, in labor history, you know Camille

Guerin-Gonzales or Vicki Ruiz, your analysis is enriched. If the names Paula Gunn Allen, Valerie Matsumoto, and Yvette Huginnie are unfamiliar, you do not know western history.

In an important historiographical essay in the *Pacific Historical Review*, the historian Antonia Castañeda argued the necessity of—supported here by Johnson's work as well—redesigning concepts in western history, not for inclusion per se (we hope to be well beyond that, although some western women's history and many survey courses still evidence this tendency, especially in syllabi or in overcrowded classrooms) but instead for a fundamental reorientation, beginning with dislocation and avoiding circular reasonings or renditions. An example of this would be to ask what Asian-American women's history affords traditional western history or U.S. history. In chronological breakdown alone, Asian-American women's stories suggest that the Civil War and the U.S.-Mexican War might not be appropriate as cutoff dates, and the structure as well as the chronology needs to be held accountable. Similarly, Native American chronologies do not abide the "western"-western dictatorial practice of a precontact/postconquest divide, as if no Native American societies practiced diplomacy or war before the Europeans arrived. These histories and the rich documentary evidence upon which they are based—when historians of the West become capable linguistically—suggest not simply revamping but severe questioning of the alignments that organize our topics, subjects, and bibliographies. As Johnson's essay demonstrates, cycles of exchange, of conquest, and of wills belie that some people won and many "others" lost in the conquest of the Mexican North, the U.S. West. The West as foregone conclusion is only a recent "fact," and books suggesting the opposite might benefit from the example of the reorientation grounding Johnson's work by taking a longer chronological and cultural view. The recommendation strikes me as one of the important missing links in our current work in this field, and it is also one Johnson could strengthen as she avoids cataloguing the contributions and perspectives of women of color when she reorganizes questions around the newer studies of race, class, ethnicity, sex, gender, and sexuality. A summation of the fresh questions to accompany the inventive concepts would mark the essay historiographically as well.

Reading Johnson's essay primarily as exhortation neglects another dimension. Her method—if historians indeed adhere to any methodology or combinations of them—teaches valuable lessons and is also the benchmark of the "new" western history. Theoretical thinking is not sufficient; rather, theorizing tagged to particular experiences, stories, and ideologies shapes the *practice* of western history. Glances in the direction of ethnic studies are insufficient, this essay emphasizes. Rather, it is the explicit message, theory, and application of bell hooks's point about multiple selves and myriad representations that Johnson takes to heart and applies to Walt Whitman and George Armstrong Custer alike. Whitman makes Custer whiter than white and masculinizes him in Whitman's own (homoerotic) tradition. Custer is neither tragic figure nor hero but a complex figure because our memories of him are not alike, and he affronts collective racial memories at every turn.

What we have failed to take into account in the new western history is precisely the notion that we too feminize-masculinize in our own image and that this textures our renderings of Calamity Jane or Babe Bean. We are not painters or artists in that sense, but we are, as good social historians, storytellers capable of "filling in" the blank spots. In fact, many of us enjoy working from the blank canvas toward the larger picture and not the reverse, as has been so common especially among the followers of Turner or Herbert Eugene Bolton. In other words, this essay informs us that the task is not to pay attention to the marginal or marginalized but to join where possible the margins for a wider reading *and* a reformulated reading of the "wild West." Honest positionings require an intellectual rigor sustained by an interdisciplinary thinking that has been absent in much western history. (As Johnson says, "I see this, then, as a specific intervention in the rewriting of western history.") An "overdetermined" male–western history relationship, as Johnson says, is precisely the point, but the conclusion also calls for a refocusing with differently trained senses; adding "bad girls," cowgirls, or widow-farmers to the list is not the task, unless we want to "sell" western women's history or overdetermine femaleness against male westerners. Euro-American men and women were equally conquerors, day laborers, poor migrants, and, before 1848, illegal immigrants. We should seek not egalitarian-companionate mythologies but revamped, far-reaching, and layered ones. What we welcome in Johnson, ultimately, and in other work like hers, is the ability to say that writing against the grain, that is, whipping past Turner, Bolton, or any number of others, is no longer the motive. Creating a new vision of a new West is more to the point, and with this work, we are approaching that goal.

Bibliography

Allen, Paula Gunn. *The Sacred Hoop: Recovering the Feminine in American Indian Traditions*. Boston, 1986.

Anzaldúa, Gloria. *Borderlands/La Frontera: The New Mestiza.*San Francisco, 1987.

Castañeda, Antonia. "Women of Color and the Rewriting of Western History: The Discourse, Politics, and Decolonization of History." *Pacific Historical Review* 61 (November 1992): 501–33.

Castillo, Ana. *So Far from God*. New York, 1993.

Cisneros, Sandra. *Woman Hollering Creek*. New York, 1991.

Cronon, William. *Changes in the Land: Indians, Colonists, and the Ecology of New England*. New York, 1983.

Gaspar de Alba, Alicia.*The Mystery of Survival and Other Stories*. Tucson, 1993.

Guerin-Gonzales, Camille. *Mexican Workers and American Dreams: Immigration, Repatriation, and California Farm Labor, 1900–1939*. New Brunswick, N.J., 1994.

hooks, bell. *Talking Back: Thinking Feminist, Thinking Black*. Boston, 1988.

Huginnie, Andrea Yvette. "'Strikitos': Race, Class, and Work in the Arizona Copper Industry, 1870–1920." Ph.D. diss., Yale University, 1992.

Kolodny, Annette. *The Land before Her: Fantasy and Experience of the American Frontiers, 1630–1860.* Chapel Hill, 1984.

Limerick, Patricia Nelson. *The Legacy of Conquest: The Unbroken Past of the American West.* New York, 1987.

Marx, Leo. *The Machine in the Garden: Technology and the Pastoral Ideal in America.* New York, 1964.

Matsumoto, Valerie. "Desperately Seeking 'Deirdre': Gender Roles, Multicultural Relations, and Nisei Women Writers of the 1930s." *Frontiers: Journal of Women's Studies* 12 (1991): 19–32.

Pascoe, Peggy. "At the Crossroads of Culture." *Women's Review of Books* 7(5) (1990): 22–23.

Pérez, Emma. *Gulf Dreams.* Berkeley, 1996.

Ruiz, Vicki. *Cannery Women, Cannery Lives: Mexican Women, Unionization, and the California Food Processing Industry, 1930–1950.* Albuquerque, 1987.

Sandoval, Anna. "Binding the Ties: Toward a Comparative Study of Chicana and Mexicana Literature." Ph.D. diss., University of California, Santa Cruz, forthcoming.

Slotkin, Richard. *Regeneration through Violence: The Mythology of the American Frontier, 1600–1860.* Middletown, Conn., 1973.

Smith, Henry Nash. *Virgin Land: The American West as Symbol and Myth.* Cambridge, Mass., 1950.

White, Richard. *Land Use, Environment, and Social Change: The Shaping of Island County, Washington.* Seattle, 1980.

9 Concluding Statements

Through the Prism of Race: The Meaning of African-American History in the West

Quintard Taylor

The new western history, with its emphasis on race, class, and gender, owes much—as David G. Gutiérrez, Susan Lee Johnson, Arnoldo De León, and other contributors to this volume have acknowledged—to the innovative scholarship on African-American history and the black studies that emerged in the 1970s and 1980s. Ironically, the scholarship they praise remains focused largely on the South or the East, since the experiences of African Americans west of the ninety-eighth meridian have yet to be addressed in any systematic, comprehensive manner. Unlike Asian-American, Chicano, or much of nineteenth- and twentieth-century Native American history, areas that are axiomatically "western" in orientation even if their field of historical vision originates from across the Pacific, the Bering Strait, or the Rio Grande, the African-American past in the West continues to be viewed by western regional historians and historians of African America as an interesting footnote to a story focused elsewhere. This dearth of black western scholarship is particularly surprising considering the size of the black population. As early as 1870, African Americans constituted 12 percent of the region's population, some 284,000 people, and resided in every state and territory in the West.[1]

Reconstructing black western history is imperative not simply because of the commendable desire to celebrate the region's rich ethnic diversity or to "correct" prevailing stereotypes. We must, in addition, ask often disturbing questions about relations of power among the various diverse peoples of the region, relations that found expression at different times in conflict, cooperation, and accommodation. The Los Angeles riot of 1992, as Gail Nomura indicated in her essay on Asians and Asian Americans in the region, made the nation aware of the complex relationships between peoples of color in the modern urban West. Yet the multiple sources of that relationship are rooted in five centuries of encounter of racially and culturally diverse peoples both as individuals and as distinct populations. African-American history in the West affords one opportunity to examine those shifting relationships, to provide a different prism for viewing the entire western experience. Moreover, western black history tests the validity of western exceptionalism as originally advanced by Frederick Jackson Turner and as posited in a quite different context by many "new West" historians. Was the West significantly different for African Americans? Given the paucity of research on blacks in the region, a preliminary answer must, of necessity, rest on superficial and inconclusive evidence. Yet that answer suggests both yes, if we note the success of post–Civil War western blacks in gaining and keeping voting rights everywhere in the region except Texas, and no, if we consider the emergence of postbellum discriminatory legislation symbolized by antimiscegenation statutes and public school segregation in states as diverse as Montana, Arizona, and Kansas. Such ambiguity arising from African-American history in the West surely complicates the region's past.[2]

That complication begins with the earliest African arrivals in the region. Accounts of Estevan, the black slave who ventured to New Spain's northern frontier in 1539 in the futile search for the fabled Seven Cities of Cíbola, or of Isabel de Olvera, who was a member of the Juan Guerra de Resa colonization expedition to New Mexico in 1600 and who became the first free black woman to enter the West (predating by nineteen years the landing of twenty Africans at Jamestown), should be removed from the "contributions" school of ethnic history and allowed to suggest myriad possibilities for reconceptualizing the region's past. Estevan's travels, for example, initiated the meeting of Indian and Spanish cultures, which shaped much of the region's history. Moreover, Estevan, Isabel de Olvera, and the hundreds of other Spanish-speaking black settlers who populated cities and towns from San Antonio to San Francisco and who in 1781 were a majority of the founders of Los Angeles, the greatest of the West's cities, confirm the "multicultural" West as the meeting place of diverse races and cultures long before the arrival of nineteenth-century English-speaking settlers. From the sixteenth through the eighteenth centuries, people of African ancestry who migrated to what now constitutes the West were far more likely to have moved north from central Mexico rather than west from the Atlantic slope. Their experiences call for a reinterpretation of Spanish-Mexican history in the Southwest to illustrate the enigmatic role of race in shaping social and cultural traditions in colonial and postcolonial Mexican society. Those traditions, in turn, confounded Anglo sensibilities on proper racial attitudes long after the Treaty of Guadalupe Hidalgo established American sovereignty over the region.[3]

African-American history in the West often reveals paradoxes and ironies as in Revolutionary Era Texas, where the liberty of Anglo slaveholders was in direct opposition to the freedom of black people. Mexico's constitution of 1821 renounced black slavery and proclaimed political equality for all of the nation's inhabitants. The promise of freedom and equality proved a powerful attraction for fugitive slaves and free blacks "from the states." The Sabine River became a political and racial frontier for the small number of intrepid African Americans who arrived in Mexican Texas in the 1820s. Many were fugitive slaves, but the immigrants also included free blacks determined to live under what they viewed as Mexican liberty rather than American tyranny. Samuel H. Hardin, for example, wrote that he and his wife had moved to Texas because Mexico's laws "invited their emigration" and guaranteed their right to own property. Yet the aspirations of free blacks and their supporters for a free, racially tolerant Texas soon conflicted with the goal of southern white planters to transform the Mexican province into an empire for slavery. By 1835 Texas slaveholders had duplicated the slave system of the United States, increasing the servile population to 10 percent of English-speaking Texans. With growing numbers of slaveholders demanding the protection of their property while openly selling black slaves, Anglo Texans and the Mexican government were on a collision course that would lead to the Alamo.[4]

African Americans would soon be engulfed in the tumultuous creation of independent Texas. For many Texas slaves the flag of Mexico rather than the revolutionaries' "lone star" seemed the banner of liberty. In February 1836, one month before his siege of the Alamo, General Antonio López de Santa Anna, commander of the Mexican Army, queried government officials in Mexico City about the liberation of the slaves. "Shall we permit those wretches to moan in chains any longer in a country whose kind laws protect the liberty of man without distinction of cast or color?" Minister of War José María Tornel provided an answer on March 18. While affirming that "the philanthropy of the Mexican nation" had already freed the slaves, he informed the commanding general to grant their "natural rights" including "the liberty to go to any point on the globe" that appealed to them, to remain in Texas, or to move to another part of Mexico. The Mexican Army seemed poised to become a legion of liberation. As that army crossed the Colorado and Brazos Rivers moving into the region heavily populated by slaves, the boldest of the bondspeople took flight toward Santa Anna's forces both when they marched into Texas and when they retreated. In return for Mexican protection, these fugitives served as spies, messengers, or provocateurs for their liberators.[5]

The victory of the Texas revolutionaries over the Mexican Army set in motion political forces that in the next decade succeeded in adding all of Mexico's northern territories to the United States. But it also initiated the status decline of the free blacks who had sought refuge in Texas, and it fixed African slavery as the predominate labor system. With the guarantee of governmental protection, the "peculiar institution" of Texas grew from three thousand African Americans held in bondage in 1835 to a quarter of a million slaves three decades later.

African-American agricultural history on the high plains provides the prism through which to explore William Deverell's theme of the West as the "place to witness the limits of the American promise of success and upward mobility." On a thousand-mile frontier from North Dakota to Oklahoma, African-American homesteaders, propelled by the twin desires for land and "political freedom" in the West, confronted the broad, virtually treeless Great Plains. The *Langston City Herald,* the newspaper for the most famous all-black town in Oklahoma Territory, proclaimed as much in 1893 when it called on southern blacks to avail themselves of the last chance to secure "free homes" on government domain. "Everyone that can should go to the [Cherokee] strip . . . and get a hundred and sixty, all you need . . . is a Winchester, a frying pan, and the $15.00 filing fee." In Graham County, Kansas, in 1879, Logan County, Oklahoma, in 1891, or Cherry County, Nebraska, in 1904, African-American women and men tried and often failed to "conquer" the plains. One gets a sense of this daunting challenge through the eyes of one settler, Willianna Hickman, who wrote excitedly of navigating across the plains by compass in the summer of 1878, destined for the first of these high plains black settlements: Nicodemus, Kansas. When fellow emigrants exclaimed, "There is Nicodemus!" she anxiously surveyed the landscape. Expecting to find buildings on the horizon, she said: "I looked with all the eyes I had. 'Where is Nicodemus? I don't see it.'" Her husband responded to her question by pointing to the plumes of smoke coming out of the ground. "The families lived in dugouts," she dejectedly recalled. "We landed and struck tents. The scenery was not at all inviting and I began to cry."[6]

Success for black western farmers rested on a tenuous foundation of ample credit and rain. The absence of either could spell disaster. Gilbert Fite did not have black farmers in mind when he wrote: "Rather than realizing their Jeffersonian dreams establishing a successful farm and living a happy, contented life . . . [farmers] were battered and defeated by nature and ruined by economic conditions over which they had no control. Many western pioneers . . . who filed on government land soon found that natural and human-made barriers defeated their hopes and aspirations." Yet the statement reflected the experience of a disproportionate number of black agriculturalists on the high plains. Moreover, statistics indicated that the general poverty of black homesteaders from the South prevented their acquiring the land necessary to sustain their farming efforts in the West. In Oklahoma, the state that received the largest number of African-American homesteaders, black farm ownership peaked at 13,000 in 1910. Perhaps more telling, 38 percent of these farmers had less than 50 acres. In a region where large landholding was a necessity, the small size of these farms ensured a rapid exit from western agriculture.[7]

Yet the experiences of black homesteaders in northwestern Nebraska suggest that farm size alone did not ensure success. The Kinkaid Homestead Act of 1904, which threw open thousands of acres of the Sandhills region of Nebraska, provided the last opportunity for black homesteading in the state. Recognizing the arid condition of the land, the federal government provided homestead claims of 640 rather than 160 acres. The first African American to file a claim, Clem Deaver, arrived in 1904. Other blacks followed, and by 1910 twenty-four families filed claim to 14,000 acres of land in Cherry County. Eight years later 185 blacks held 40,000 acres. Yet in a pattern much like that in Oklahoma, Kansas, and eastern Colorado, black farm families, unable to render the land productive enough for sustainable incomes, began leaving the isolated region in the early 1920s for Denver, Omaha, or Lincoln. The disappearance of black homesteaders from the high plains constitutes one of many crucial areas in need of scholarly investigation.[8]

Nowhere are the possibilities of re-envisioning the West through the prism of African-American history greater than in an assessment of the struggle of people of color for their civil rights. Patricia Nelson Limerick and Gary Y. Okihiro have called for a reorientation of civil rights history away from the southern movement of the 1950s and 1960s to incorporate the longer campaigns of people of color in the West. As Okihiro wrote elsewhere in this volume, "Racial minorities, in their struggles for inclusion and equality, helped to preserve and advance the very privileges that were denied to them." The long black struggle for civil rights in the West is an example. That struggle, so identified with twentieth-century southern history, was already engaged in the West a century before Rosa Parks's fateful refusal to relinquish her seat on a Montgomery, Alabama, bus in 1955. Its multiple sources include the legal and extralegal campaigns of California African Americans to free Robert Perkins, Biddy Mason, Archy Lee, and numerous other slaves held in the state in the 1850s, their efforts to repeal discriminatory laws, and their sponsorship of four statewide conventions between 1855 and 1865 to present their political grievances.

Indeed, California's "Rosa Parks" emerged when the rest of the nation was still in the throes of the Civil War. On April 17, 1863, Charlotte Brown was ejected from a San Francisco streetcar because of her race. In her subsequent suit against the Omnibus Company for $200 in damages, the jury awarded her just five cents (the cost of the fare). Three days after the trial she was again ejected from an Omnibus streetcar, and she brought a second suit for $3,000 in damages; this suit ended on January 17, 1865, with a jury awarding her $500. When she was forced to file suit a third time, the Omnibus Company in October 1866 finally rescinded its policy of exclusion.[9]

That civil rights struggle intensified during "western" Reconstruction. Black westerners were understandably anxious that the Reconstruction process in the ex-Confederate states ensure political participation for the ex-slaves, but they also understood their own grievances. Denial of the right to vote and exclusion from public schools, the jury box, public transportation, and accommodations were painful reminders of the limitations on black freedom despite the formal end of slavery in 1865. For western blacks, Reconstruction meant obtaining full citizenship within their states and territories as well as urging comparable rights for the freedpeople of the South.

The right to vote epitomized complete African-American political emancipation. In 1865 black women and men in Virginia City, Nevada, initiated a series of meetings, which led to the formation of the Nevada Executive Committee, to petition the next legislature for voting rights. The following year a convention of black men meeting in Lawrence, Kansas, challenged the widely held idea that black voting was a privilege that the white male electorate could embrace or reject at its pleasure. Then the convention issued this warning to the Euro-American majority in the state: "Since we are going to remain among you, we believe it unwise to . . . take from us as a class, our natural rights. Shall our presence conduce to the welfare, peace, and prosperity of the state, or . . . be a cause of dissension, discord, and irritation[?] We must be a constant trouble in the state until it extends to us equal and exact justice."[10]

The victory that black westerners gained in their campaign for suffrage in Colorado Territory had national implications. Between 1864 and

1867, Colorado Territory's 150 African Americans, including Lewis and Frederick Douglass Jr., sons of the national civil rights leader, waged a relentless campaign to press Congress to delay statehood for the territory until their suffrage rights were guaranteed. William J. Hardin, who had arrived in Denver in 1863, quickly assumed the leadership of this effort, contacting Massachusetts Senator Charles Sumner by letter and telegram to outline the grievances of the territory's African Americans. Hardin issued an ominous warning in his February 1866 letter to Senator Sumner when he declared, "Slavery went down in a great deluge of blood, and I greatly fear, unless the american [*sic*] people learn from the past to do justice now & in the future, that their cruel prejudices will go down in the same crimson blood." Senator Sumner declared his opposition to Colorado statehood after reading the black leader's telegram before the U.S. Senate.[11]

The debate over black suffrage restrictions in Colorado prompted Congress to pass the Territorial Suffrage Act in January 1867, which gave black male residents the right to vote. Consequently Colorado blacks and those in the remaining territories were guaranteed suffrage months before similar rights were extended to African Americans in the southern states and three years before ratification of the Fifteenth Amendment ensured similar rights for African American men in northern and western states. Yet the suffrage campaign revealed the ambiguities and contradictions of nineteenth-century western reform movements. Leading white Republican advocates of black voting rights—leaders such as Nevada Senator William Stewart, a sponsor of the Fifteenth Amendment—nonetheless opposed Chinese voting rights. But so did much of California's African-American leadership. Philip A. Bell, a veteran of both the New York abolitionist movement and the antebellum California civil rights campaign and editor of the *San Francisco Elevator,* was unequivocally blunt regarding Chinese suffrage. "We make no issue in the Chinese question," Bell declared during the post–Civil War black suffrage campaign in his state. "Let them 'paddle their own canoe.'" Respective leaders of the parallel suffrage campaigns in Kansas for women and for black men bitterly resented the linking of their two reforms on an 1867 Kansas referendum and correctly predicated that both would fail. Yet when women were allowed to vote in Wyoming Territory in 1869 and Washington Territory in 1883, African-American women quickly embraced their new civic responsibilities.[12]

The struggle for civil rights intensified in the twentieth century, particularly after the arrival of World War II–era black defense workers and their families in the urban West, increasing the region's African-American population 33 percent from 1.3 million to 1.8 million between 1940 and 1950.[13] Determined to challenge local and national racial restrictions and obtain a double victory over the Axis and Jim Crow, black activists reinvigorated moribund civil rights organizations (the Seattle chapter of the National Association for the Advancement of Colored People increased from 85 to 1,550 members between 1941 and 1945) and launched a full-scale assault on western citadels of racial discrimination, including some of the most powerful labor unions in the nation. In Seattle the enlarged black community, supported by white and Asian allies and ultimately the federal government, challenged the exclusionary practices of the International Association of Machinists (IAM) Local 751, prompting the local to admit people of color and white women on a nondiscriminatory basis at Boeing Aircraft and forcing the IAM itself to remove its color bar at its national convention in 1946. A similar campaign by black shipyard workers against the International Boilermakers' Union in Portland, in the San Francisco Bay area, in Los Angeles, and in Honolulu led to the union's postwar admission of African-American workers and put in place important legal precedents that would be used in the 1960s and 1970s to challenge workplace discrimination throughout the nation.[14]

World War II–era efforts were mere preparation, however, for the civil rights activity that exploded onto the western scene in the 1960s. From San Antonio to Seattle, African Americans took to the streets as an integral part of the national campaign that attempted to eradicate racism, empower black communities, and achieve the full and final democratization of the United States. The Seattle "Movement," for example, an entirely local effort mounted by blacks and sympathetic whites and Asians, employed sit-ins, economic boycotts, protest marches, and other forms of nonviolent demonstration to confront the three major grievances of the black community—job discrimination, housing bias, and de facto school segregation. When Reverend John H. Adams, a local civil rights activist, proudly proclaimed in 1963 that the civil rights movement had "finally leaped the Cascade Mountains," he was simply confirming the rise of a nonviolent crusade that had already engaged the energies and aspirations of thousands of Seattleites. Although the "direct action" efforts of western black civil rights activists and their allies did not eliminate all of their racial grievances, the campaign nonetheless demolished decades-old barriers to opportunity and equality throughout the region, confirming what nineteenth-century black westerners had long known: the struggle for racial justice was not simply a southern campaign but had to be waged in every corner of the nation including the American West.[15]

The study of race, ethnicity, and the interaction of the various "cul-

tures" constitutes a crucial pillar of the "new" western history. In an influential article published in 1986, Richard White argued that the peculiar
pattern of race relations in the region provides much of the foundation for
western distinctiveness. Without it the West "might as well be New Jersey
with mountains and deserts." African-American history in the West affords us the opportunity to test the validity of that thesis. It also signals a
challenge to African-Americanist historians to write truly "national" history and to western regional historians, as Limerick has urged, to define
the West as a reflection of its complex, varied, paradoxical history of dominance and resistance, of conflict, competition, and cooperation, of success
and failure, rather than as a collage of heroic stereotypes.[16]

Notes

1. See U.S. Bureau of the Census, *Negro Population in the United States,
1790–1915* (Washington, D.C., 1918), 43, 44. W. Sherman Savage's *Blacks in the
West* (Westport, Conn., 1976) remains the only synthesis of black history in the region, although it ends, in classic Turnerian fashion, in 1890. Virtually all other history
of African Americans in the region can be found in articles or in the few monographs
usually on nineteenth-century black soldiers, histories of individual states, or twentieth-century urban communities. See for example William L. Leckie, *Buffalo Soldiers:
A Narrative of the Negro Cavalry in the West* (Norman, 1967); Alwyn Barr, *Black Texans: A History of Negroes in Texas, 1528–1971* (Austin, 1973); Albert S. Broussard,
Black San Francisco: The Struggle for Racial Equality in the West, 1900–1950
(Lawrence, 1993); or Quintard Taylor, *The Forging of a Black Community: Seattle's
Central District from 1870 to the Civil Rights Era* (Seattle, 1994).

2. See for example Donald A. Grinde Jr. and Quintard Taylor, "Red vs. Black:
Conflict and Accommodation in the Post Civil War Indian Territory, 1865–1907,"
American Indian Quarterly 8 (Summer 1984): 211–29, and Quintard Taylor, "Blacks
and Asians in a White City: Japanese Americans and African Americans in Seattle,
1890–1940," *Western Historical Quarterly* 22 (November 1991): 401–29. I am indebted to my colleague Jeff Ostler for sharing his ideas and preliminary findings for a
forthcoming article he and Robert Johnston are writing on "exceptionalism" and the
new western history.

3. For an example of that impact, see Arnoldo De León, *They Called Them
Greasers: Anglo Attitudes toward Mexicans in Texas, 1821–1900* (Austin, 1983), and
Neil Francis Foley, "The New South in the Southwest: Anglos, Blacks, and Mexicans
in Central Texas, 1880–1930" (Ph.D. diss., University of Michigan, 1990). On Este-
van, see A. D. F. Bandelier, ed., *The Journey of Alvar Nuñez Cabeza de Vaca* (New
York, 1905), 8–9, 30–34, 53–54, and John Upton Terrell, *Estevanico the Black* (Los
Angeles, 1968). Isabel de Olvera is described in Carroll L. Riley, "Blacks in the Early
Southwest," *Ethnohistory* 19 (Summer 1972): 257. The black founders of Los Angeles are profiled in Jack D. Forbes, "Black Pioneers: The Spanish-Speaking Afroameri-
cans of the Southwest," *Phylon* 27 (Fall 1966): 234. The literature on blacks in

colonial Mexico is extensive and sophisticated. Representative examples are Gonzalo Aguirre Beltran, "The Integration of the Negro into the National Society of Mexico," in *Race and Class in Latin America,* ed. Magnus Morner (New York, 1970), 11–27; Colin Palmer, *Slaves of the White God: Blacks in Mexico, 1570–1650* (Cambridge, Mass., 1976); and Patricia Seed, "Social Dimensions of Race: Mexico City, 1753," *Hispanic American Historical Review* 62 (November 1982): 569–602.

4. The Hardin quotation appears in George Ruble Woolfolk, *The Free Negro in Texas, 1800–1860: A Study in Cultural Compromise* (Ann Arbor, 1976), 23. See also Paul Lack, *The Texas Revolutionary Experience: A Political and Social History, 1835–1836* (College Station, Tex., 1992), chap. 12, and Randolph B. Campbell, *An Empire for Slavery: The Peculiar Institution in Texas, 1821–1865* (Baton Rouge, 1989), chaps. 1, 2.

5. Quoted in Lack, *The Texas Revolutionary Experience,* 244.

6. See *Langston City Herald,* 15 June 1893, 4. The Hickman quotation appears in Glen Schwendemann, "Nicodemus: Negro Haven on the Solomon," *Kansas Historical Quarterly* 34 (Spring 1986): 14. Willianna Hickman's initial response to Nicodemus supports Anne Hyde's claim that women often viewed the West far differently than men, often correctly sensing far less economic opportunity and far greater danger. See Anne F. Hyde, "Cultural Filters: The Significance of Perception in the History of the American West," *Western Historical Quarterly* 24 (August 1993): 360–61 (reprinted this volume, pages 175–201). For a detailed discussion of black settlement on the high plains, see Nell Irwin Painter, *Exodusters: Black Migration to Kansas after Reconstruction* (Lawrence, 1986); Robert G. Athearn, *In Search of Canaan: Black Migration to Kansas, 1879–80* (Lawrence, 1878); and James D. Bish, "The Black Experience in Selected Nebraska Counties, 1854–1920" (Master's thesis, University of Nebraska at Omaha, 1989).

7. The Fite quotation appears in Gilbert C. Fite, "A Family Farm Chronicle," in *Major Problems in the History of the American West,* ed. Clyde A. Milner (Lexington, Mass., 1989), 431–32. See also Jimmie Lewis Franklin, *Journey toward Hope: A History of Blacks in Oklahoma* (Norman, 1982), 22–23. It should be noted that some farmers, such as Nebraska homesteader Robert Anderson, became the epitome of success. Anderson's claim of 160 acres in Box Butte County in 1884 grew to 1,120 acres by the end of the century. "I lived alone, saved, worked hard, lived cheaply as I could," recalled Anderson in his 1927 autobiography, satisfied with his status as one of the most prosperous farmers in the state. The Anderson quotation appears in Daisy Anderson Leonard, ed., *From Slavery to Affluence: Memoirs of Robert Anderson, Ex-Slave* (Steamboat Springs, Colo., 1967), 57. See also Darold D. Wax, "Robert Ball Anderson, Ex-Slave: A Pioneer in Western Nebraska, 1884–1930," *Nebraska History* 64 (Summer 1983): 163–70.

8. Bish, "The Black Experience in Selected Nebraska Counties," 157, 209–20.

9. See Robert J. Chandler, "Friends in Time of Need: Republicans and Black Civil Rights in California during the Civil War Era," *Arizona and the West* 24 (Winter 1982): 333–34.

10. Quoted in the *Kansas Tribune,* 28 October 1866, 2. See Elmer Rusco, *"Good Time Coming?" Black Nevadans in the Nineteenth Century* (Westport, Conn., 1975), 73–75.

11. See Eugene Berwanger, *The West and Reconstruction* (Urbana, 1981), 145–55, and Eugene Berwanger, "William J. Hardin: Colorado Spokesman for Racial Justice, 1863–1873," *Colorado Magazine* 52 (Winter 1975): 55–56.

12. Philip Bell's statements appear in Leigh Dana Johnsen, "Equal Rights and the 'Heathen Chinee': Black Activism in San Francisco, 1865–1875," *Western Historical Quarterly* 11 (January 1980): 61. See also Berwanger, *The West and Reconstruction,* 132–33, 166–68; T. A. Larson, "Wyoming's Contribution to the Regional and National Women's Rights Movement," *Annals of Wyoming* 52 (Spring 1980): 2–15, and T. A. Larson, "The Woman Suffrage Movement in Washington," *Pacific Northwest Quarterly* 67 (April 1976): 52–55.

13. The black population of the West grew more rapidly than the entire population of the region, which registered a 26 percent gain, yet the black percentage of the total population remained virtually unchanged—from 4.9 percent in 1940 to 5.2 percent ten years later. There was also a significant intraregional shift of African-American residence. Oklahoma, for example, lost 23,346 black residents in the decade while Washington gained 23,267. See U.S. Bureau of the Census, *Sixteenth Census of the United States: 1940, Population,* vol. 2, *Characteristics of the Population,* part i (Washington, D.C., 1943), 52; and U.S. Bureau of the Census, *Census of Population: 1950,* vol. 2, *Characteristics of the Population,* part 1, *United States Summary* (Washington, D.C., 1953), 1–106.

14. On Seattle, see Taylor, *The Forging of a Black Community,* 164–65, 170. For a discussion of the campaigns in Portland, Los Angeles, San Francisco, and Honolulu, see Alonzo Smith and Quintard Taylor, "Racial Discrimination in the Workplace: A Study of Two West Coast Cities during the 1940s," *Journal of Ethnic Studies* 8 (Spring 1980): 35–54; Broussard, *Black San Francisco,* 158–65; and Beth Bailey and David Farber, "The 'Double-V' Campaign in World War II Hawaii: African Americans, Racial Ideology, and Federal Power," *Journal of Social History* 26 (Summer 1993): 831–35.

15. The Adams quotation appears in Larry S. Richardson, "Civil Rights in Seattle: A Rhetorical Analysis of a Social Movement" (Ph.D. diss., Washington State University, 1975), 77. There is a growing body of literature on the black civil rights movement in the 1950s and 1960s. One of the few firsthand accounts of the civil rights movement in the West is Lubertha Johnson and Jamie Coughtry, *Lubertha Johnson: Civil Rights Efforts in Las Vegas, 1940s–1960s: An Oral History Interview* (Reno, 1988). See also Elmer R. Rusco, "The Civil Rights Movement in Nevada," in *Nevada Public Affairs Review: Ethnicity and Race in Nevada,* ed. Elmer R. Rusco and Sue Fawn Chung (Reno, 1987), No. 2, 75–81; Mary Melcher, "Blacks and Whites Together: Interracial Leadership in the Phoenix Civil Rights Movement," *Journal of Arizona History* 32 (Summer 1991): 195–216; Robert A Goldberg, "Racial Change on the Southern Periphery: The Case of San Antonio, Texas, 1960–1965," *Journal of Southern History* 49 (August 1983): 349–74; W. Edwin Derrick and J. Herschel Barnhill, "With 'All' Deliberate Speed: Desegregation of the Public Schools in Oklahoma City and Tulsa, 1954 to 1972," *Red River Valley Historical Review* 6 (Spring 1981): 78–90; Doris Pieroth, "With All Deliberate Caution: School Integration in Seattle, 1954–1968," *Pacific Northwest Quarterly* 73 (April 1982): 50–61; Joseph N. Crowley, "Race and Residence: The Politics of Open Housing in Nevada," in *Sagebrush*

and Neon: Studies in Nevada Politics, ed. Eleanore Bushnell (Reno, 1973), 55–73; Franklin, *Journey toward Hope,* chap. 8; and Taylor, *The Forging of a Black Community,* chap. 7.

16. See Richard White, "Race Relations in the American West," *American Quarterly* 38 (1986): 396–97, and Patricia Nelson Limerick, *The Legacy of Conquest: The Unbroken Past of the American West* (New York, 1987), 349.

Reintroducing a Re-envisioned West

Anne F. Hyde and William Deverell

As we write this, that summer in Logan, where we first talked about these varieties of significances, seems a long time ago. Yet the debates sparked there continue to invigorate historical discussion. Ironically, though the conference was supposed to commemorate the centennial of Frederick Jackson Turner's frontier thesis, Turner did not seem to be a big presence. Although the participants of the symposium wore nametags that read "Frederick Jackson Gutiérrez" and "Anne Hyde Jackson Turner," none of us seemed very worried about where we stood in that debate. Some writers honored Turner, some attacked him, but most of us never mentioned him at all, even though we had been told by the organizers of the conference that we would be like Turner—young historians taking our stands on the significance of the West in American history.

Perhaps in part because the idea of emulating Turner was so intimidating, all of us hoped that our ideas would initiate discussion on a variety of Wests rather than propose the final word on Turner. We hoped that our talks in Logan might spark interesting commentary, find their way into western history bibliographies, and initiate further work by scholars at all levels of the profession. Sometimes you get what you wish for, and our talks did create immediate debate—among ourselves, among the commentators, and among the people watching the show. And the show became heated. At a session for graduate students, some wondered how a group of people who could argue so passionately and so publicly could still eat, drink, and tell jokes together. It was a good question. We do feel passionately about these issues, but we also feel that there is enormous room for debate, development, and changing ideas among colleagues who share a powerful mutual respect. This debate began with the commentaries about our work at the conference and continues with the discussion published in this book.

A place as varied as the West, and a process as complex as its history, can never be captured in a single definition or paradigm. It all depends, of course, on where you stand and in whose shoes you are standing. However, this place and its continuing process are worth arguing about. As Bill Deverell put it in his essay, these are "Fighting Words." As less an attempt at the last word and more a kind of inverted introduction, we close this volume with some ideas about how we might think about recent scholarship on the American West and why it is important.

Perhaps more so than our colleagues who study other regional subsets of America, western historians remain fixed (some would say fixated) on regional definition and regional identity. Each of the essays and the commentaries responding to them is concerned, to some degree, with questions about "whose West" we are talking about, "what West" we are choosing to define our focus, and "where is the West" we are discussing. Of course too much attention paid to such questions can result in long discussions that inevitably get in the way of substantive analysis. However, our group contemplation of these problems created some compelling insights.

David G. Gutiérrez tackles the question of "whose West" very squarely in his essay, "Significant to Whom?" He argues that the very use of the word *significant* re-creates modes of analysis that place one group in relation to a dominant group, that is, how Mexican Americans are significant to Anglo Americans. Gutiérrez refuses to play this game, choosing instead to write a powerful historiographical essay. Gutiérrez effectively argues that a "history" constructed by Anglo Americans who won the war of conquest, thus giving them the privilege "to *explain* what had occurred there," rendered Mexican Americans "insignificant as human beings." He then points out the crucial work of several generations of Mexican-American historians to recover a past of significance. This work of excavating history from the weight of myth had more importance than simply correcting the historical record: it had profound political consequences because it gave Mexican Americans a voice and a story, which they used to create the Chicano movement in the 1960s and 1970s, in which the question of "whose West" took on an entirely new meaning.

Gutiérrez takes his argument one crucial step further. He argues that the history of ethnic Mexicans is now driving the most crucial parts of western history by fundamentally reconfiguring the way identity is determined. Identity is a formulation of relationships between peoples, political structures, and histories—and it is always changing. In a West that is, and always has been, a world of majority minorities, looking seriously at the way in which peoples have created themselves is crucial. This history has demanded new categories of analysis and a rejection of traditional methodologies that created hegemonic explanations. The significance of Mexican Americans, Gutiérrez says finally, is that through the recovery of their history, the entire concept of "mainstream" and "minority" has been demolished.

In a similar way, Susan Lee Johnson points out the way that the traditional equation of "the West" and "the man's West" has allowed us to remain ignorant of large parts of western history. Her essay is, in simplest terms, a critique of the entire premise of western history as identifiably man's history—a gold rush camp that lasted a century. In a deftly handled theoretical discussion, she argues that because the West is perceived as a "preserve for white masculinity," the identities and histories of people who do not fit into this category are ignored, even though several decades of women's history and ethnic history have demonstrated that other kinds of people were present. She worries too (as should we all) that western women's historians and historians of ethnic minorities have been so busy carving out a place for themselves in this heavily white male world that they have forgotten to see the crucial relationships between various groups. By wondering again about "whose West" it was, Johnson reminds us to remember the complexity inherent in the stories we all tell.

Johnson also offers some solutions to the problem of western place. By looking at several classic texts and taking the gender issues in them seriously, she demonstrates a powerful new way of seeing the West. Instead of a place where genders and races are oddly separate in their loci of action and in the ways they are portrayed, the West could provide us some clues about how much static notions of gender have "reinforced relations of domination." She argues that precisely because the West was a place of hyper-masculinity and of "disrupted gender relations," where women packed pistols and generals were revered for their long cinnamon-scented hair, we can disentangle what gender might mean and how it affects what people do. Gender might even, Johnson hopes, allow us to see the real complexity of western history that has been buried underneath a dominant myth.

David Rich Lewis likewise wonders about both "who" and "where" in his essay, "Still Native," arguing that the Native American place in the American West is as significant now as ever. Lewis takes his cue from a blind spot in Turner's work. Noting that Turner considered Native Americans "of little significance," Lewis not only effectively demonstrates the vitality of Native American life and community in the twentieth century but also highlights the vibrancy in scholarly work. Turner is rendered naive and his thesis so environmentally determined as to have missed the forest for the trees.

The straightforward and intelligent essay Lewis has written presents issues that force any latter-day Turner to rethink the role and presence of Indians in the "postfrontier" West. Throughout, the emphasis is on Indian persistence and perseverance in this century. Lewis is careful to insist that "Native American" is itself far too generic a category to provide more than a general overview of Indian history and life; yet he nonetheless offers a brief but compelling passage on the symbolic role Native Americans continue to play—for better or for worse—in contemporary American culture. One persistent cause of trouble, Lewis notes, is easy to spot: "Euro-Americans have placed American Indians outside history, relegating them to an idealized past that never existed, refusing to allow them to be or become modern." In other words, Turner's West of marginalized Indians lives on in geographies of today. The essay closes with an assessment of the scholarship that is coming out of native communities and that might bring Native Americans out of Turner's imaginary woods and into the present—where they have always been.

Gail M. Nomura plays with similar ideas. Her essay, "Significant Lives," demonstrates that "which West" is determined by "whose West" one inhabits. Where Johnson and Lewis talk about the unseen places created by gender and race, Nomura speaks in terms of a more regimented cartographic axis. Her essay is particularly useful in reorienting geography. Recall that Turner thought explicitly in an east-west direction; that was how the country had to move, that was how the trees had to fall in order for the theory to hold together and explain the lockstep of Manifest Destiny. Nomura reminds us—and insists that we not forget again—that east to west is only one trajectory among many. West to east is a truly significant journey into the history of the American West, and within those byways of ocean, land bridges, and commercial exchange is the real story of western America's Asian "significances."

Questions of place drive Susan Rhoades Neel's essay, "A Place of Extremes," in which she ponders the work of the new regionalist historians who insist on the role of the environment in determining the history of the West. She worries that the tendency in much of this new history is to make nature do all the work, to make the "facts" of place explain everything. Neel shows that the regionalists' clear answers to the big questions of "where" and "what"—west of the one hundredth meridian and aridity—have real limitations. Aridity is culturally biased because it assumes that lack of water is a problem and that lushness is normal, but not everyone sees it that way. In fact, Neel points out that major parts of the West are not particularly arid. She argues for replacing the trait of aridity with extreme variability and unpredictability, and she further suggests that we don't know enough about the western environment to make it a central actor in the western drama. Her essay ends with an important warning to western and environmental historians that nature cannot carry history any more than history can carry nature.

Another essay that takes western place and western places seriously is Anne F. Hyde's "Cultural Filters." In many ways, the essay itself is a piece of time travel to a series of different places. Hyde starts out by accompanying early western explorers on their journeys. Stunned, amazed, even speechless at the sights presented before them, these early interpreters of the region had to search for descriptive language. When they did find language, it often reflected what explorers had been told they should find. The West had been imagined long before it had been explored, and consequently, it lived up to expectations—not because image matched reality but because there was no alternative. Hyde notes that the West has always been saddled with such expectations. At the heart of so much of this tautology was the marriage of national fulfillment and western dreams. The formulas were simple: Anglo farmers formed the center of a virtuous American nation that had to spread to the Pacific; therefore the West had to be good for farming and must be described as so.

Hyde's essay is complex in that it wrestles with all varieties of perception and wanders through a long period, essentially from horseback views of the region to superhighway journeys. It demonstrates that culture drives vision and perception, that culture demands certain realities imposed by racial, commercial, or other filters. These filters are hard to remove, as Hyde shows. But in comparing Anglo-American views of the West through time with those of other groups, she has initiated a discussion that promises to cast much-needed light on this important aspect of western history and historiography. As Hyde points out, different visions indicate different Wests, different truths, different histories.

William Deverell had the somewhat unenviable task of *really* asking "who," "what," and "where," of describing *the* significance of the West in the history of the United States. Whereas the rest of us could dodge the question, Deverell had to face it squarely. Is there one West, a place that can be described by a "supernarrative" like Turner's, or are there many Wests, creating a collage that defies a narrative approach? Wisely, and persuasively, Deverell argues that the West is neither and both. Undeniably, many different people have inhabited the West and have used and interpreted it in different ways. Any community's or person's definitions of "West" and its significance vary in distinctive ways. Deverell points out that historians know too much about the histories of women, men, environments, ethnic groups, and political groups to deny the fact of a variety of Wests. However, something larger is there. Deverell senses that none of us can completely deny the attraction of the big picture, that there is a West that holds together in a coherent way. Physically, the West stands distinctively. Its extremes of wet and dry, high and low, arable and sterile, urban and rural, demand more of its residents, no matter who they are. He hints at a new "supernarrative," the story of the imposition of power to use and interpret such a distinctive place.

Using the concept of the ward and guardian, Deverell explains that looking at the way in which the broadest conception of state wields power over all of the people living in and moving through the West might help us out of our dilemma. Everyone, from a Chinese railroad worker to a mine owner to a tribal medicine man to a lettuce picker to a sod-house farmer to an urban schoolteacher, felt the power of the state. In fact, Deverell argues that the state made everyone into some sort of a dependent, telling when and how much to plant, mine, marry, pick, eat, water, and build. Deverell says finally that the West's significance might be that it is the place where the American faith in progress and success came to a grinding halt despite the fact that the West was also the place where the state had invested heavily to make sure that it worked. Thus, the region is both West and Wests, an idea of promise and progress that foundered on a variety of realities.

Deverell does us a great service by suggesting that the source of "fighting words" is our exhilaration at the possibilities and our frustration with our failure to live up to them in this place and process that is the West. Our failures as historians are just as clear. These essays demonstrate that despite a century of arguing about the "who," "what," and "where," we have a lot of work to do. It is our hope that the result of these essays and the commentary they inspired is a renewed sense of the West as a region that is as significant as it is complex. Accepting complexity and approaching it with new tools will create a new West—which, like the old West, will demand our redoubled attentions and our thoughtful re-envisionings.

Contributors

The Editor

Clyde A. Milner II is the editor of the *Western Historical Quarterly* and a professor of history at Utah State University. He has written on a range of subjects, including the work of eastern Quakers among the Plains Indians and the role of memory in creating a western identity. He is the editor of *Major Problems in the History of the American West* and the coeditor, with Carol A. O'Connor and Martha A. Sandweiss, of *The Oxford History of the American West*.

The Authors

Allan G. Bogue is Frederick Jackson Turner Professor of History emeritus at the University of Wisconsin–Madison. He has been president of the Organization of American Historians, the Agricultural History Society, the Economic History Association, and the Social Science History Association. He is the author of many books on American western and political history and has recently completed a biographical study of Frederick Jackson Turner.

Richard Maxwell Brown is Beekman Professor of Northwest and Pacific History emeritus at the University of Oregon. He was 1991–92 president of the Western History Association and a consultant to the National Commission on the Causes and Prevention of Violence in 1968–69. Among his publications are *Strain of Violence: Historical Studies of American Violence and Vigilantism* and *No Duty to Retreat: Violence and Values in American History and Society.*

Arnoldo De León is C. J. "Red" Davidson Professor of History at Angelo State University. His books include *They Called Them Greasers, The Tejano Community, 1836–1900*, and with Kenneth L. Stewart, *Tejanos and the Numbers Game.*

William Deverell is an associate professor of history in the Division of the Humanities and Social Sciences at the California Institute of Technology and adjunct associate professor of history at the University of California, San Diego. He is the author of *Railroad Crossing: Californians and the Railroad, 1850–1910* and coeditor of *California Progressivism Revisited.*

Dan Flores is A. B. Hammond Professor of Western History at the University of Montana. He has written extensively on the environmental history of the American West. His works include *Caprock Canyonlands: Journeys into the Heart of the Southern Plains* and *Jefferson and Southwestern Exploration.*

Deena J. González is an associate professor of history at Pomona College and the chair of Chicano Studies at the Claremont Colleges. Her publications include *Refusing the Favor: The Spanish-Mexican Women of Santa Fe, 1820–1880* (forthcoming) and *Dictionary of Latinas in the United States.*

David G. Gutiérrez is an associate professor of history and the codirector of the Southwest History Project at the University of California, San Diego. He is the author of *Walls and Mirrors: Mexican Americans, Mexican Immigrants, and the Politics of Ethnicity* and the editor of *Between Two Worlds: Mexican Immigrants in the United States.*

Albert L. Hurtado is an associate professor of history at Arizona State University. The Organization of American Historians awarded him the Billington Prize for his book *Indian Survival on the California Frontier* (1988). He has published articles in *Pacific Historical Review, Western Historical Quarterly,* and other scholarly journals and is writing a biography of the borderlands historian Herbert Eugene Bolton.

Anne F. Hyde is an associate professor of history at Colorado College and is the author of *An American Vision: Far Western Landscape and National Culture, 1820–1920.*

Peter Iverson is a professor of history at Arizona State University. His books include *The Navajo Nation, Carlos Montezuma, The Plains Indians of the Twentieth Century, The Navajos,* and *When Indians Became Cowboys.*

Susan Lee Johnson is an assistant professor of history at the University of Colorado at Boulder. Her first book, on gender and race relations in the California Gold Rush, is forthcoming from W. W. Norton. Her essay published in the *Western Historical Quarterly* and reprinted in this collection received the Joan Jensen–Darlis Miller Award from the Coalition for Western Women's History and the Don D. Walker Award from the Western Literature Association.

David Rich Lewis is an associate professor of history at Utah State University and the associate editor of the *Western Historical Quarterly.* He is the author of *Neither Wolf Nor Dog: American Indians, Environment, and Agrarian Change.*

He is now engaged in research and writing on Native American gambling in the twentieth century.

Patricia Nelson Limerick, a professor of history at the University of Colorado, Boulder, is the author of *Desert Passages* and *The Legacy of Conquest: The Unbroken Past of the American West*. She also edited, with Clyde A. Milner II and Charles E. Rankin, *Trails: Toward a New Western History*.

Sucheta Mazumdar is an assistant professor of history at Duke University. Her publications include *Sugar and Society in China: Peasants, Technology, and the World Market* (forthcoming). She also coedited *Making Waves: Writings by and about Asian American Women* and is the founder-editor of the *South Asia Bulletin: Comparative Studies of South Asia, Middle East, and Africa*.

Susan Rhoades Neel is an associate professor of history in the Department of History and Philosophy at Montana State University. Her first book is on Echo Park and the rise of modern environmentalism. She is presently researching and writing on tourism and the commodification of nature in Yellowstone National Park.

Gail M. Nomura is director of the Asian/Pacific American Studies Program and a faculty member of the Program in American Culture and Residential College at the University of Michigan. She has coedited two anthologies— *Frontiers of Asian American Studies* and *Bearing Dreams, Shaping Visions: Asian Pacific American Perspectives*—and has published numerous chapters and articles on the history of Asian Americans.

Gary Y. Okihiro is the director of Cornell University's Asian American Studies Program and a professor of history. He is the author of *Margins and Mainstreams: Asians in American History and Culture* and *Cane Fires: The Anti-Japanese Movement in Hawaii, 1865–1945*.

Robert W. Righter is a professor of history at the University of Texas at El Paso. Included among his books are *Crucible for Conservation: The Creation of Grand Teton National Park* and *The Making of a Town: Wright, Wyoming*. He has published articles in many journals, including "National Monuments to National Parks: The Use of the Antiquities Act of 1906," in the *Western Historical Quarterly*.

Vicki L. Ruiz is a professor of women's studies and history at Arizona State University. She is the author of *Cannery Women, Cannery Lives* and the coeditor of *Western Women: Their Land, Their Lives, Women on the U.S.-Mexico Border,* and *Unequal Sisters: A Multicultural Reader in U.S. Women's History*. Forthcoming is *From Out of the Shadows: A History of Mexican Women in the United States, 1900–1990*.

Martha A. Sandweiss is director of the Mead Art Museum and an associate professor of American Studies at Amherst College. A former curator of photographs at the Amon Carter Museum, she has written widely on western photography and art. She is the author of *Laura Gilpin: An Enduring Grace* and the editor of *Photography in Nineteenth-Century America.* With Clyde A. Milner II and Carol A. O'Connor, she coedited *The Oxford History of the American West,* which received the Western Heritage Award of the National Cowboy Hall of Fame.

Quintard Taylor is a professor of history at the University of Oregon. He is the author of *The Forging of a Black Community: Seattle's Central District from 1870 through the Civil Rights Era* and *In Search of the Racial Frontier: African Americans in the American West, 1528–1990* (forthcoming).

Barre Toelken is a professor of English and history and is the director of the Folklore Program and the American Studies Graduate Program at Utah State University. A former president of the American Folklore Society, he is the author of *The Dynamics of Folklore* and of *Morning Dew and Roses.* He also has published more than fifty articles on folklore, folksong, Native American and ethnic traditions, and related topics.

Elliott West is a professor of history at the University of Arkansas, Fayetteville. A specialist in the social history of the West and the frontier, he is the author of *Growing Up with the Country: Childhood on the Far-Western Frontier* and *The Saloon on the Rocky Mountain Mining Frontier.*

Index